EASY GUITAR

100 GREATEST HARD ROCK SONGS

ISBN 978-1-4234-8013-6

HAL•LEONARD® CORPORATION

7777 W. BLUEMOUND RD. P.O. BOX 13819 MILWAUKEE, WI 53213

D1088635

Visit Hal Leonard Online at
www.halleonard.com

	SONG TITLE	ARTIST	YEAR
1	Welcome to the Jungle	Guns N' Roses	1987
2	Back in Black	AC/DC	1981
3	Whole Lotta Love*	Led Zeppelin	1969
4	Paranoid	Black Sabbath	1970
5	Enter Sandman*	Metallica	1991
6	Won't Get Fooled Again	The Who	1971
7	Smells Like Teen Spirit	Nirvana	1991
8	Walk This Way	Aerosmith	1975
9	Runnin' with the Devil	Van Halen	1978
10	Ace of Spades	Motorhead	1980
11	Smoke on the Water	Deep Purple	1972
12	Breaking the Law	Judas Priest	1980
13	Photograph	Def Leppard	1983
14	Run to the Hills	Iron Maiden	1982
15	Dr. Feel Good	Mötley Crüe	1989
16	Rock and Roll All Nite	Kiss	1975
17	I Wanna Rock	Twisted Sister	1984
18	Rock You Like a Hurricane	Scorpions	1984
19	Tom Sawyer	Rush	1981
20	You Give Love a Bad Name	Bon Jovi	1986
21	Kashmir*	Led Zeppelin	1975
22	Hey Joe	Jimi Hendrix Experience	1966
23	Crazy Train	Ozzy Osbourne	1980
24	In-A-Gadda-Da-Vida	Iron Butterfly	1968
25	Blitzkrieg Bop*	The Ramones	1976
26	Free Bird	Lynyrd Skynyrd	1974
27	Still of the Night*	Whitesnake	1987
28	Everlong	Foo Fighters	1997
29	Bad Reputation	Joan Jett	1981
30	Even Flow	Pearl Jam	1992
31	Dirty Deeds Done Dirt Cheap	AC/DC	1976
32	Cat Scratch Fever*	Ted Nugent	1977
33	Basket Case*	Green Day	1993
33	School's Out	Alice Cooper	1972
34	Barracuda	Heart	1977
36	Hot for Teacher	Van Halen	1984
37	My Generation	The Who	1965
38	Stone Cold Crazy	Queen	1974
39	More Than a Feeling	Boston	1976
40	Talk Dirty to Me	Poison	1987
41	Cum On Feel the Noize	Quiet Riot	1983
42	Should I Stay or Should I Go	The Clash	1982
43	Holy Diver	Dio	1983
44	Sunshine of Your Love	Cream	1968
45	Slow Ride	Foghat	1975
46	Madhouse	Anthrax	1985
47	Bawitdaba	Kid Rock	1999
48	Freak on a Leash	Korn	1998
49	Search and Destroy	The Stooges	1973
50	Give It Away	Red Hot Chili Peppers	1991

51	Peace Sells	Megadeth	1986
52	Cherry Bomb	The Runaways	1976
53	Born to Be Wild	Steppenwolf	1968
54	Epic	Faith No More	1990
55	Don't Fear the Reaper	Blue Öyster Cult	1976
56	Cherry Pie	Warrant	1990
57	You Really Got Me	The Kinks	1964
58	Interstate Love Song	Stone Temple Pilots	1994
59	The Stroke	Billy Squier	1981
60	18 and Life	Skid Row	1989
61	Round and Round	Ratt	1984
62	Breaking the Chains	Dokken	1983
63	Eye of the Tiger	Survivor	1982
64	Liar*	Rollins Band	1994
65	Kick Out the Jams	MC5	1969
66	Final Countdown	Europe	1986
67	Tush	ZZ Top	1975
68	More Human Than Human	White Zombie	1995
69	Cult of Personality	Living Colour	1988
70	Hot Blooded	Foreigner	1978
71	Mountain Song	Jane's Addiction	1988
72	Heartbreaker	Pat Benetar	1979
73	Jailbreak	Thin Lizzy	1976
74	Love Removal Machine	The Cult	1987
75	Seven Nation Army	The White Stripes	2003
76	Kiss Me Deadly	Lita Ford	1988
77	Black Hole Sun	Soundgarden	1994
78	Feel Like Making Love	Bad Company	1975
79	Rebel Yell	Billy Idol	1984
80	Any Way You Want It	Journey	1980
81	Heaven and Hell	Black Sabbath	1980
82	Since You Been Gone	Rainbow	1976
83	Bring Me to Life*	Evanescence	2003
84	I Wanna Be Somebody	W.A.S.P.	1984
85	Slither	Velvet Revolver	2004
86	The Beautiful People	Marilyn Manson	1996
87	Seventeen	Winger	1989
88	Would?	Alice in Chains	1992
89	Party Hard	Andrew W.K.	2001
90	Aqualung	Jethro Tull	1971
91	Bullet with Butterfly Wings*	Smashing Pumpkins	1995
92	Don't Tell Me You Love Me	Night Ranger	1983
93	Turn Up the Radio	Autograph	1984
94	I Believe in a Thing Called Love*	The Darkness	2003
95	Higher	Creed	2000
96	Carry On Wayward Son	Kansas	1976
97	Frankenstein	The Edgar Winter Group	1973
98	Lit Up	Buckcherry	1999
99	We're an American Band	Grand Funk Railroad	1973
100	I Can't Drive 55	Sammy Hagar	1984

* Omitted from this publication because of licensing restrictions.

STRUM AND PICK PATTERNS

This chart contains the suggested strum and pick patterns that are referred to by number at the beginning of each song in this book. The symbols ⊓ and ∨ in the strum patterns refer to down and up strokes, respectively. The letters in the pick patterns indicate which right-hand fingers play which strings.

p = **thumb**
i = **index finger**
m = **middle finger**
a = **ring finger**

For example; Pick Pattern 2
is played: thumb - index - middle - ring

Strum Patterns   ## Pick Patterns

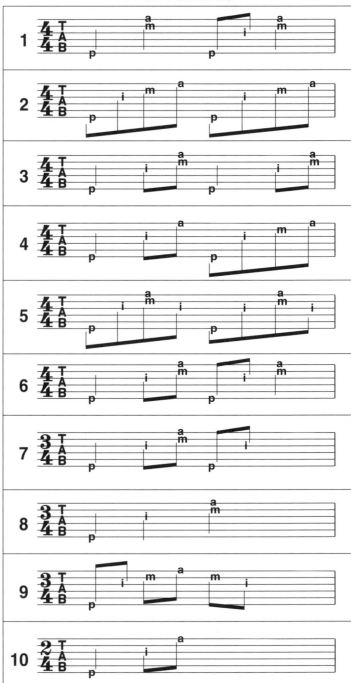

You can use the 3/4 Strum and Pick Patterns in songs written in compound meter (6/8, 9/8, 12/8, etc.). For example, you can accompany a song in 6/8 by playing the 3/4 pattern twice in each measure. The 4/4 Strum and Pick Patterns can be used for songs written in cut time (¢) by doubling the note time values in the patterns. Each pattern would therefore last two measures in cut time.

Ace of Spades

Words and Music by Ian Kilmister, Edward Clarke and Philip Taylor

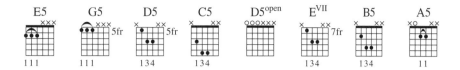

*Drop D tuning, down 1/2 step:
(low to high) D♭-A♭-D♭-G♭-B♭-E♭

Strum Pattern: 3, 4

Intro
Fast Rock, in 2

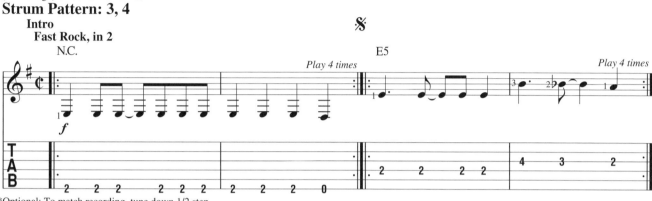

*Optional: To match recording, tune down 1/2 step.

Verse

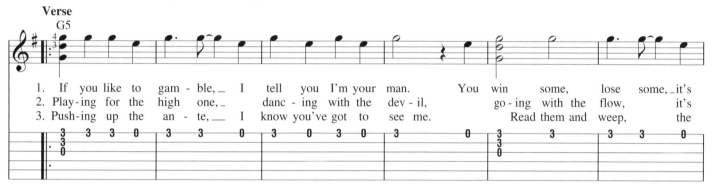

1. If you like to gam - ble, __ I tell you I'm your man. You win some, lose some, _ it's
2. Play - ing for the high one, __ danc - ing with the dev - il, go - ing with the flow, it's
3. Push - ing up the an - te, __ I know you've got to see me. Read them and weep, the

all the same __ to me.
all a game __ to me.
dead man's __ hand __ a - gain.

The pleas - ure is to play, it
Sev - en or e - lev - en,
I see it in your eyes,

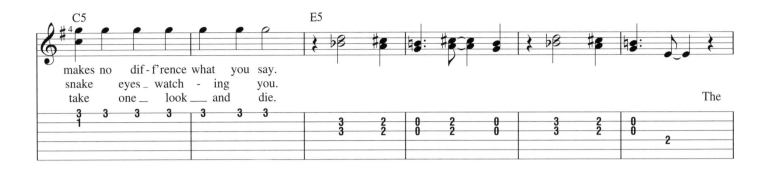

makes no dif-f'rence what you say.
snake eyes _ watch - ing you.
take one _ look _ and die.

The

I don't share your greed, the on - ly card I need is the ace of _ spades, _ the
Dou - ble up or quit, dou - ble stakes or split. The ace of _ spades, _ the
on - ly thing you see, you know it's gon - na be the ace of _ spaces, _ the

To Coda

ace of _ spades. _
ace of _ spades. _
ace of _ spades. _

Bridge
E5   N.C.

You know I'm born to

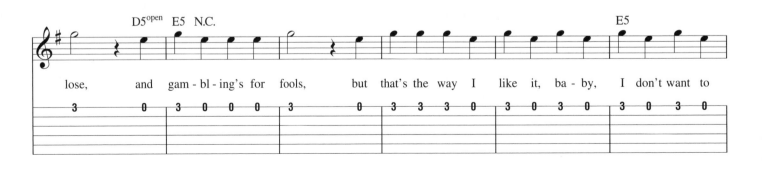

lose, and gam - bl - ing's for fools, but that's the way I like it, ba - by, I don't want to

live for - ev - er.

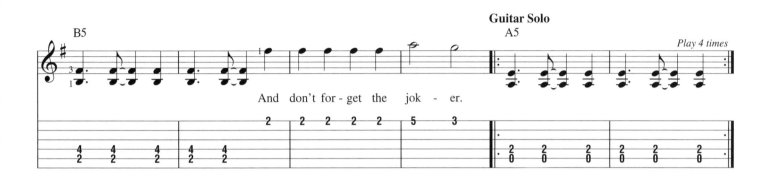

Guitar Solo

And don't for - get the jok - er.

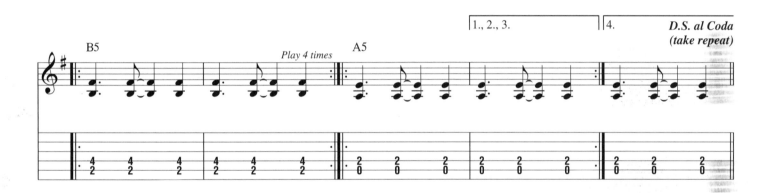

1., 2., 3. | 4. | ***D.S. al Coda*** *(take repeat)*

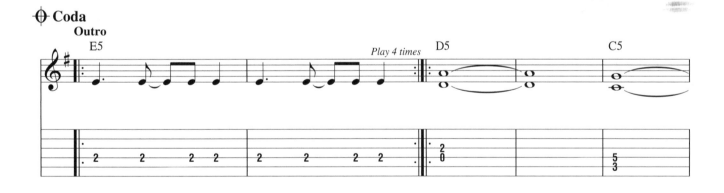

Coda
Outro

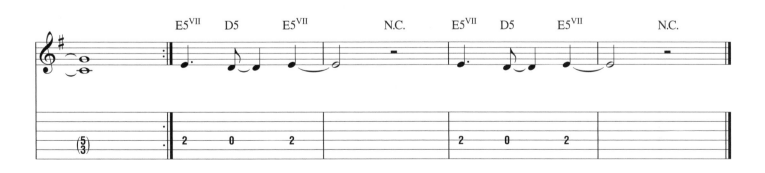

Any Way You Want It

Words and Music by Steve Perry and Neal Schon

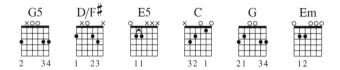

Strum Pattern: 1
Pick Pattern: 5

Intro
Moderate Rock

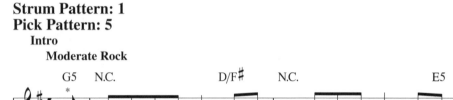

Sung one octave higher.

Verse

**Sung as written.

She loves to move.___
___ then ___ we touched, ___

She loves to groove. _
then ___ we sang ___

She loves the lov - in' things. }
a - bout the lov - in' things. }

*Sung one octave higher.

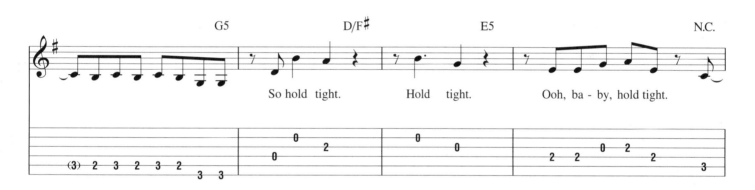

Ooh, all night.   All   night.   Oh,   ev -'ry night.

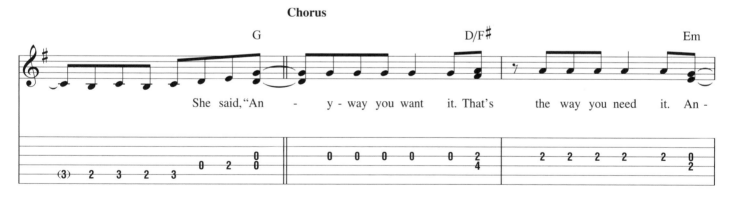

So hold tight.   Hold   tight.   Ooh, ba - by, hold tight.

Chorus

She said, "An - y - way you want it. That's   the   way you need   it. An-

- y way you want ___ it."   { She } said, "An - y way you want   it. That's
{ I }

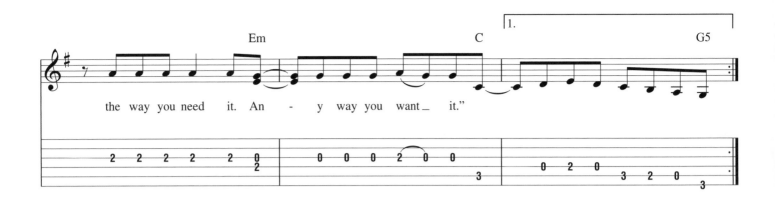

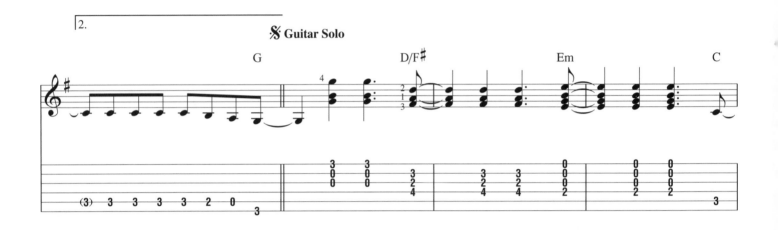

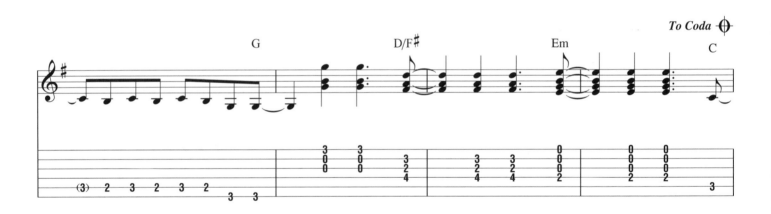

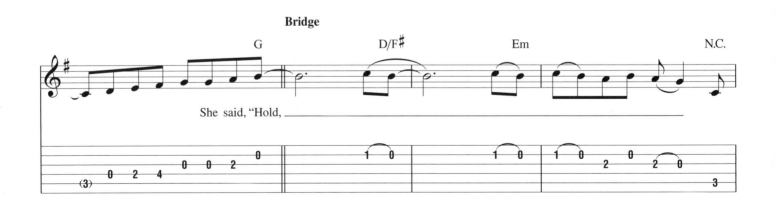

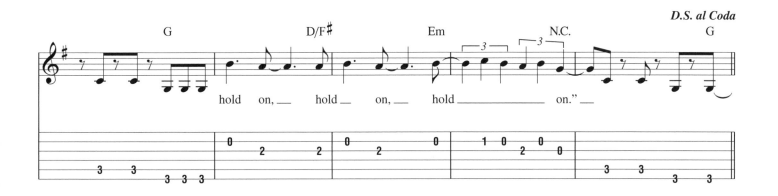

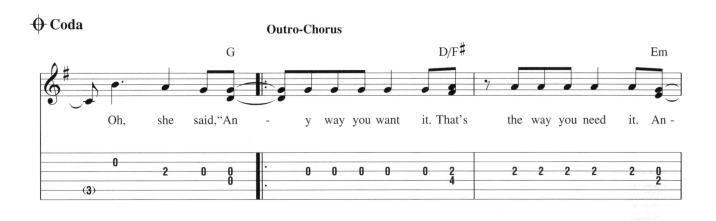

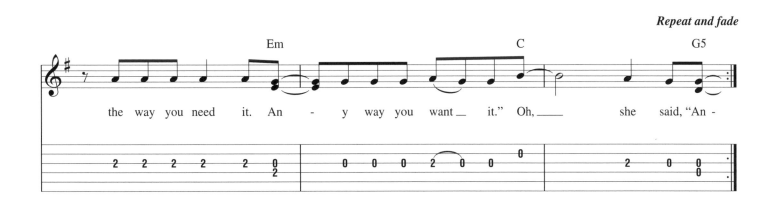

Aqualung

Music by Ian Anderson
Lyrics by Jennie Anderson

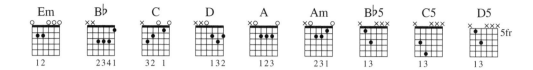

*Capo III

Strum Pattern: 2, 5
Pick Pattern: 3, 4

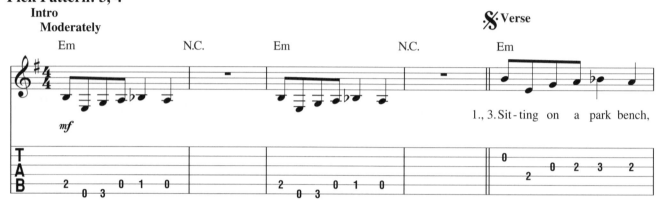

*Optional: To match recording, place capo at 3rd fret.

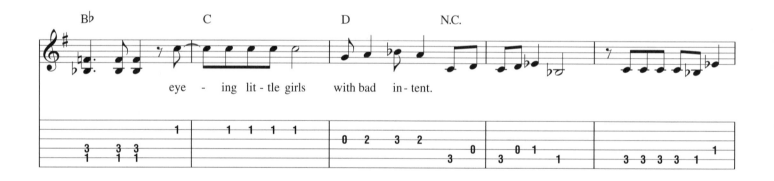

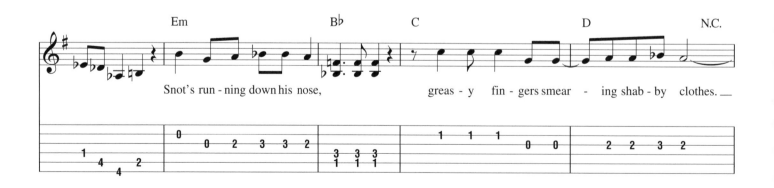

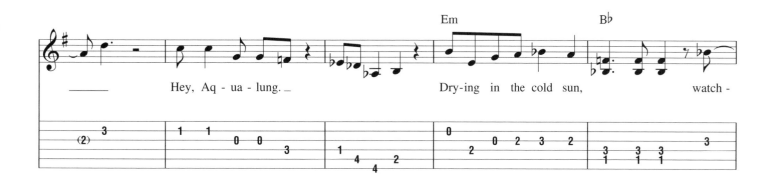

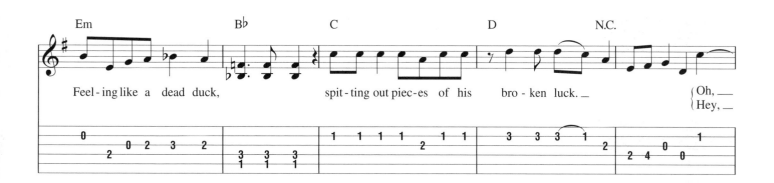

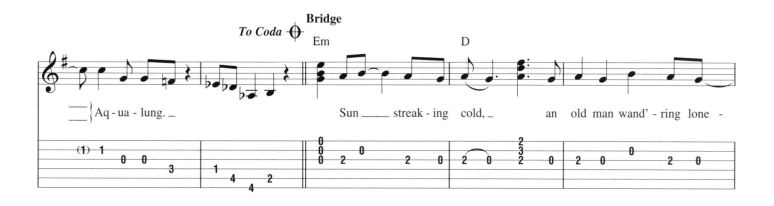

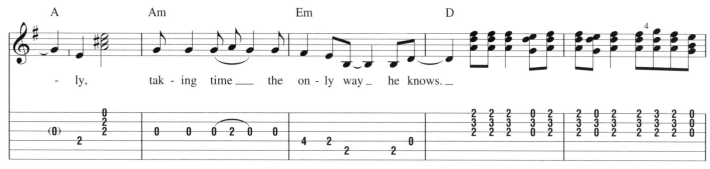

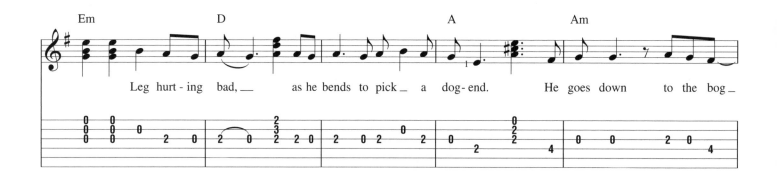

Leg hurt-ing bad, __ as he bends to pick __ a dog-end. He goes down to the bog __

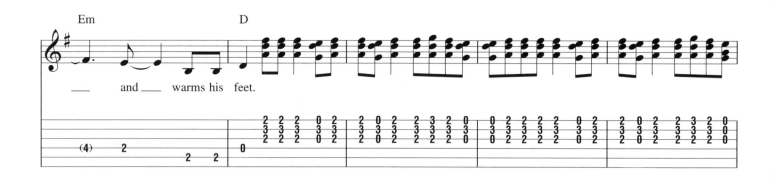

__ and __ warms his feet.

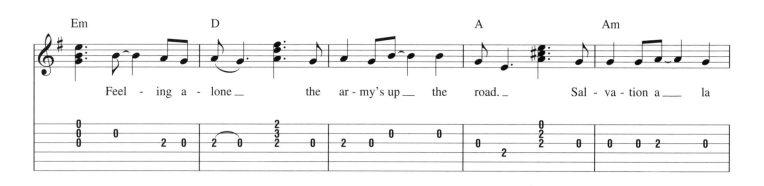

Feel - ing a - lone __ the ar - my's up __ the road. __ Sal - va - tion a __ la

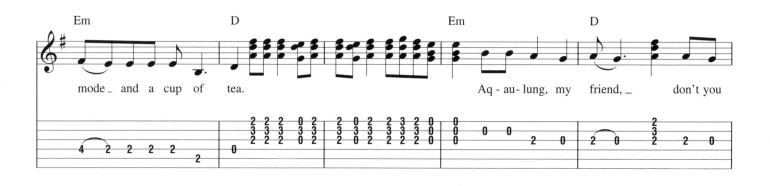

mode __ and a cup of tea. Aq - au - lung, my friend, __ don't you

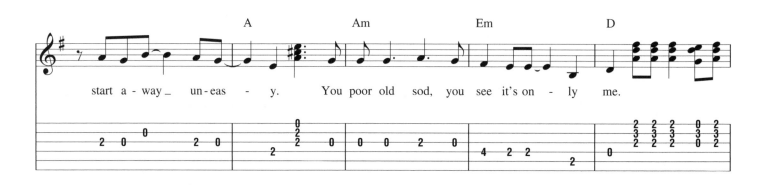

start a - way __ un - eas - y. You poor old sod, you see it's on - ly me.

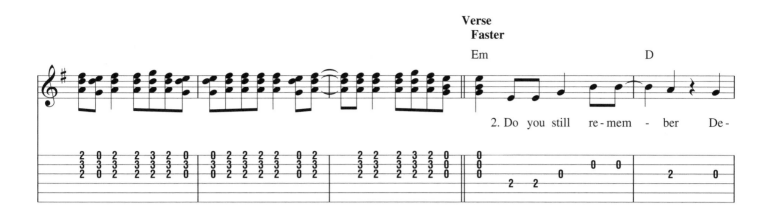

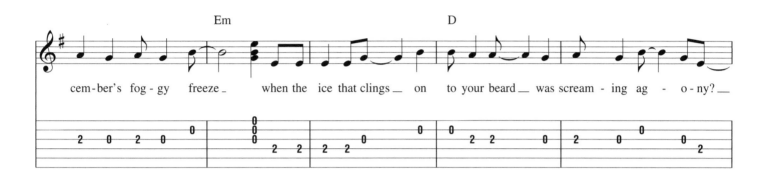

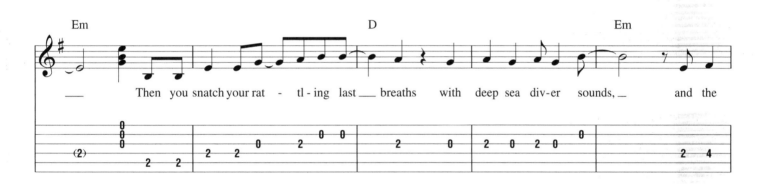

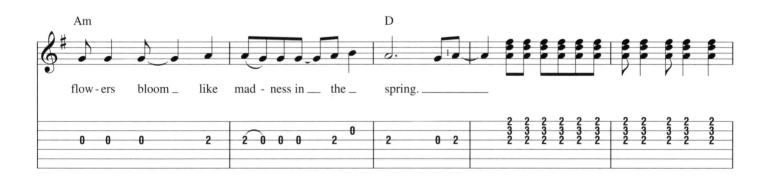

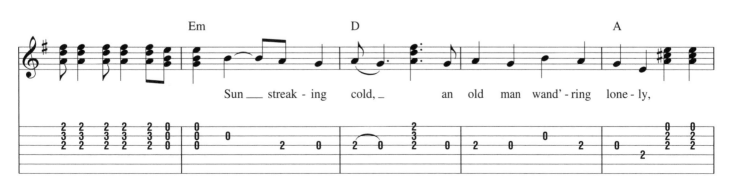

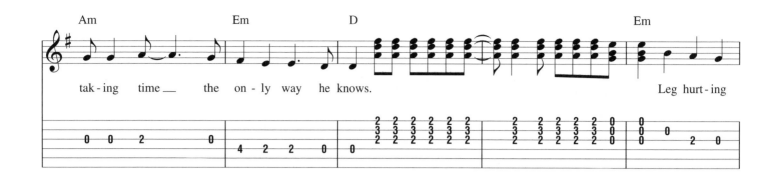

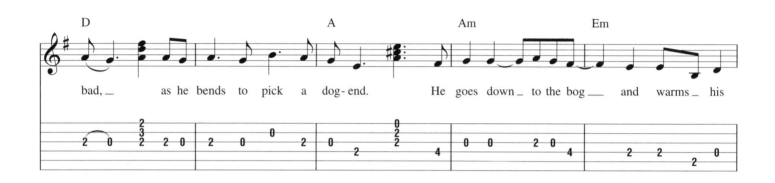

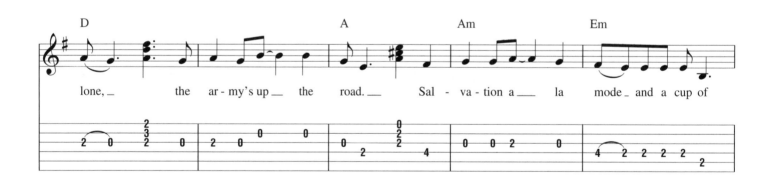

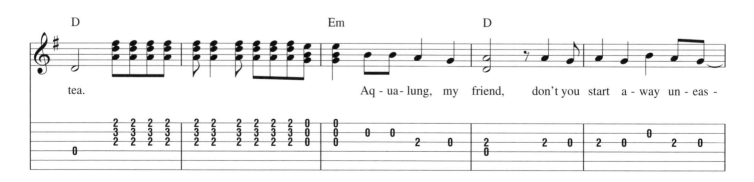

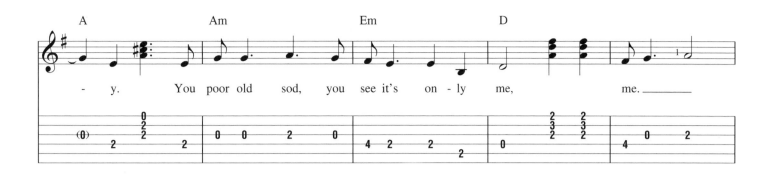

-y. You poor old sod, you see it's on-ly me, me. _____

Interlude

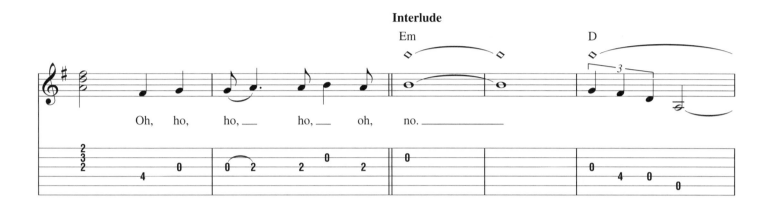

Oh, ho, ho, ___ ho, ___ oh, no.

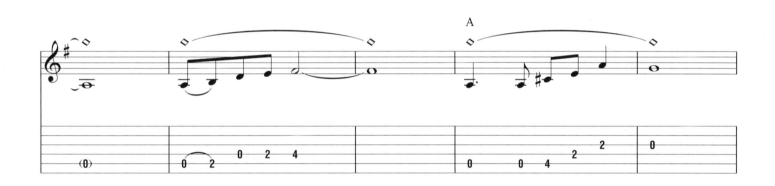

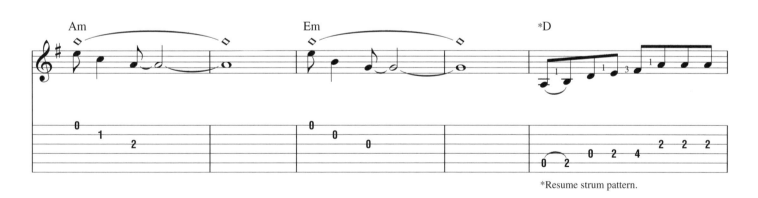

*Resume strum pattern.

Guitar Solo

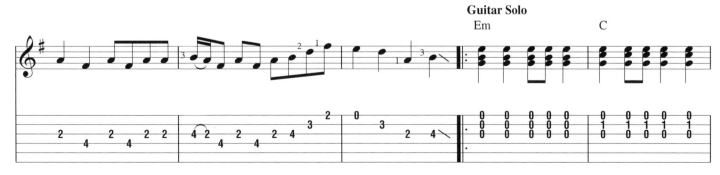

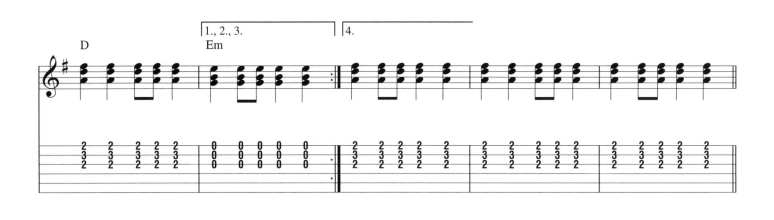

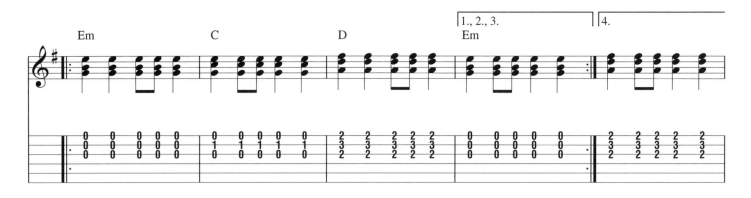

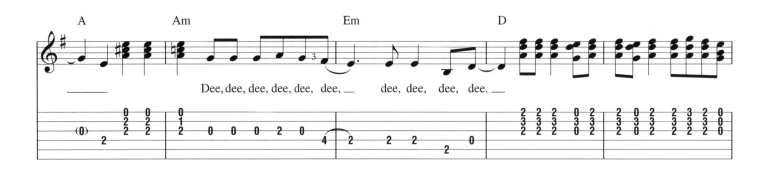

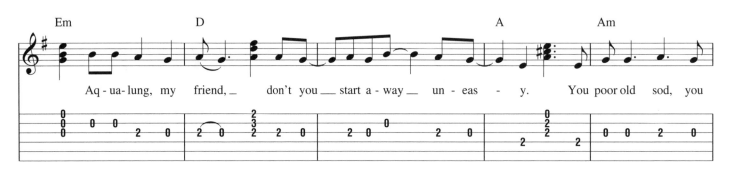

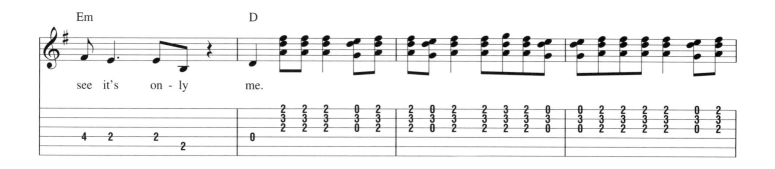

see it's on - ly me.

Interlude *D.S. al Coda*

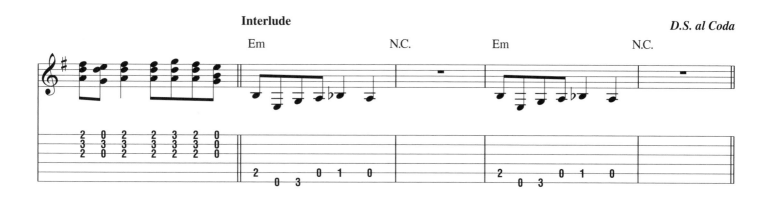

Coda

Outro

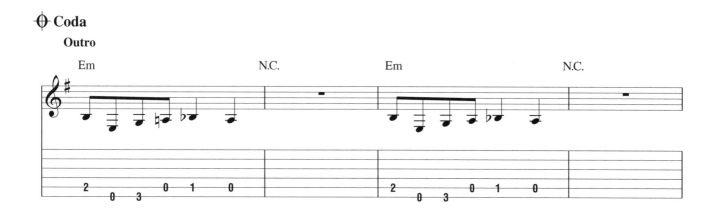

Free Time

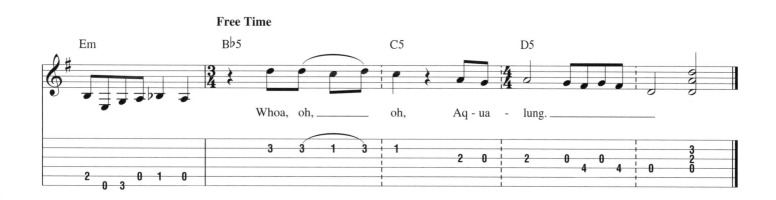

Whoa, oh, _____ oh, Aq - ua - lung. _____

Back in Black

Words and Music by Angus Young, Malcolm Young and Brian Johnson

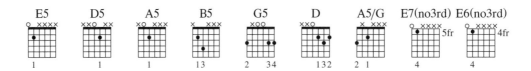

Strum Pattern: 3
Pick Pattern: 3

Intro

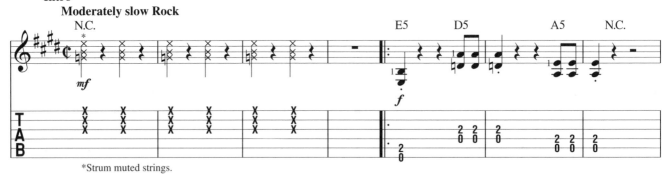

*Strum muted strings.

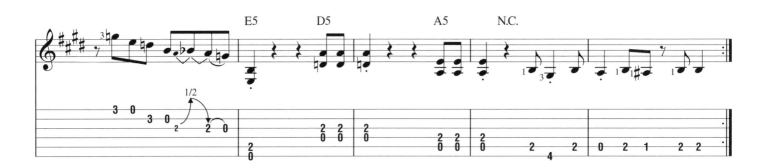

Verse
w/ Intro rhythm

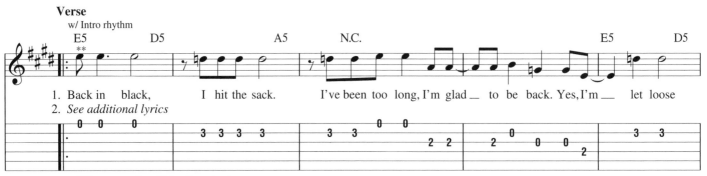

1. Back in black, I hit the sack. I've been too long, I'm glad ___ to be back. Yes, I'm ___ let loose
2. *See additional lyrics*

**Sung one octave higher throughout.

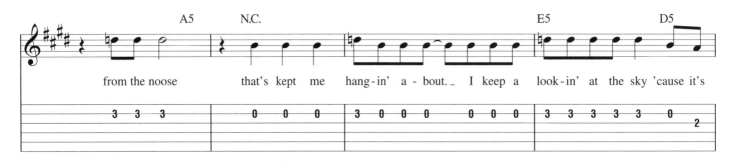

from the noose that's kept me hang-in' a-bout. ___ I keep a look-in' at the sky 'cause it's

get-tin' me high.   For-get the hearse 'cause I'll nev-er die.   I got   nine lives,   cat's eyes.   A-

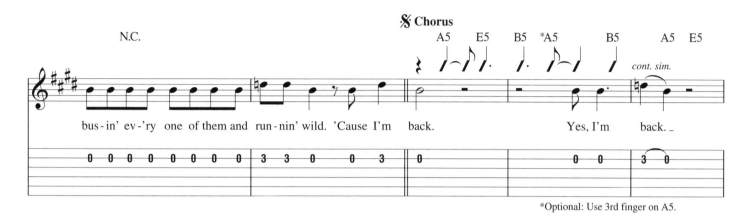

§ **Chorus**

bus-in' ev-'ry one of them and run-nin' wild. 'Cause I'm   back.   Yes, I'm   back.

*Optional: Use 3rd finger on A5.

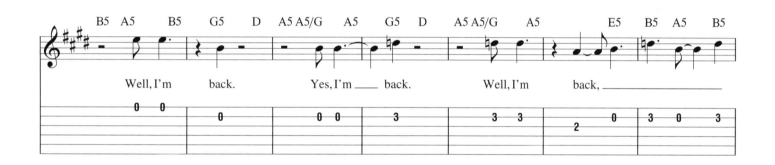

Well, I'm   back.   Yes, I'm ___ back.   Well, I'm   back, _____

To Coda ⊕

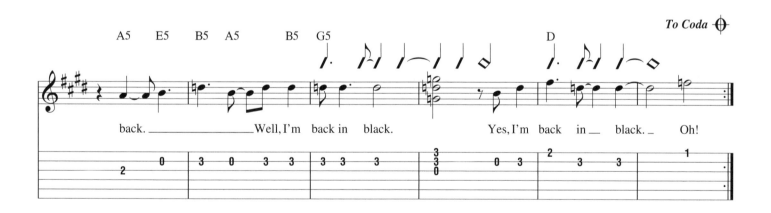

back. _____ Well, I'm back in black.   Yes, I'm back in ___ black. ___ Oh!

Guitar Solo

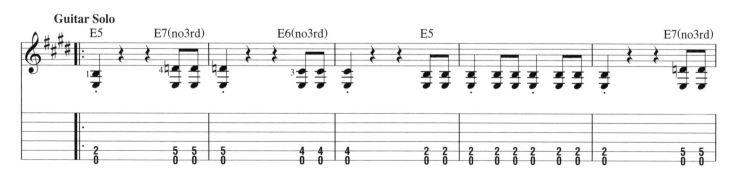

23

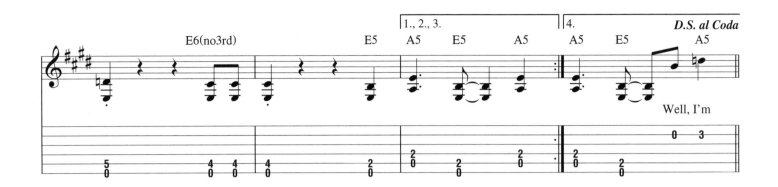

*Chords in parentheses reflect implied harmony.

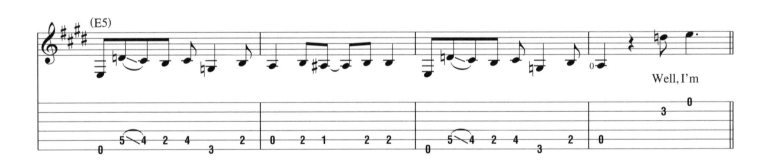

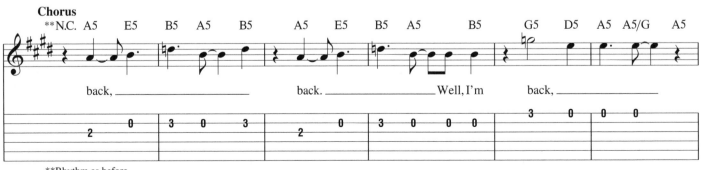

**Rhythm as before.

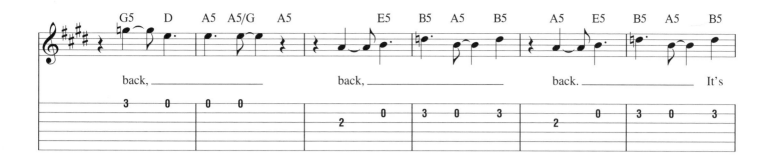

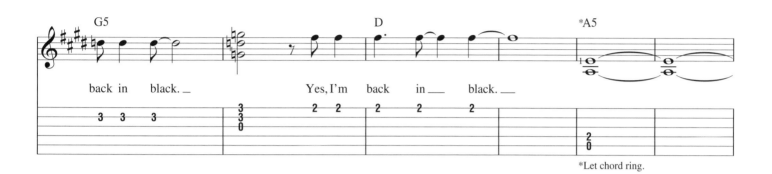

*Let chord ring.

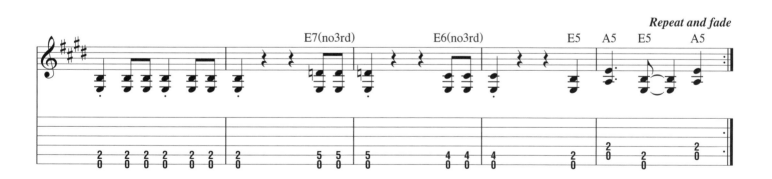

Additional Lyrics

2. Back in the back of a Cadillac.
   Number one with a bullet, I'm a power pack.
   Yes, I'm in the band, with the gang.
   They got to catch me if they want me to hang
   'Cause I'm back on the track, and I'm beatin' the flack.
   Nobody's gonna get me on another rap.
   So look at me now, I'm just a makin' my play.
   Don't try to push your luck, just get outta my way.

Bad Reputation

Words and Music by Joan Jett, Kenny Laguna, Ritchie Cordell and Marty Kupersmith

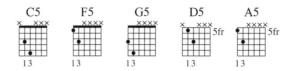

*Tune down 1/2 step:

(low to high) E♭-A♭-D♭-G♭-B♭-E♭

Strum Pattern: 1, 6

*Optional: To match recording, tune down 1/2 step.

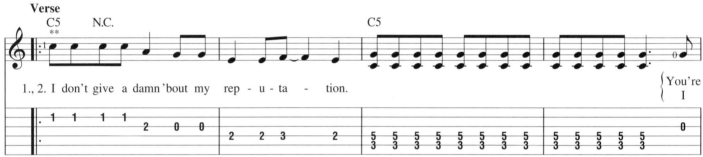

**Sung one octave higher throughout.

1., 2. I don't give a damn 'bout my rep-u-ta - tion.

You're / I

liv-ing in the past, it's a new gen-er-a-tion.
nev-er said I want-ed to im-prove my ___ sta - tion.

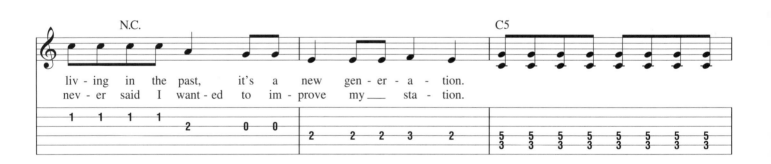

And a girl can do ___ what she wants to do, ___ and that's what I'm gon-na
And I'm al-ways feel-ing good when I'm hav-ing fun, ___ and I don't have to please no

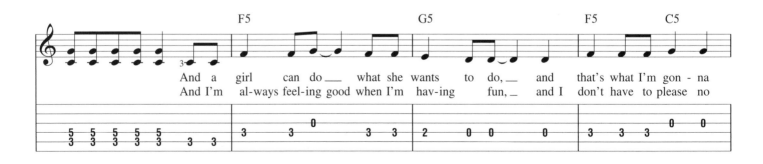

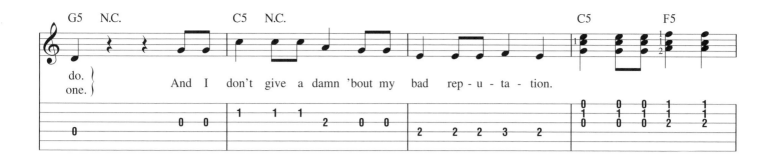

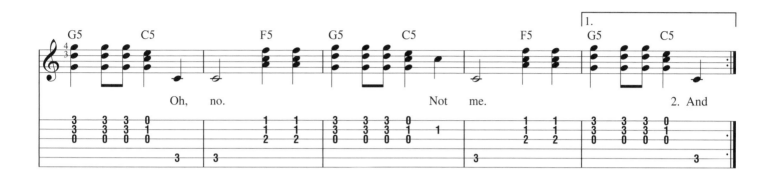

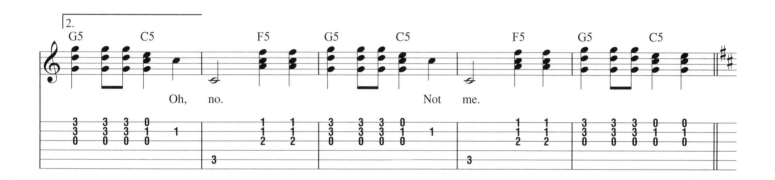

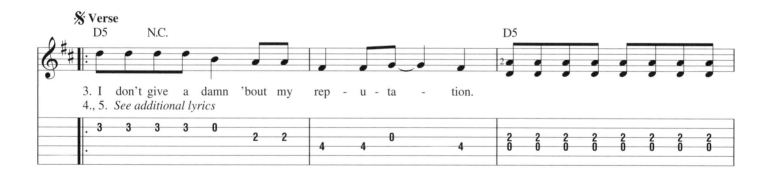

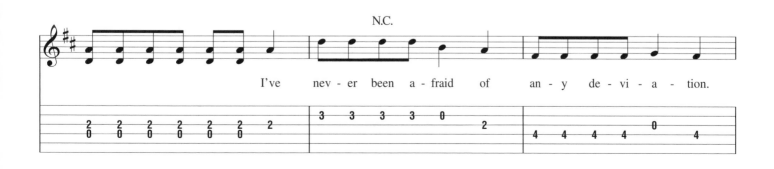

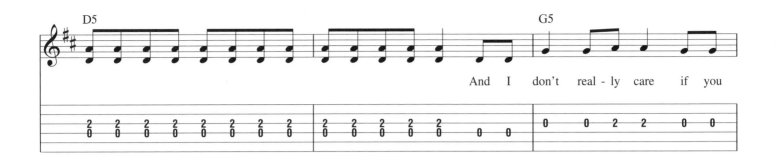

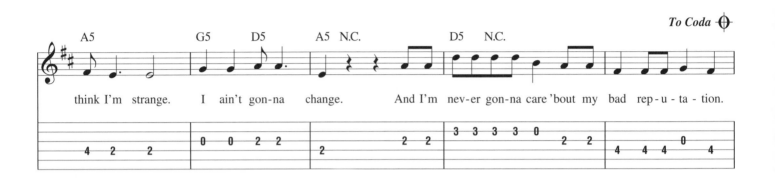

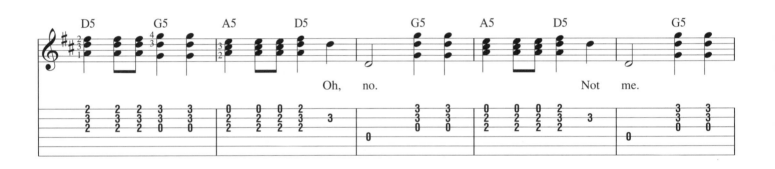

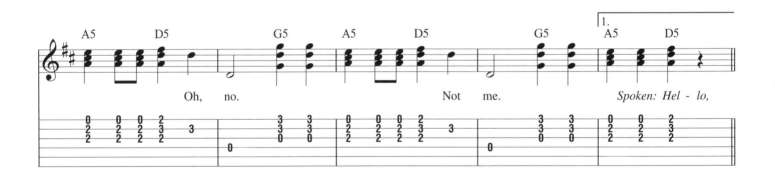

Interlude

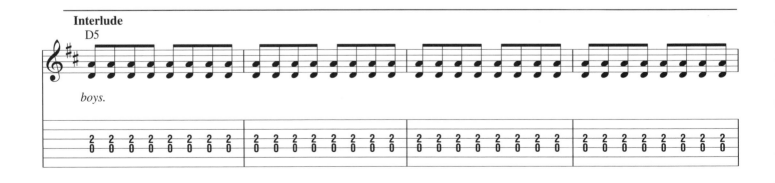

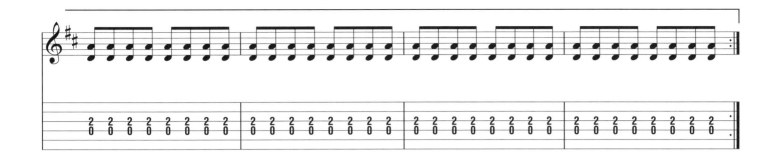

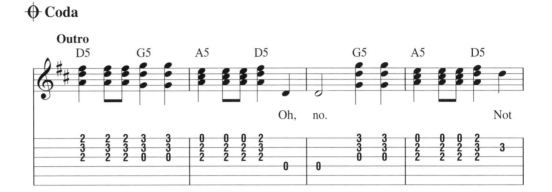

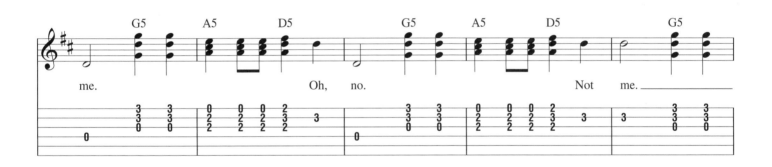

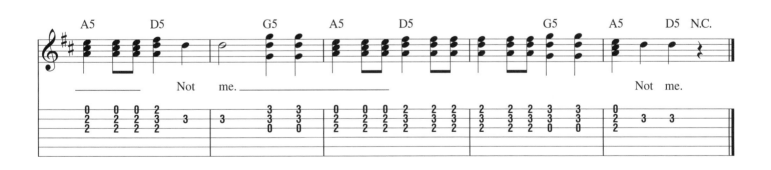

Additional Lyrics

4. I don't give a damn 'bout my reputation.
   The world's in trouble, there's no communication.
   And ev'ryone can say what they wanna say.
   It never gets better anyway.
   So why should I care 'bout a bad reputation anyway?
   Oh, no. Not me. Oh, no. Not me.

5. I don't give a damn 'bout my reputation.
   You're living in the past, it's a new generation.
   And I only feel good when I got no pain,
   And that's how I'm gonna stay.
   And I don't give a damn 'bout my bad reputation.
   Oh, no. Not me. Oh no. Not me. Not me. Not me.

Barracuda

Words and Music by Nancy Wilson, Ann Wilson, Michael Derosier and Roger Fisher

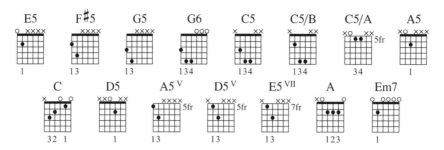

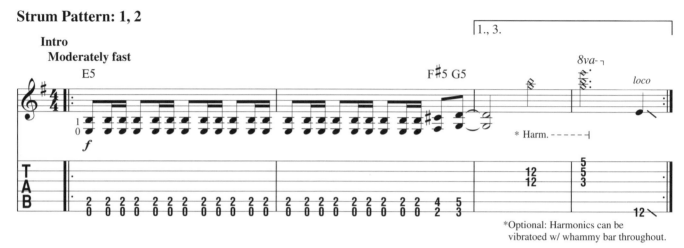

Strum Pattern: 1, 2

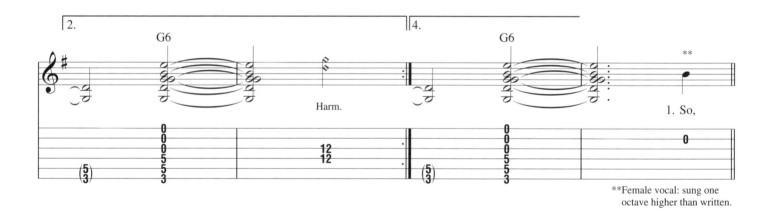

*Optional: Harmonics can be
vibratoed w/ whammy bar throughout.

**Female vocal: sung one
octave higher than written.

this ain't the end, I saw you a-gain, to-day.
2. See additional lyrics

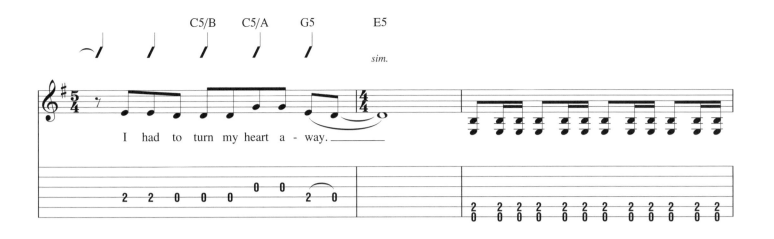

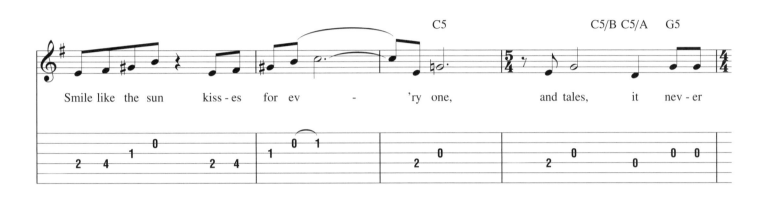

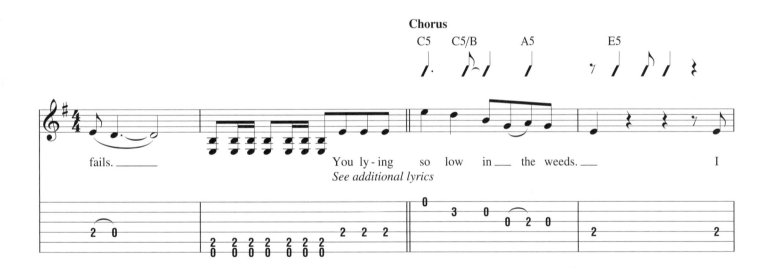

See additional lyrics

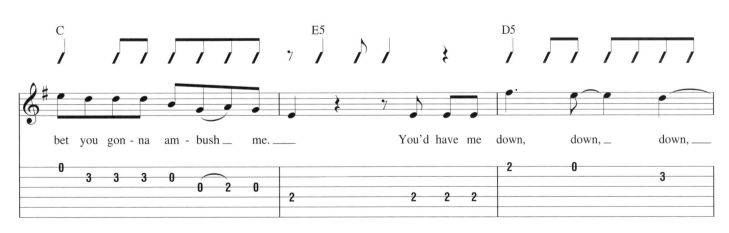

down on my knees, now would-n't you, bar-ra-cu-da?

Oh.

Harm.

Harm.

Ooh, bar-ra-cu-da.

Oh, yeah.

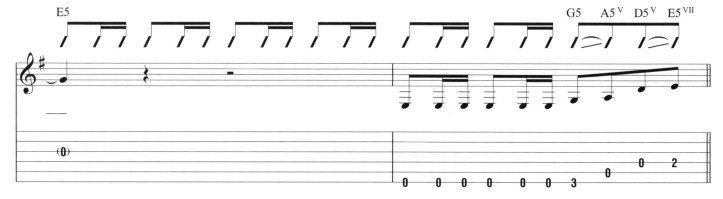

Bridge

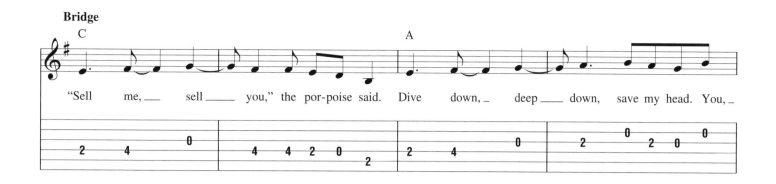

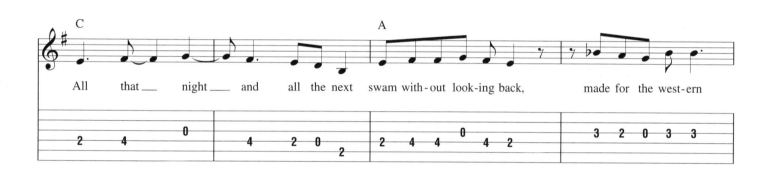

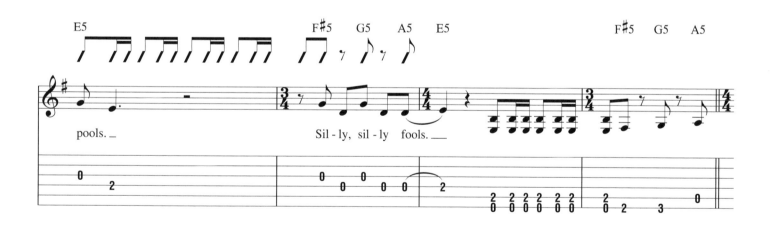

Guitar Solo

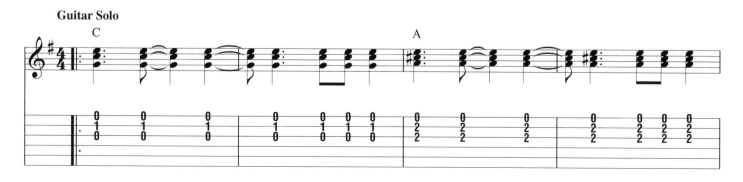

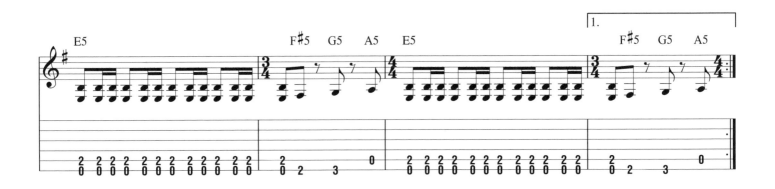

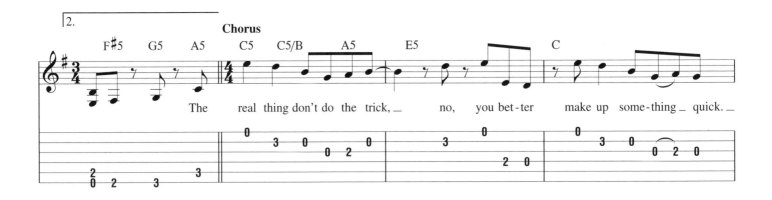

Outro

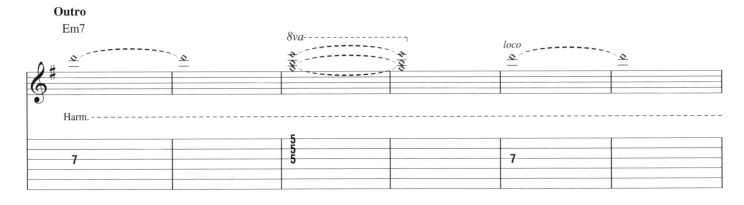

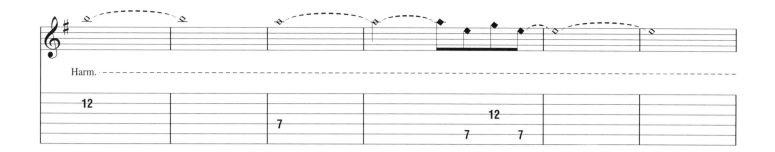

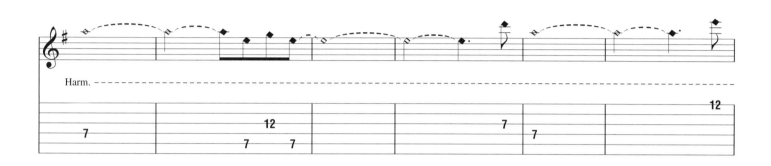

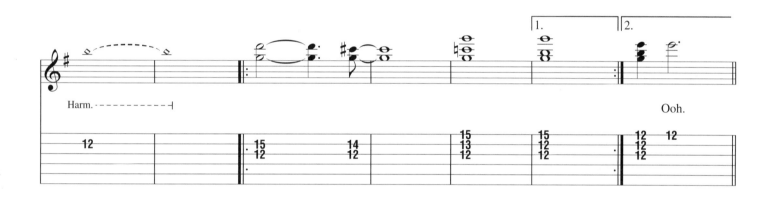

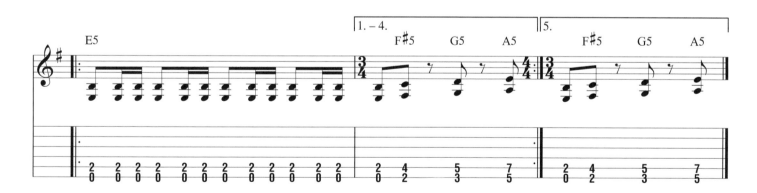

Additional Lyrics

2. Back over time we were all trying for free,
   You met the porpoise and me. Uh huh.
   No right, no wrong; selling a song,
   A name. Whisper games.

Chorus   And if the real thing don't do the trick,
   You better make up something quick.
   You gonna burn, burn, burn, burn,
   Burn it to the wick.

Bawitdaba

Words and Music by Jason Krause, David Parker,
R.J. Ritchie, Sylvia Robinson and Matthew Shafer

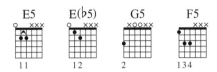

Strum Pattern: 5

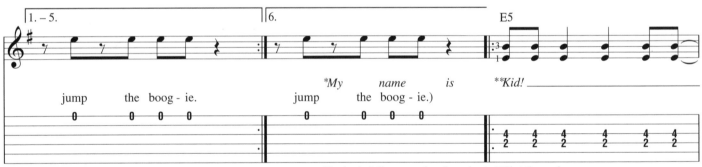

*Lyrics in italics are spoken throughout. **First time only.

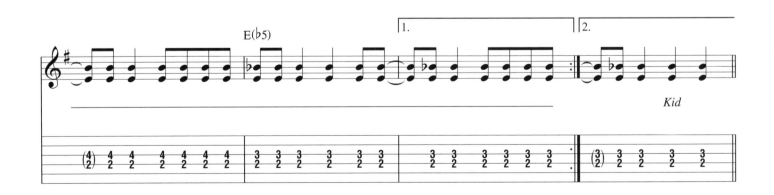

Gs with the for-ties and the chicks with beep-ers. The North-ern Lights _ and the
pints of love _ and the fifths of stress. _ For the hook-ers all trick-ing out in
ho - mies in the coun-ty in cell _ block six. _ The grits when there ain't e-nough

South-ern Com - fort and it don't e - ven mat-ter if the veins are punc - tured.
Hol - ly - wood, and for my hoods of the world mis - un - der-stood. _ I said
eggs to cook _ and for D. B. Coop - er and the mon-ey he took. _ You can

To Coda 1

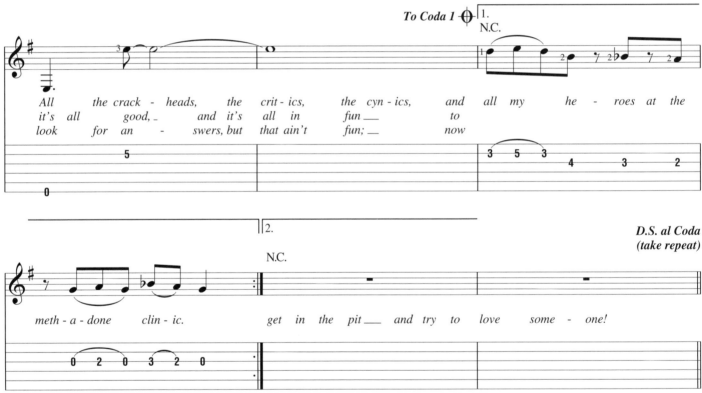

All the crack - heads, the crit - ics, the cyn - ics, and all my he - roes at the
it's all good, _ and it's all in fun _ to
look for an - swers, but that ain't fun; _ now

D.S. al Coda
(take repeat)

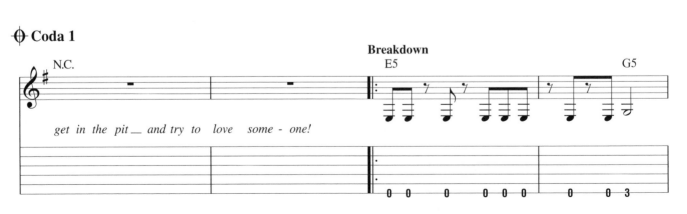

meth - a - done clin - ic. get in the pit _ and try to love some - one!

Coda 1

Breakdown

get in the pit _ and try to love some - one!

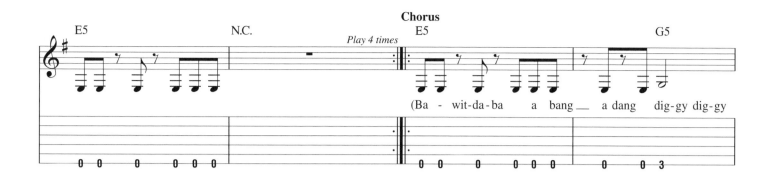

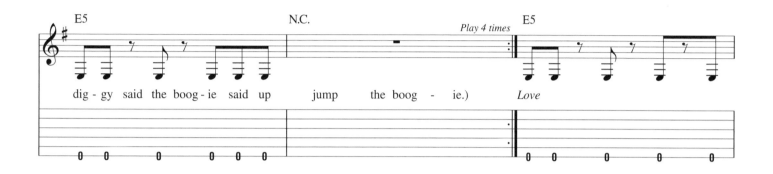

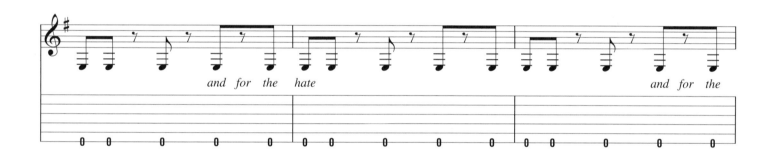

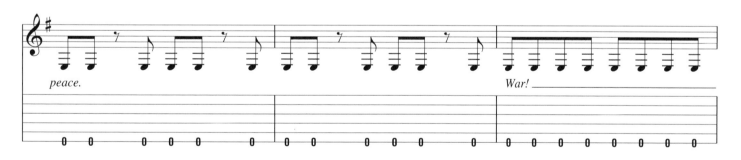

Coda 2

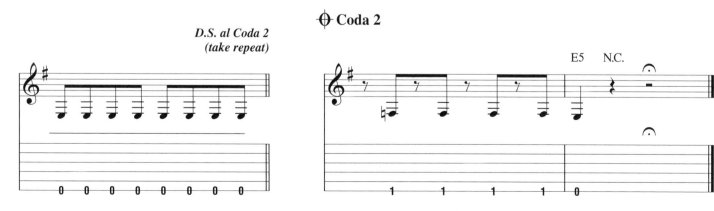

The Beautiful People

Words and Music by Brian Warner and Jeordie White

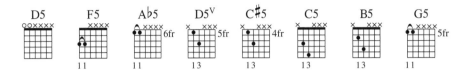

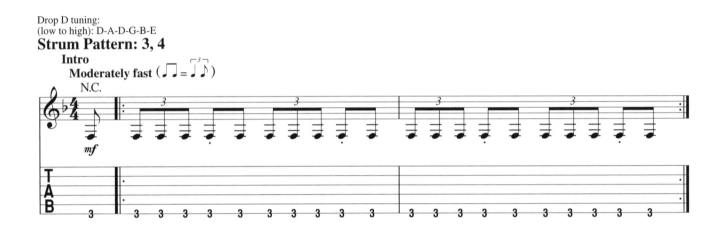

Drop D tuning:
(low to high): D-A-D-G-B-E

Strum Pattern: 3, 4

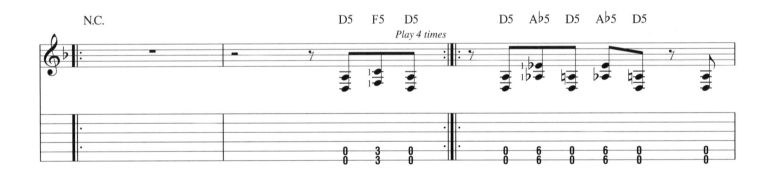

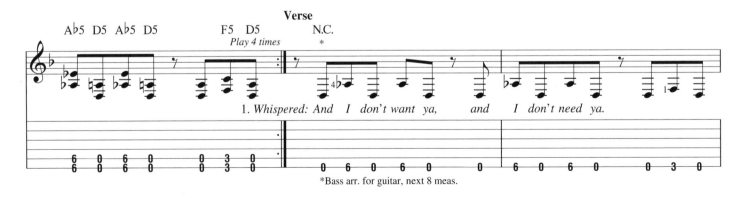

1. *Whispered: And I don't want ya, and I don't need ya.*

*Bass arr. for guitar, next 8 meas.

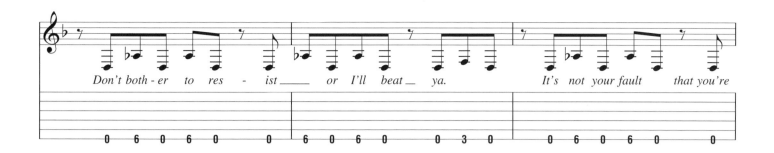

Don't both - er to res - ist _____ or I'll beat _ ya.   It's not your fault   that you're

al - ways   wrong. _   The   weak   ones are there to jus - ti - fy the   strong. _

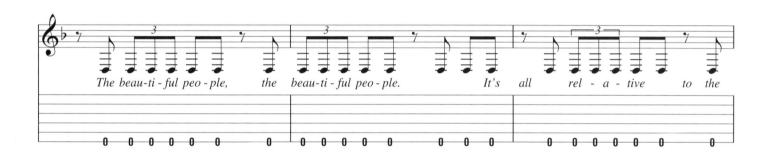

The beau - ti - ful peo - ple,   the   beau - ti - ful peo - ple.   It's   all   rel - a - tive   to the

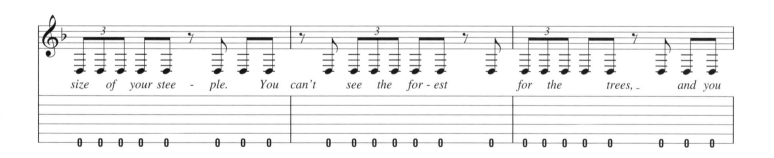

size   of   your stee - ple.   You   can't   see   the   for - est   for   the   trees, _   and you

§ **Pre-Chorus**

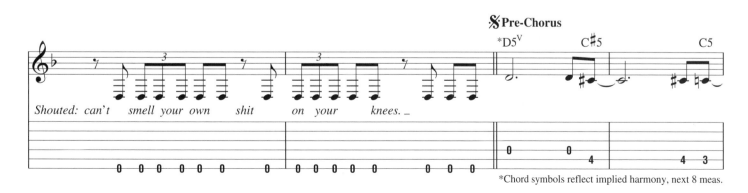

Shouted: can't   smell your   own   shit   on   your   knees. _

*Chord symbols reflect implied harmony, next 8 meas.

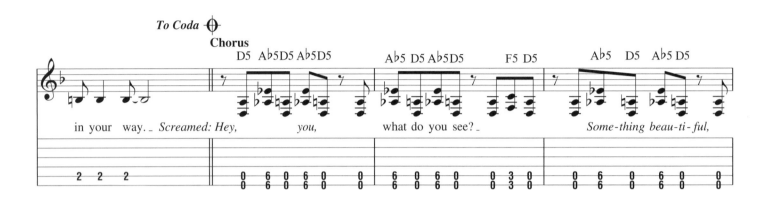

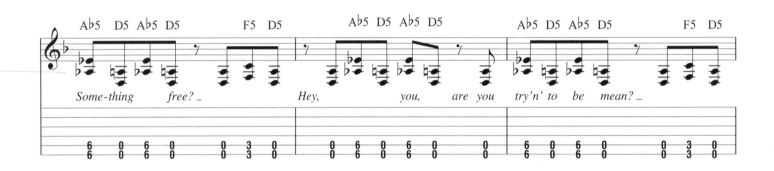

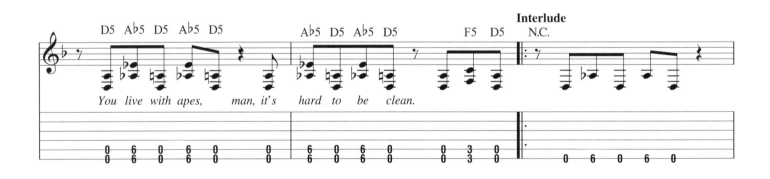

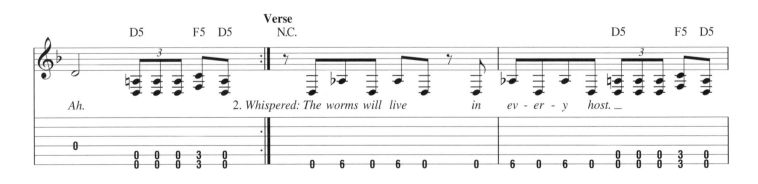

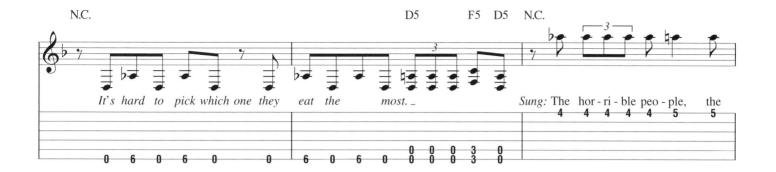

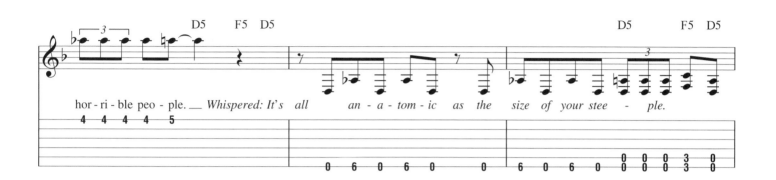

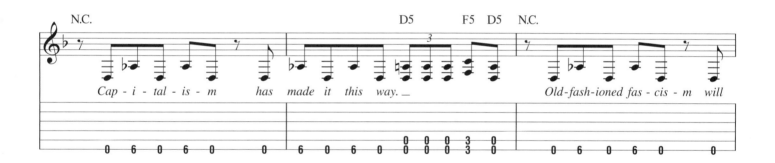

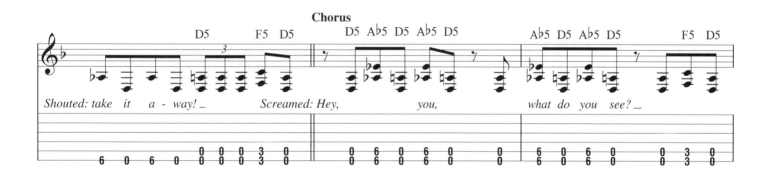

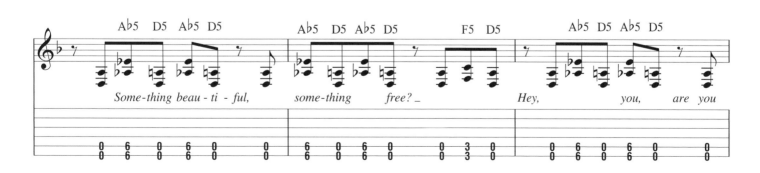

D.S. al Coda

try'n' to be mean? _ You live with apes, man it's hard to be clean. _

Coda

Chorus

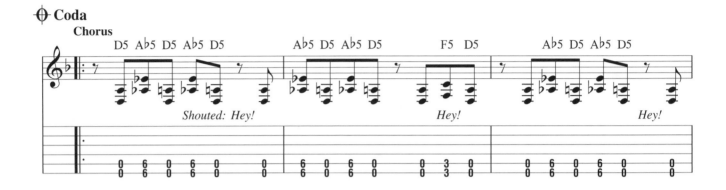

Shouted: Hey! Hey! Hey!

Interlude

Hey! Whispered: The beau-ti-ful peo-ple, the beau-ti-ful peo-ple.
(Ah.)

Play 4 times

Chorus

Screamed: Hey, you, what do you see? _ Some-thing beau-ti-ful,

some-thing free? _ Hey, you, are you try'n' to be mean? _

44

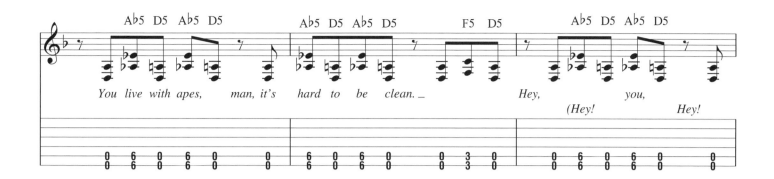

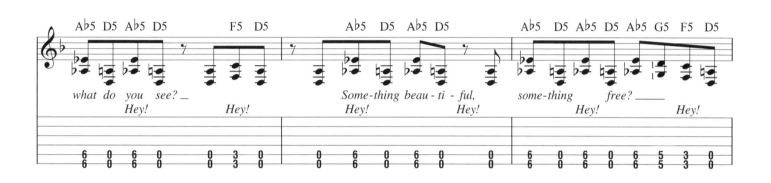

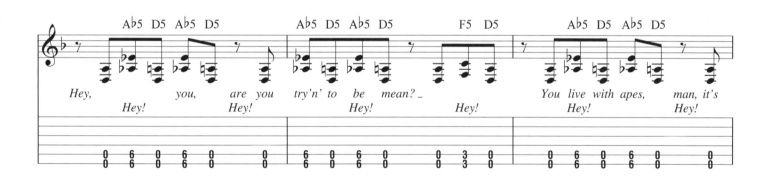

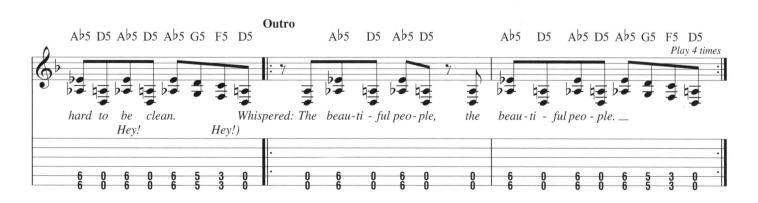

Black Hole Sun

Words and Music by Chris Cornell

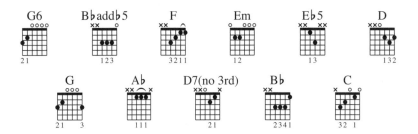

Strum Pattern: 3
Pick Pattern: 3

Verse

Slow Rock

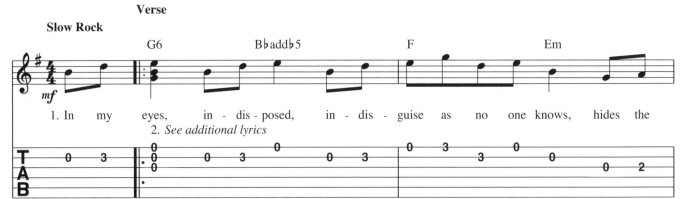

1. In my eyes, in - dis - posed, in - dis - guise as no one knows, hides the
2. *See additional lyrics*

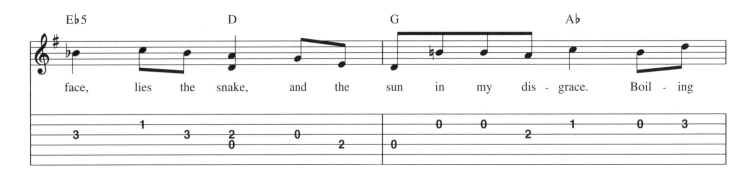

face, lies the snake, and the sun in my dis - grace. Boil - ing

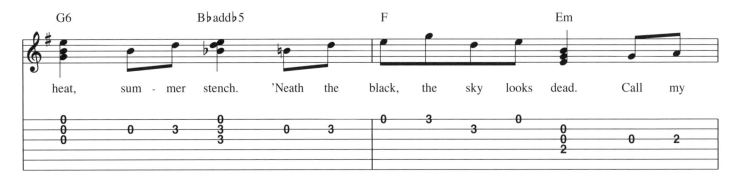

heat, sum - mer stench. 'Neath the black, the sky looks dead. Call my

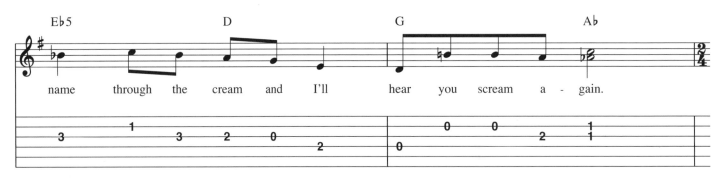

name through the cream and I'll hear you scream a - gain.

% Chorus

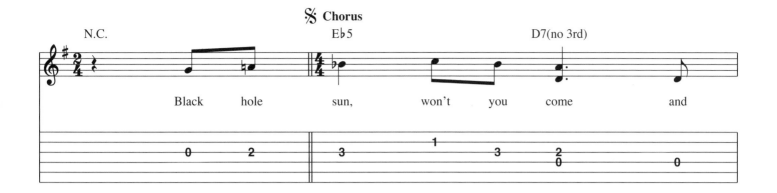

Black hole sun, won't you come and

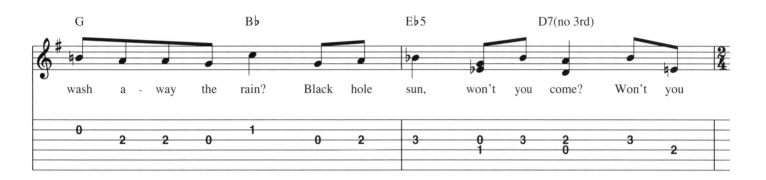

wash a - way the rain? Black hole sun, won't you come? Won't you

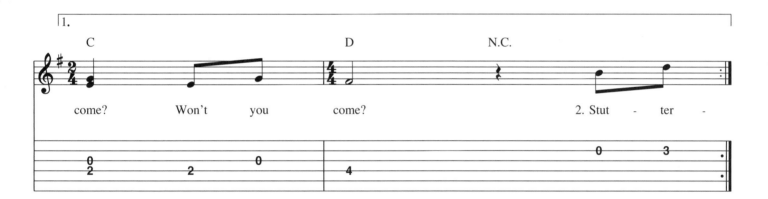

come? Won't you come? 2. Stut - ter -

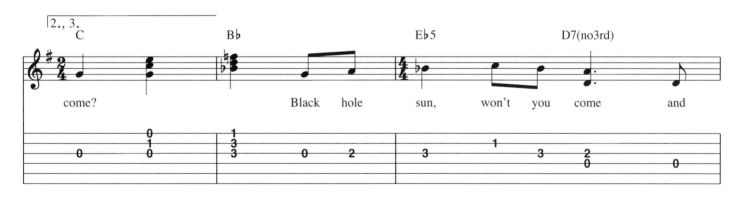

come? Black hole sun, won't you come and

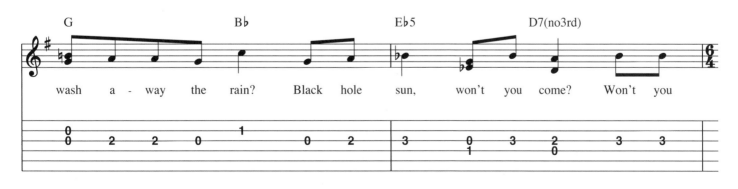

wash a - way the rain? Black hole sun, won't you come? Won't you

47

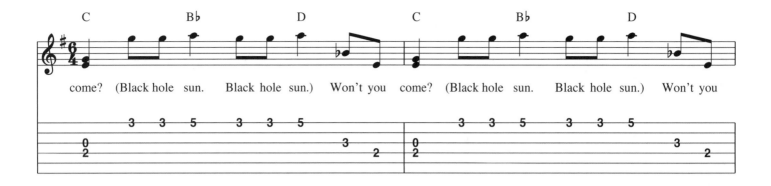

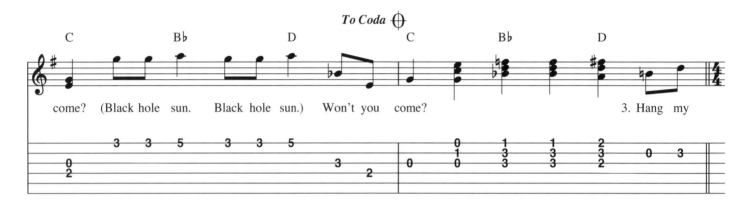

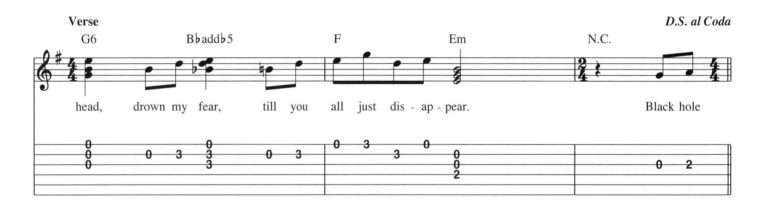

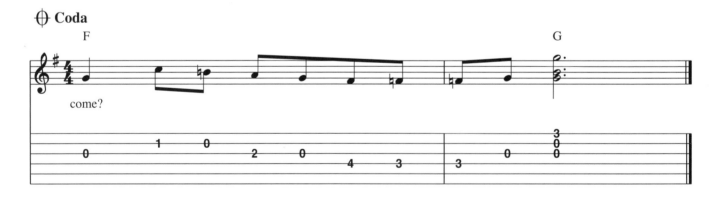

Additional Lyrics

2. Stuttering, cold and damp.
   Steal the warm wind, tired friend.
   Times are gone for honest men,
   And sometimes far too long for snakes.
   In my shoes, a walking sleep.
   In my youth I pray to keep.
   Heaven send hell away.
   No one sings like you anymore.

Breaking the Law

Words and Music by Glenn Tipton, Rob Halford and K.K. Downing

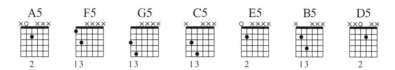

Strum Pattern: 1

Intro
Moderately fast Rock

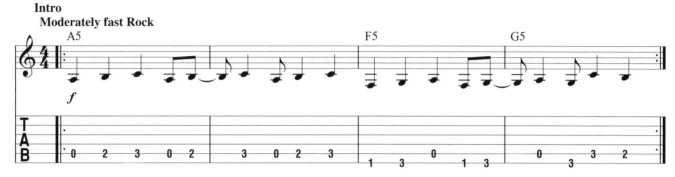

Verse

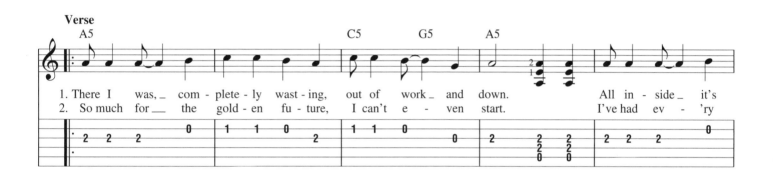

1. There I was, __ com-plete-ly wast-ing, out of work __ and down. All in-side __ it's
2. So much for __ the gold-en fu-ture, I can't e-ven start. I've had ev-'ry

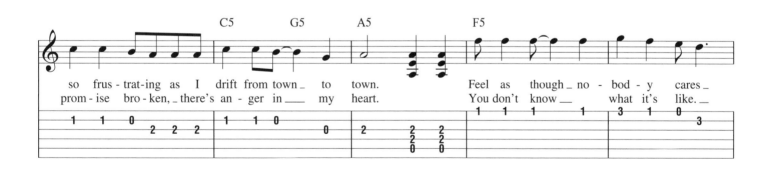

so frus-trat-ing as I drift from town __ to town. Feel as though __ no-bod-y cares __
prom-ise bro-ken, __ there's an-ger in ___ my heart. You don't know __ what it's like. __

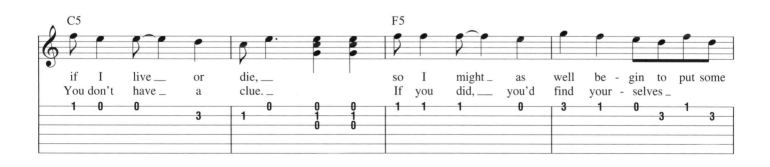

if I live __ or die, __ so I might __ as well be-gin to put some
You don't have __ a clue. __ If you did, __ you'd find your-selves __

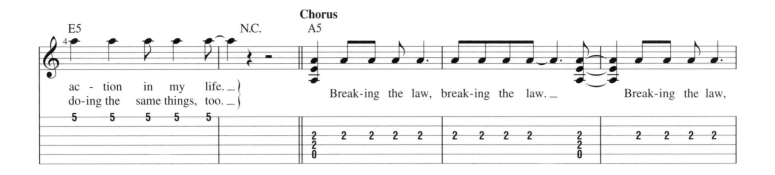

*Bass plays B, next 8 meas.

**Bass plays D, next 8 meas.

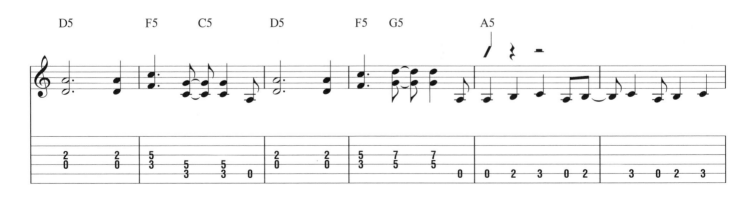

*Resume Strum Pattern 1.

Outro-Chorus

Spoken:
Break-ing the law,   break-ing   the law.   Break-ing the law,   break-ing   the law.

Break-ing the law,   break-ing the law.   Break-ing the law,   break-ing the law.

Break-ing the law,   break-ing the law.   Break-ing the law,   break-ing the law.

Born to Be Wild

Words and Music by Mars Bonfire

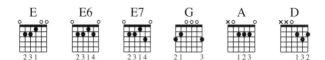

Strum Pattern: 2, 4
Pick Pattern: 3, 4

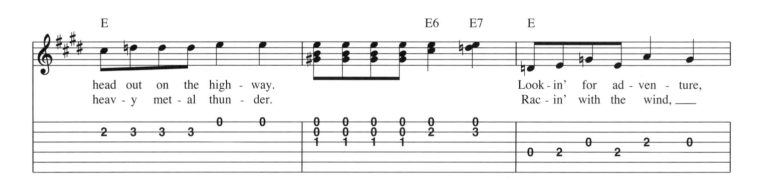

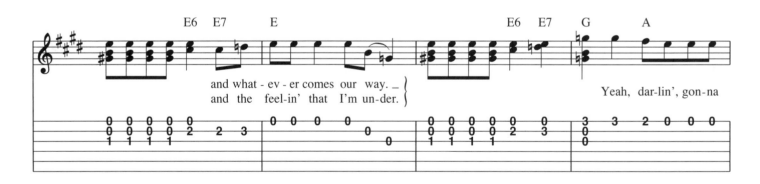

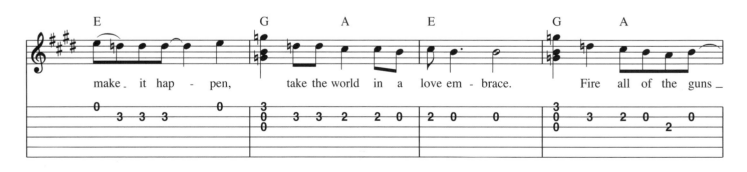

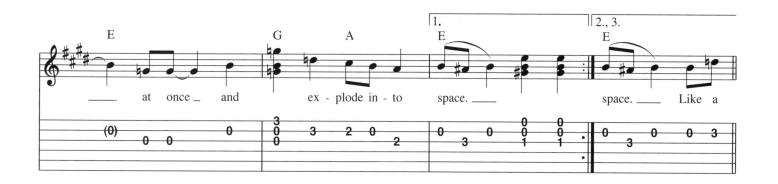

Pre-Chorus

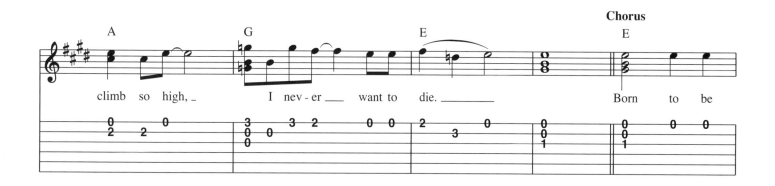

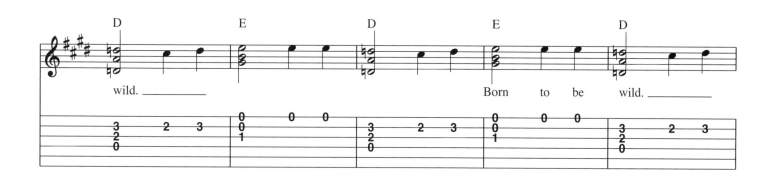

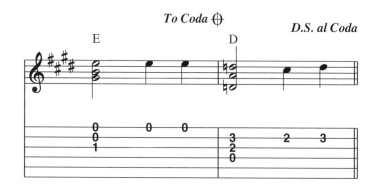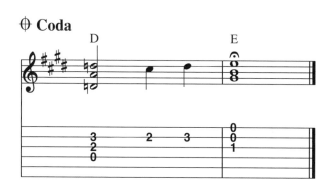

Breaking the Chains

Words and Music by Don Dokken, George Lynch and Mick Brown

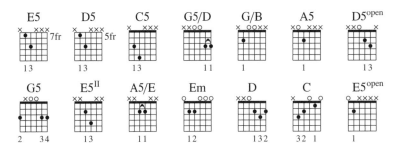

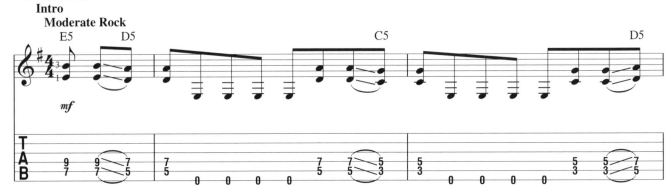

Strum Pattern: 1

Intro
Moderate Rock

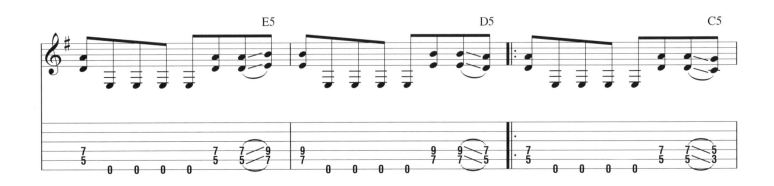

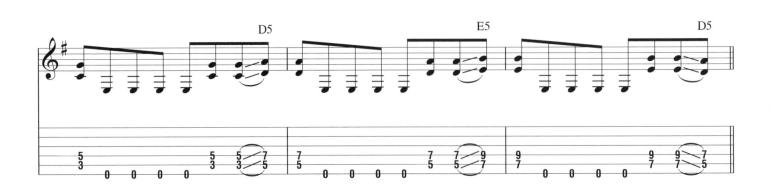

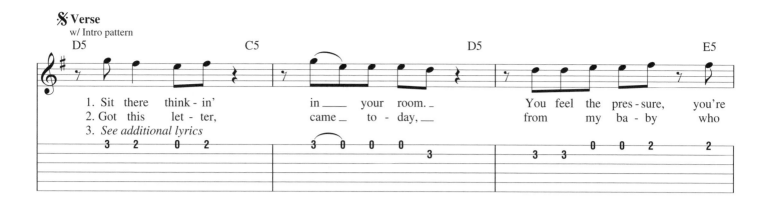

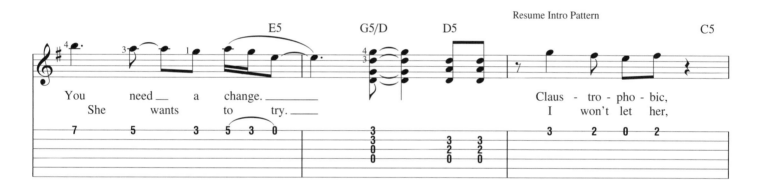

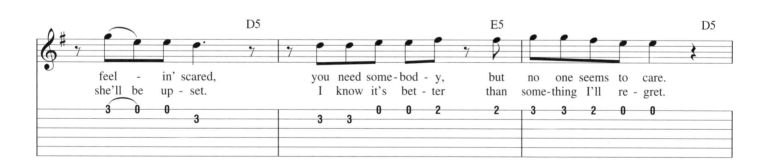

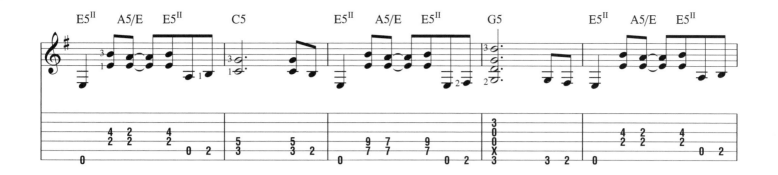

Coda

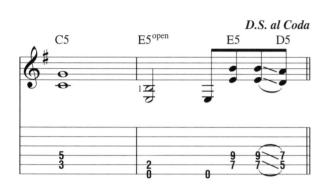

D.S. al Coda

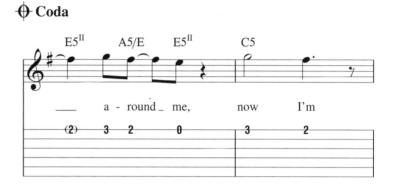

___ a - round ___ me,   now   I'm

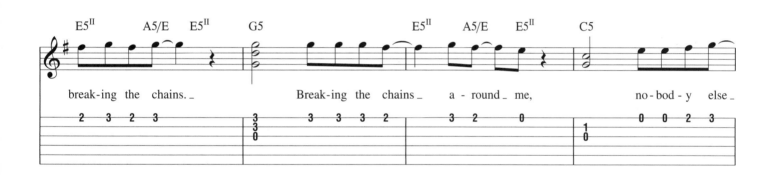

break-ing the chains. ___   Break-ing the chains ___   a - round ___ me,   no - bod - y   else ___

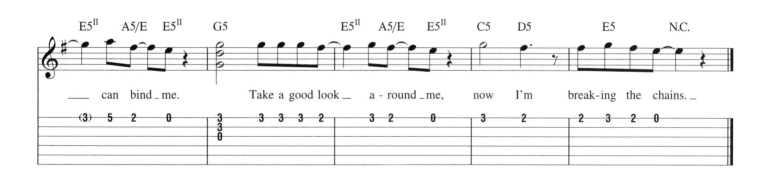

___ can bind ___ me.   Take a good look ___ a - round ___ me,   now   I'm   break-ing the chains. ___

Additional Lyrics

3. Woke up today, I'm alone.
   I look around but baby, you are gone.
   But I don't mind and I don't worry.
   I will survive.
   I'm alone now that you're gone.
   Don't need nobody to hold or tie me down.
   I broke the chains, so let me be.
   I've gotta be free.

Carry On Wayward Son

Words and Music by Kerry Livgren

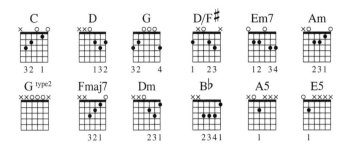

Strum Pattern: 3
Pick Pattern: 2, 3

Intro
Moderate Rock

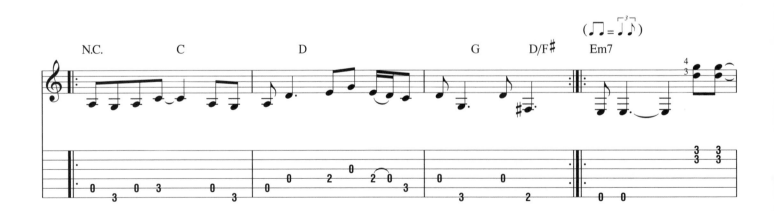

Car-ry on my way - ward son, _____ there'll be peace when you ___ are done. ___

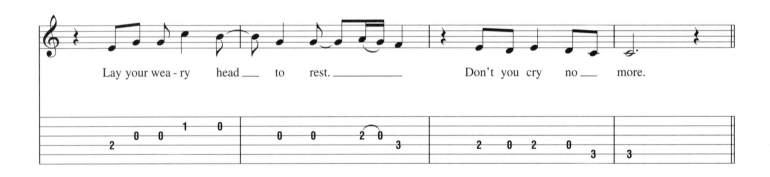

Lay your wea - ry head ___ to rest. _____ Don't you cry no ___ more.

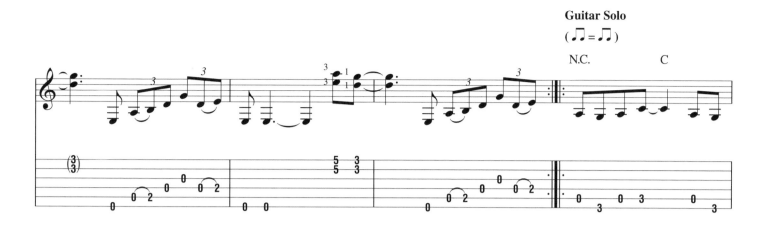

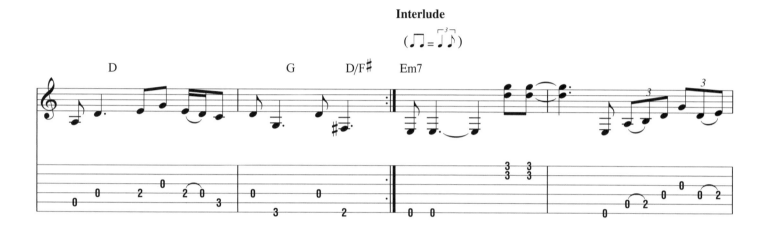

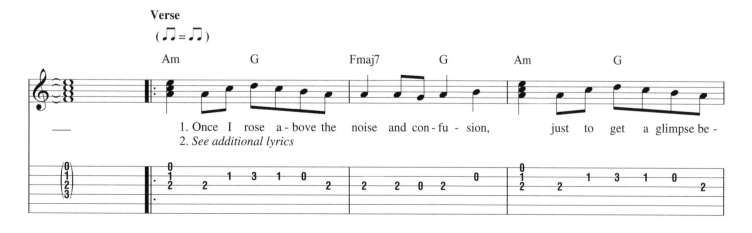

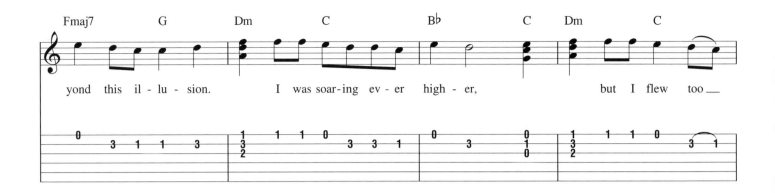

Chorus

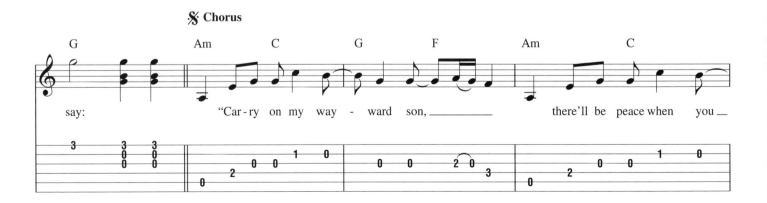

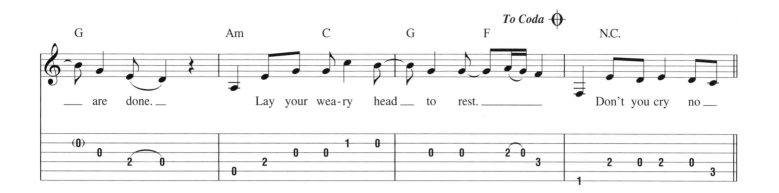

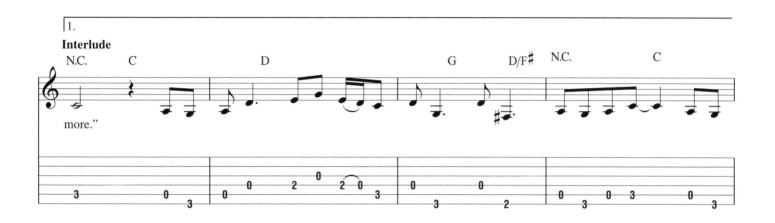

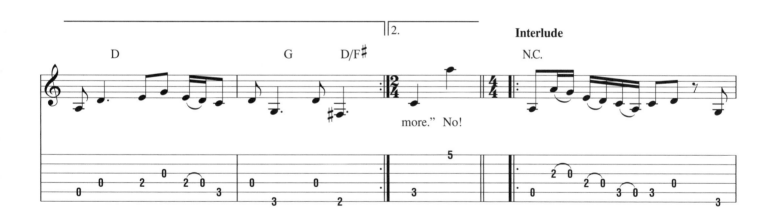

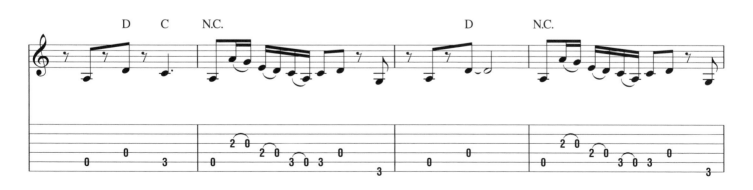

Solos

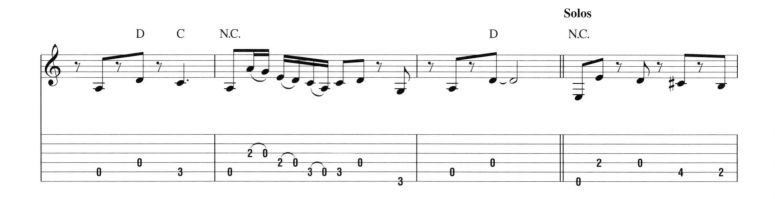

Interlude

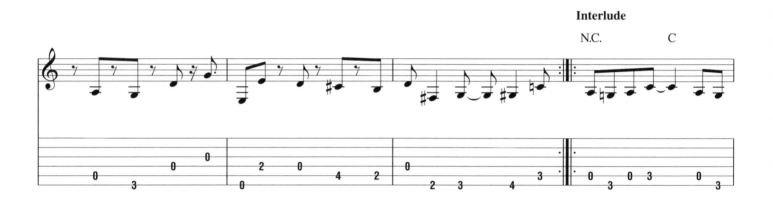

Bridge

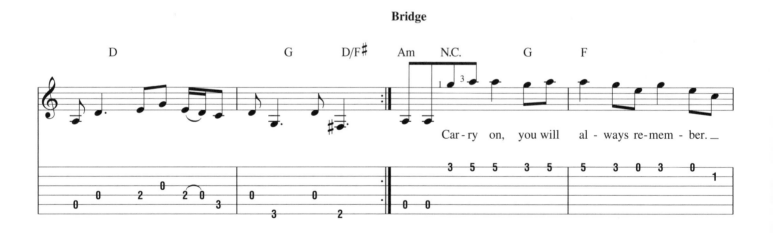

Car - ry on, you will al - ways re - mem - ber. __

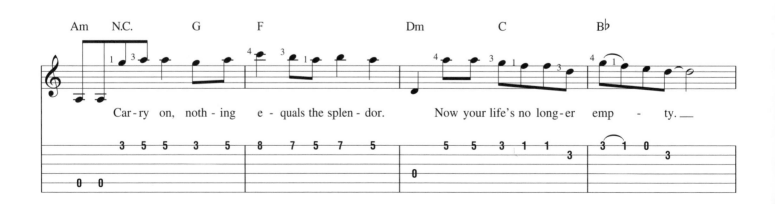

Car - ry on, noth - ing e - quals the splen - dor. Now your life's no long - er emp - ty. __

Interlude

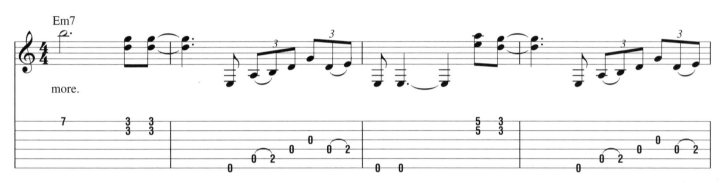

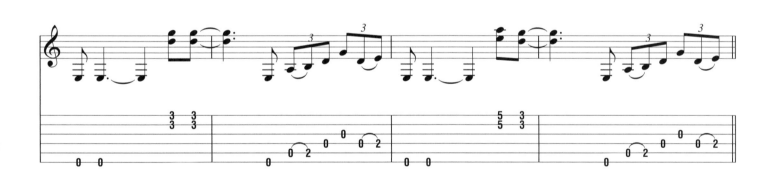

Guitar Solo

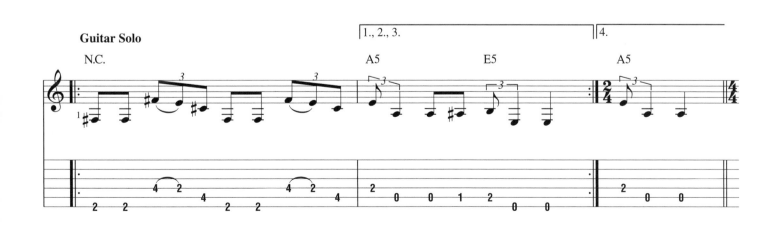

Interlude

Guitar Solo

Outro

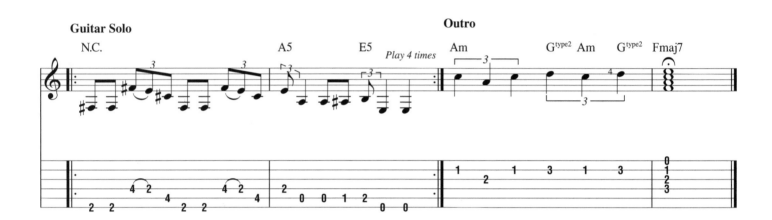

Additional Lyrics

2. Masquerading as a man with a reason.
   My charade is the event of the season.
   And if I claim to be a wise man, well,
   It surely means that I don't know.
   On a stormy sea of moving emotion,
   Tossed about, I'm like a ship on the ocean.
   I set a course for winds of fortune.
   But I hear the voices say:

Dirty Deeds Done Dirt Cheap

Words and Music by Angus Young, Malcolm Young and Bon Scott

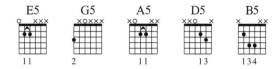

Strum Pattern: 1
Pick Pattern: 1

Intro

Moderate Rock

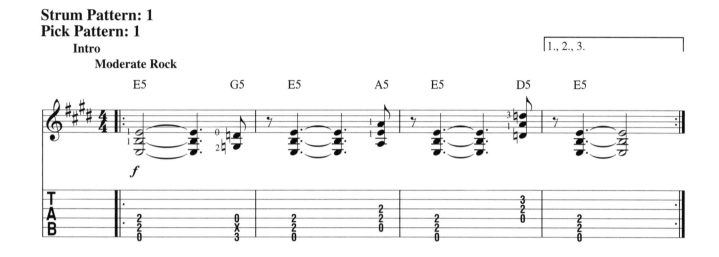

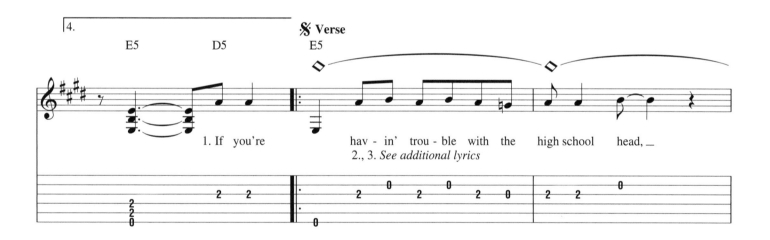

1. If you're hav - in' trou - ble with the high school head, _
2., 3. *See additional lyrics*

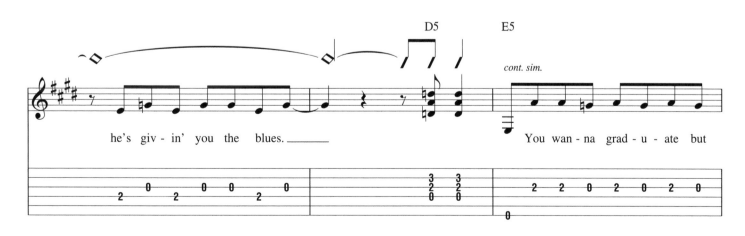

he's giv - in' you the blues. _____

You wan - na grad - u - ate but

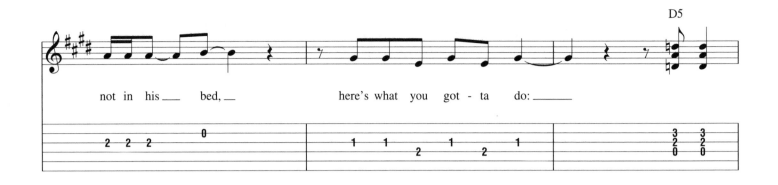

not in his ___ bed, ___   here's what you got - ta do: _____

pick up the phone, I'm ___ al - ways home.   Call me an - y - time. ___   Just ring

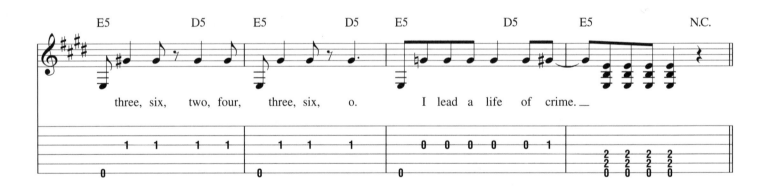

three, six, two, four, three, six, o.   I lead a life of crime. _

Chorus

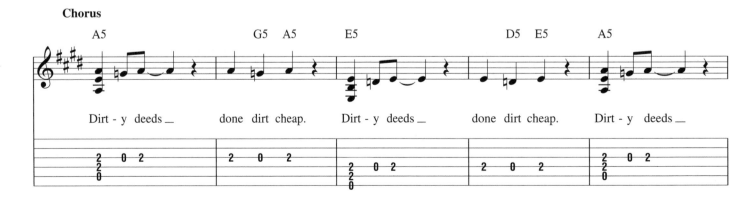

Dirt - y deeds ___ done dirt cheap.   Dirt - y deeds ___ done dirt cheap.   Dirt - y deeds ___

done dirt cheap.   Dirt - y deeds ___ and they're done dirt cheap.   Dirt - y deeds ___ and they're

*Let chord ring.

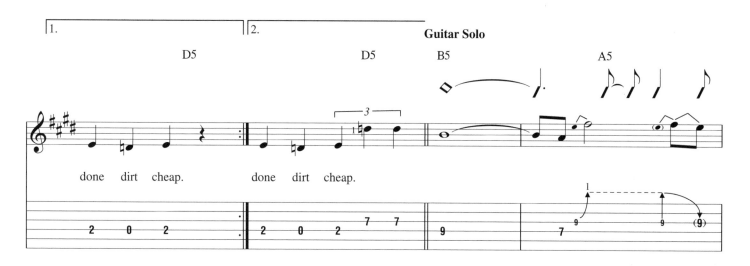

done dirt cheap.   done dirt cheap.

Guitar Solo

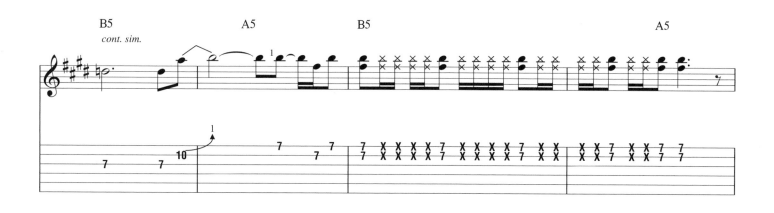

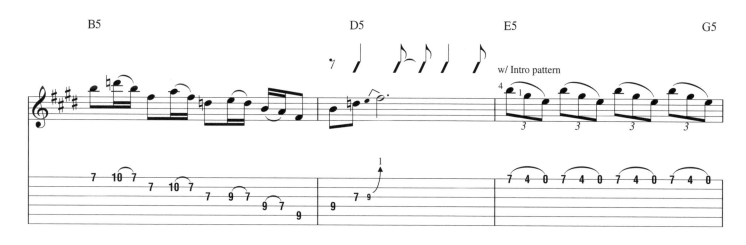

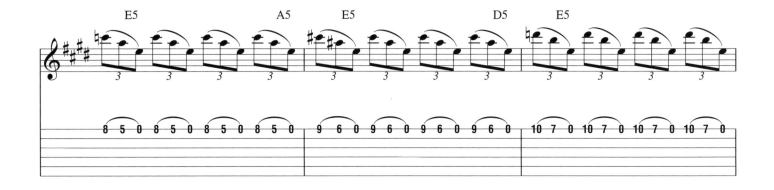

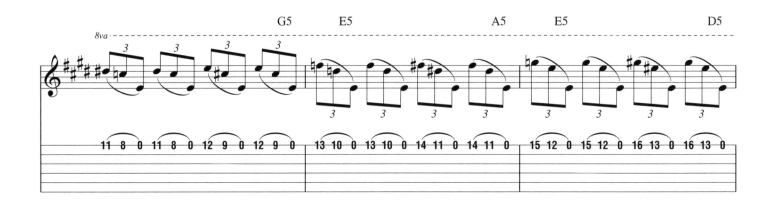

D.S. al Coda   ⊕ **Coda**

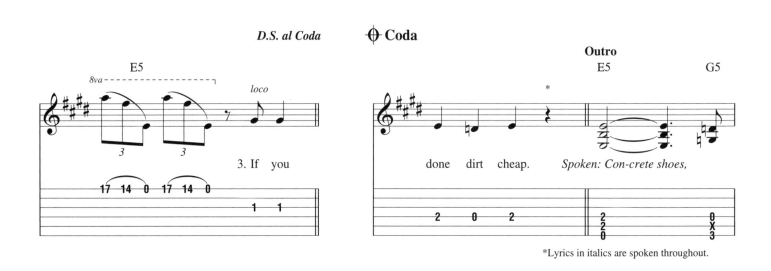

*Lyrics in italics are spoken throughout.

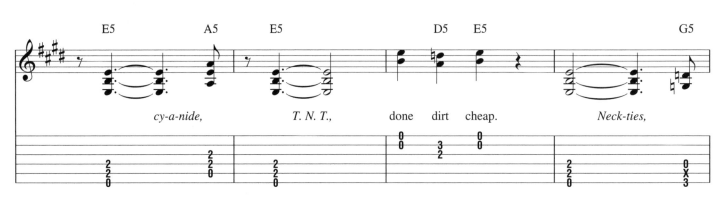

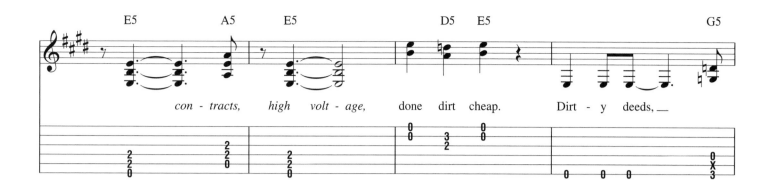

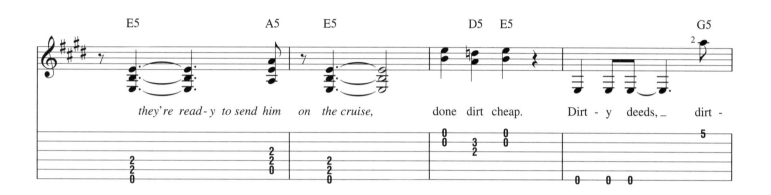

Additional Lyrics

2. You got problems in your life of love,
   You got a broken heart.
   He's double-dealin' with your best friend,
   That's when the teardrops start, fella.
   Pick up the phone, I'm here alone,
   Or make a social call.
   Come right in, forget about him,
   We'll have ourselves a ball.

3. If you got a lady and you want her gone,
   But you ain't got the guts.
   She keeps naggin' at you night and day,
   Enough to drive you nuts.
   Pick up the phone, leave her alone,
   It's time you made a stand.
   For a fee, I'm happy to be
   Your back door man. Whoo!

Cherry Bomb

Words and Music by Kim Fowley and Joan Jett

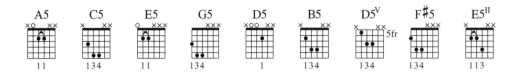

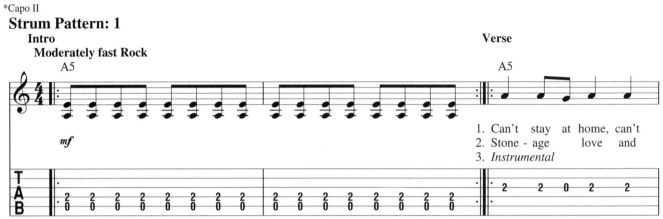

*Capo II

Strum Pattern: 1

*Optional: To match recording, place capo at 2nd fret.

Verse
1. Can't stay at home, can't stay at school, old folks say, "You poor lit-tle fool." Down the street, I'm the
2. Stone - age love and strange sounds too, come on, ba - by, let me get to you. Bad nights caus-ing

girl next door, **I'm the fox you've been wait-ing for.**
teen - age blues, *get down lad - ies, you've got noth-ing to lose.*

**Lyrics in italics are spoken throughout.

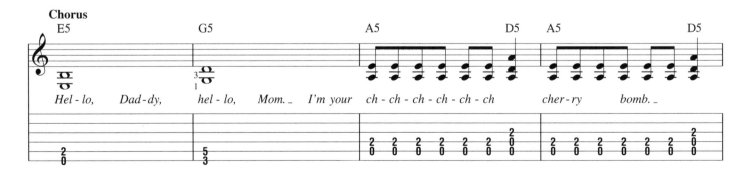

Chorus

Hel - lo, Dad-dy, hel - lo, Mom. I'm your ch - ch - ch - ch - ch - ch cher-ry bomb.

Cherry Pie

Words and Music by Jani Lane

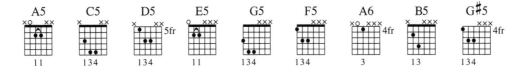

Strum Pattern: 3, 5

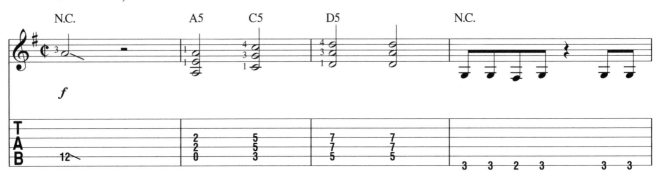

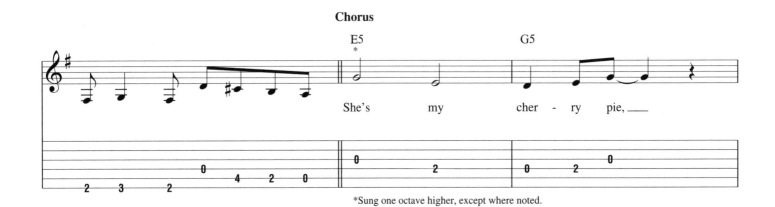

*Sung one octave higher, except where noted.

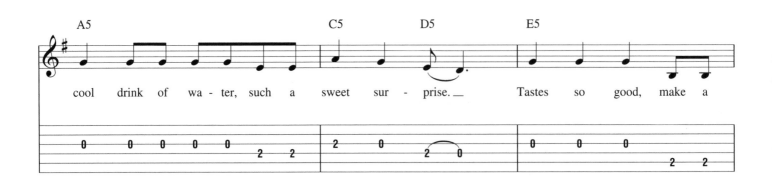

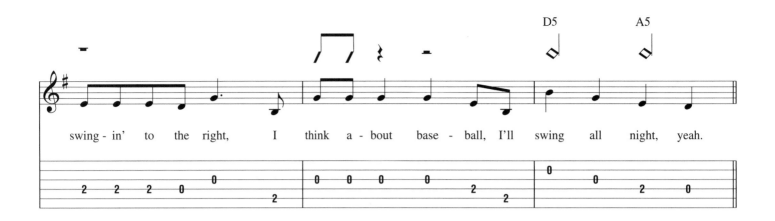

swing-in' to the right, I think a-bout base-ball, I'll swing all night, yeah.

Interlude

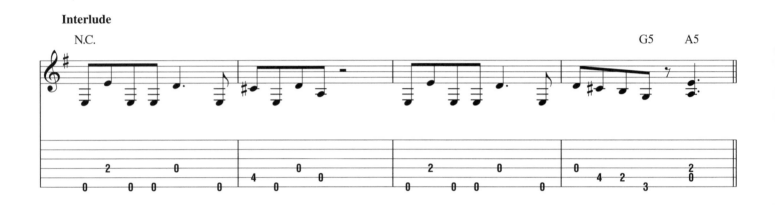

Verse

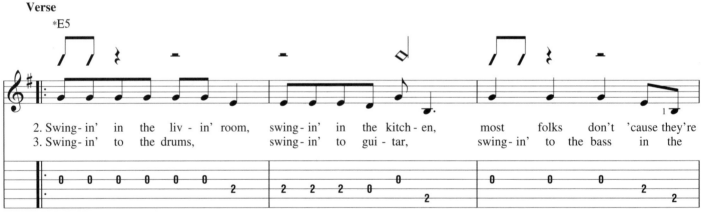

2. Swing-in' in the liv-in' room, swing-in' in the kitch-en, most folks don't 'cause they're
3. Swing-in' to the drums, swing-in' to gui-tar, swing-in' to the bass in the

*2nd time, N.C. 3 meas.

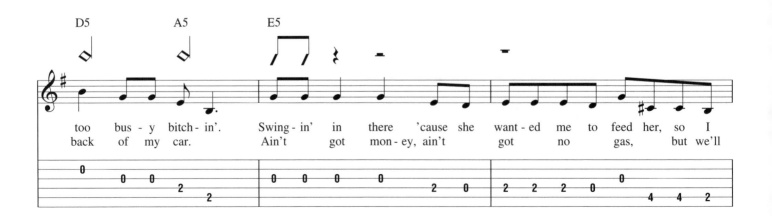

too bus-y bitch-in'. Swing-in' in there 'cause she want-ed me to feed her, so I
back of my car. Ain't got mon-ey, ain't got no gas, but we'll

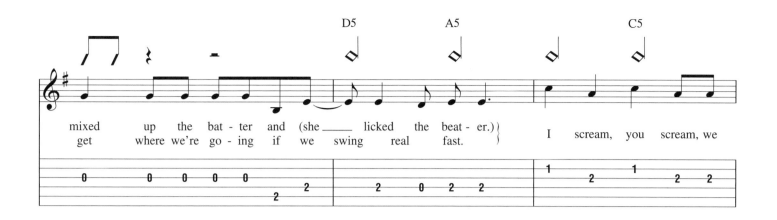

mixed up the bat - ter and (she ___ licked the beat - er.)

get where we're go - ing if we swing real fast.

I scream, you scream, we

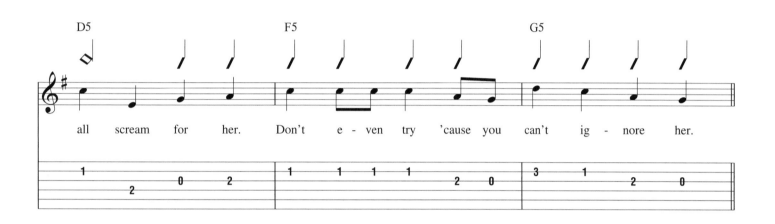

all scream for her. Don't e - ven try 'cause you can't ig - nore her.

Chorus

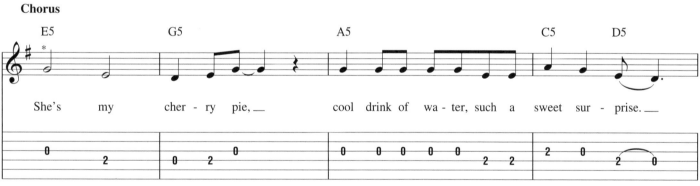

She's my cher - ry pie, ___ cool drink of wa - ter, such a sweet sur - prise. ___

* Sung one octave higher.

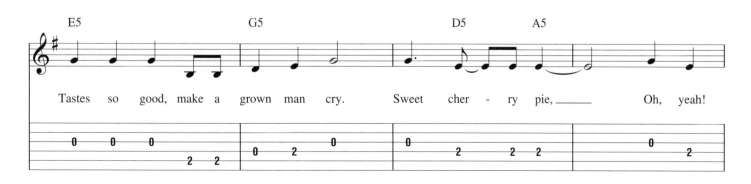

Tastes so good, make a grown man cry. Sweet cher - ry pie, ___ Oh, yeah!

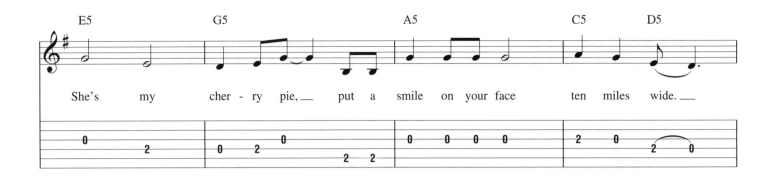

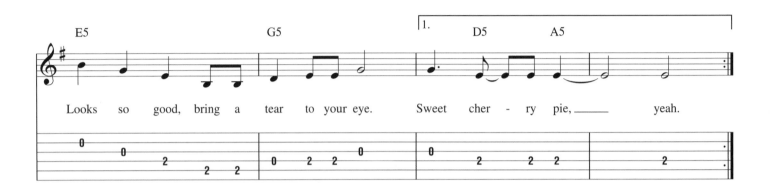

*Let chord ring.   **Sung as written, next 2 meas.   ***Let chord ring.

Guitar Solo

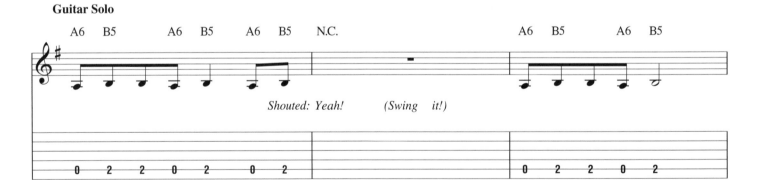

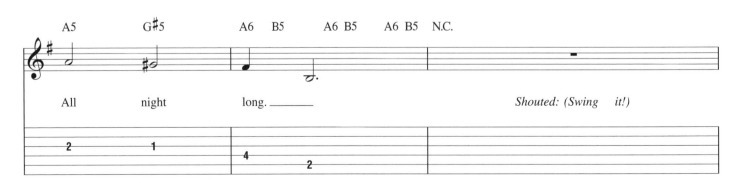

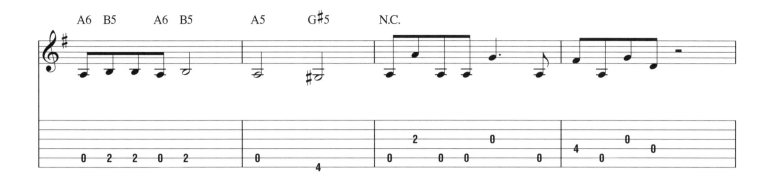

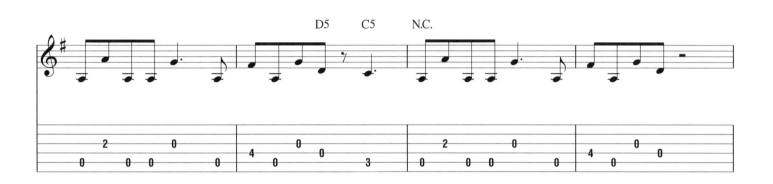

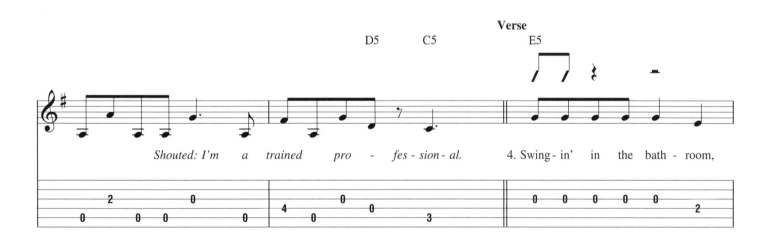

Shouted: I'm a trained pro - fes - sion - al. 4. Swing-in' in the bath - room,

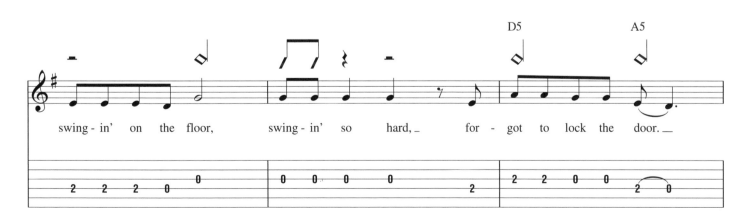

swing-in' on the floor, swing-in' so hard, __ for - got to lock the door. __

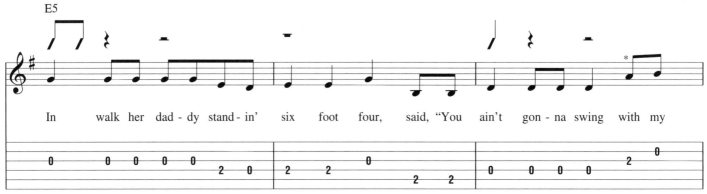

In walk her dad-dy stand-in' six foot four, said, "You ain't gon-na swing with my

* Sung as written.

Outro-Chorus

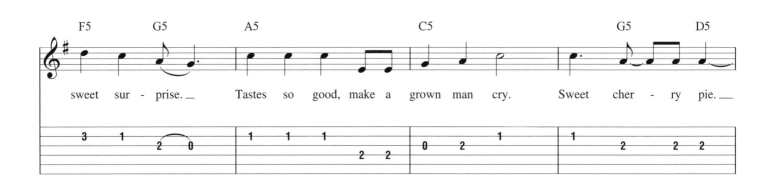

daugh-ter no more." She's my cher-ry pie, ___ cool drink of wa-ter, such a

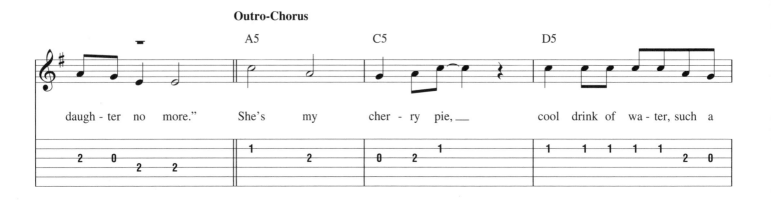

sweet sur-prise. ___ Tastes so good, make a grown man cry. Sweet cher-ry pie. ___

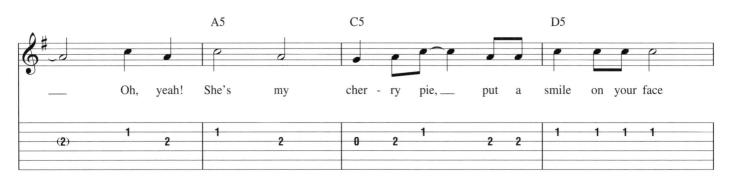

___ Oh, yeah! She's my cher-ry pie, ___ put a smile on your face

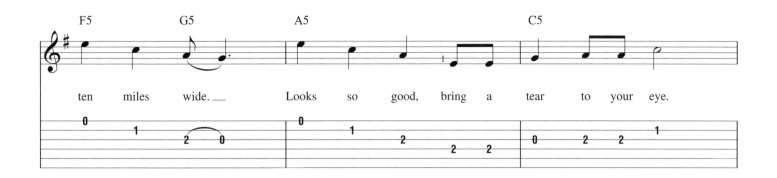

ten   miles   wide. ___   Looks   so   good,   bring   a   tear   to   your   eye.

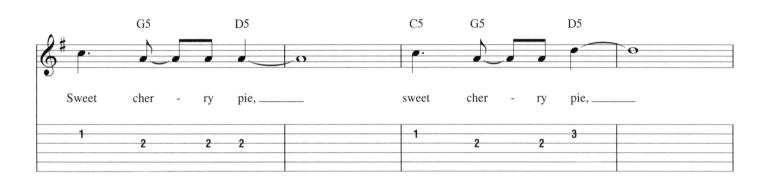

Sweet   cher - ry   pie, _____   sweet   cher - ry   pie, _____

yeah!

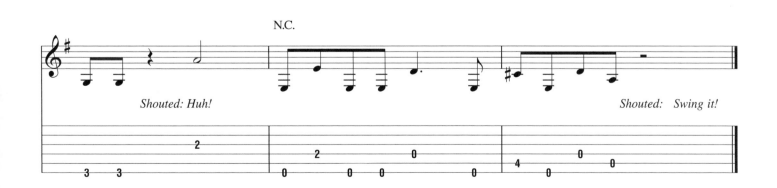

Shouted: Huh!   *Shouted: Swing it!*

Crazy Train

Words and Music by Ozzy Osbourne, Randy Rhoads and Bob Daisley

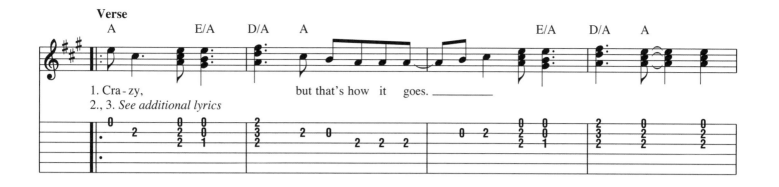

Verse

1. Cra-zy, but that's how it goes. ____
2., 3. *See additional lyrics*

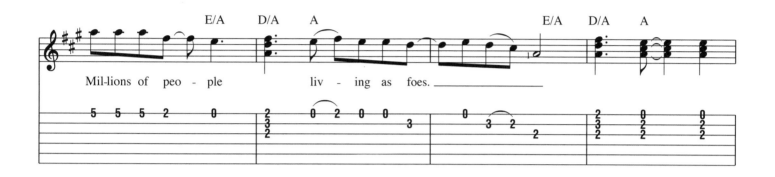

Mil-lions of peo-ple liv - ing as foes. ____

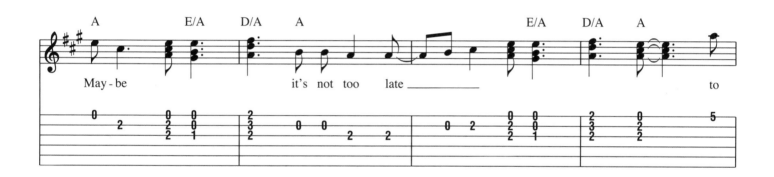

May - be it's not too late ____ to

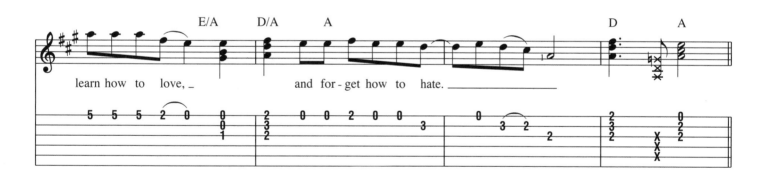

learn how to love, _ and for - get how to hate. ____

Chorus

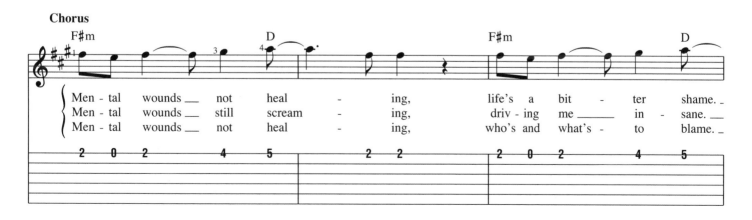

Men - tal wounds __ not heal - ing, life's a bit - ter shame. _
Men - tal wounds __ still scream - ing, driv - ing me _____ in - sane. _
Men - tal wounds __ not heal - ing, who's and what's - to blame. _

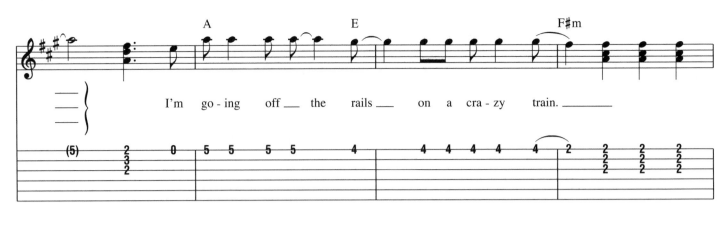

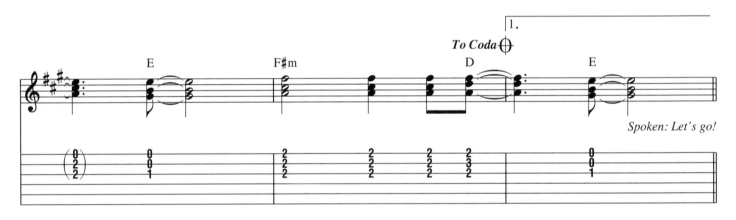

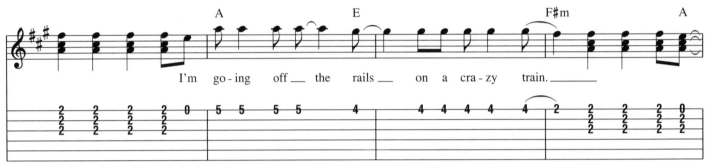

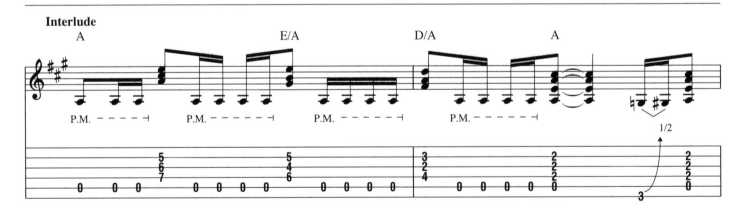

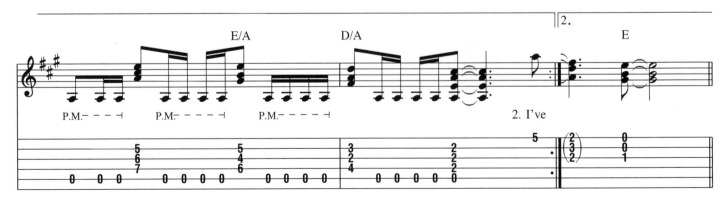

Bridge

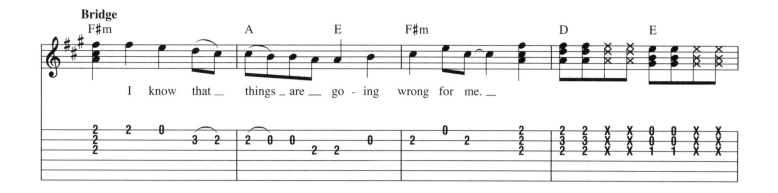

I know that __ things _ are _ go - ing wrong for me. __

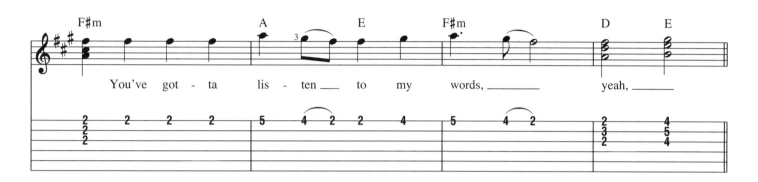

You've got - ta lis - ten __ to my words, _____ yeah, _____

Guitar Solo

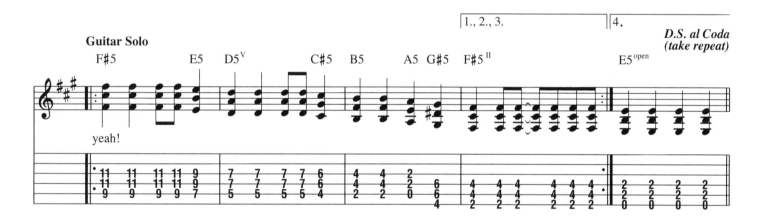

yeah!

🜋 **Coda**

Outro

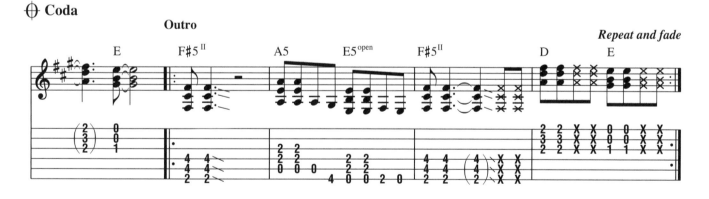

Additional Lyrics

2. I've listened to preachers, I've listened to fools.
   I've watched all the dropouts who make their own rules.
   One person conditioned to rule and control.
   The media sells it, and you live the role.

3. Heirs of a cold war, that's what we've become.
   Inheriting troubles, I'm mentally numb.
   Crazy, I just cannot bear.
   I'm living with something that just isn't fair.

Cult of Personality

Words and Music by William Calhoun, Corey Glover,
Muzz Skillings and Vernon Reid

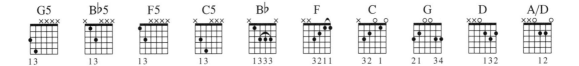

Strum Pattern: 2, 6

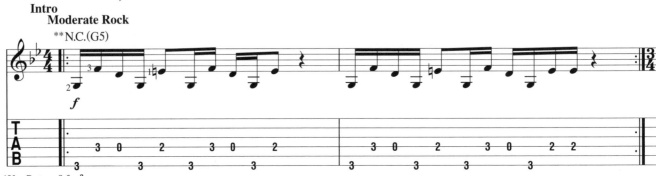

*Use Pattern 8 for ¾ meas.
Use Pattern 10 for ¾ meas.
**Chords in parentheses reflect implied harmony.

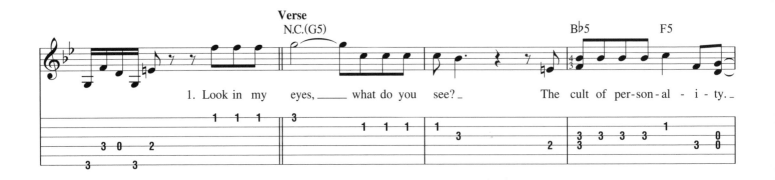

1. Look in my eyes, ___ what do you see? ___ The cult of per-son-al - i - ty. ___

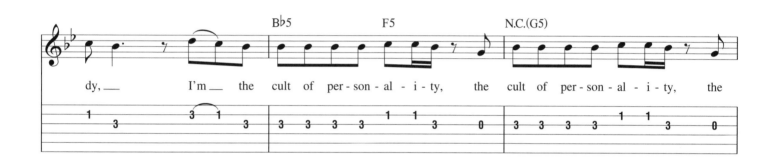

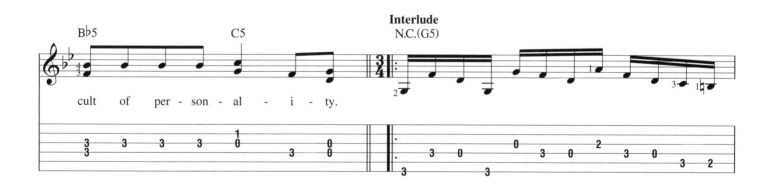

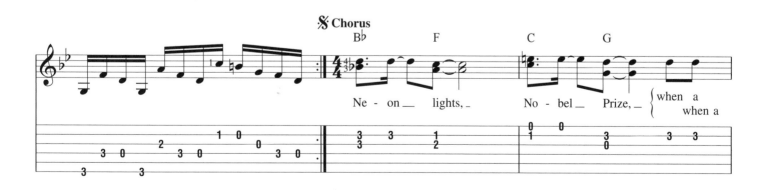

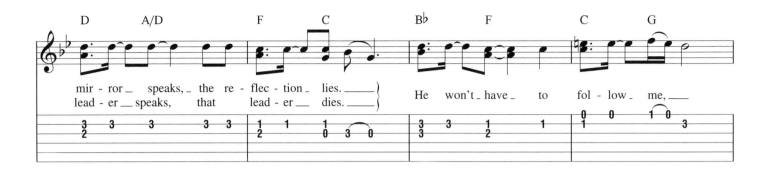

mir - ror _ speaks, _ the re - flec - tion _ lies. _____
lead - er _ speaks, that lead - er _ dies. _____
He won't _ have _ to fol - low _ me, _____

To Coda ⊕

Interlude

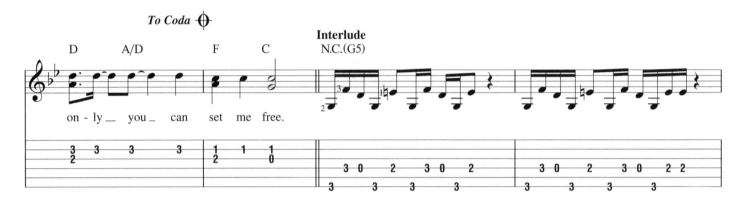

on - ly _ you _ can set me free.

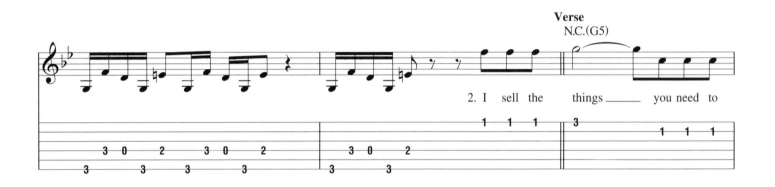

Verse
N.C.(G5)

2. I sell the things _____ you need to

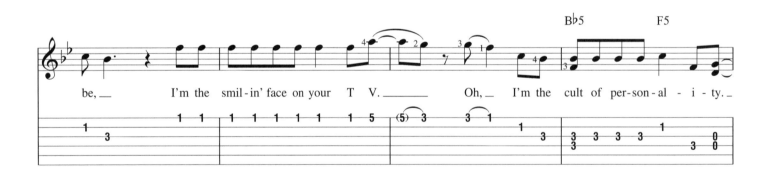

be, _ I'm the smil-in' face on your T V. _____ Oh, _ I'm the cult of per-son-al - i - ty. _

N.C.(G5)

_ I ex-ploit you, still you love me. _ I tell you one an' one makes

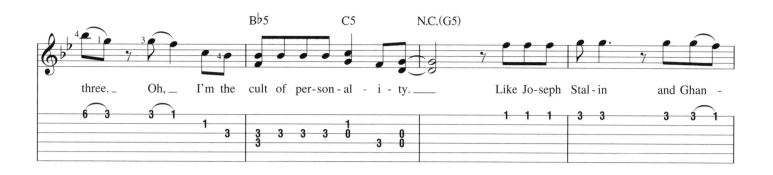

three. ___ Oh, ___ I'm the cult of per-son-al - i - ty. ___ Like Jo-seph Stal-in and Ghan -

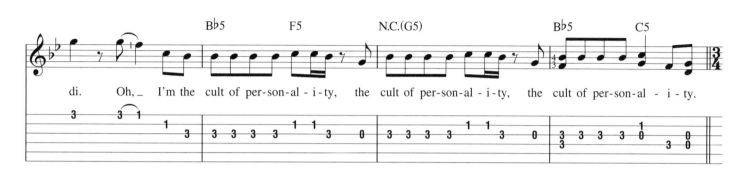

di. Oh, ___ I'm the cult of per-son-al - i - ty, the cult of per-son-al - i - ty, the cult of per-son-al - i - ty.

Interlude

Coda

Guitar Solo

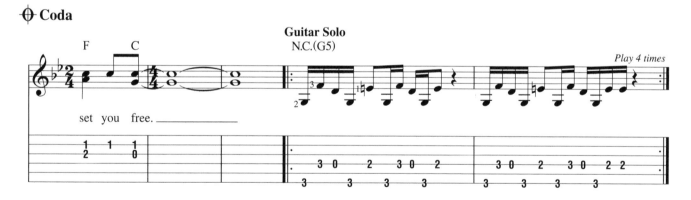

set you free. _____

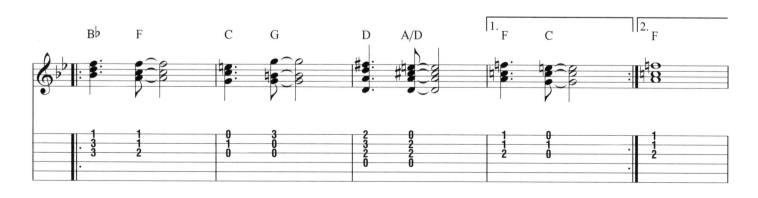

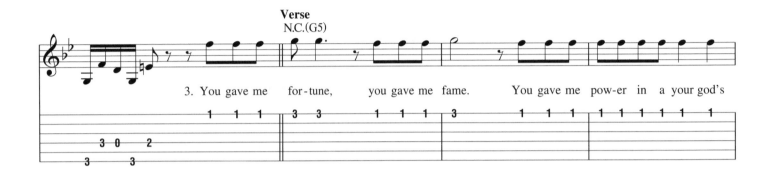

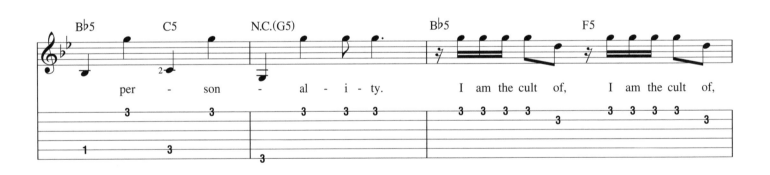

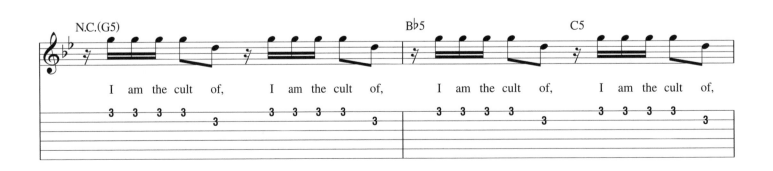

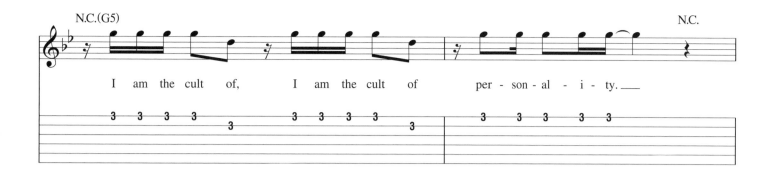

I am the cult of,   I am the cult of   per - son - al - i - ty. ____

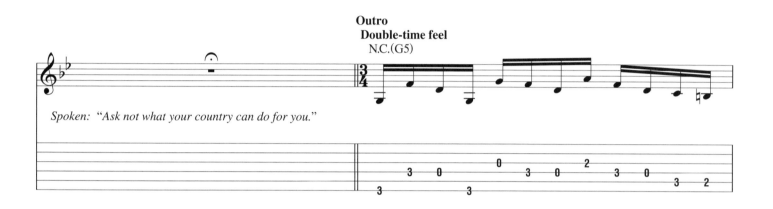

Outro
Double-time feel

Spoken: "Ask not what your country can do for you."

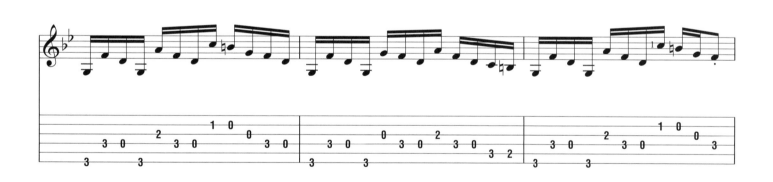

Spoken: "The only thing we have to fear is fear itself."

Cum On Feel the Noize

Words and Music by Neville Holder and James Lea

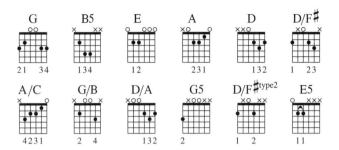

Strum Pattern: 3, 6
Pick Pattern: 3, 4

Intro
Moderately fast

*Sung one octave higher throughout.

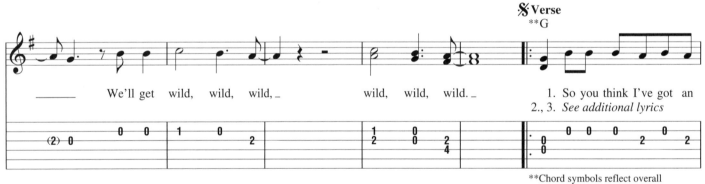

**Chord symbols reflect overall harmony throughout.

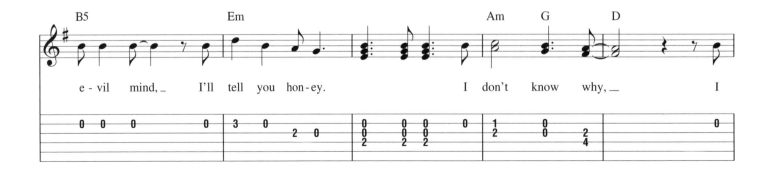

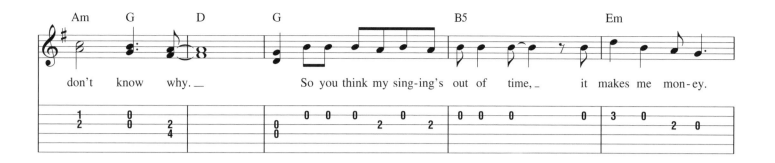

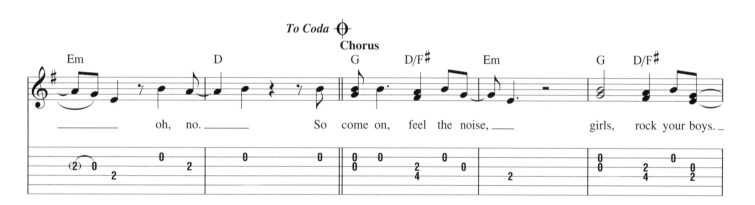

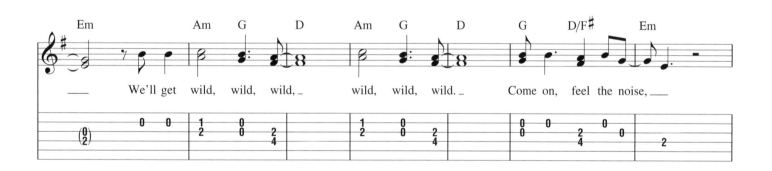

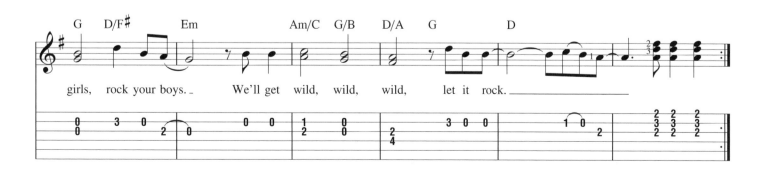

Interlude

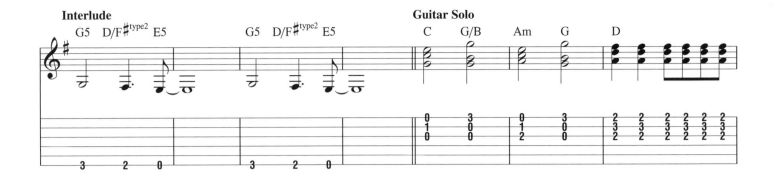

Guitar Solo

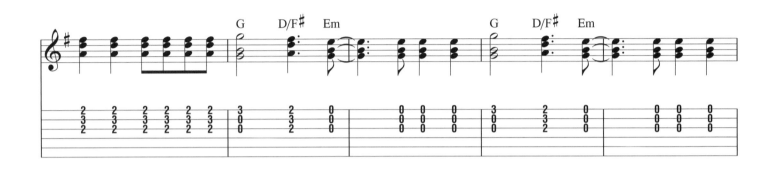

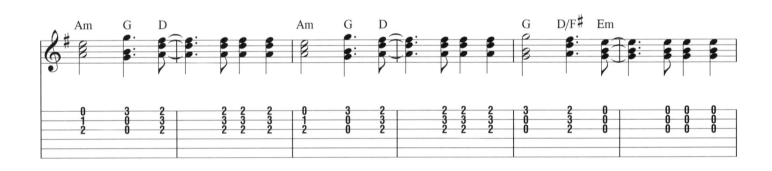

D.S. al Coda

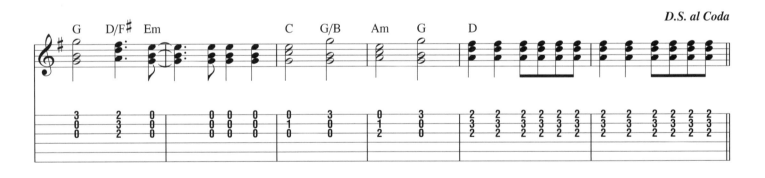

Coda
Chorus

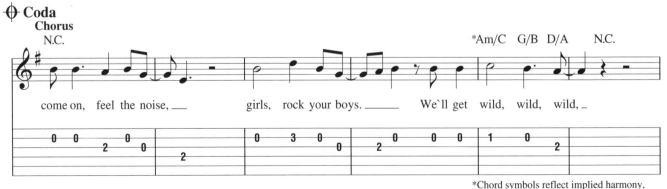

come on, feel the noise, ___ girls, rock your boys. ___ We'll get wild, wild, wild, _

*Chord symbols reflect implied harmony,
next 4 meas.

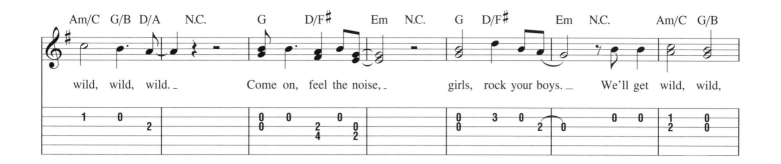

Outro-Chorus
w/ Lead voc. ad lib.

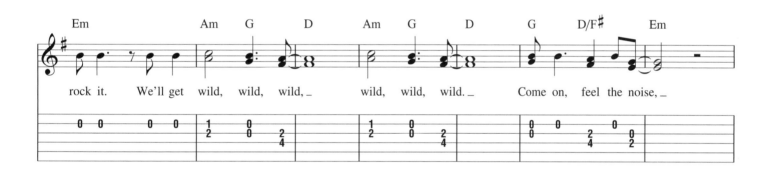

Repeat and fade

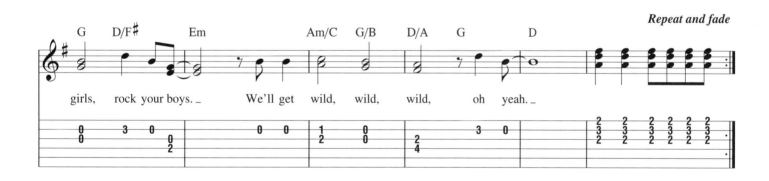

Additional Lyrics

2. So you say I got a funny face; I've got no worries.
   And I don't know why, I don't know why.
   Oh, I've got to sing with some disgrace, I'm in no hurry.
   And I don't know why, I don't know why anymore, no, no, no.

3. Well, you think we have a lazy time, you should know better.
   I don't know why, I don't know why.
   So you say I got a dirty mind; I'm a mean go-getter.
   I don't know why, I don't know why anymore, oh, no.

Dr. Feel Good

Words by Nikki Sixx
Music by Mick Mars and Nikki Sixx

*Tune down 1 step:
(low to high) D-G-C-F-A-D

Strum Pattern: 4, 5

*Optional: To match recording, tune down 1 step.

1. Rat-tailed Jim-my is a sec-ond-hand hood, deals ___ out in Hol-ly-wood. ___
___ on the cor-ner al-ways ig-nore, some-bod-y's get-ting paid. ___

Got a six-ty-five Chev-y, prim-ered flames ___ trad-ed for some pow-dered goods. ___
Jim-my's got it wired, law's ___ for hire; got it made in the shade. ___

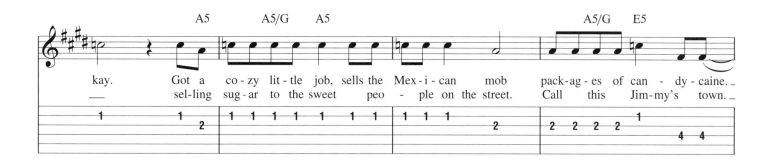

*Sung one octave higher till end.

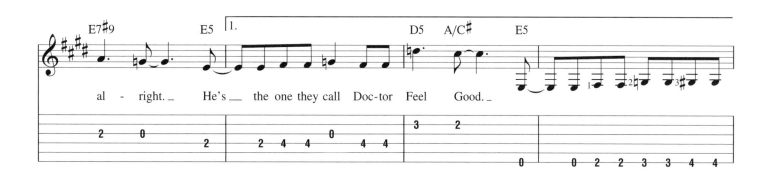

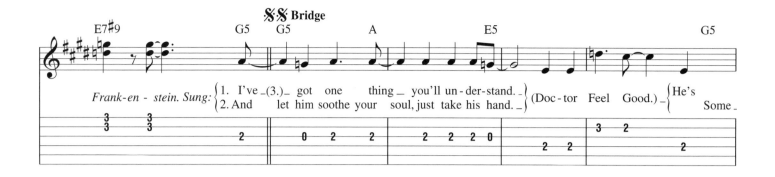

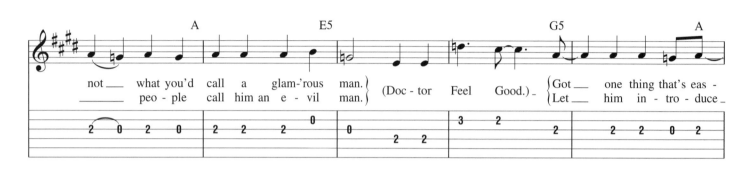

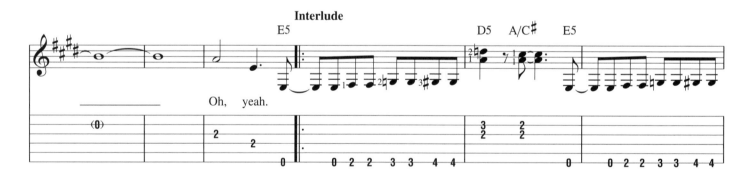

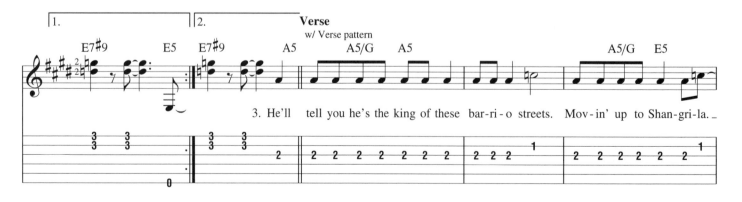

Came by his wealth as a mat-ter of luck. Says he nev-er broke no law. Two

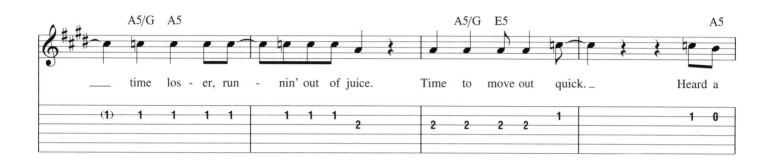

time los - er, run - nin' out of juice. Time to move out quick. Heard a

D.S. al Coda 1
(take 2nd ending)

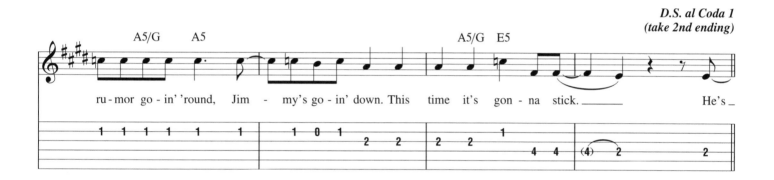

ru - mor go - in' 'round, Jim - my's go - in' down. This time it's gon - na stick. He's

Coda 1

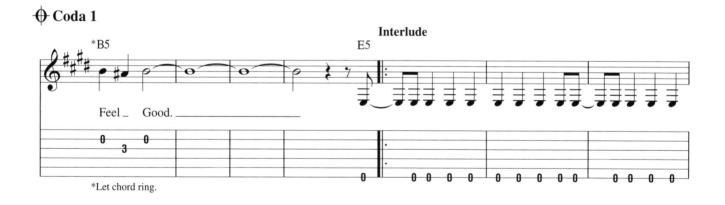

Interlude

Feel _ Good.

*Let chord ring.

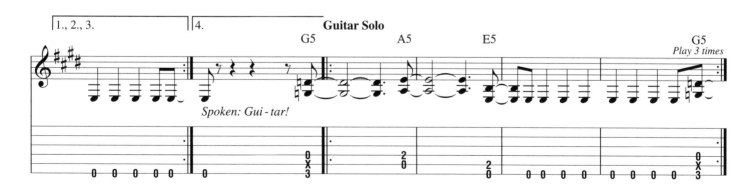

1., 2., 3. | 4. | Guitar Solo

Spoken: Gui - tar!

Play 3 times

Don't Fear the Reaper

Words and Music by Donald Roeser

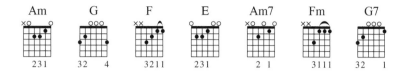

Strum Pattern: 3
Pick Pattern: 2

Intro
Moderate Rock

Verse

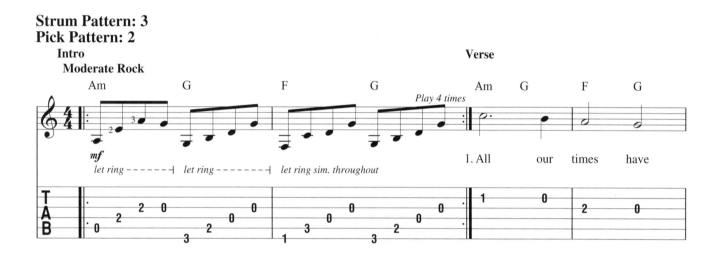

Play 4 times

1. All our times have

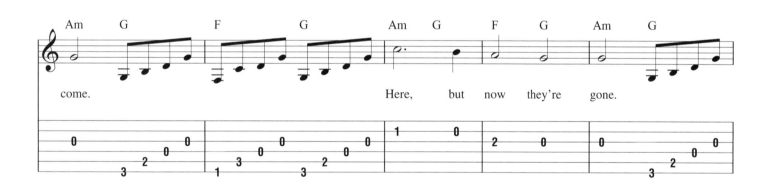

come. Here, but now they're gone.

Sea - sons don't fear the reap - er, nor do the

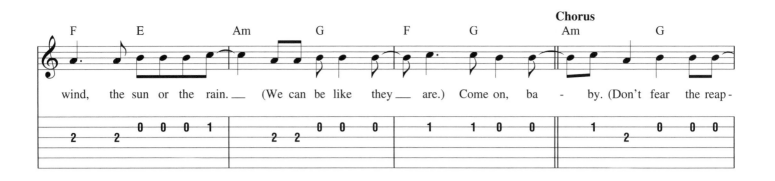

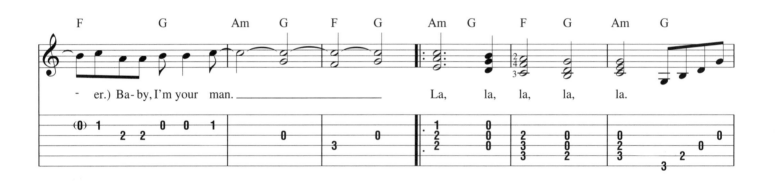

*Let chord ring.

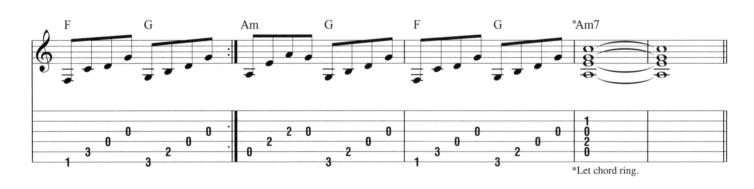

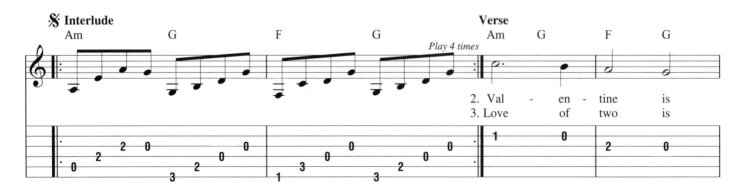

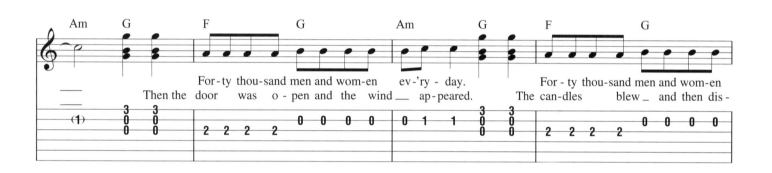

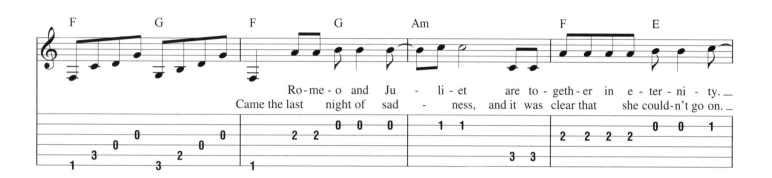

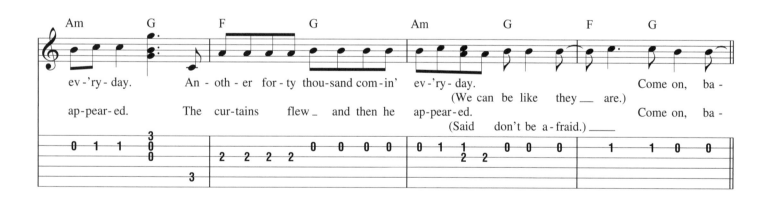

Chorus

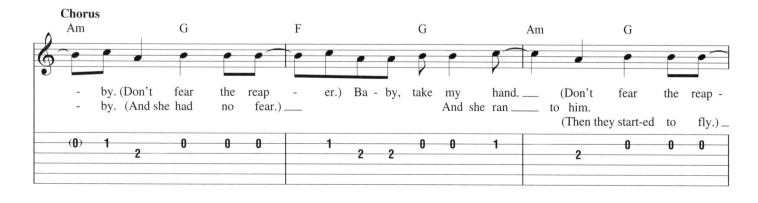

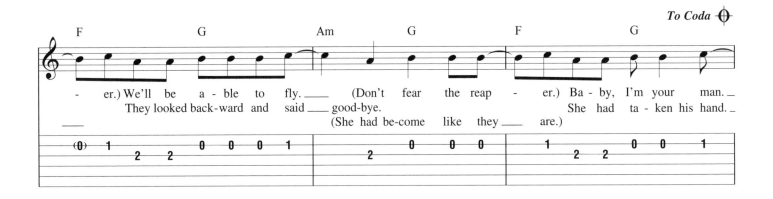

To Coda

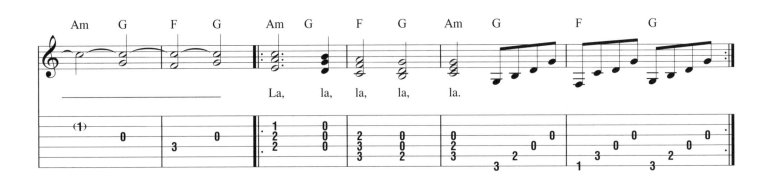

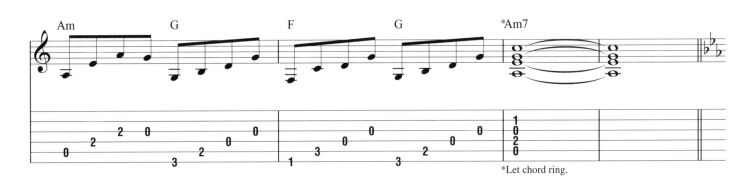

*Let chord ring.

Bridge

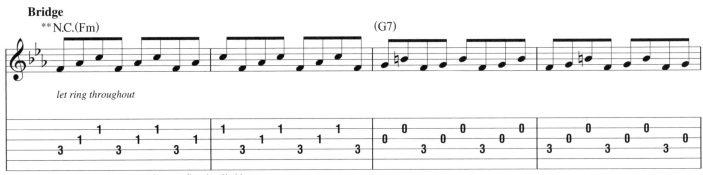

let ring throughout

**Chord symbols in parentheses reflect implied harmony.

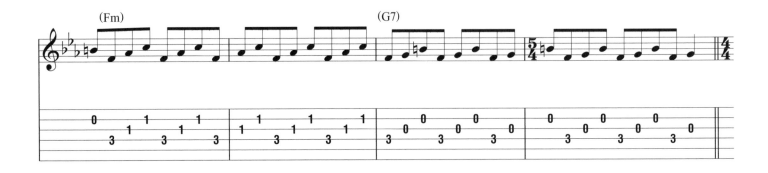

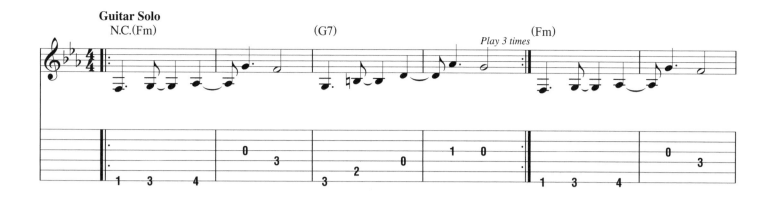

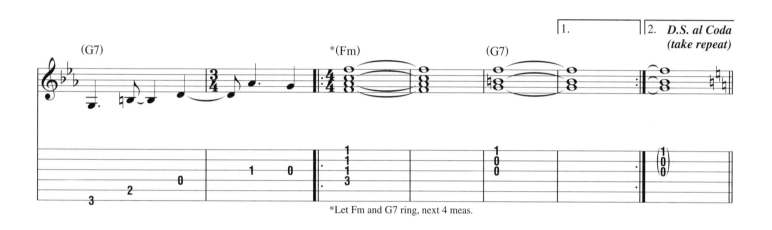

*Let Fm and G7 ring, next 4 meas.

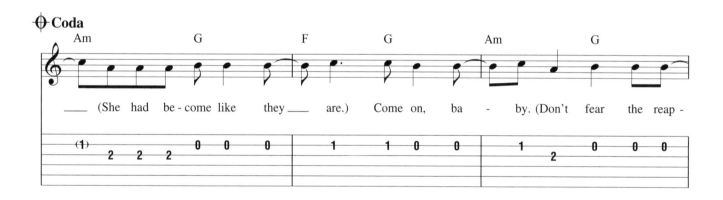

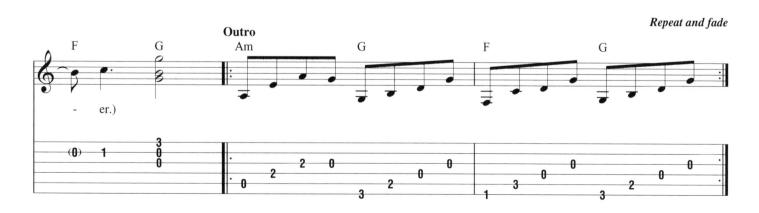

Don't Tell Me You Love Me

Words and Music by Jack Blades

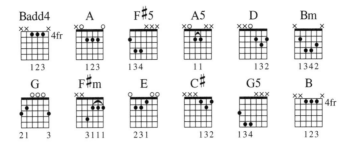

Strum Pattern: 1, 2
Pick Pattern: 2, 3

Intro
Moderately fast

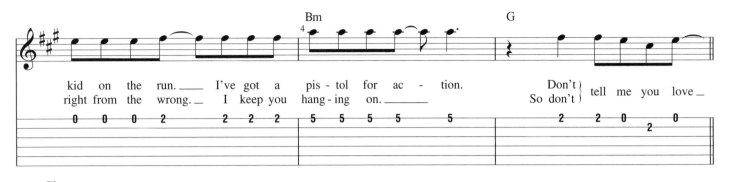

Chorus
Half-time feel

End half-time feel

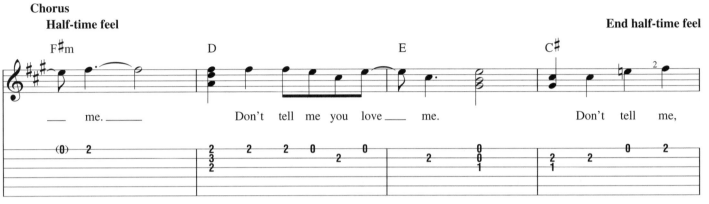

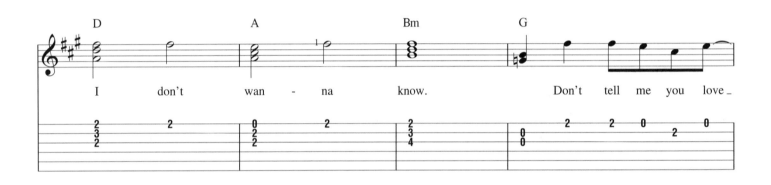

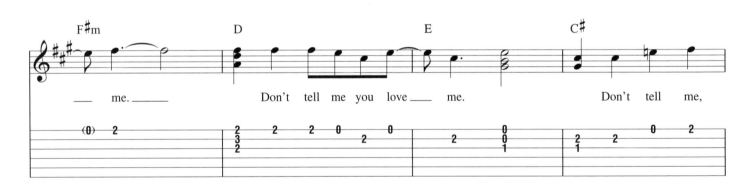

To Coda ⊕

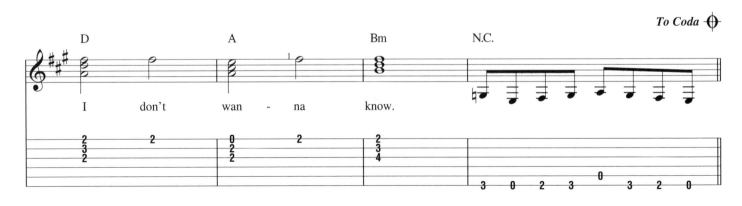

Interlude

D.S. al Coda

Coda

Guitar Solo

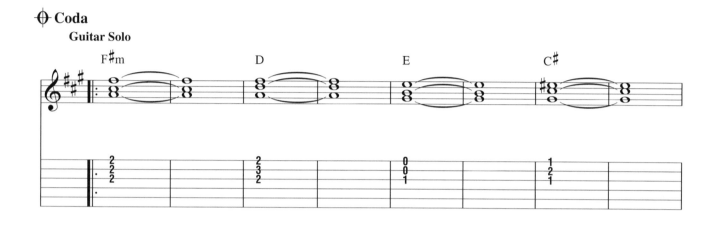

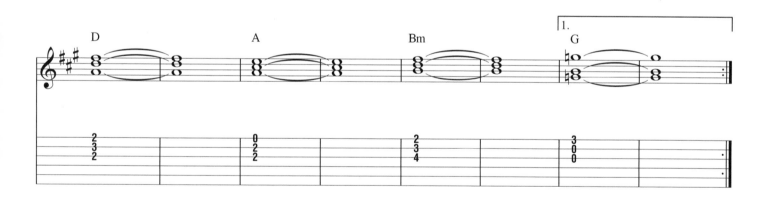

Bridge

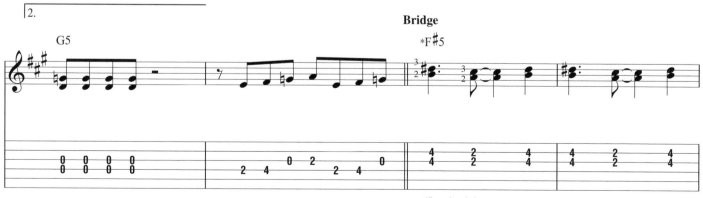

*Let chord ring.

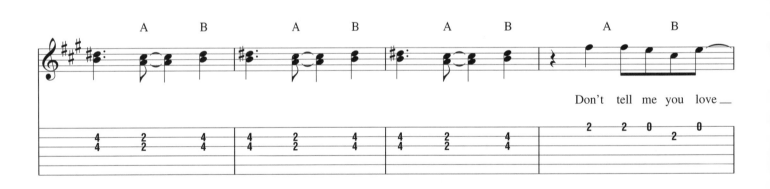

Don't tell me you love ___ me.

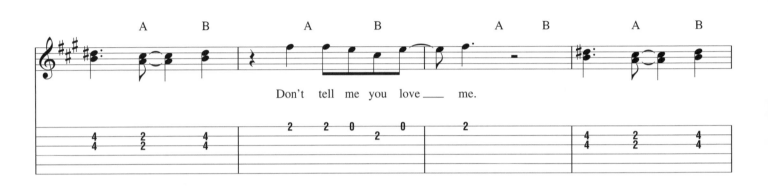

Don't tell me you love ___

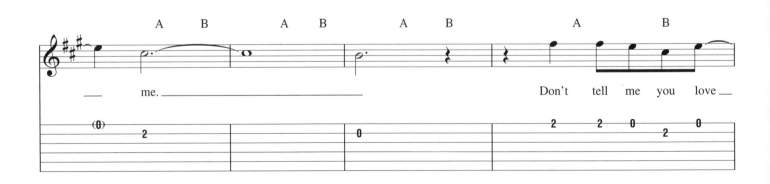

___ me. _____

Don't tell me you love ___

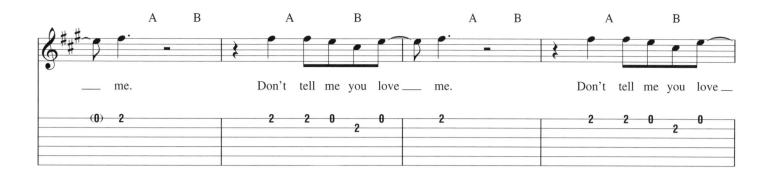

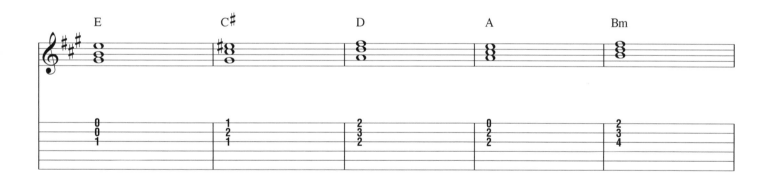

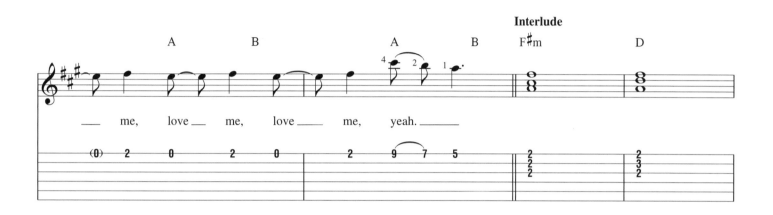

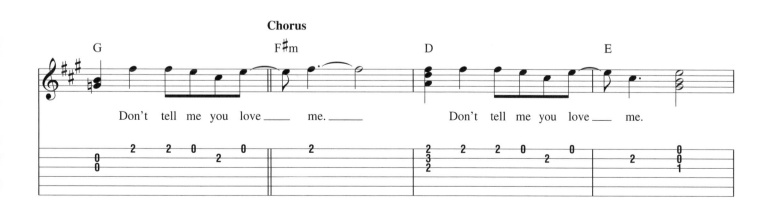

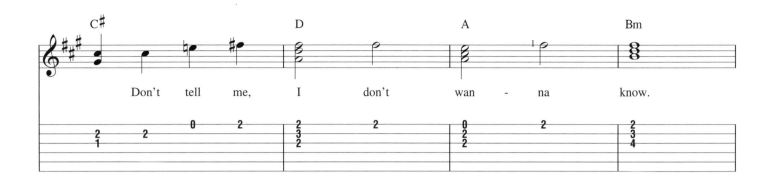

Don't tell me, I don't wan - na know.

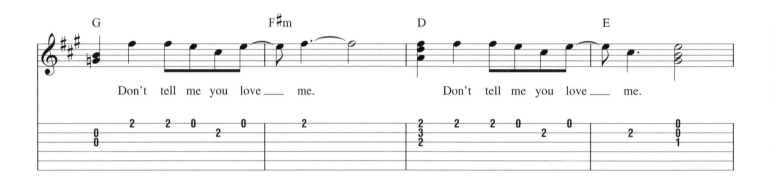

Don't tell me you love ____ me. Don't tell me you love ____ me.

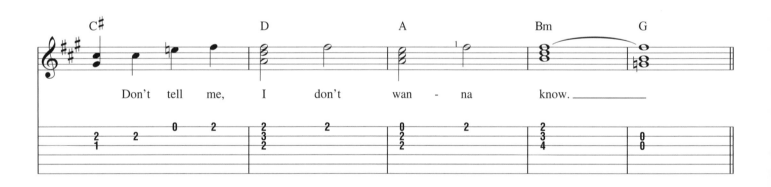

Don't tell me, I don't wan - na know. _____

Outro-Guitar Solo

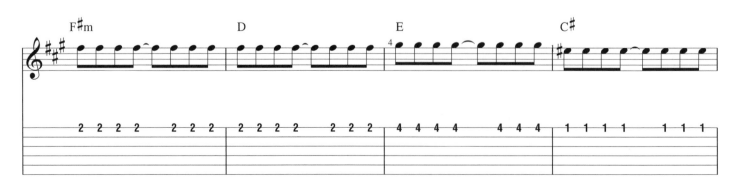

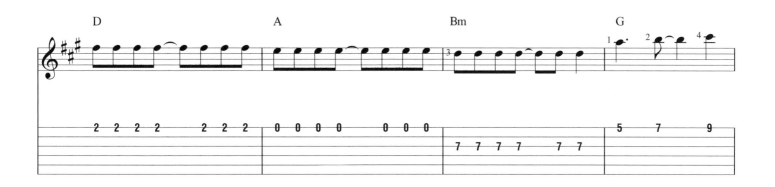

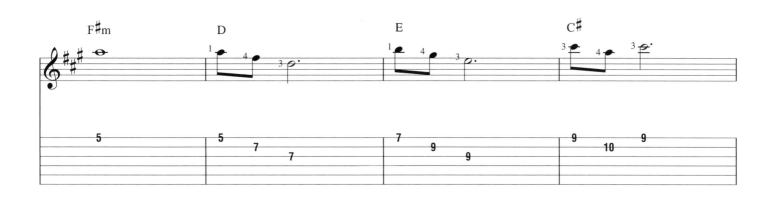

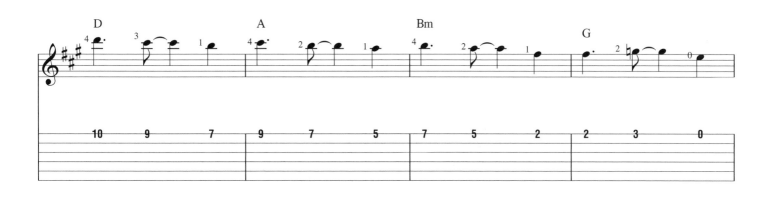

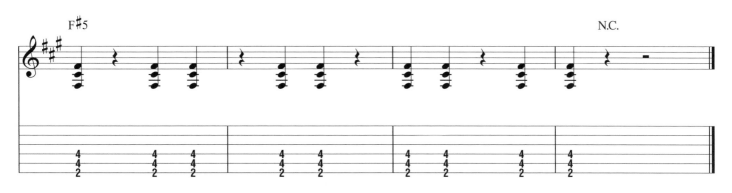

18 and Life

Words and Music by Rachael Bolan Southworth and David Michael Sabo

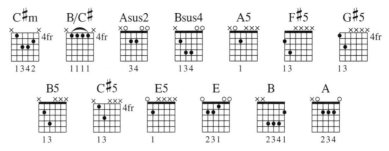

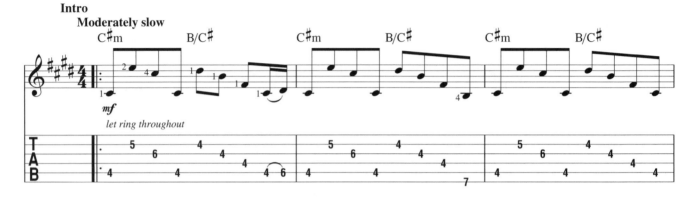

Strum Pattern: 1, 4
Pick Pattern: 5

Intro
Moderately slow

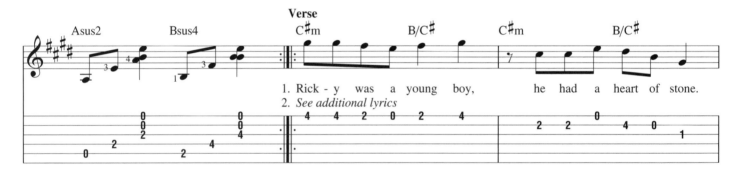

let ring throughout

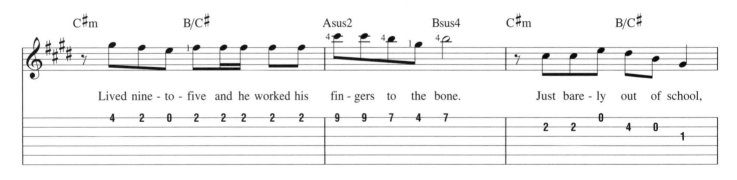

1. Rick - y was a young boy, he had a heart of stone.
2. *See additional lyrics*

Lived nine - to - five and he worked his fin - gers to the bone. Just bare - ly out of school,

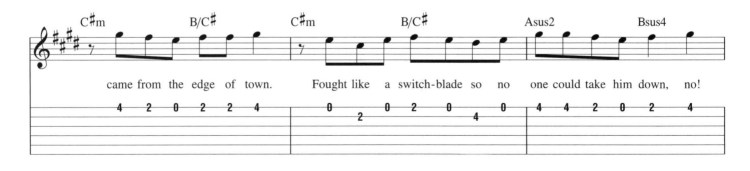

came from the edge of town. Fought like a switch-blade so no one could take him down, no!

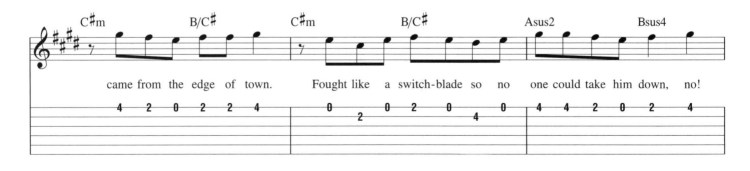

He had no mon-ey, no, no good at home.__ Walked the streets a sol-dier and he

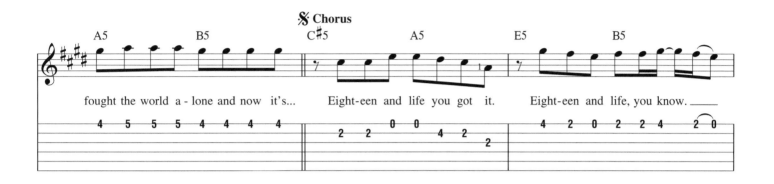

♪§ **Chorus**

fought the world a-lone and now it's... Eight-een and life you got it. Eight-een and life, you know.____

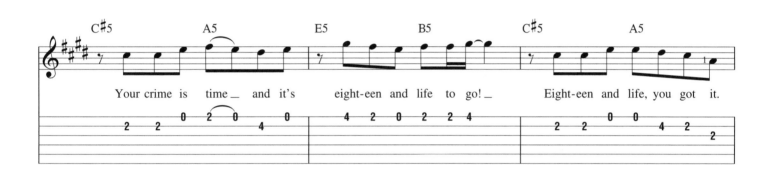

Your crime is time__ and it's eight-een and life to go!__ Eight-een and life, you got it.

To Coda ⊕

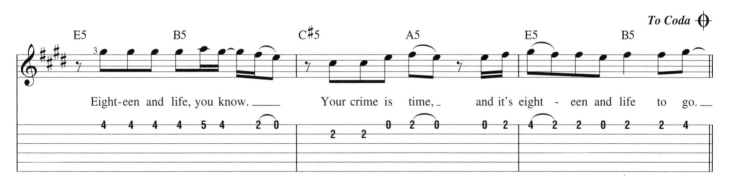

Eight-een and life, you know.____ Your crime is time,_ and it's eight-een and life to go.__

1.

Interlude
w/ Intro pattern

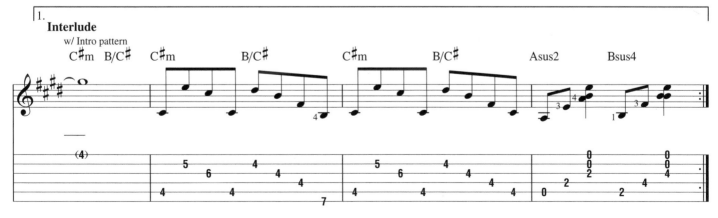

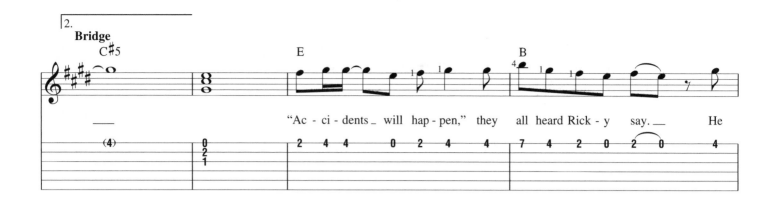

"Ac-ci-dents_ will hap-pen," they all heard Rick-y say. __ He

*Sung one octave higher.

D.S. al Coda

Coda

Outro

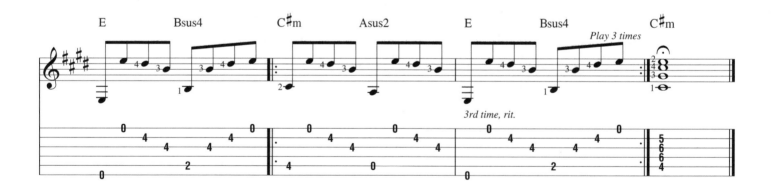

Play 3 times

3rd time, rit.

Additional Lyrics

2. Tequila in his heartbeat, his veins burned gasoline.
   It kept his motor running, but it never kept him clean.
   They say he loved adventure, Ricky's the wild one.
   He married trouble, had a courtship with a gun.
   Bang, bang, shoot 'em up, the party never ends.
   You can't think of dying when the bottle's your best friend
   And now it's...

Eye of the Tiger

Theme from ROCKY III

Words and Music by Frank Sullivan and Jim Peterik

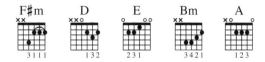

Strum Pattern: 1
Pick Pattern: 2

Verse

Moderate Rock

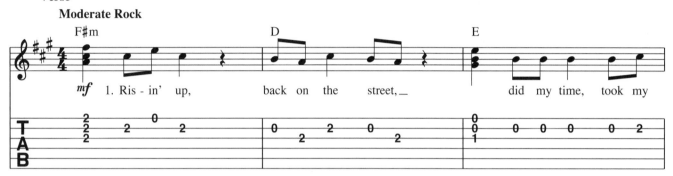

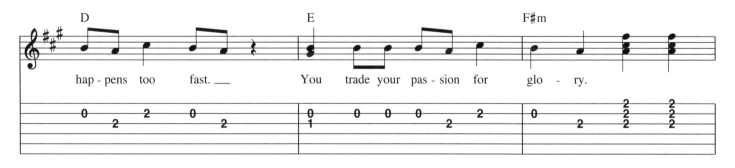

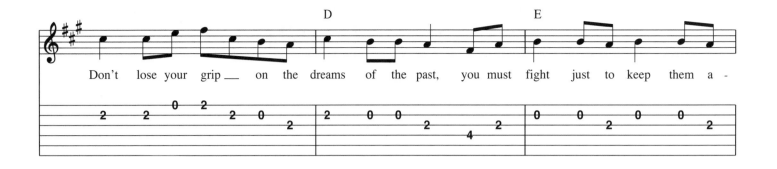

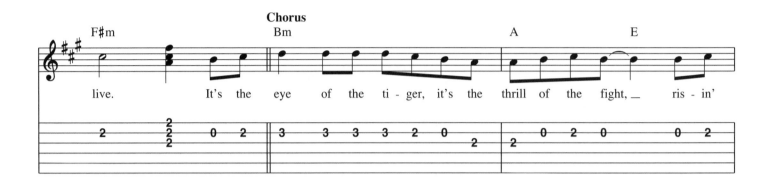

Chorus

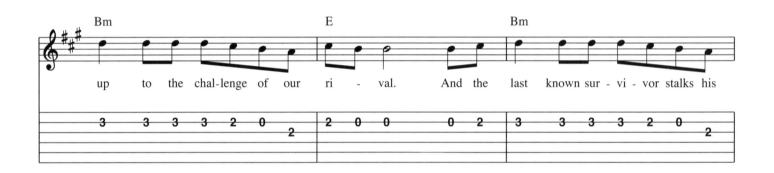

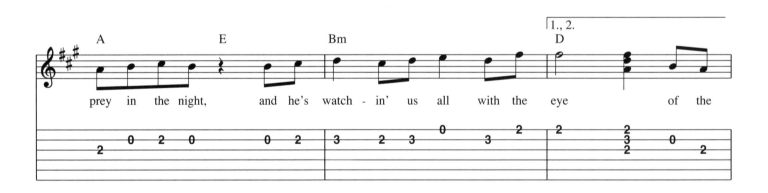

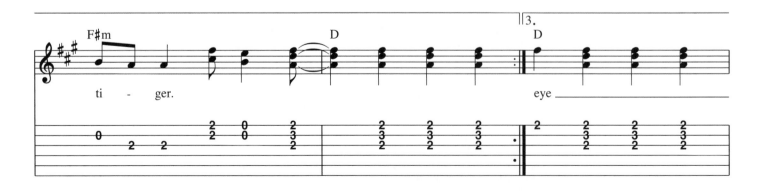

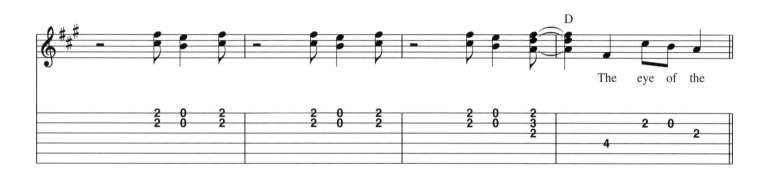

Additional Lyrics

3. Face to face, out in the heat,
   Hangin' tough, stayin' hungry.
   They stack the odds,
   Still we take to the street
   For the kill with the skill to survive.

4. Risin' up, straight to the top,
   Had the guts, got the glory.
   Went the distance,
   Now I'm gonna stop,
   Just a man and his will to survive.

Epic

**Words and Music by Michael Bordin, Roddy Bottum,
Bill Gould, James Martin and Michael Patton**

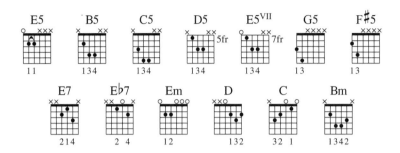

Strum Pattern: 2, 3
Pick Pattern: 3, 4

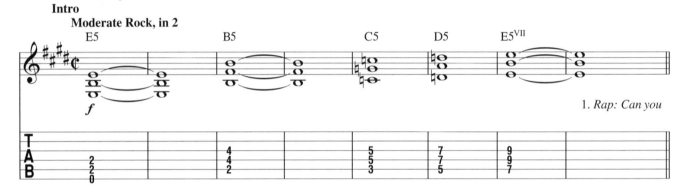

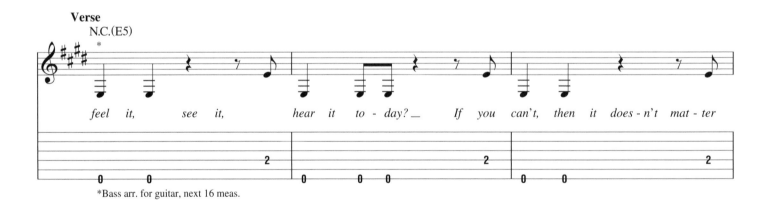

*Bass arr. for guitar, next 16 meas.

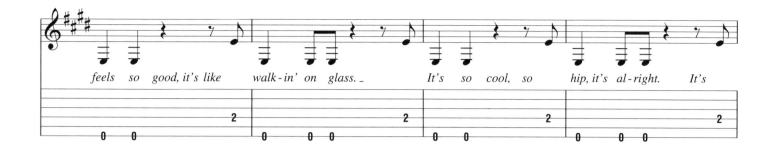

feels so good, it's like walk-in' on glass. _____ It's so cool, so hip, it's al-right. It's

so groov-y, it's out-ta sight. You can touch it, smell it, taste it so sweet. But it

Chorus

E5   B5

makes no dif-f'rence 'cause it knocks you off your feet. *Sung:* You want ___ it all, ___ but you ___ can't have ___

C5   D5   E5^VII   G5 F#5 G5 N.C.(E5)

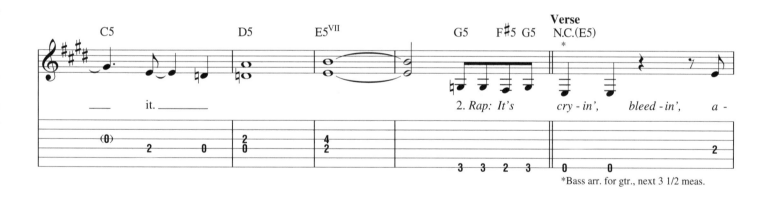

___ it. _____ 2. *Rap:* It's cry-in', bleed-in', a-

*Bass arr. for gtr., next 3 1/2 meas.

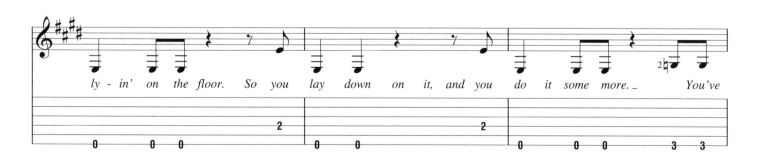

ly-in' on the floor. So you lay down on it, and you do it some more. _____ You've

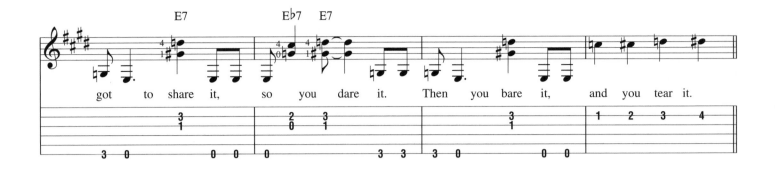

got to share it, so you dare it. Then you bare it, and you tear it.

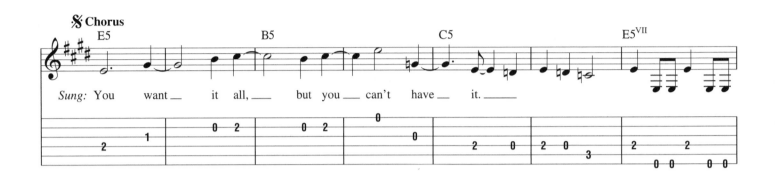

Sung: You want __ it all, __ but you __ can't have __ it. ____

It's in __ your face, __ but you __ can't grab __ it. ____

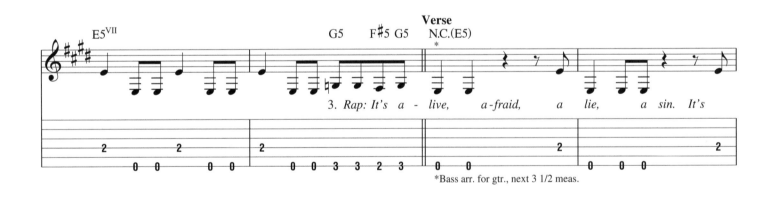

3. *Rap:* It's a - live, a-fraid, a lie, a sin. It's

*Bass arr. for gtr., next 3 1/2 meas.

mag - ic, it's trag - ic, it's a loss, it's a win. __ It's dark, it's moist, it's a bit - ter pain. __ It's

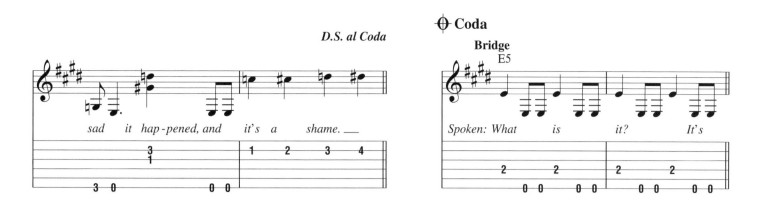

D.S. al Coda

sad   it   hap - pened, and   it's   a   shame. __

Spoken: What   is   it?   It's

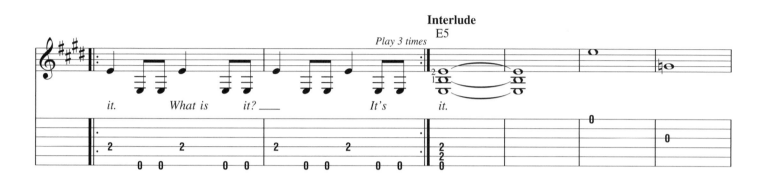

Interlude

it. __   What is   it? __   It's   it.

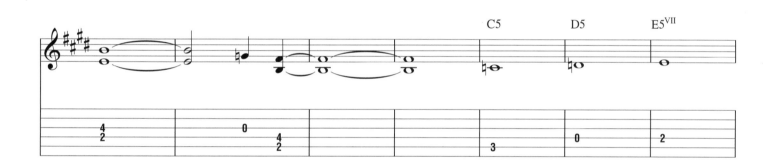

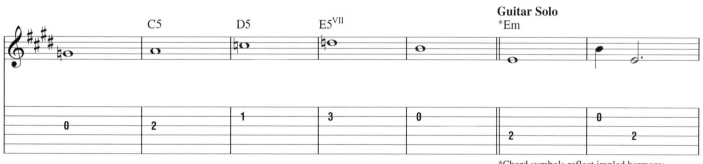

*Chord symbols reflect impled harmony,
next 16 meas.

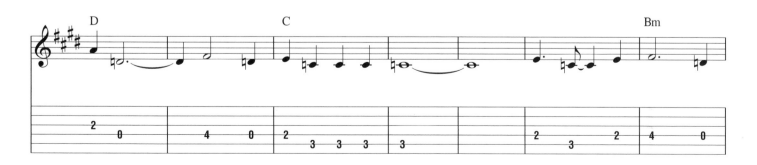

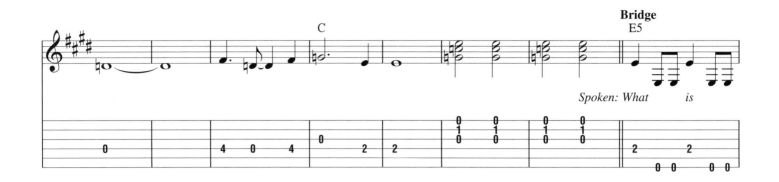

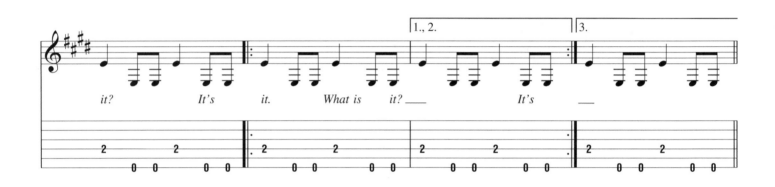

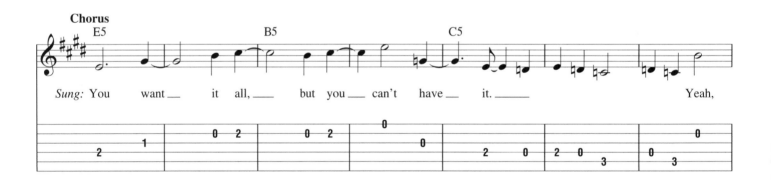

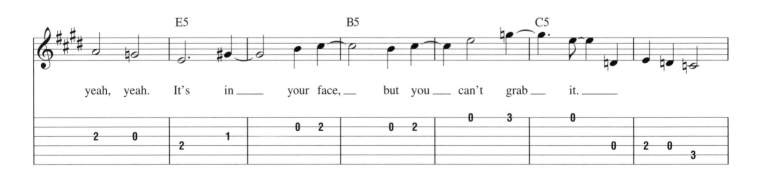

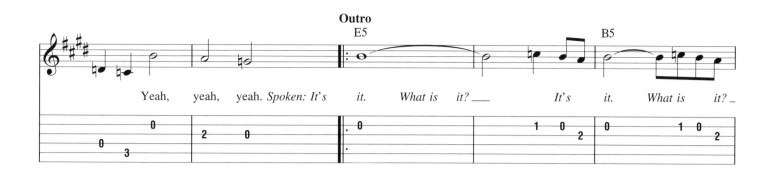

Outro

Yeah, yeah, yeah. *Spoken: It's it. What is it? ___ It's it. What is it? _*

— *It's it. What is it? ___ It's it. What is it? ___ It's it.*

Play 4 times

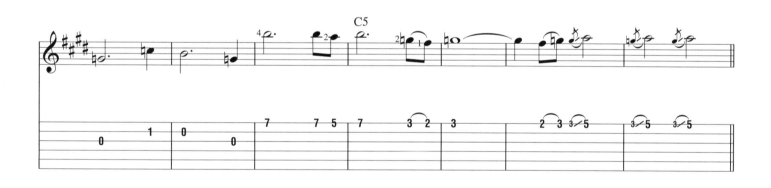

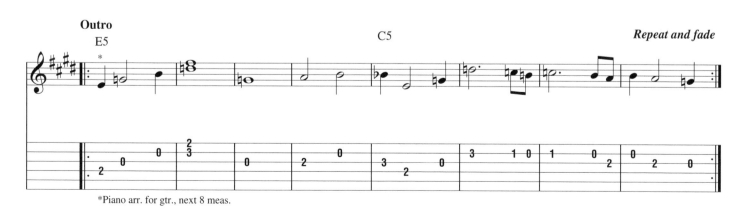

Outro

Repeat and fade

*Piano arr. for gtr., next 8 meas.

Even Flow

Music by Stone Gossard
Lyric by Eddie Vedder

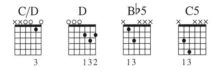

*Drop D tuning:
(low to high) D-A-D-G-B-E

Strum Pattern: 3, 5
Pick Pattern: 1, 2

Intro
Moderately

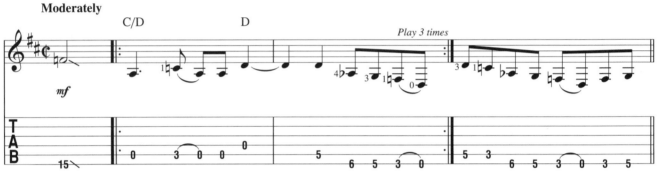

Verse
w/ Intro pattern

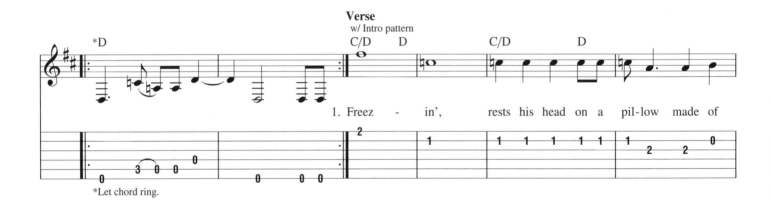

*Let chord ring.

1. Freez - in', rests his head on a pil-low made of con - crete _ a - gain. _ Oh, feel - in' may-be he'll see a lit-tle

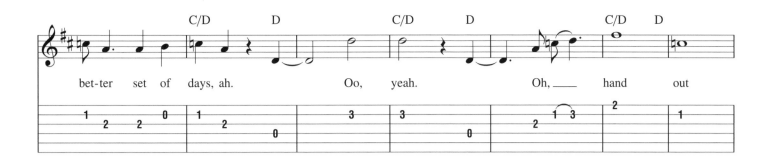

bet-ter set of days, ah. Oo, yeah. Oh,____ hand out

fac-es that he sees time a - gain ain't that fa - mil - iar.____ Oo, yeah. Oh,____ dark

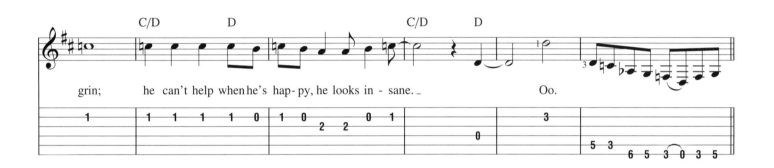

grin; he can't help when he's hap-py, he looks in - sane.____ Oo.

Interlude

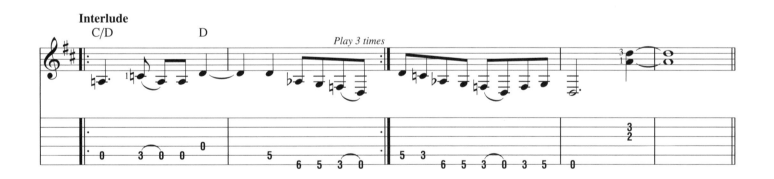

Play 3 times

𝄋 Chorus

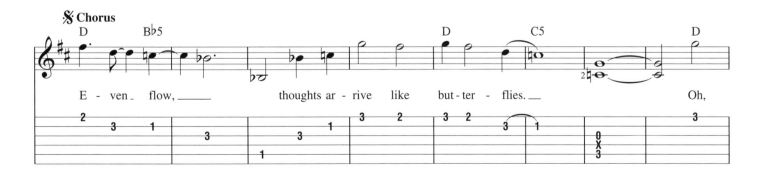

E - ven____ flow,_____ thoughts ar - rive like but - ter - flies.____ Oh,

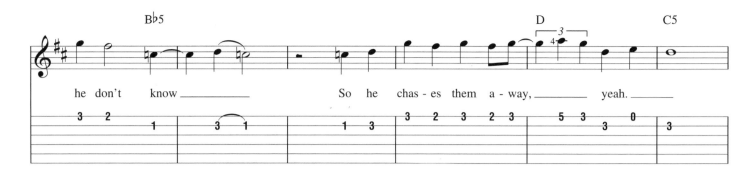

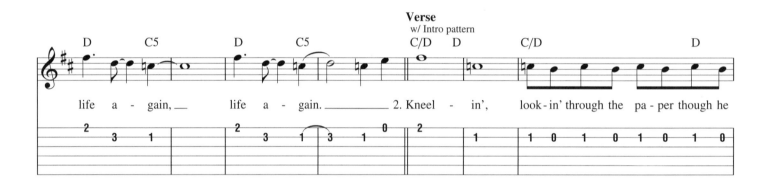

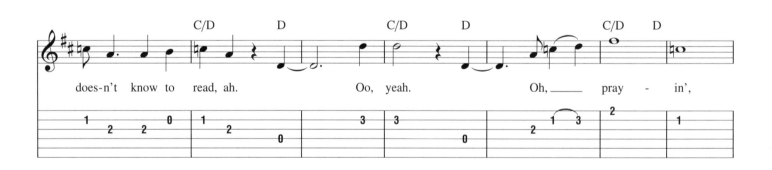

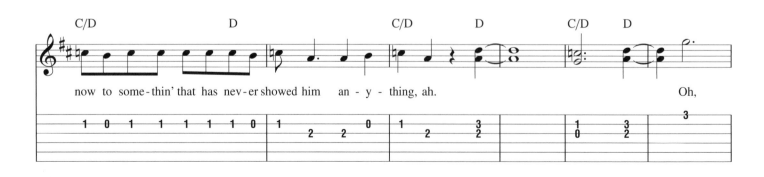

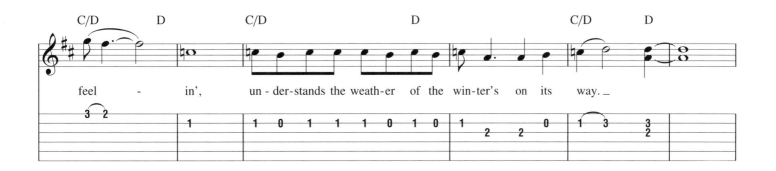

feel - in', un - der-stands the weath-er of the win-ter's on its way.

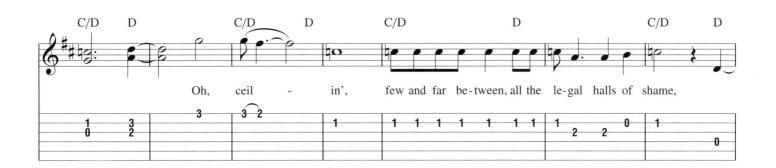

Oh, ceil - in', few and far be-tween, all the le-gal halls of shame,

D.S. al Coda 1

⊕ **Coda 1**

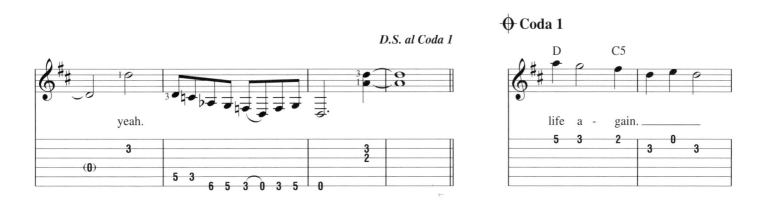

yeah.

life a - gain.

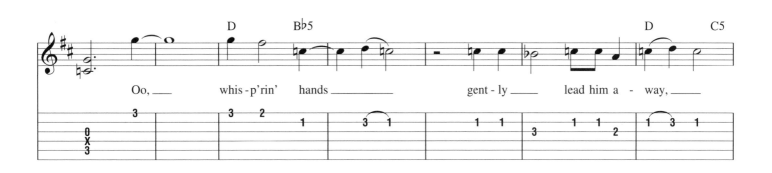

Oo, ___ whis-p'rin' hands _____ gent - ly ___ lead him a - way, ___

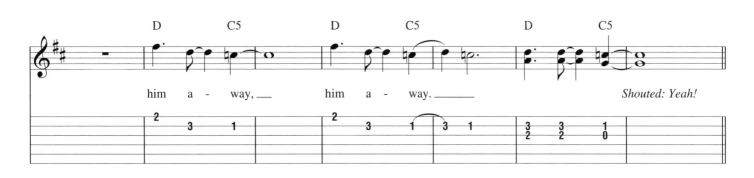

him a - way, ___ him a - way. ___

Shouted: Yeah!

Interlude

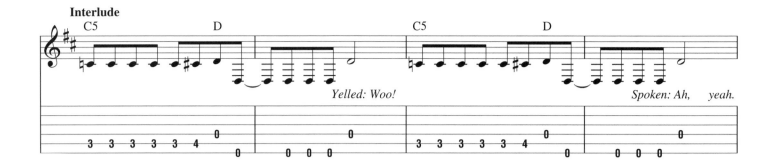

Yelled: Woo!

Spoken: Ah, yeah.

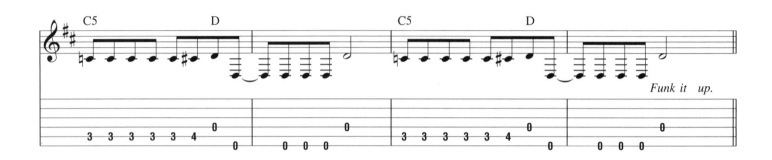

Funk it up.

Guitar Solo

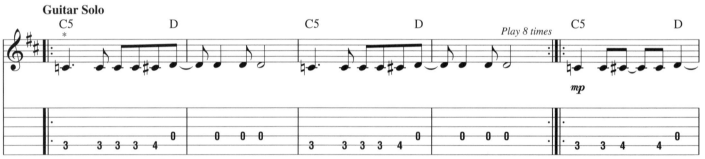

*Bass arr. for gtr., next 8 meas.

4th time, D.S. al Coda 2

⊕ **Coda 2**

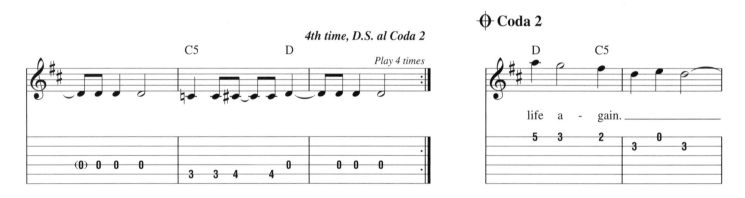

life a - gain.

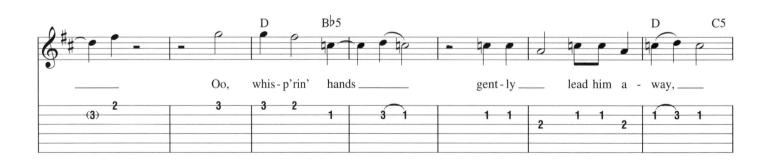

Oo, whis - p'rin' hands _____ gent - ly _____ lead him a - way, _____

128

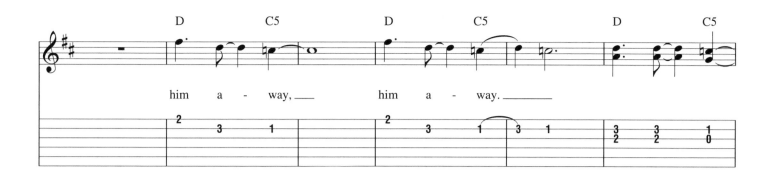

him a - way, _____ him a - way. _____

Outro
2nd time, voc. tacet

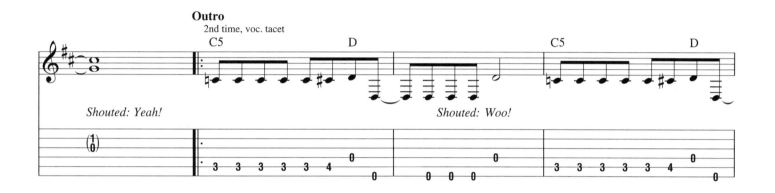

Shouted: Yeah! _____ *Shouted: Woo!*

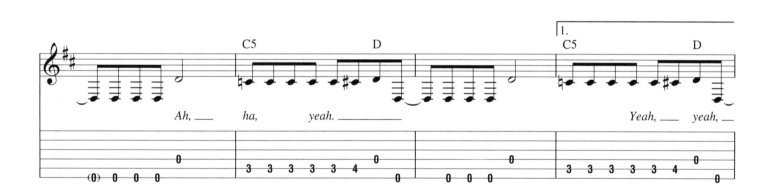

Ah, ___ *ha,* *yeah.* _____ *Yeah,* ___ *yeah,* __

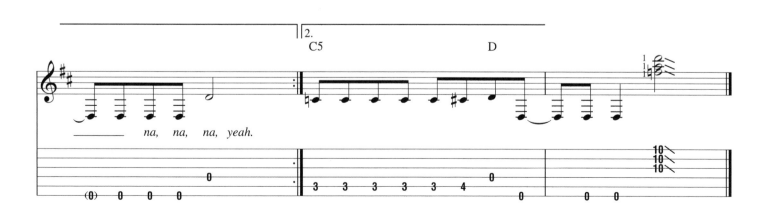

_____ *na,* *na,* *na,* *yeah.*

Everlong

Words and Music by David Grohl

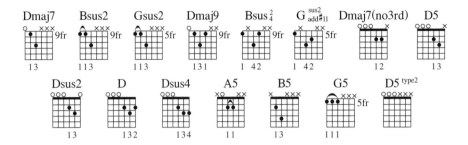

Drop D tuning:
(low to high) D-A-D-G-B-E

Strum Pattern: 1
Pick Pattern: 4

Intro

Moderate Rock

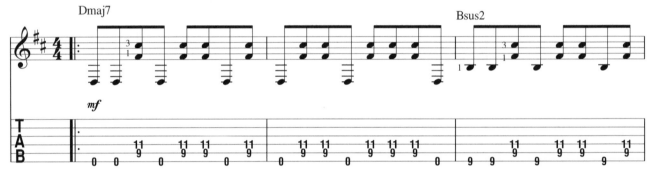

Interlude

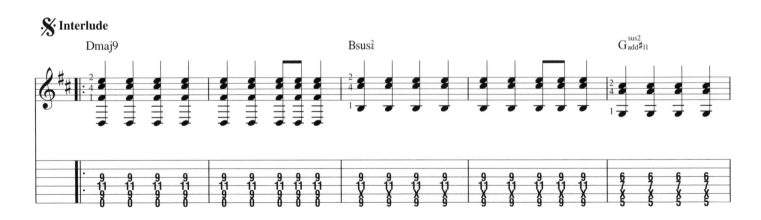

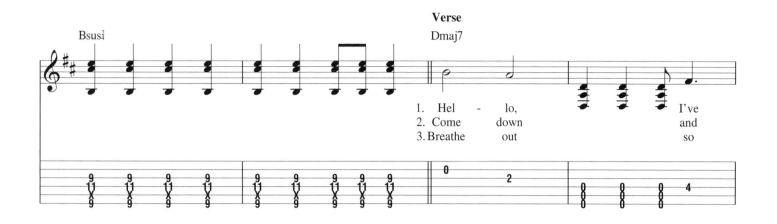

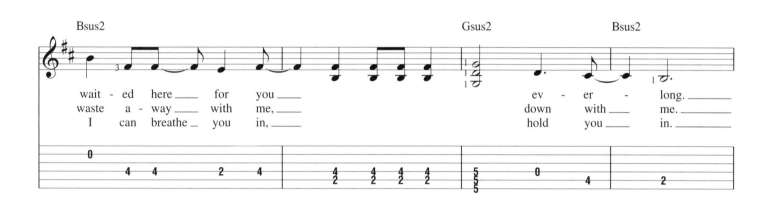

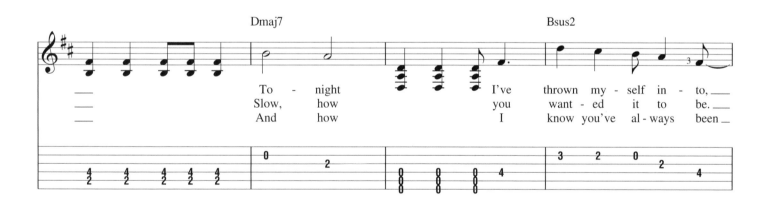

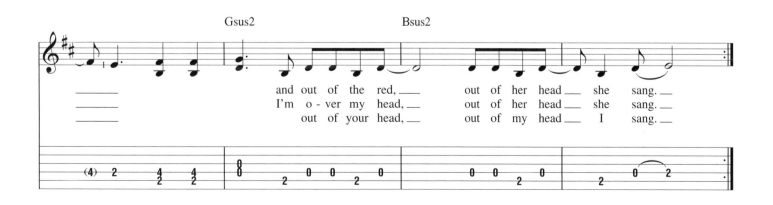

Feel Like Makin' Love

Words and Music by Paul Rodgers and Mick Ralphs

*Strum Pattern: 3, 4
*Pick Pattern: 3, 4

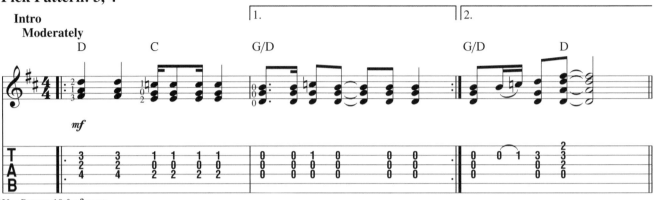

*Use Pattern 10 for 2/4 meas.

1. Ba - by, when I think a - bout you, I think a-bout love. _____
2. *See additional lyrics*

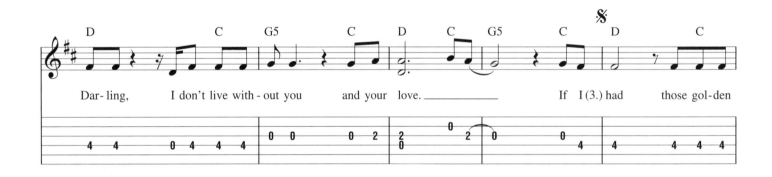

Dar - ling, I don't live with - out you and your love. _____ If I (3.) had those gol - den

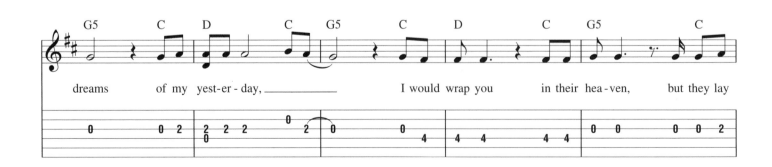

dreams of my yest - er - day, _____ I would wrap you in their hea - ven, but they lay

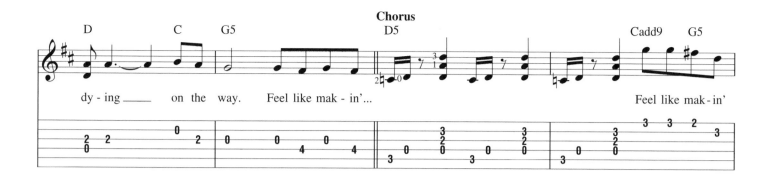

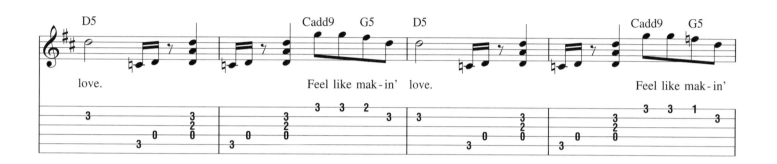

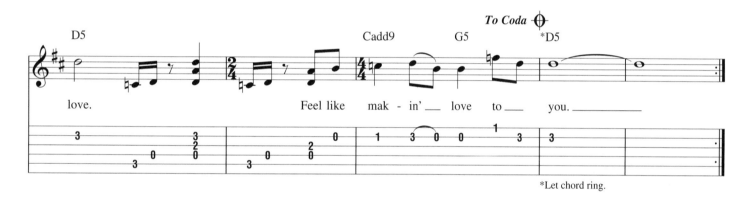

*Let chord ring.

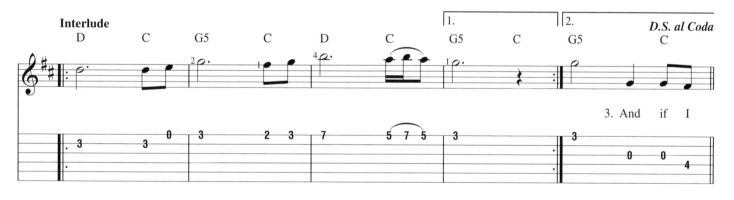

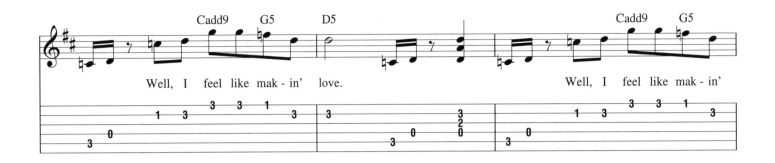

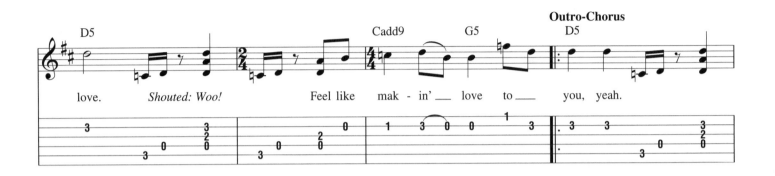

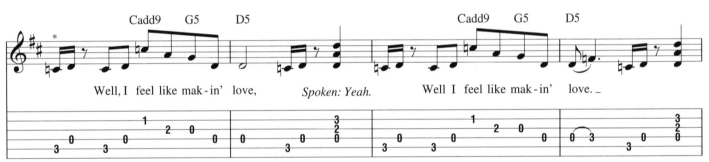

*Sung one octave higher, next 6 meas.

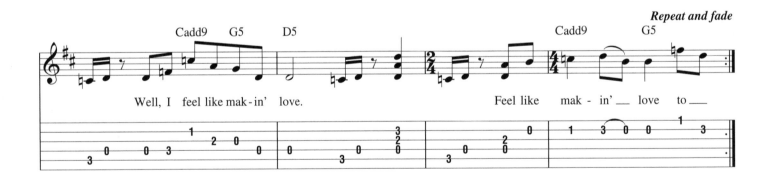

Additional Lyrics

2. Baby, if I think about you,
   I think about love.
   Darling, if I live without you,
   I live without love.
   And if I had the sun and moon,
   And they were shining,
   I would give you both night and day,
   Love satisfying.
   Feel like makin'...

Frankenstein

By Edgar Winter

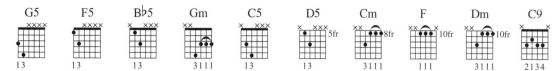

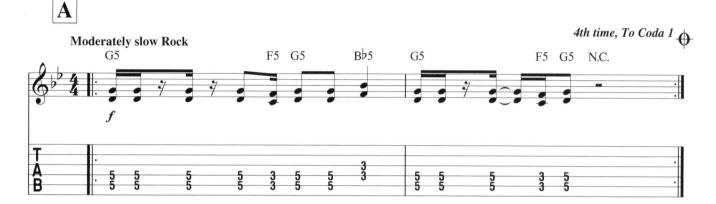

Strum Pattern: 1

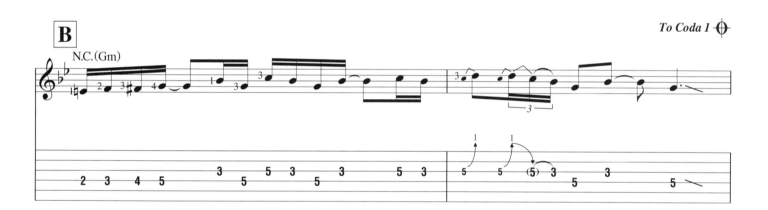

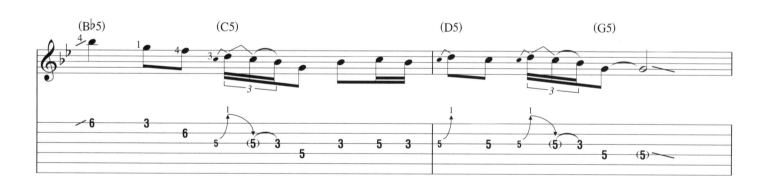

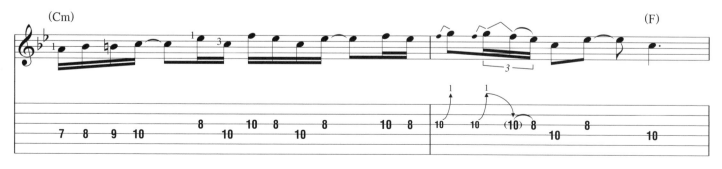

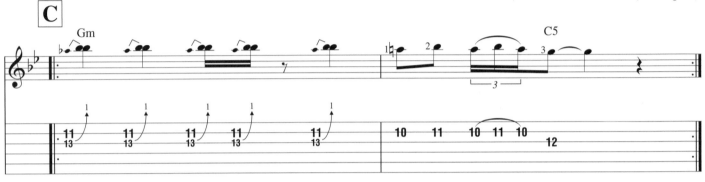

2nd time, D.C. al Coda 1
(take repeat)

C

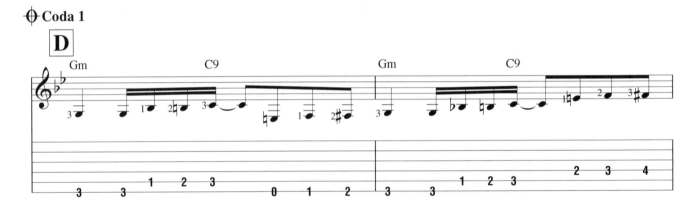

Coda 1

D

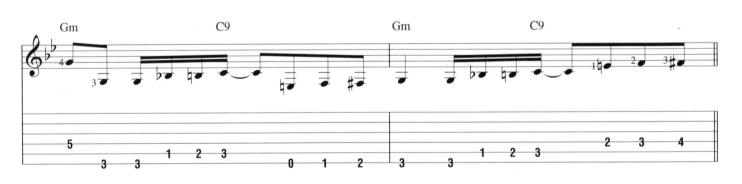

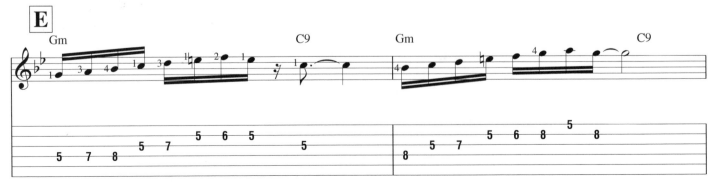

E

138

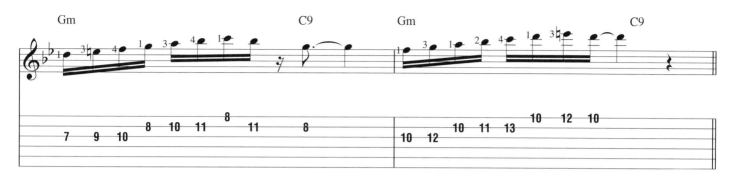

2nd time, D.C. al Coda 2
(take repeat)

F

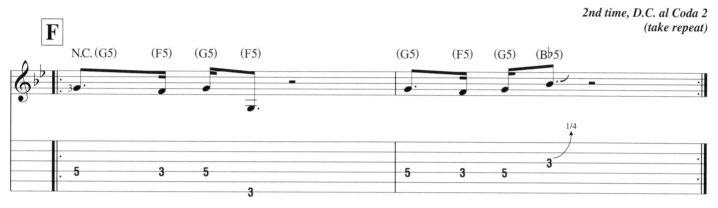

⊕ Coda 2

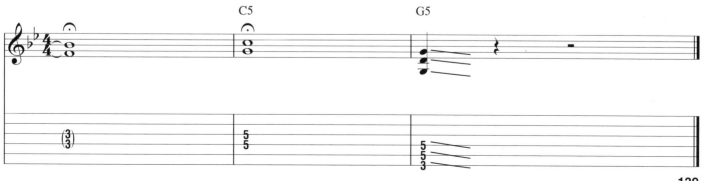

Final Countdown

Words and Music by Joey Tempest

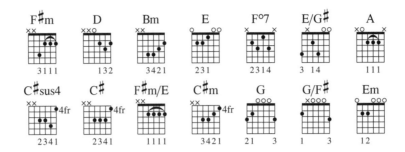

Strum Pattern: 4
Pick Pattern: 4

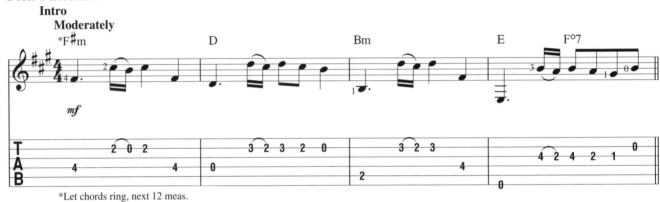

*Let chords ring, next 12 meas.

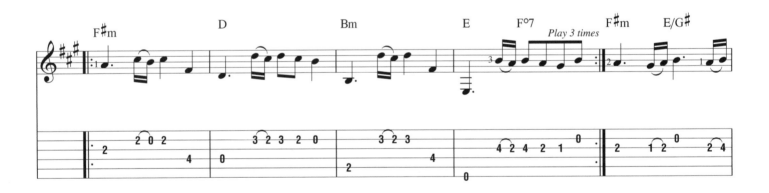

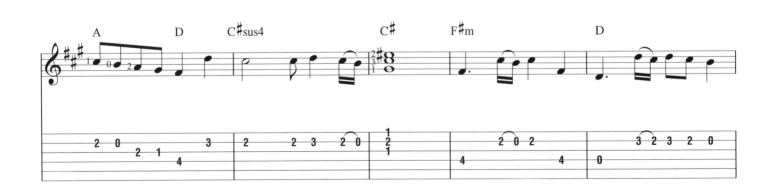

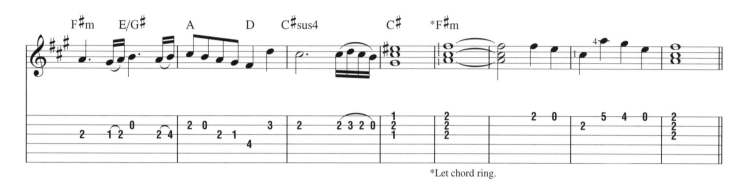

*Let chord ring.

Verse

1. We're leav-ing to-geth - er, but still it's fare-well. And ma-be we'll come _ back _
2. We're head-ed for Ve - nus, and still we stand tall, 'cause may-be they've seen _ us _

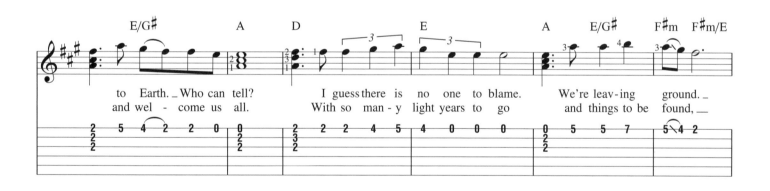

to Earth. _ Who can tell? I guess there is no one to blame. We're leav-ing ground. _
and wel - come us all. With so man - y light years to go and things to be found, _

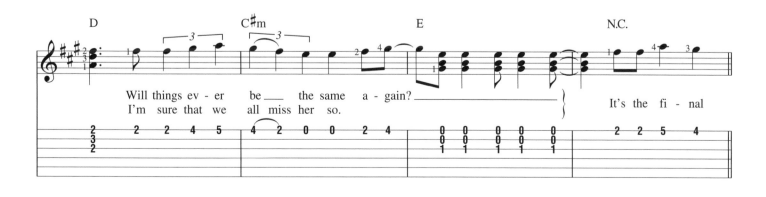

Will things ev - er be _ the same a - gain? _ It's the fi - nal
I'm sure that we all miss her so.

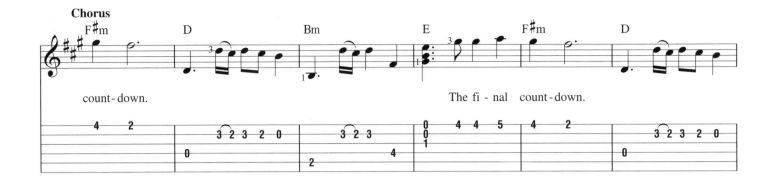

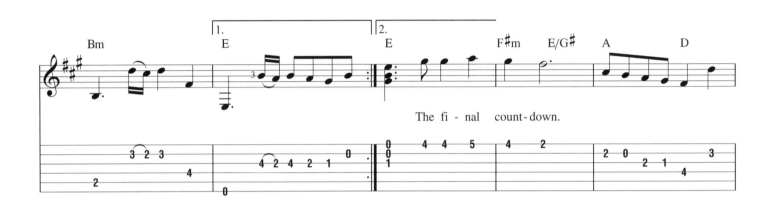

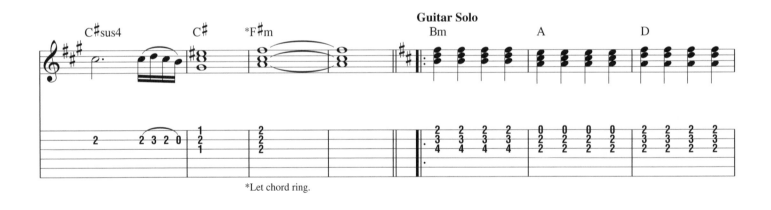

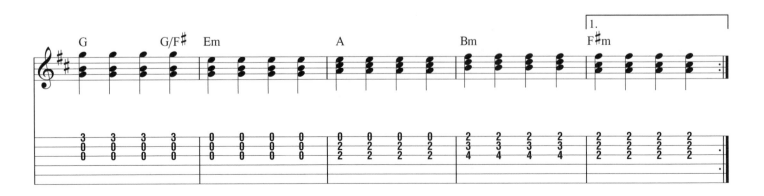

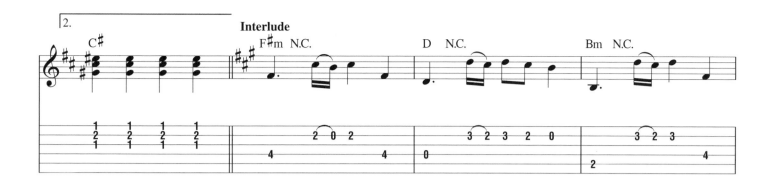

Interlude

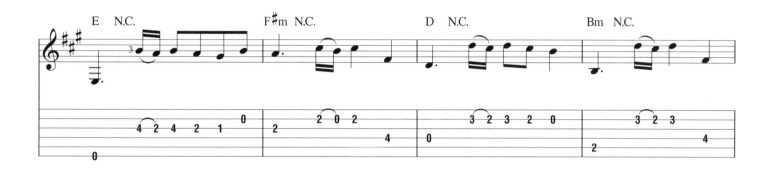

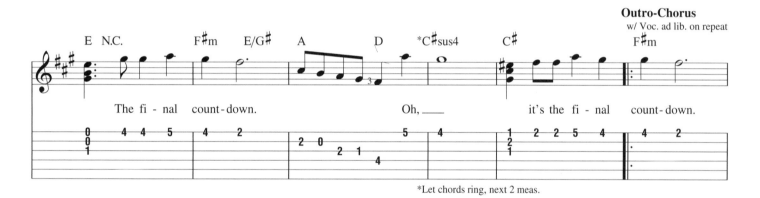

The fi - nal count-down. Oh, ___ it's the fi - nal count-down.

*Let chords ring, next 2 meas.

The fi - nal count-down.

Repeat and fade

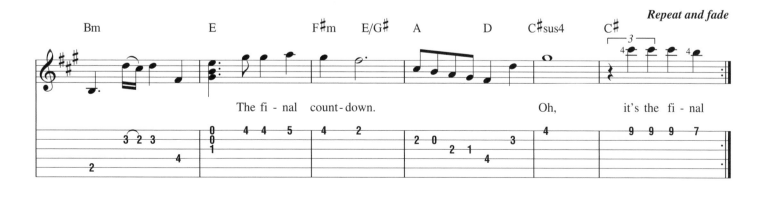

The fi - nal count-down. Oh, it's the fi - nal

Freak on a Leash

**Words and Music by Jonathan Davis, Reginald Arvizu, Brian Welch,
James Christian Schaffer and David Randall Silveria**

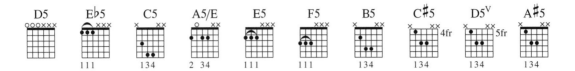

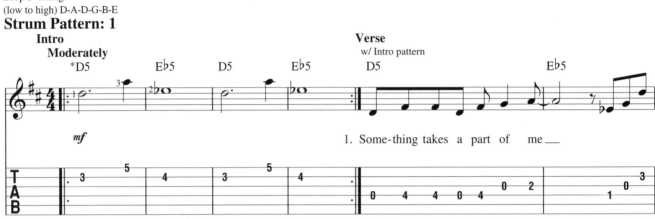

*Chord symbols reflect implied harmony, next 20 meas.

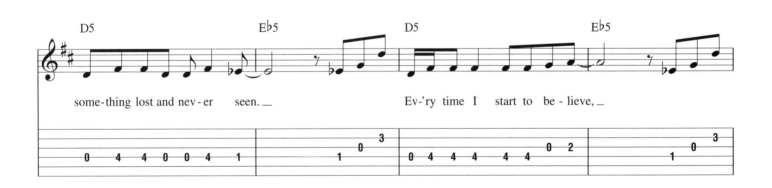

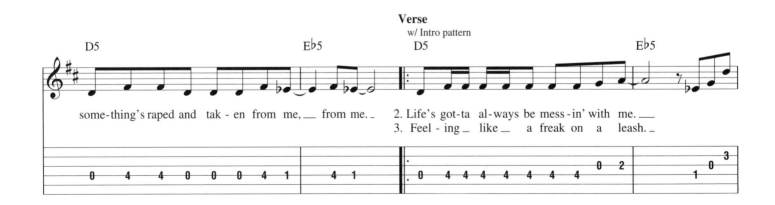

Can't it chill and let me be free? —
Feel-ing like I have no re - lease. —

Can't I take a - way all this pain? —
How man-y times have I felt dis - ease? —

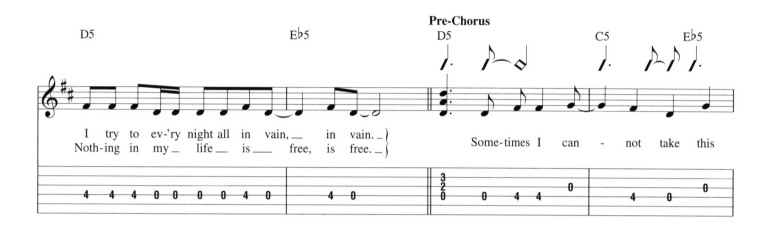

Pre-Chorus

I try to ev-'ry night all in vain, __ in vain. __
Noth-ing in my __ life __ is __ free, is free. __

Some-times I can - not take this

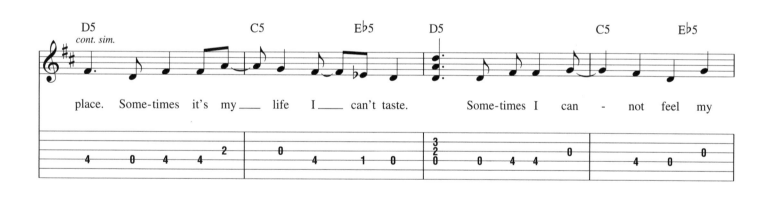

place. Some-times it's my ___ life I ___ can't taste.

Some-times I can - not feel my

%. Chorus

face. You'll nev-er see __ me fall from grace.

Some - thing takes_ a part _

*Let chord ring.

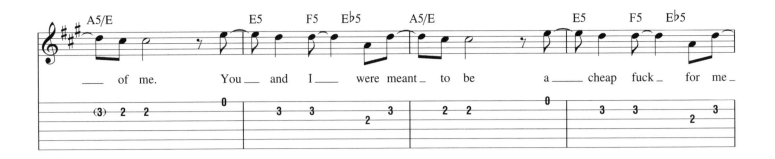

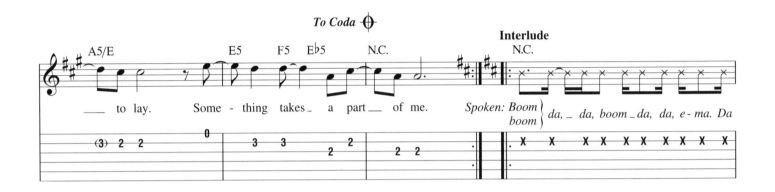

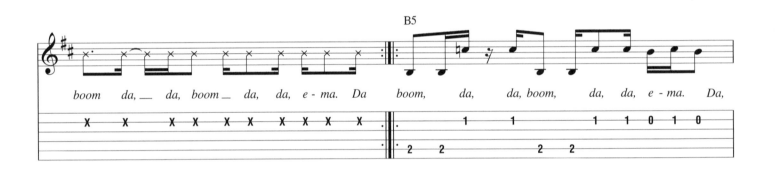

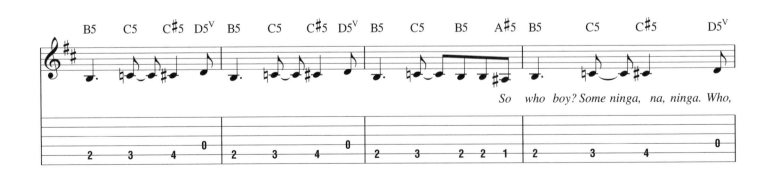

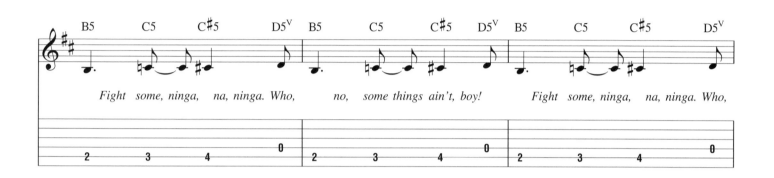

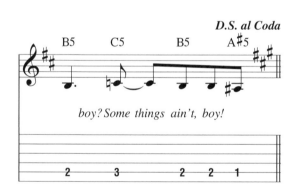

D.S. al Coda

$\oplus$ **Coda**

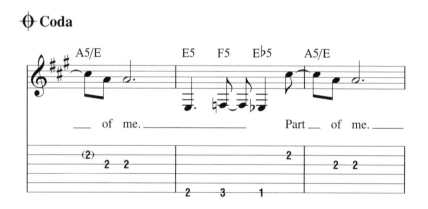

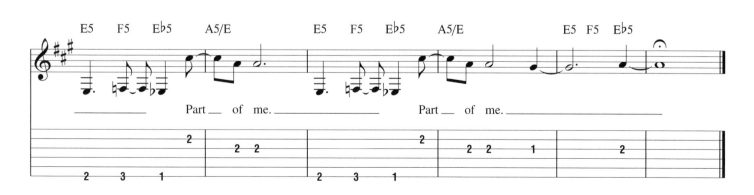

Free Bird

Words and Music by Allen Collins and Ronnie Van Zant

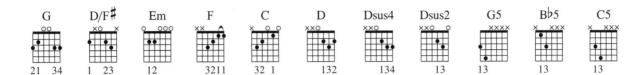

Strum Pattern: 3, 4
Pick Pattern: 3, 4

Intro
Slowly

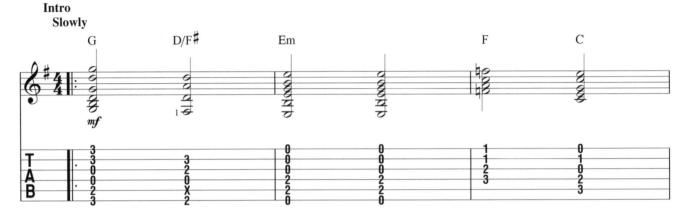

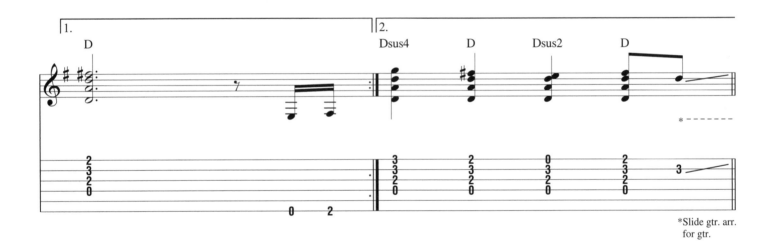

*Slide gtr. arr.
for gtr.

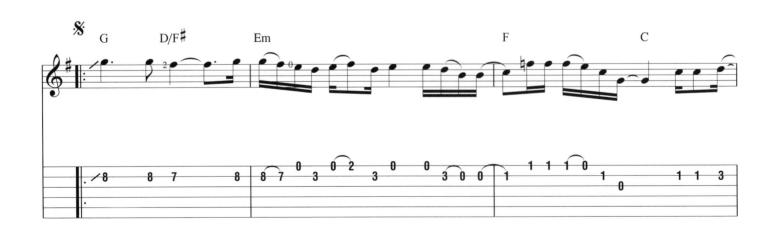

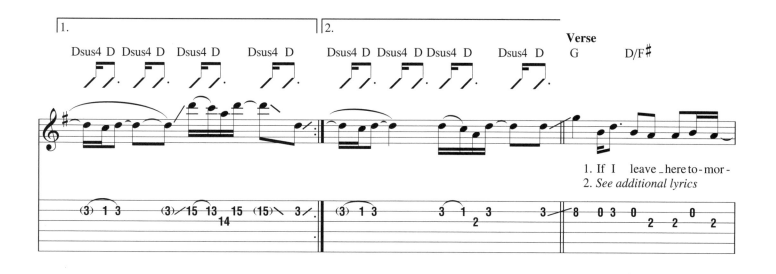

1. If I leave _ here to-mor-
2. *See additional lyrics*

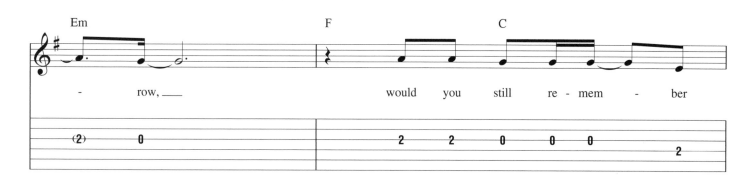

-row, ___ would you still re-mem - ber me?

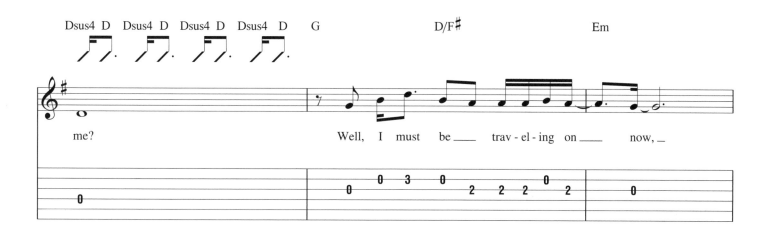

me? Well, I must be ___ trav - el - ing on ___ now, _

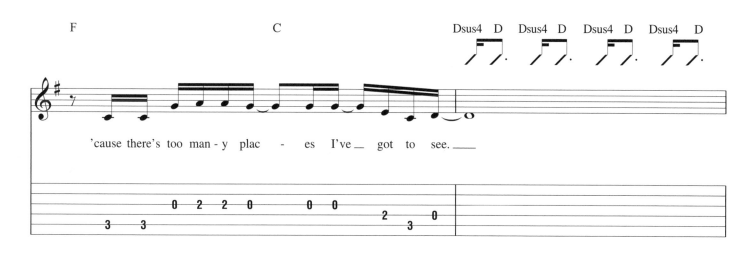

'cause there's too man - y plac - es I've _ got to see. ___

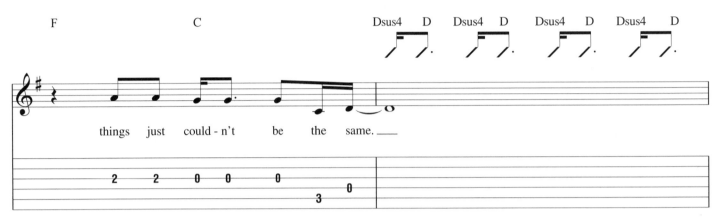

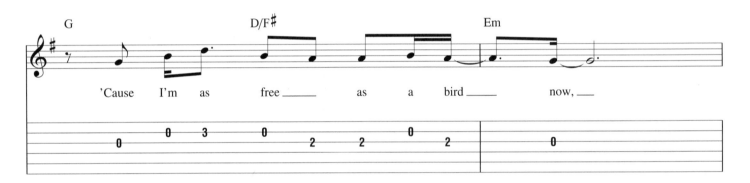

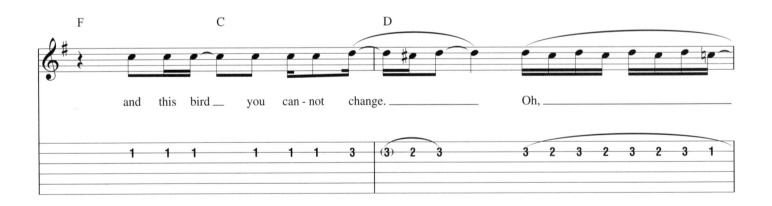

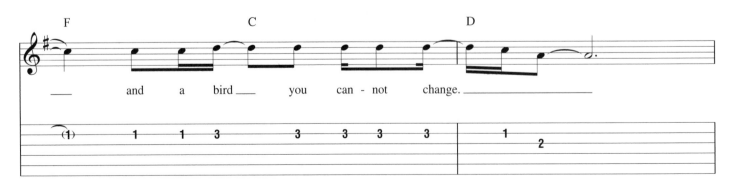

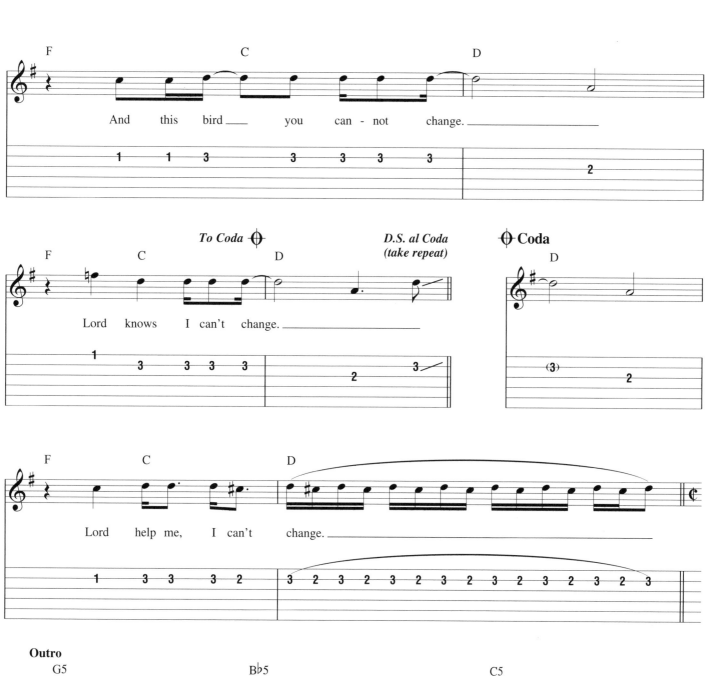

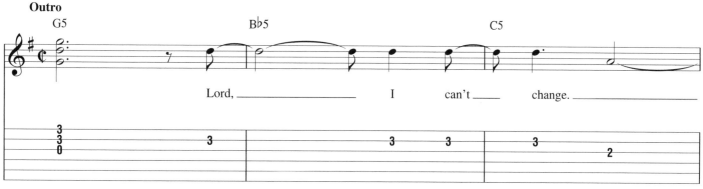

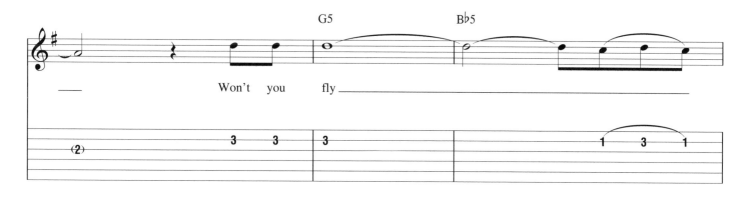

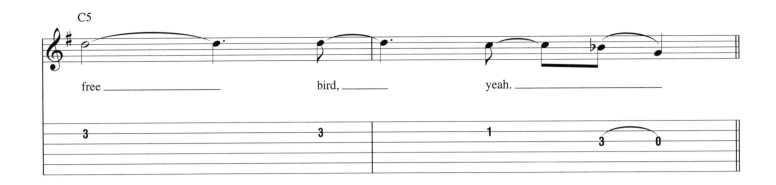

free _____ bird, _____ yeah. _____

Guitar Solo

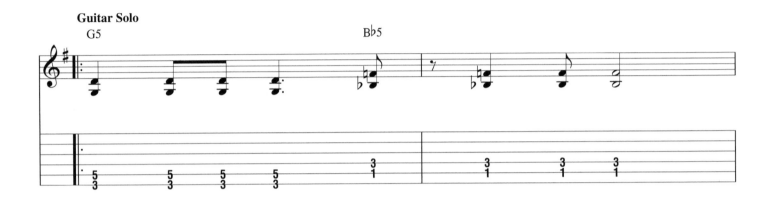

Repeat and fade

Additional Lyrics

2. Bye bye, baby, it's been sweet now, yeah, yeah.
   Though this feelin' I can't change.
   A please don't take it so badly,
   'Cause Lord knows I'm to blame.
   But if I stay here with you, girl,
   Things just couldn't be the same.
   'Cause I'm as free as a bird now,
   And this bird you cannot change.
   Oh, and a bird you cannot change.
   And this bird you cannot change.
   Lord knows I can't change.
   Lord help me, I can't change.

Heartbreaker

Words and Music by Cliff Wade and Geoff Gill

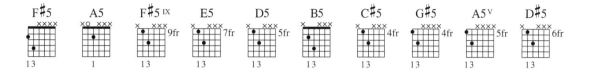

*Tune down 1/2 step:
(low to high) Eb-Ab-Db-Gb-Bb-Eb

Strum Pattern: 1

Intro
Moderately fast

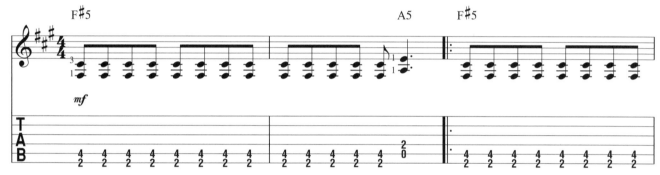

*Optional: To match recording, tune down 1/2 step.

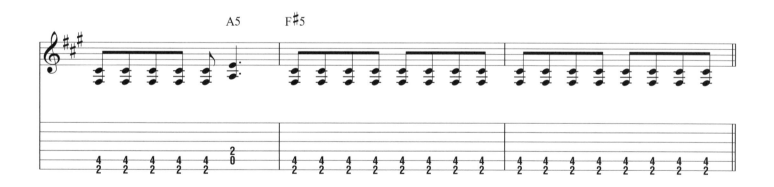

Verse

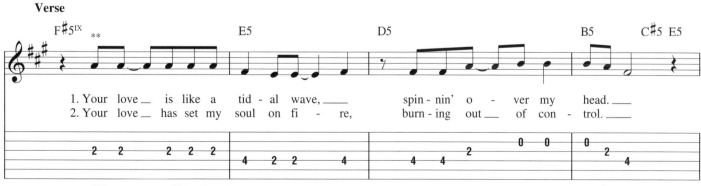

1. Your love __ is like a tid-al wave, ____ spin-nin' o — ver my head. ____
2. Your love __ has set my soul on fi — re, burn-ing out __ of con - trol. ____

**Sung one octave higher throughout.

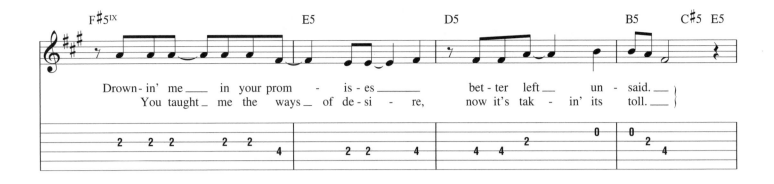

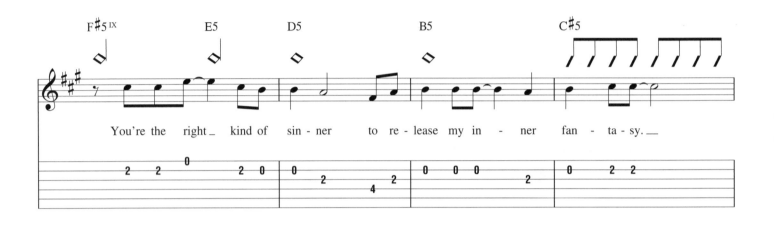

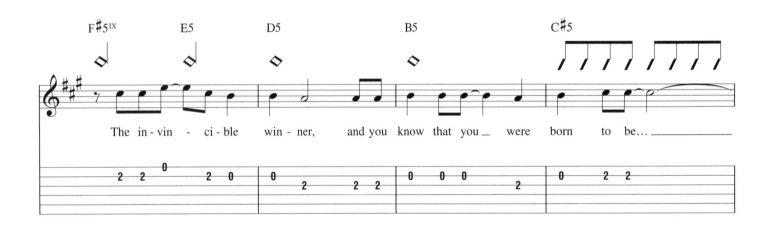

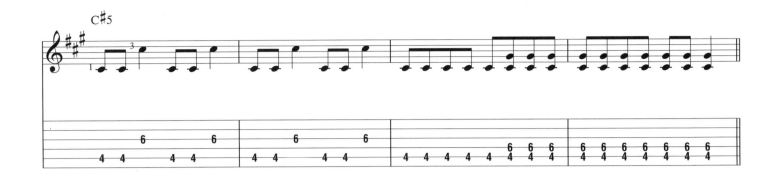

Bridge

You're the right __ kind of sin - ner to re - lease my in - ner fan - ta - sy. __

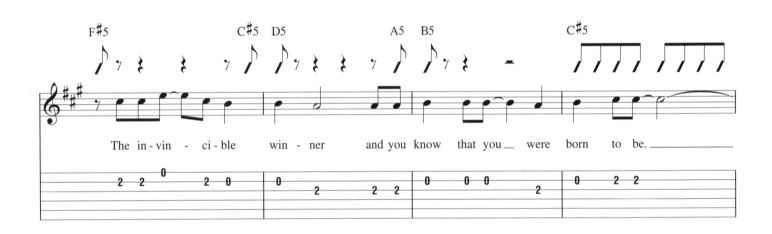

The in - vin - ci - ble win - ner and you know that you __ were born to be. __

Chorus

N.C.

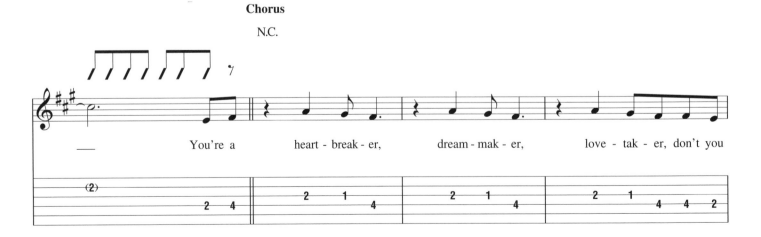

You're a heart - break - er, dream - mak - er, love - tak - er, don't you

Give It Away

Words and Music by Anthony Kiedis, Flea, John Frusciante and Chad Smith

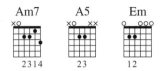

Strum Pattern: 2

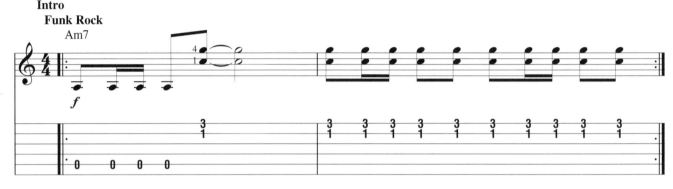

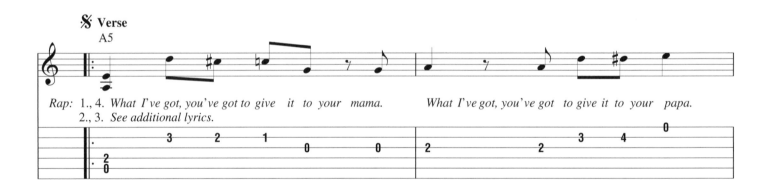

Rap: 1., 4. What I've got, you've got to give it to your mama.　　What I've got, you've got to give it to your papa.
2., 3. See additional lyrics.

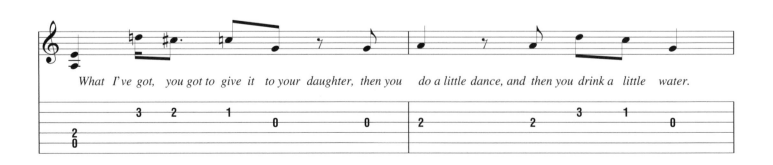

What I've got, you got to give it to your daughter, then you　do a little dance, and then you drink a little water.

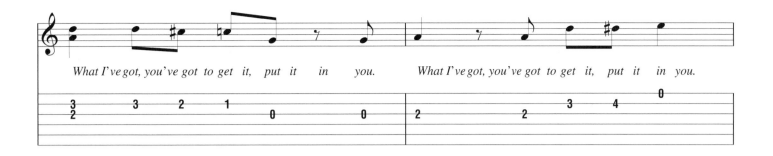

What I've got, you've got to get it, put it in you.   What I've got, you've got to get it, put it in you.

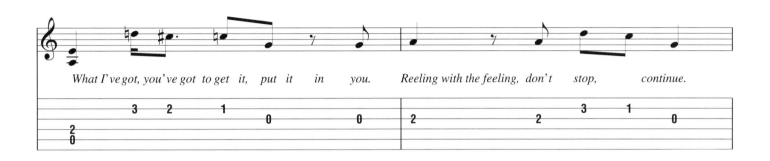

What I've got, you've got to get it, put it in you.   Reeling with the feeling, don't stop, continue.

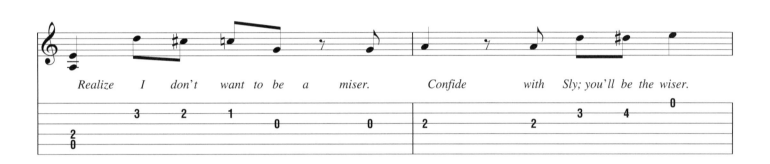

Realize I don't want to be a miser.   Confide with Sly; you'll be the wiser.

To Coda 1 ⊕

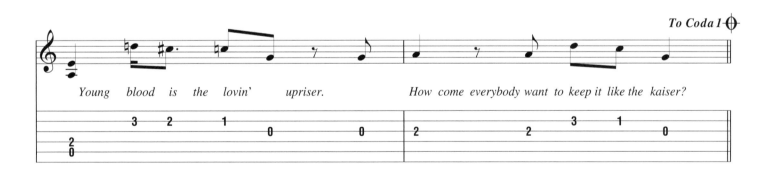

Young blood is the lovin' upriser.   How come everybody want to keep it like the kaiser?

Chorus

A5

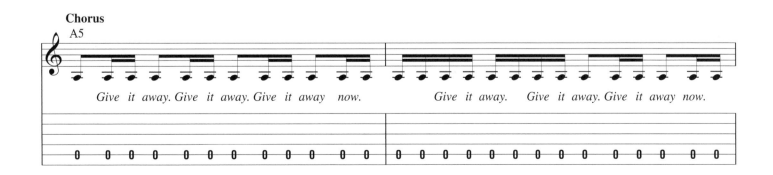

Give it away. Give it away. Give it away now.   Give it away. Give it away. Give it away now.

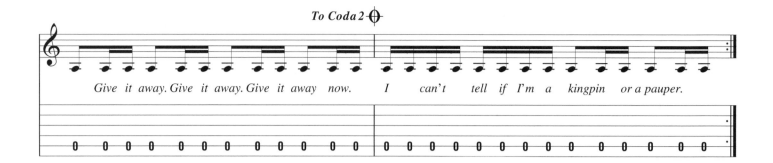

Give it away. Give it away. Give it away now.   I   can't   tell if I'm a   kingpin   or a pauper.

Chorus

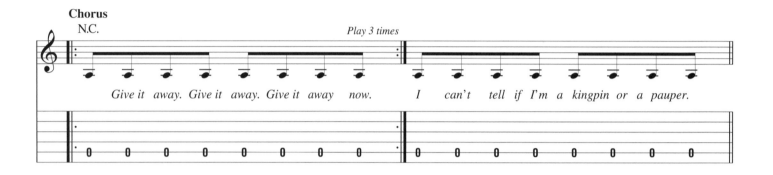

Give it away. Give it away. Give it away   now.   I   can't   tell if I'm a kingpin or a pauper.

Guitar Solo

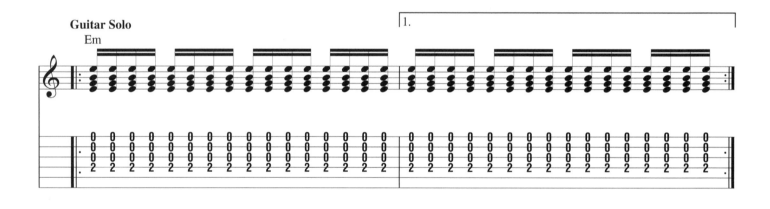

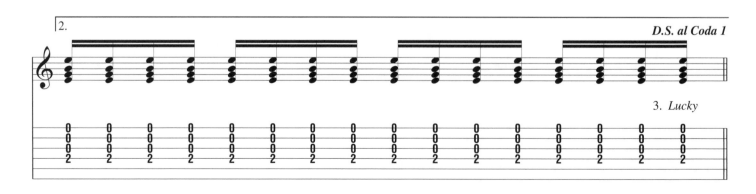

3. Lucky

⊕ Coda 1

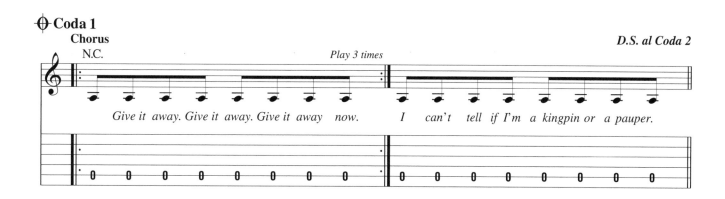

⊕ Coda 2

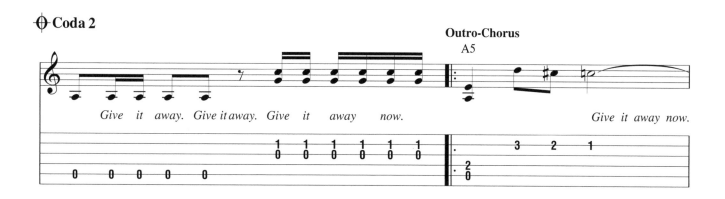

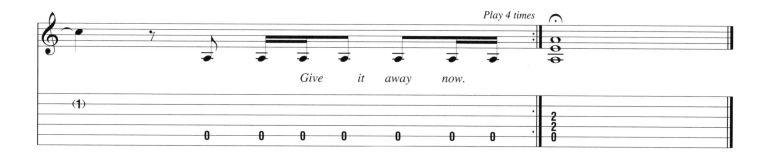

Additional Lyrics

2. *Spoken:* *Greedy little people in a sea of distress,*
   Keep your more to receive your less.
   Unimpressed by material excess,
   Love is free, love me, say, "Hell yes!"
   Lowbrow, but I rock a little know-how.
   No time for the piggies or the hoosegow.
   Get smart, get down with the power,
   Never been a better time than right now.
   Bob Marley, poet and a prophet,
   Bob Marley taught me how to off it.
   Bob Marley, walkin' like he talk it.
   Goodness me, can't you see, I'm gonna caught it?

3. *Spoken:* *Lucky me, swimmin' in my ability,*
   Dancin' down on life with agility.
   Come and drink it up from my fertility,
   Blessed with a bucket of lucky mobility.
   My mom, I love her 'cause she love me,
   Long gone are the times when she scrub me.
   Feelin' good, my brother gonna hug me,
   Drink up my juice, young love, chug-a-lug me.
   There's a river born to be a giver,
   Keep you warm, won't let you shiver.
   His heart is never gonna wither,
   Come on everybody, time to deliver.

Heaven and Hell

Words by Ronnie James Dio
Music by Ronnie James Dio, Terence Butler,
Anthony Iommi and William Ward

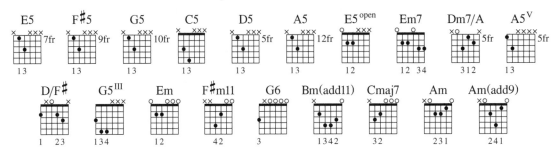

*Tune down 1/2 step:
(low to high) Eb-Ab-Db-Gb-Bb-Eb

Strum Pattern: 1, 2
Pick Pattern: 5

Intro
Moderately slow

*Optional: To match recording, tune down 1/2 step.

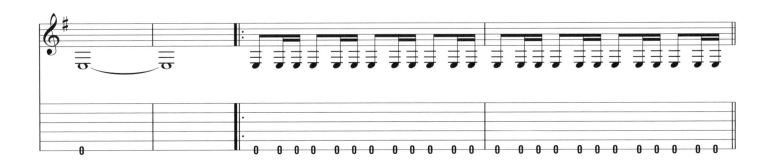

% Verse
N.C.(E5 open)

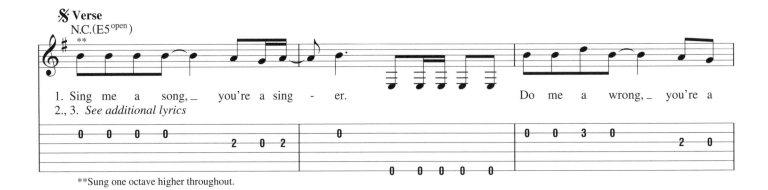

1. Sing me a song,_ you're a sing - er. Do me a wrong,_ you're a
2., 3. *See additional lyrics*

**Sung one octave higher throughout.

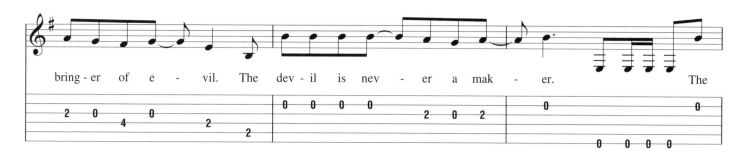

bring-er of e-vil. The dev-il is nev-er a mak-er. The

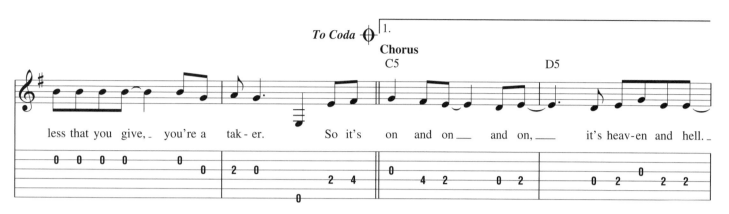

less that you give, you're a tak-er. So it's on and on and on, it's heav-en and hell.

Oh, well.

on and on and on. Whoa, it's on and on and on. It goes

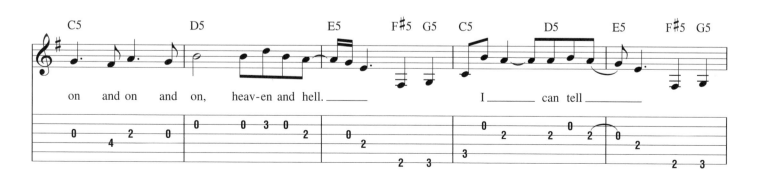

on and on and on, heav-en and hell. I can tell

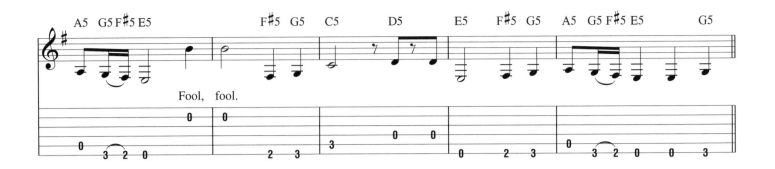

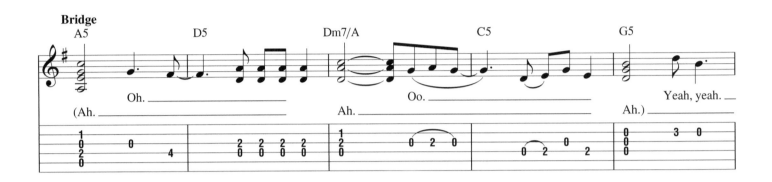

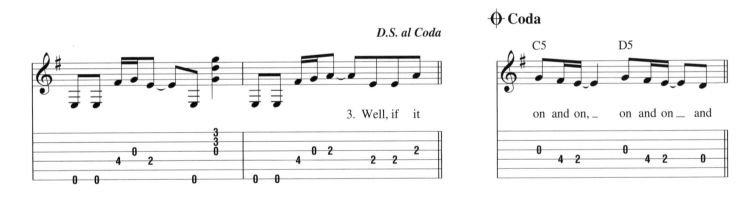

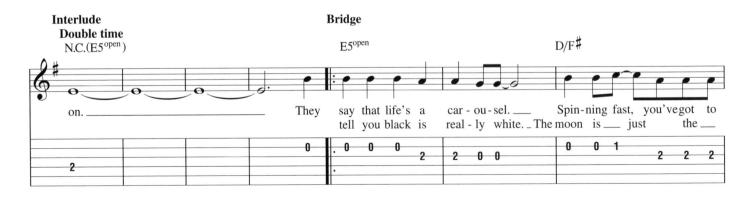

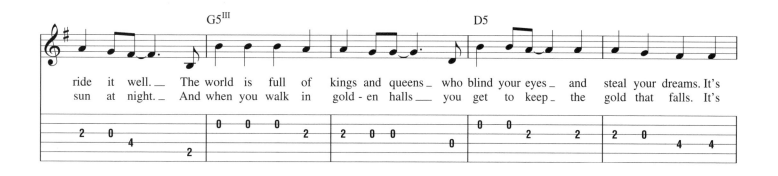

ride it well. __ The world is full of kings and queens __ who blind your eyes __ and steal your dreams. It's
sun at night. __ And when you walk in gold-en halls __ you get to keep __ the gold that falls. It's

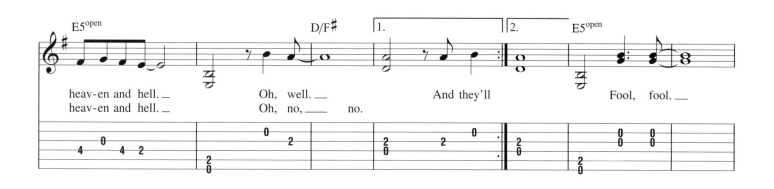

heav-en and hell. __   Oh, well. __   And they'll   Fool, fool. __
heav-en and hell. __   Oh, no, ___ no.

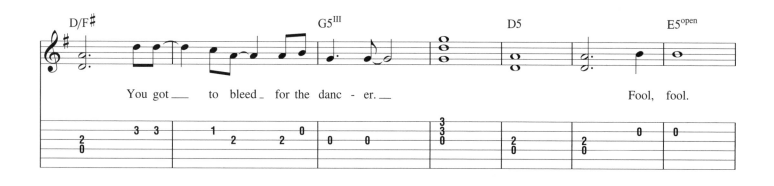

You got __ to bleed __ for the danc-er. __   Fool, fool.

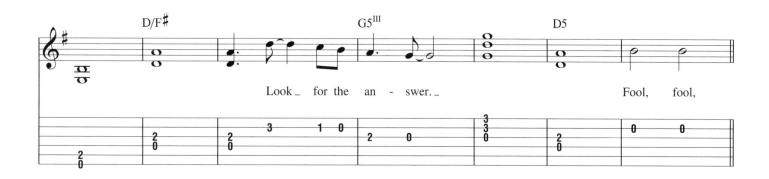

Look __ for the an-swer. __   Fool, fool,

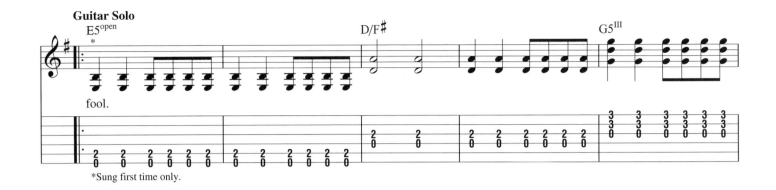

fool.

*Sung first time only.

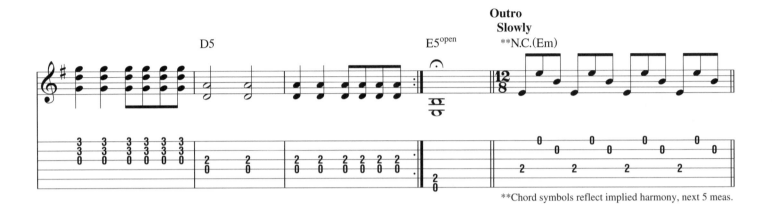

Outro
Slowly

**Chord symbols reflect implied harmony, next 5 meas.

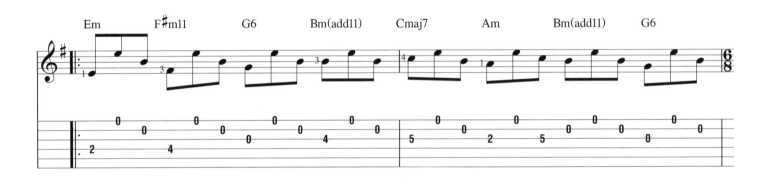

Repeat and fade

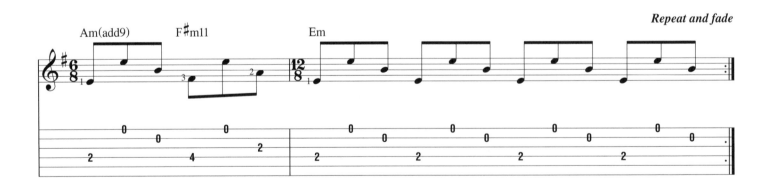

Additional Lyrics

2. The lover of life's not a sinner.
   The ending is just a beginner.
   The closer you get to the meaning,
   The sooner you know that you're dreaming.
   So it's...

3. Well if it seems to be real, it's illusion.
   For ev'ry moment of truth, there's confusion in life.
   Love can be seen as the answer,
   But nobody bleeds for the dancer.
   And if it's...

Higher

Words and Music by Mark Tremonti and Scott Stapp

Drop D tuning:
(low to high D-A-D-G-B-E

Strum Pattern: 2, 6
Pick Pattern: 4

Intro
Slow Rock

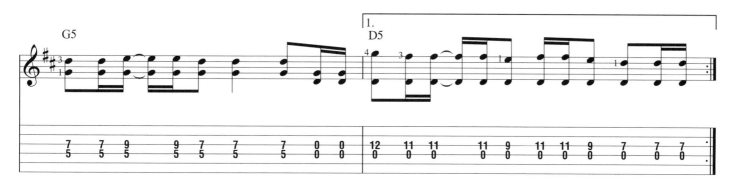

1. When dream - in', _____ I got in - to _____ an -
2. *See additional lyrics*

oth - er world _ time and time _ a - gain. _____ At

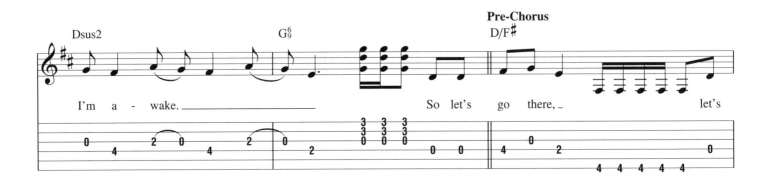

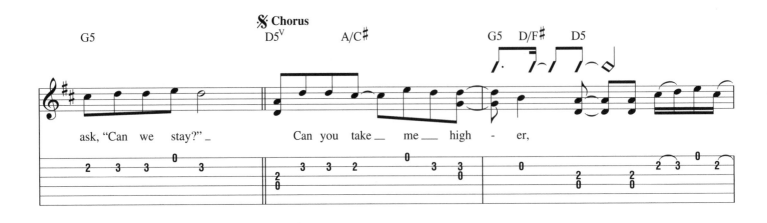

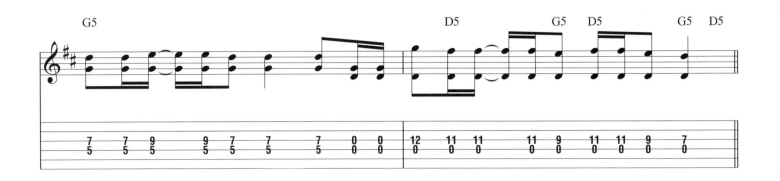

Bridge

Up high ___ I feel ___ like ___ I'm ___ a - live ___ for ___ the ___ ver - y ___

___ first ___ time. ___ Said up high, ___ I'm strong ___ e - nough ___ to take ___

Interlude

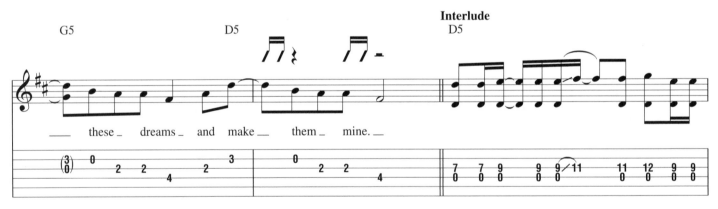

___ these ___ dreams ___ and make ___ them ___ mine. ___

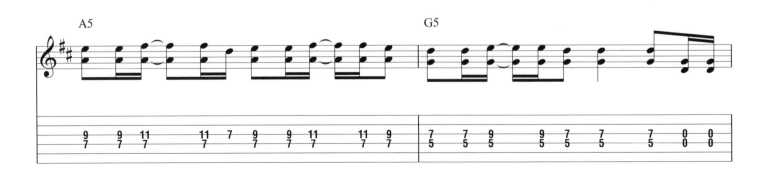

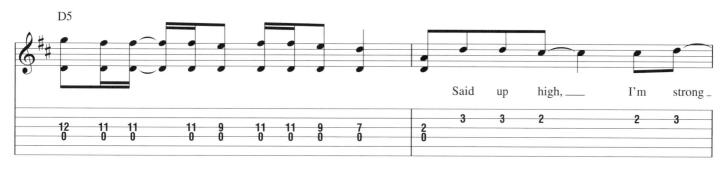

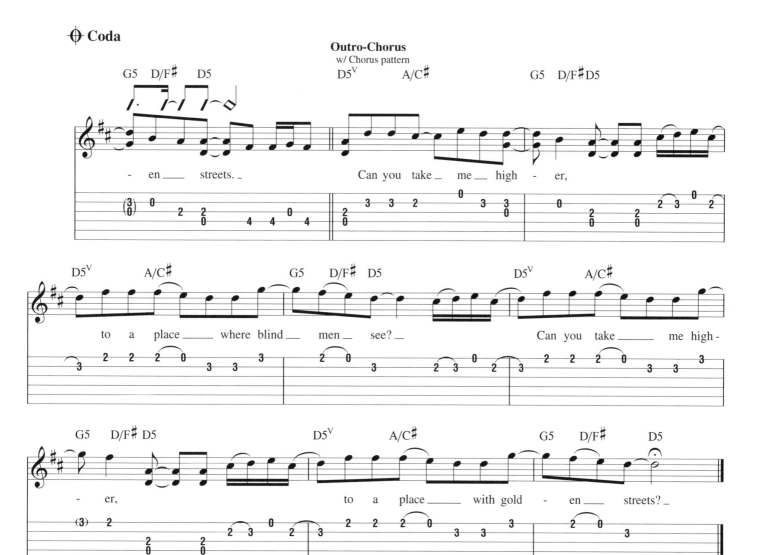

Additional Lyrics

2. Although I would like the world to change,
   It helps me to appreciate those nights and those dreams.
   But, my friend, I'd sacrifice all those nights
   If I could make the earth and my dreams the same.
   The only difference is to let love replace all our hate.

Hey Joe

Words and Music by Billy Roberts

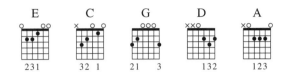

E   C   G   D   A

Strum Pattern: 4
Pick Pattern: 2

Intro
Moderately slow Rock, in 2

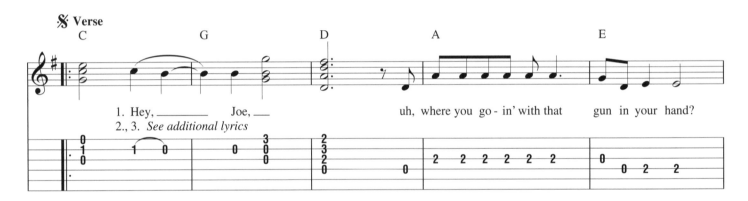

1. Hey, _____ Joe, _____ uh, where you go - in' with that gun in your hand?
2., 3. *See additional lyrics*

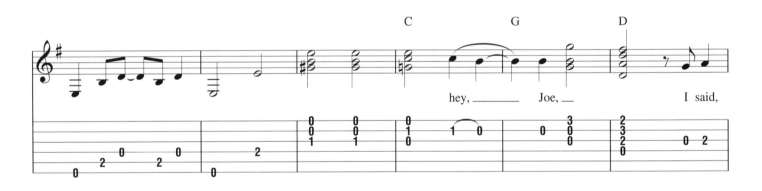

hey, _____ Joe, _____ I said,

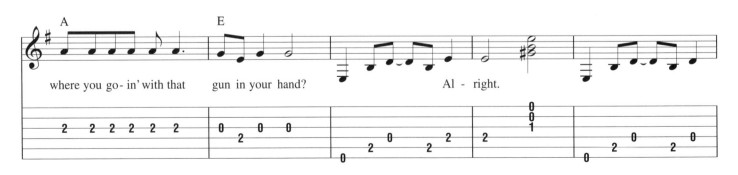

where you go - in' with that gun in your hand? Al - right.

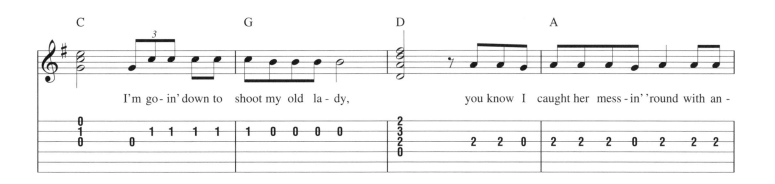

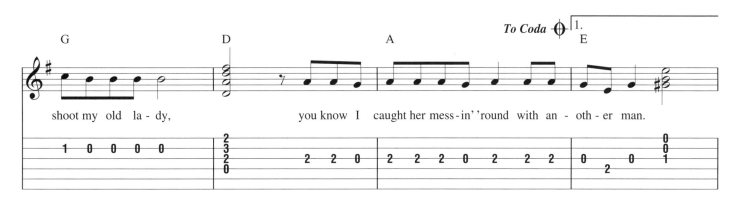

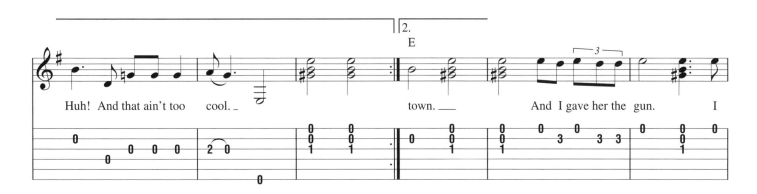

Guitar Solo

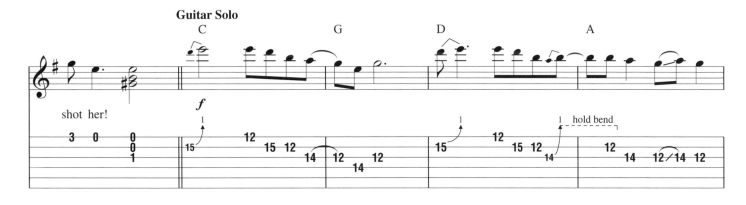

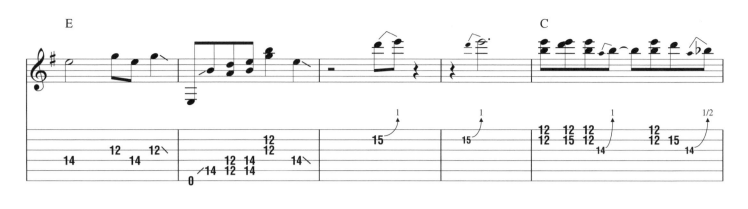

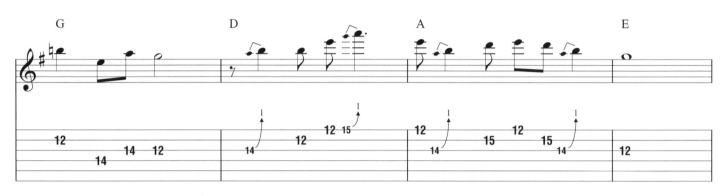

Interlude

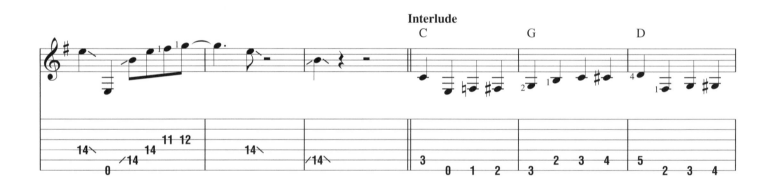

D.S. al Coda

Coda

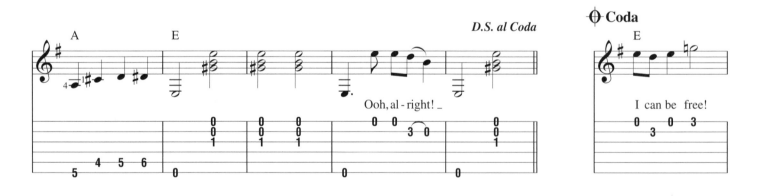

Ooh, al-right! _

I can be free!

Outro

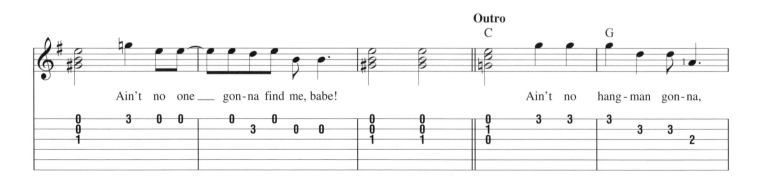

Ain't no one __ gon-na find me, babe!

Ain't no hang-man gon-na,

174

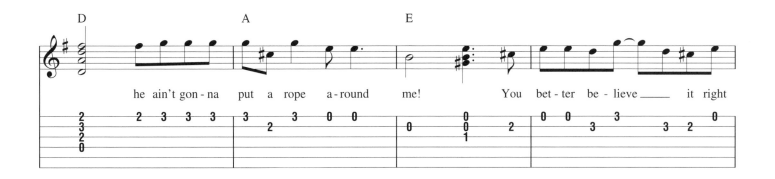

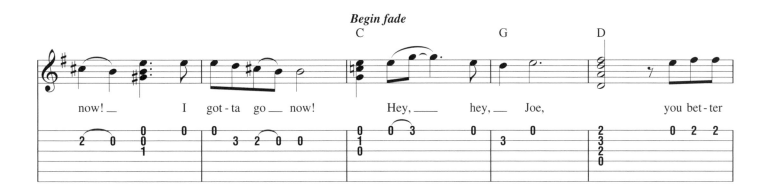

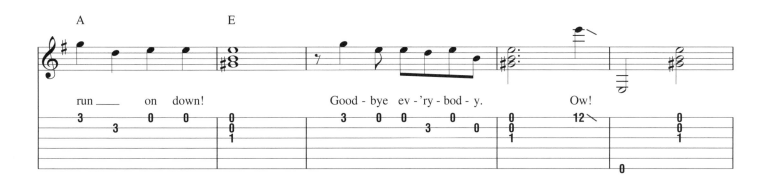

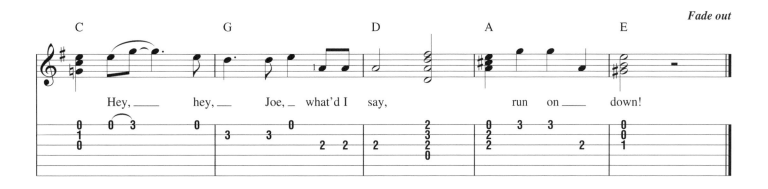

Additional Lyrics

2. Uh, hey, Joe, I heard you shot your woman down,
   You shot her down now.
   Uh, hey, Joe, I heard you shot your old lady down,
   You shot her down in the ground. Yeah!
   Yes I did, I shot her,
   You know I caught her messin' 'round, messin' round town.
   Uh, yes I did, I shot her,
   You know I caught my old lady messin' 'round town.
   And I gave her the gun. I shot her!

3. Hey, Joe, said now, uh, where you gonna run to now,
   Where you gonna run to? Yeah.
   Hey, Joe, I said, where you gonna run to now, where you,
   Where you gonna go? Well, dig it!
   I'm goin' way down south, way down to Mexico way! Alright!
   I'm goin' way down south, way down where I can be free!
   Ain't no one gonna find me, babe!

Holy Diver

Words and Music by Ronnie James Dio

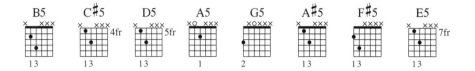

*Capo I

Strum Pattern: 1

Intro

Moderately slow Rock

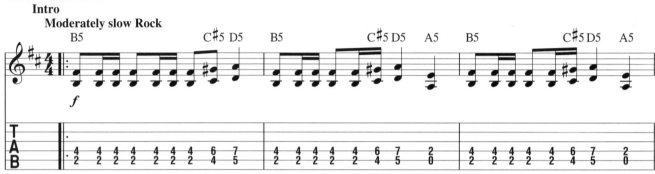

*Optional: To match recording, place capo at 1st fret.

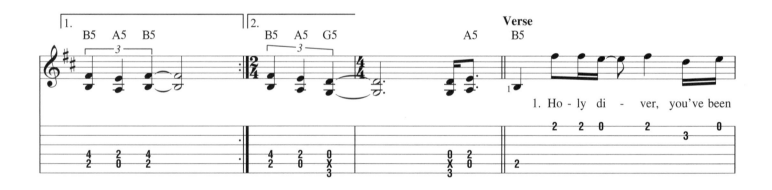

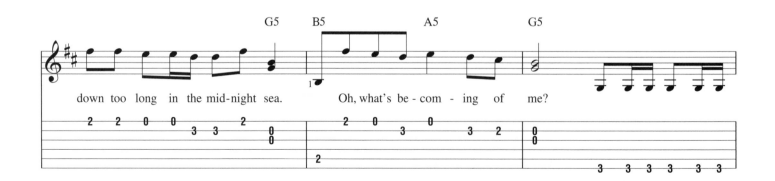

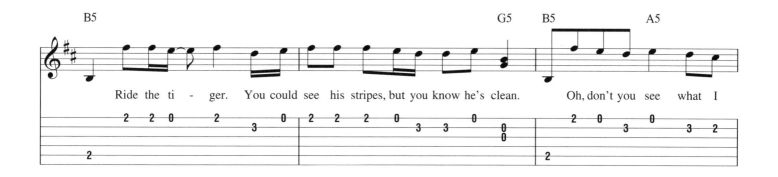

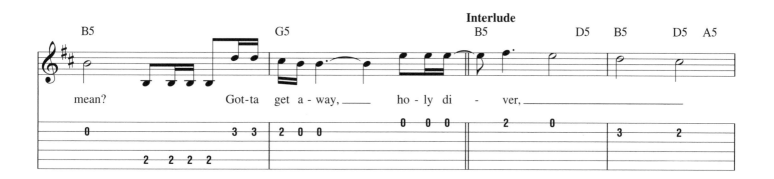

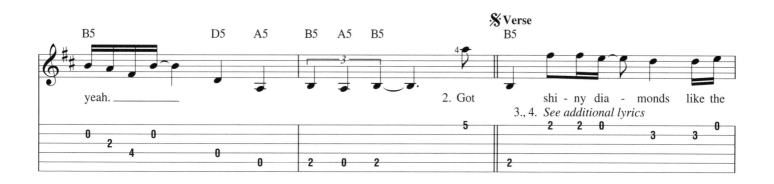

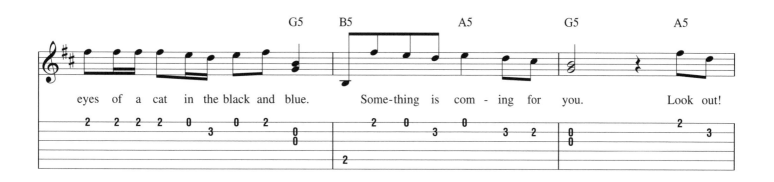

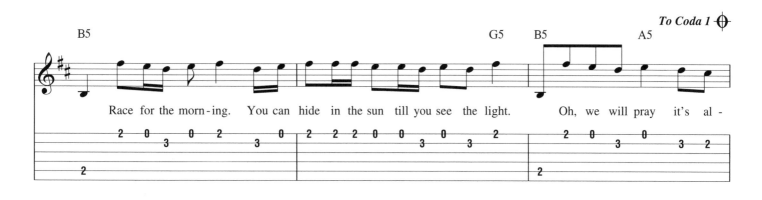

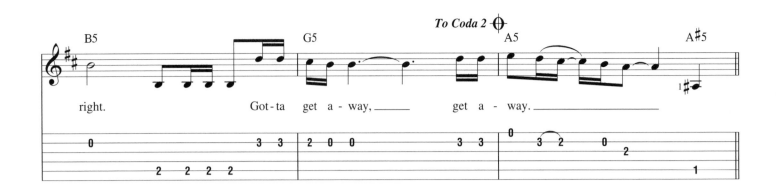

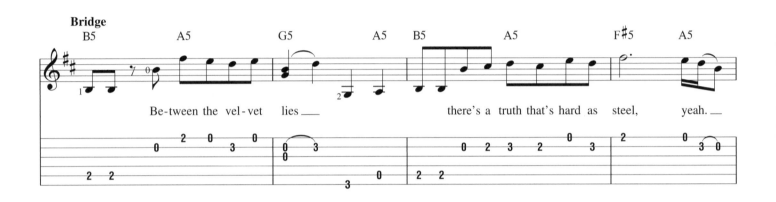

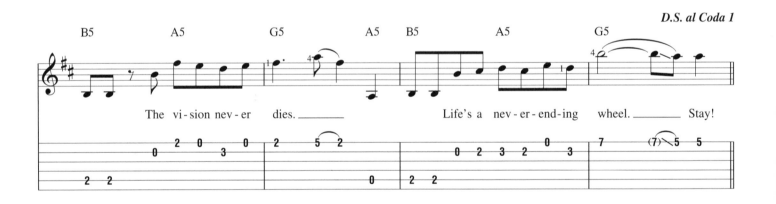

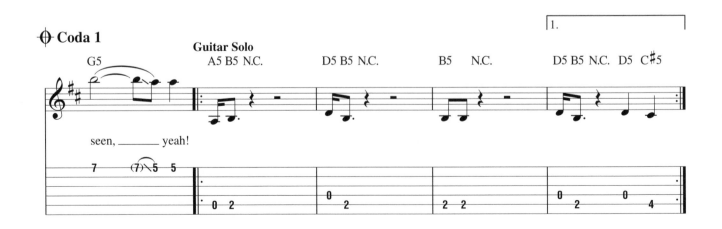

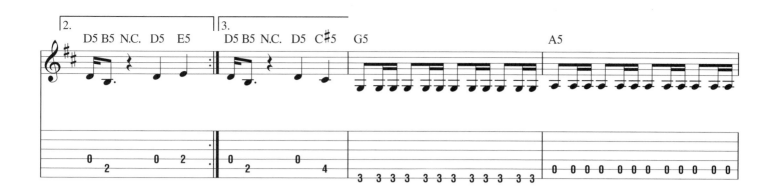

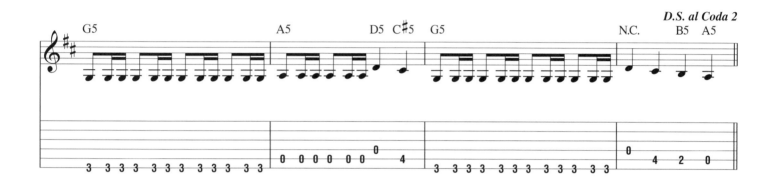

⊕ Coda 2

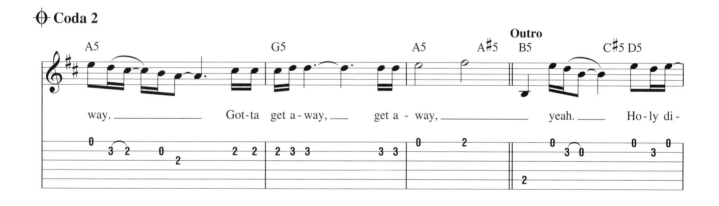

way. _____ Got-ta get a-way, _____ get a-way, _____ yeah. _____ Ho-ly di-

- ver, _____ sole sur-viv - or, you're the one who's clean. __ Ho-ly di - ver. __ Ho-ly di -

*Sung one octave higher till end.

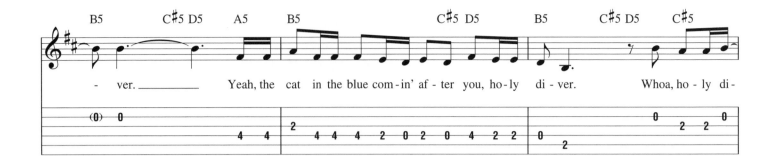

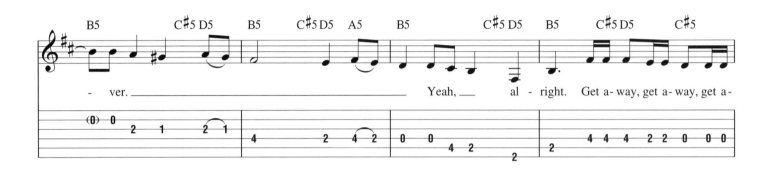

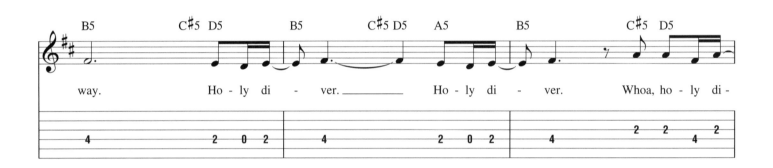

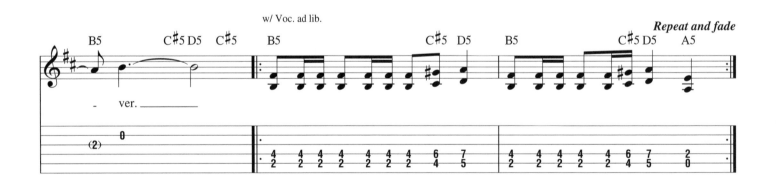

Additional Lyrics

3. Holy diver, you're the star of the masquerade.
   No need to look so afraid. Jump, jump,
   Jump from the tiger. You could feel his heart but you know he's mean.
   Some light can never be seen, yeah!

4. Holy diver, you've been down too long in the midnight sea.
   Oh, what's becoming of me? No! No!
   Ride the tiger. You could see his stripes but you know he's clean.
   Oh, don't you see what I mean? Gotta get away, get away.

Hot Blooded

Words and Music by Mick Jones and Lou Gramm

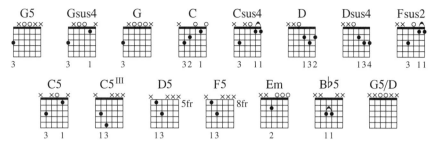

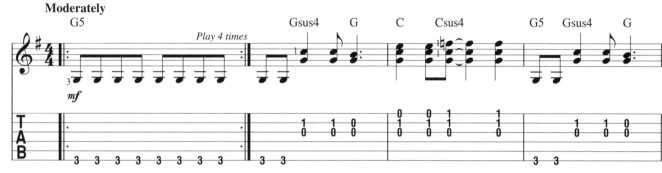

Strum Pattern: 1, 2
Pick Pattern: 2, 4

Intro
Moderately

Play 4 times

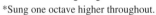

Chorus

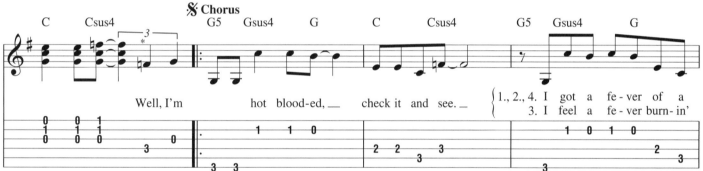

Well, I'm hot blood-ed, __ check it and see. __
1., 2., 4. I got a fe - ver of a
3. I feel a fe - ver burn-in'

*Sung one octave higher throughout.

To Coda 1

To Coda 2

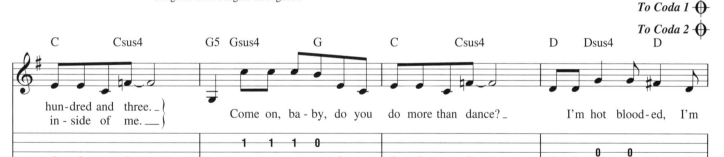

hun-dred and three. __
in-side of me. __
Come on, ba - by, do you do more than dance? _ I'm hot blood-ed, I'm

Verse

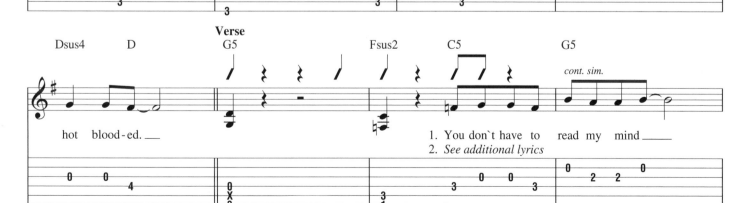

hot blood-ed. __
1. You don`t have to read my mind ____
2. See additional lyrics

Additional Lyrics

2. If it feels all right,
   Maybe you can stay all night.
   Should I leave you my key?
   But you've got to give me a sign.
   Come on, girl, some kind of sign.
   Tell me, are you hot momma?
   You sure look that way to me.

Pre-Chorus Are you old enough?
   Will you be ready when I call your bluff?
   Is my timing right?
   Did you save your love for me tonight?

Hot for Teacher

**Words and Music by David Lee Roth, Edward Van Halen,
Alex Van Halen and Michael Anthony**

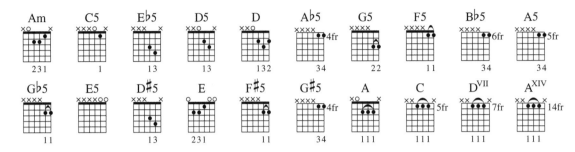

Strum Pattern: 1, 6

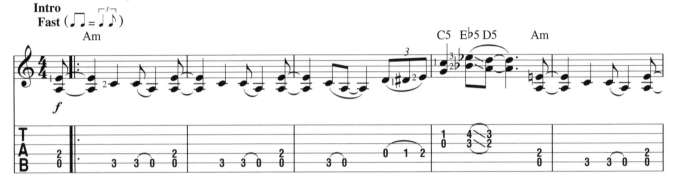

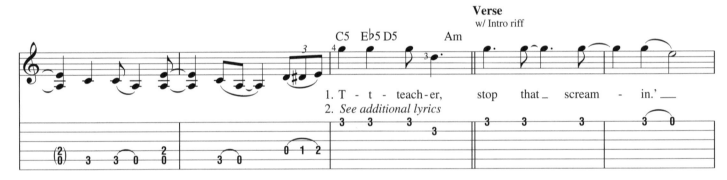

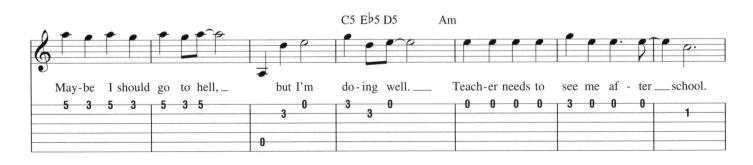

Pre-Chorus

*One strum per chord throughout Pre-Chorus

I think of all ___ the ed - u - ca - tion that I missed, ___ but then my

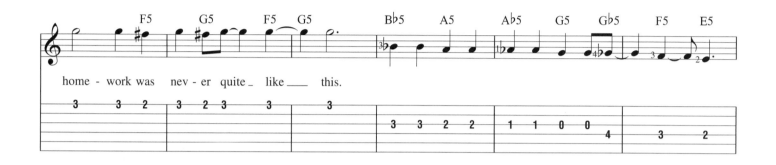

home - work was nev - er quite ___ like ___ this.

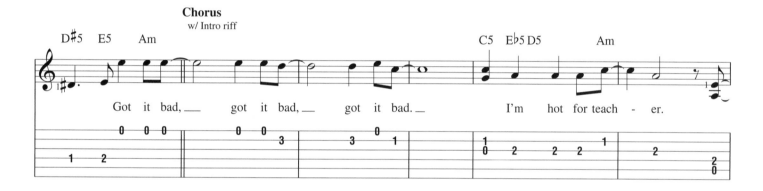

Chorus
w/ Intro riff

Got it bad, ___ got it bad, ___ got it bad. ___ I'm hot for teach - er.

I've got it bad, ___ so bad. I'm hot for teach-

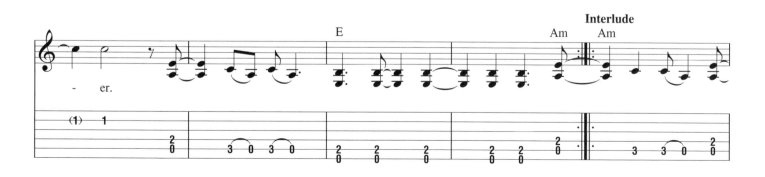

- er.

Interlude

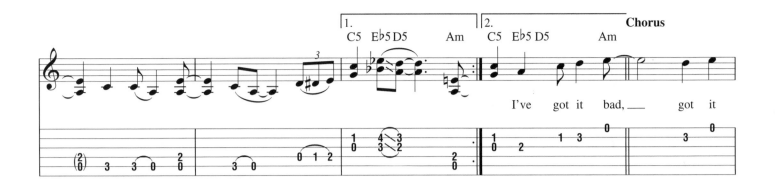

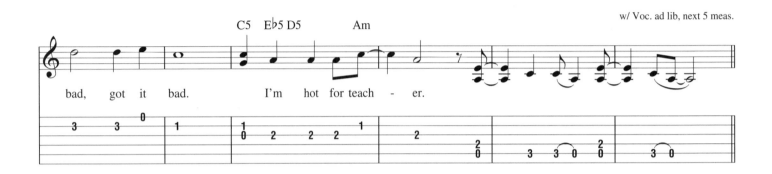

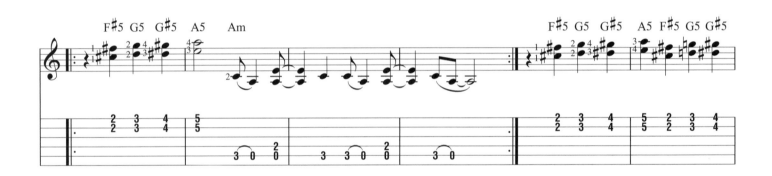

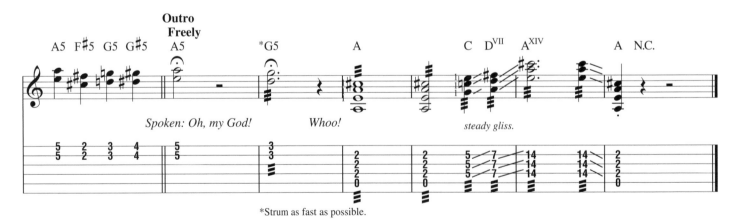

*Strum as fast as possible.

Additional Lyrics

2. I heard about your lessons,
   But lessons are so cold.
   I know about this school.
   Little girl from Cherry Lawn,
   How can you be so bold?
   How did you know that golden rule?

I Wanna Rock

Words and Music by D. Snider

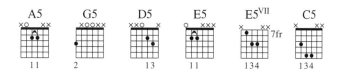

Strum Pattern: 1, 4

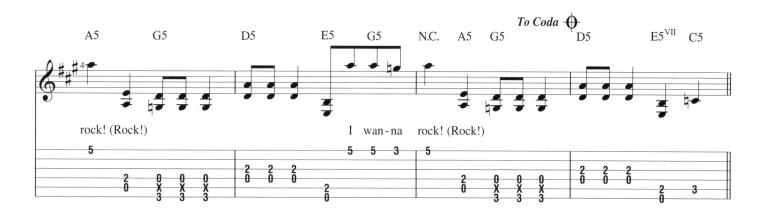

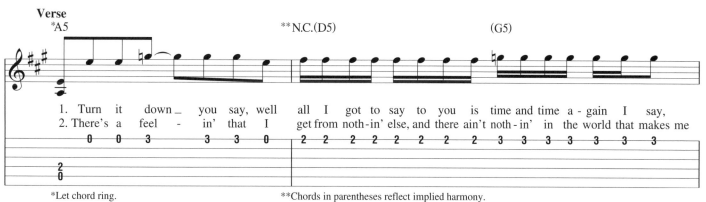

*Let chord ring.

**Chords in parentheses reflect implied harmony.

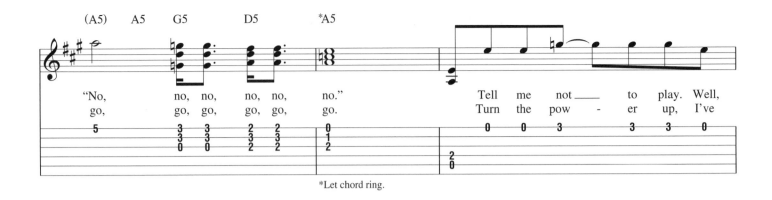

"No, no, no, no, no, no."
go, go, go, go, go, go.

Tell me not _____ to play. Well,
Turn the pow - er up, I've

*Let chord ring.

all I got-ta say to when you tell me not to play, I say, "No, no, no, no, no, no."
wait-ed for so long so I could hear my fav-'rite song, so let's go, go, go, go, go, go.

Pre-Chorus

G5   D5   G5

So if you ask me why I like the way I play it, there's on - ly one thing I can
When it's like this, I feel the mu - sic shoot - in' through me, there's noth - in' else that I would

1.   2.

D.S. al Coda

⊕ **Coda**

Bridge

C5 G5 D5 N.C.   C5 G5 D5 N.C.   D5   E5^{VII} C5   A5

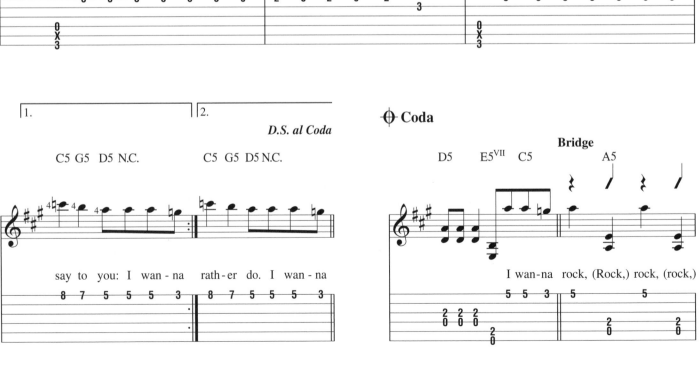

say to you: I wan - na rath - er do. I wan - na

I wan-na rock, (Rock,) rock, (rock,)

188

I Can't Drive 55

Words and Music by Sammy Hagar

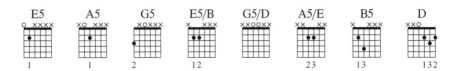

Strum Pattern: 1

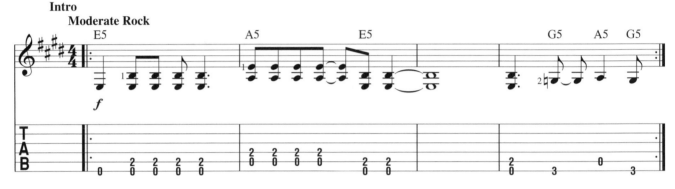

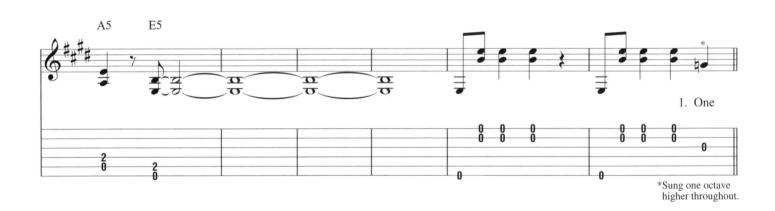

1. One

*Sung one octave
higher throughout.

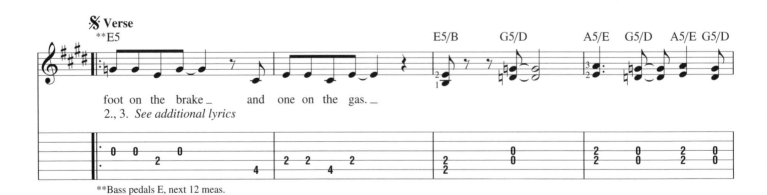

foot on the brake __ and one on the gas. __
2., 3. *See additional lyrics*

**Bass pedals E, next 12 meas.

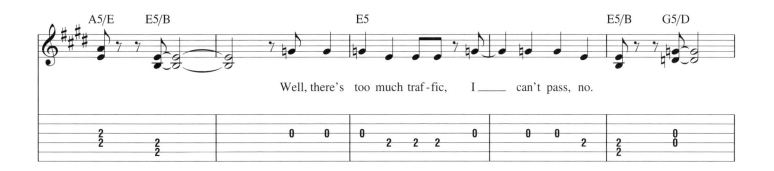

Well, there's too much traf-fic, I ___ can't pass, no.

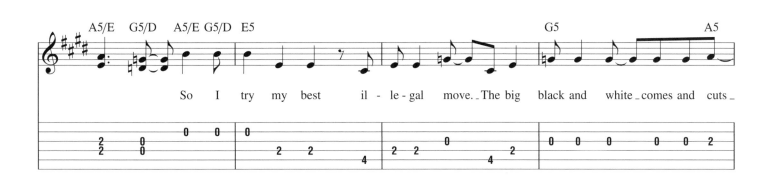

So I try my best il - le - gal move. The big black and white ___ comes and cuts ___

Chorus

___ my ___ groove ___ a - gain. ___ {1., 3. Go on and write / 2. Write} me up for one - twen-ty - five. ___

Post my face; want-ed dead or a - live. ___ Take my li-cense and all ___ that jive. ___ I ___

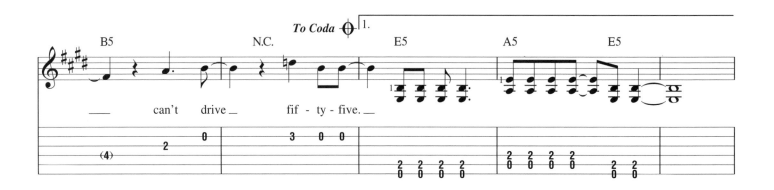

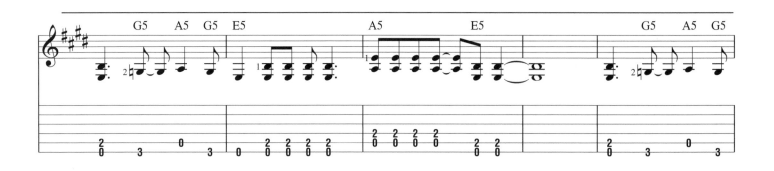

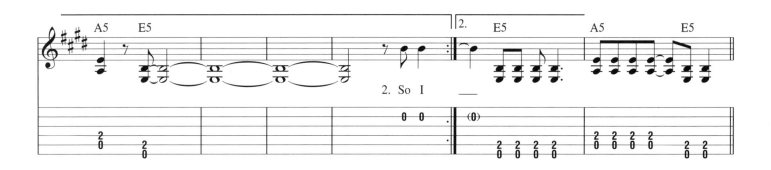

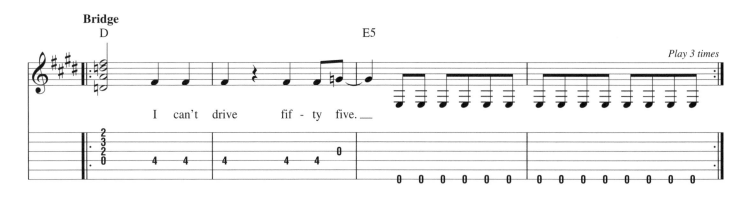

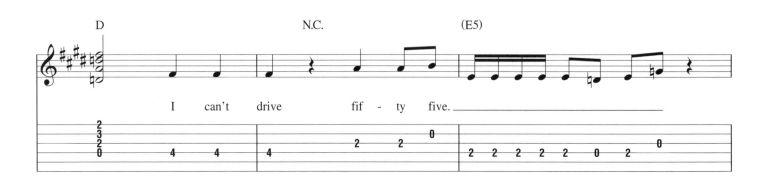

Uh!

Guitar Solo

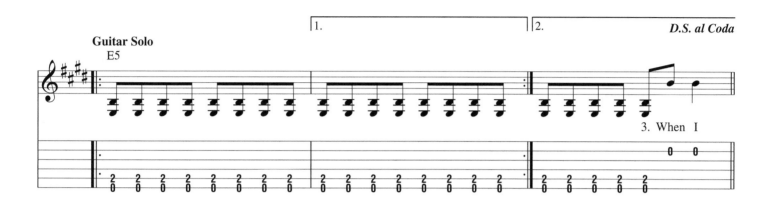

1.

2.

D.S. al Coda

3. When I

Coda

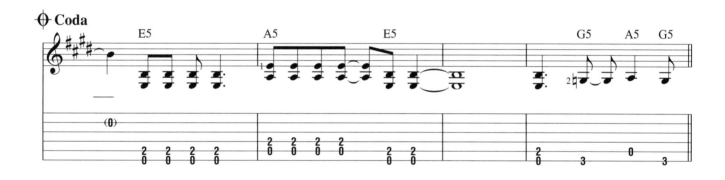

Outro
w/ Intro pattern, 1st 4 meas.

Repeat and fade

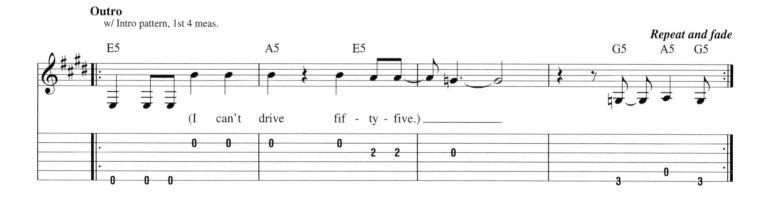

(I can't drive fif - ty - five.)

Additional Lyrics

2. So I signed my name on number twenty-four.
   And the judge said, "Boy, just one more,
   I'm gonna throw your ass in the city joint."
   He looked at me in the eye and said, "You get my point?"
   I said, "Yeah."

3. When I drive that slow, you know it's hard to steer,
   And I can't get my car outta second gear.
   What used to take two hours now takes all day.
   It took me sixteen hours to get to L.A.

I Wanna Be Somebody

Words and Music by Steve Duren

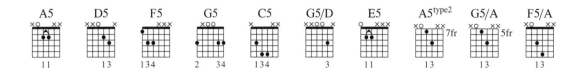

*Tune down 1/2 step:
(low to high) E♭-A♭-D♭-G♭-B♭-E♭

Strum Pattern: 1, 4
Pick Pattern: 4

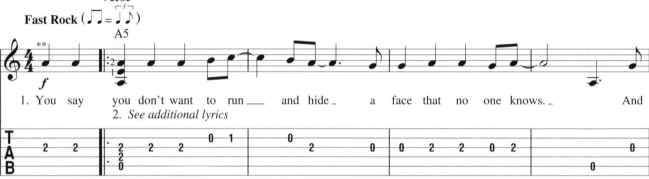

Verse

Fast Rock

1. You say you don't want to run___ and hide___ a face that no one knows.___ And
2. *See additional lyrics*

*Optional: To match recording, tune down 1/2 step.
**Sung one octave higher throughout.

ev-'ry-one___ you meet___ ya gon-na show.___ You're no-bod-y's slave;

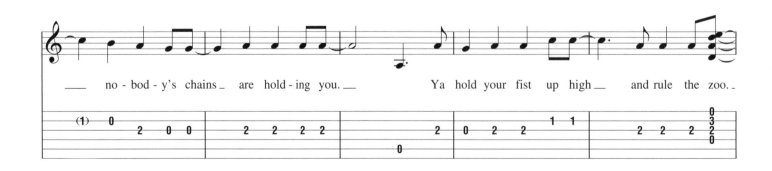

___ no-bod-y's chains___ are hold-ing you.___ Ya hold your fist up high___ and rule the zoo.___

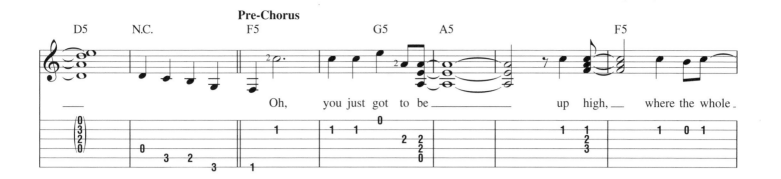

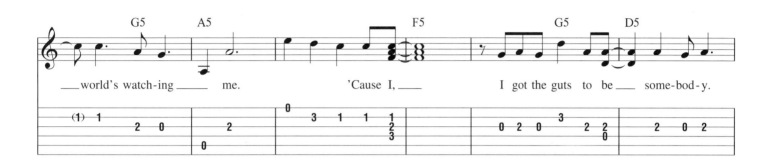

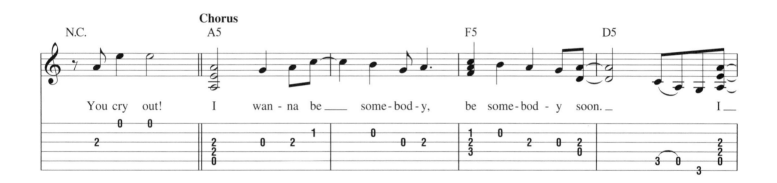

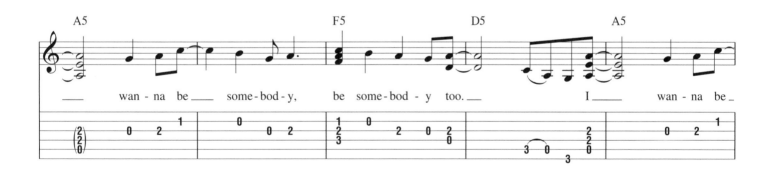

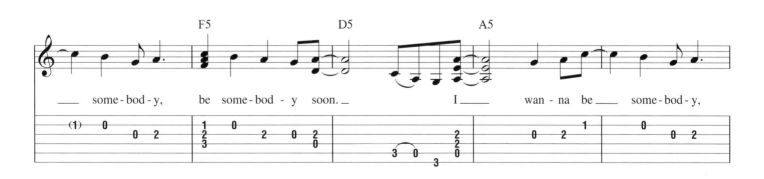

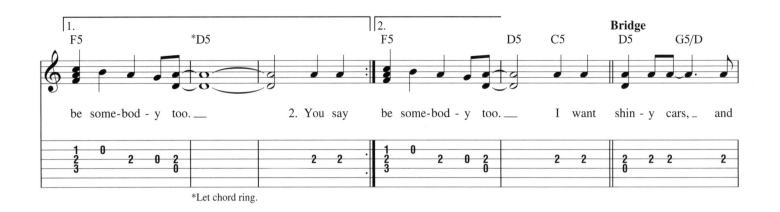

be some-bod - y too. __ 2. You say be some-bod - y too. __ I want shin - y cars, __ and

*Let chord ring.

dirt - y mon - ey, lots of rock 'n' roll. __ I will live in fame __ and die in flames. I'm

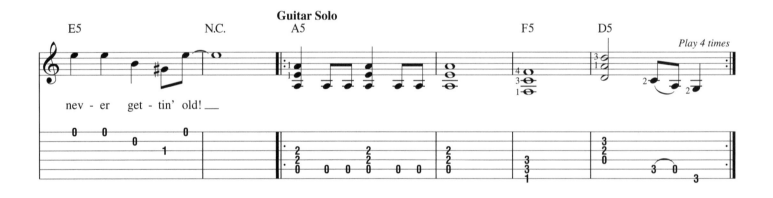

nev - er get - tin' old! __

I wan - na be __ some-bod - y, be some-bod - y soon. __

**Let chord ring.   ***Chords in parentheses reflect implied harmony.

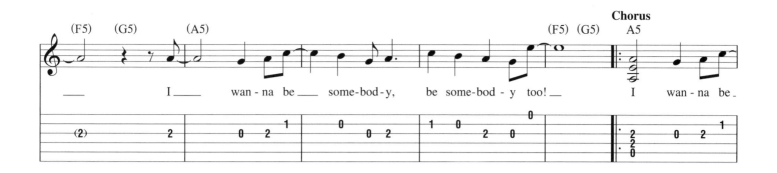

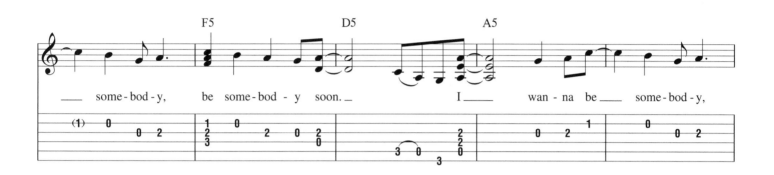

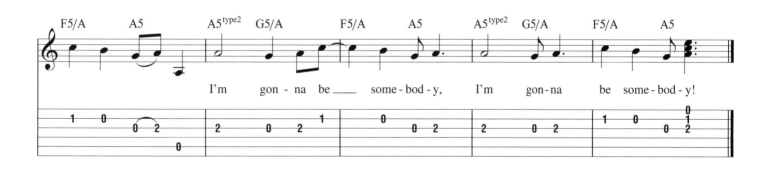

Additional Lyrics

2. You say you don't wanna starve
   Or take the table crumbs that fall.
   Uh, you don't wanna beg or plead at all.
   You don't want no nine-to-five
   Your fingers to the bone.
   You don't want the rock pile's bloody stones!

In-A-Gadda-Da-Vida

Words and Music by Doug Ingle

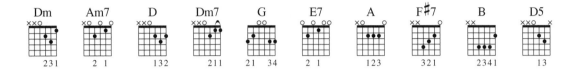

Strum Pattern: 5
Pick Pattern: 1

Intro
Moderately

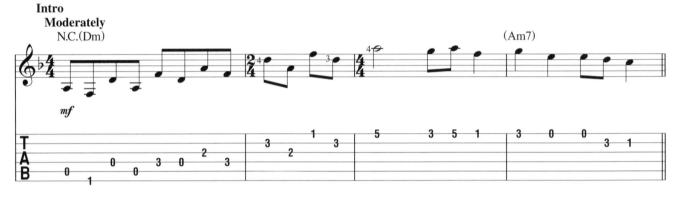

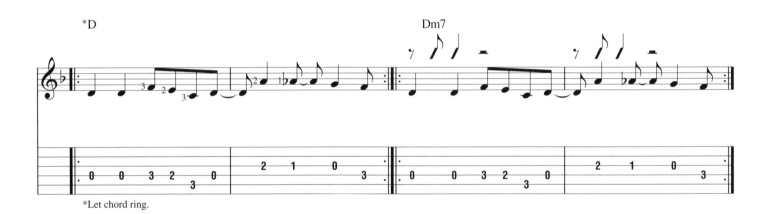

*Let chord ring.

Verse
w/ Intro pattern

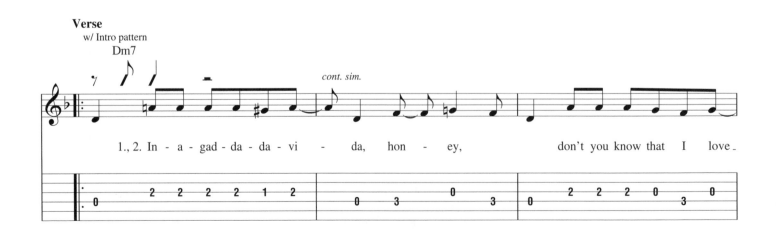

1., 2. In - a - gad - da - da - vi - da, hon - ey, don't you know that I love

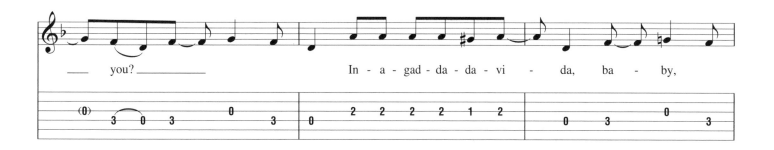

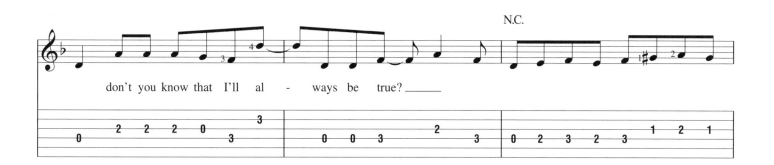

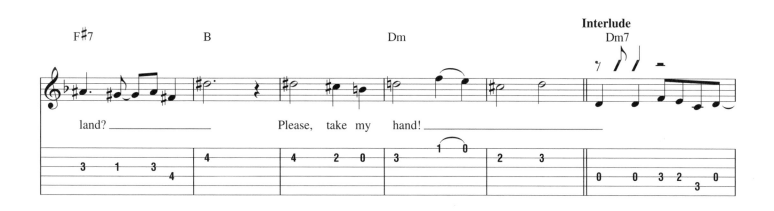

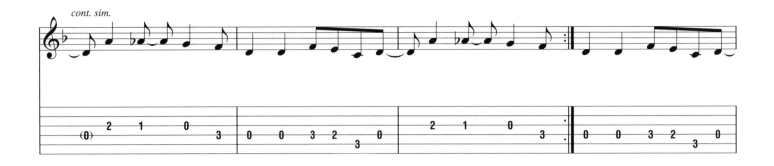

Drum Solo

Interlude

Outro

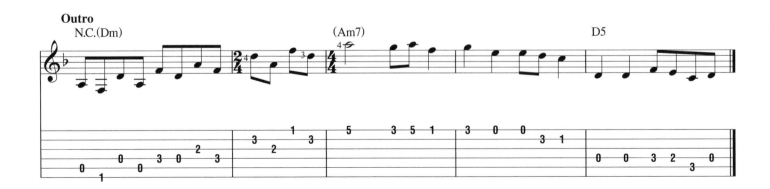

Interstate Love Song

Words and Music by Dean De Leo, Robert De Leo, Eric Kretz and Scott Weiland

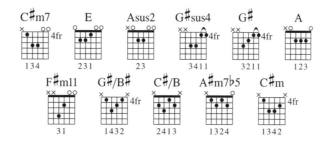

Strum Pattern: 3, 5
Pick Pattern: 1, 3

Intro
Moderately slow

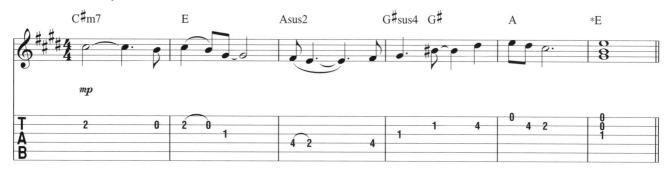

*Let chord ring.

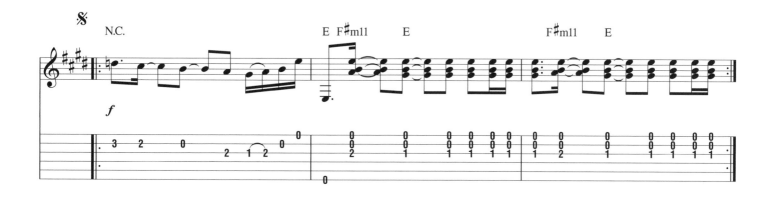

Verse

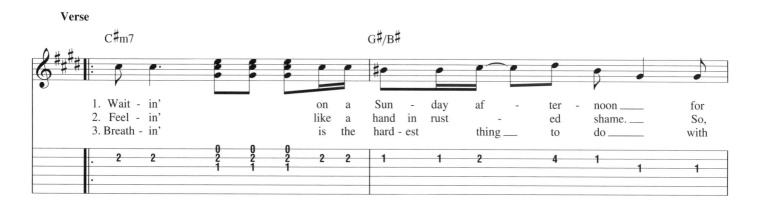

1. Wait - in'   on a Sun - day af - ter - noon ____ for
2. Feel - in'   like a hand in rust - ed shame. ____ So,
3. Breath - in'   is the hard - est thing ____ to do ____ with

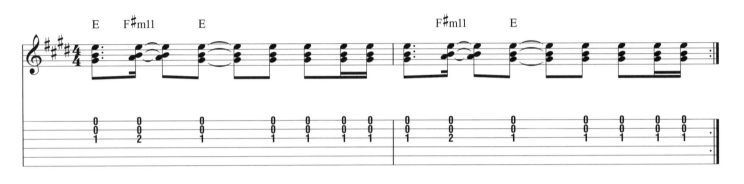

Interlude

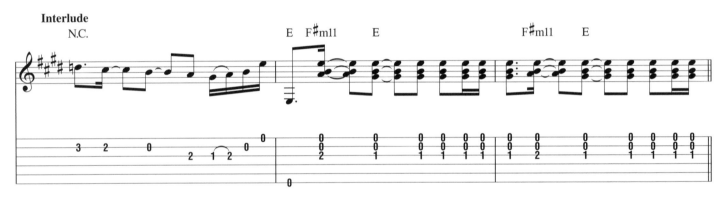

Chorus

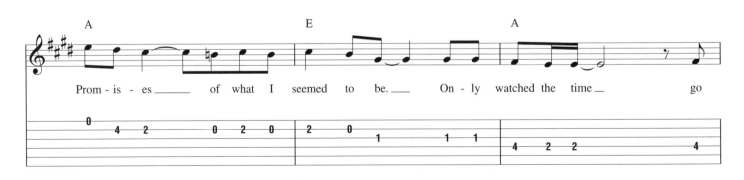

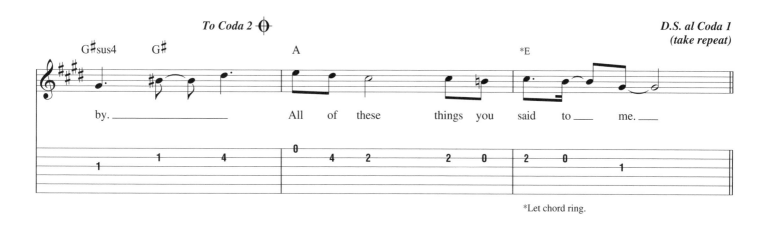

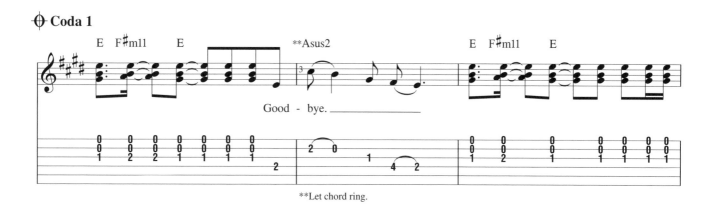

*Let chord ring.

**Let chord ring.

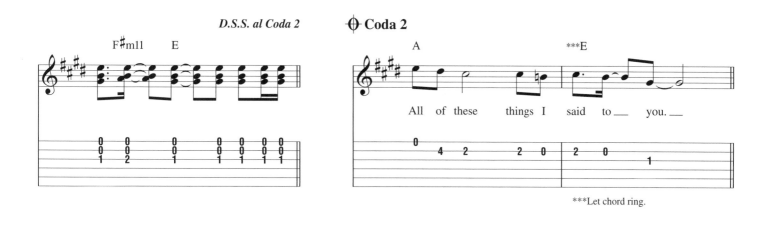

***Let chord ring.

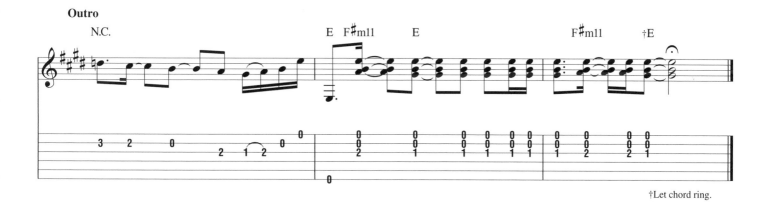

†Let chord ring.

Jailbreak

Words and Music by Philip Parris Lynott

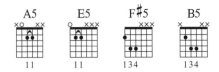

*Tune down 1/2 step:
(low to high) Eb-Ab-Db-Gb-Bb-Eb

Strum Pattern: 5, 6

Intro
Moderately fast

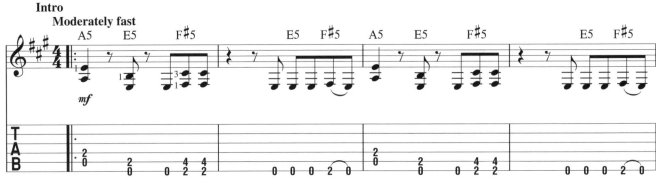

*Optional: To match recording, tune down 1/2 step.

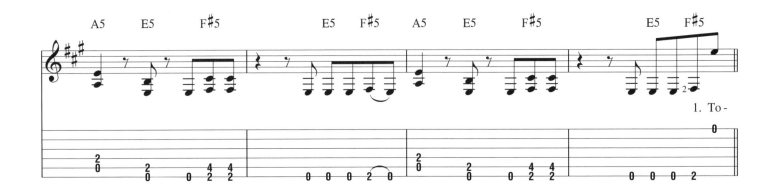

1. To-

Verse
w/ Intro pattern

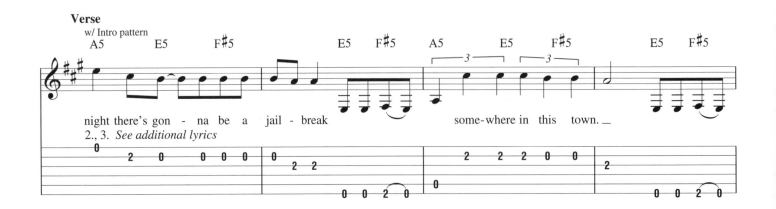

night there's gon - na be a jail - break   some-where in this town. _

2., 3. *See additional lyrics*

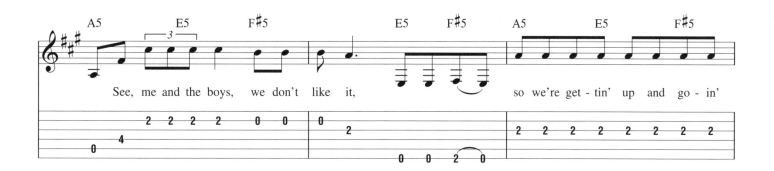

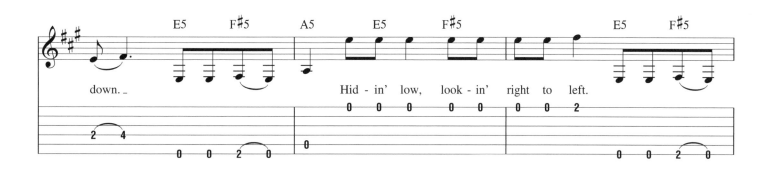

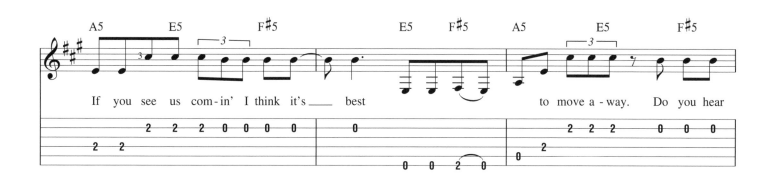

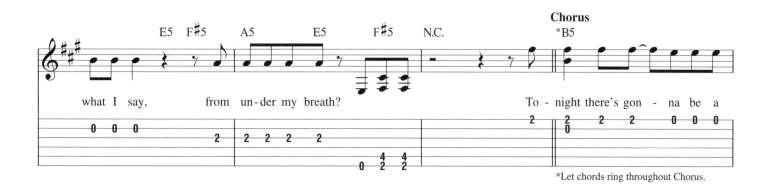

*Let chords ring throughout Chorus.

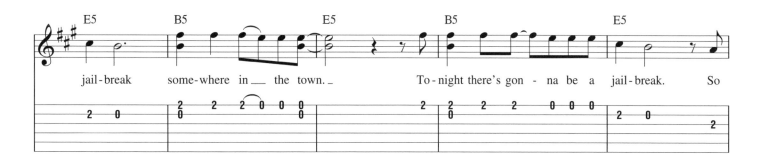

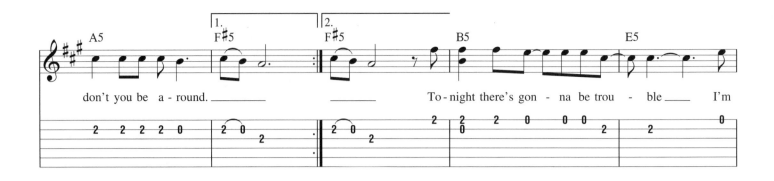

don't you be a - round._____ _____ To - night there's gon - na be trou - ble_____ I'm

To Coda ⊕

gon - na find___ my - self in. To - night there's gon - na be trou - ble,_____ so

Interlude

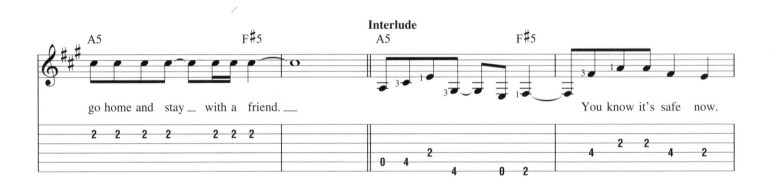

go home and stay___ with a friend.___ You know it's safe now.

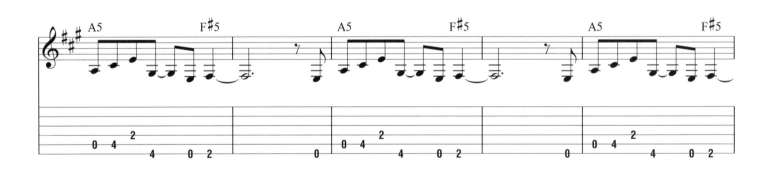

Bridge

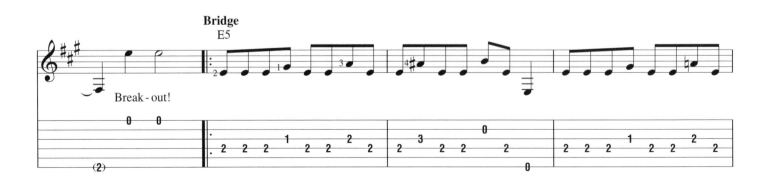

Break - out!

206

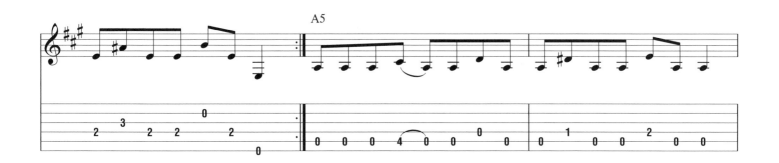

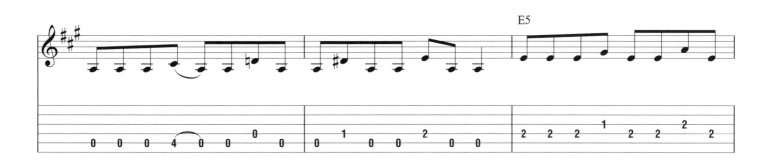

Coda

D.C. al Coda
(take 2nd ending)

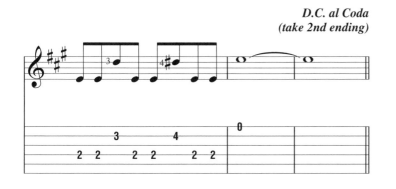

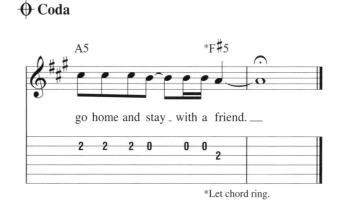

go home and stay with a friend.

*Let chord ring.

Additional Lyrics

2. Tonight there's gonna be trouble.
   Some of us won't survive.
   See, the boys and me mean business.
   Bustin' out dead or alive.
   I can hear hound dogs on my trail.
   All hell breaks loose, alarm and sirens wail.
   Like a game, if you lose, go to jail!

3. Tonight there's gonna be a breakout
   Into the city zones.
   Don't you dare to try to stop us,
   No one could for long.
   Search light on my trail.
   Tonight's the night, all systems fail.
   Good lookin' female, come here.

Kick Out the Jams

**Words and Music by Frederick Smith, Wayne Kramer,
Dennis Tomich, Robert Derminer and Michael Davis**

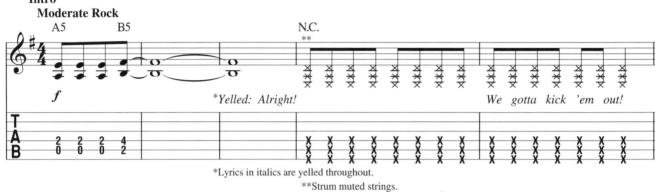

Strum Pattern: 3

Intro
Moderate Rock

Yelled: Alright!

We gotta kick 'em out!

*Lyrics in italics are yelled throughout.
**Strum muted strings.

Play 3 times

1. Well, I feel   pret - ty good   and I guess
2., 3. *See additional lyrics*

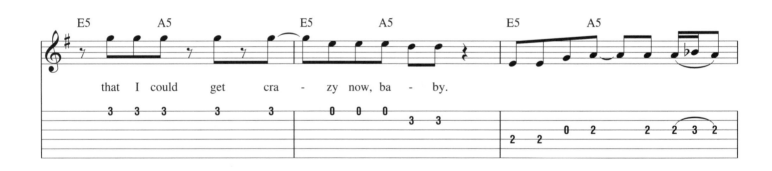

that I could   get   cra - zy now, ba - by.

We all got___ in___ tune___ where the dress - ing   room___ got haz - y.

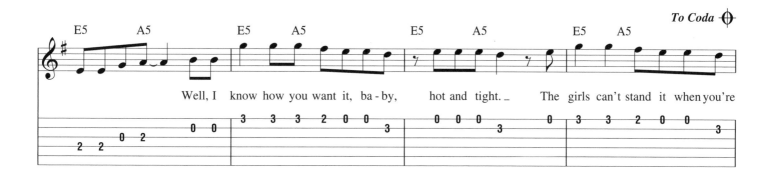

Well, I know how you want it, ba - by, hot and tight. _ The girls can't stand it when you're

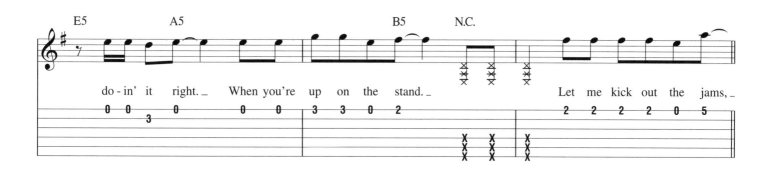

do - in' it right. _ When you're up on the stand. _ Let me kick out the jams, _

Chorus

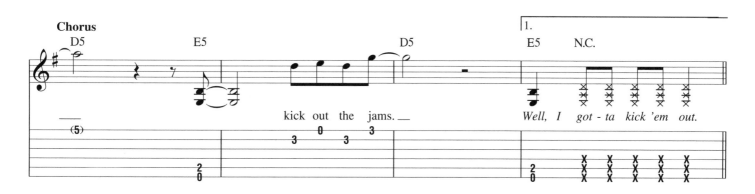

kick out the jams. _ *Well, I got - ta kick 'em out.*

Interlude

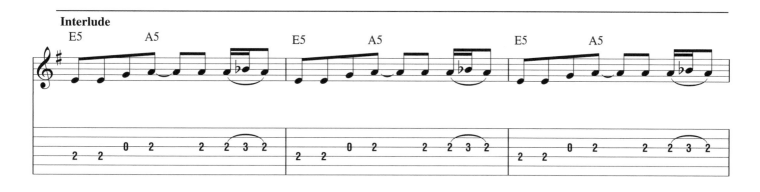

Guitar Solo

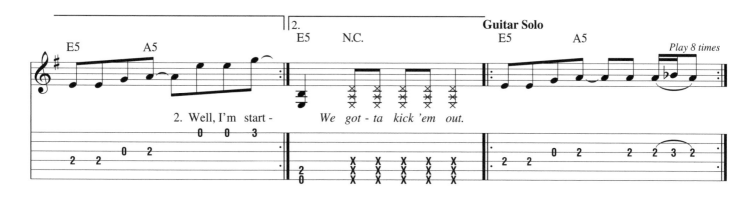

2. Well, I'm start - *We got - ta kick 'em out.*

Play 8 times

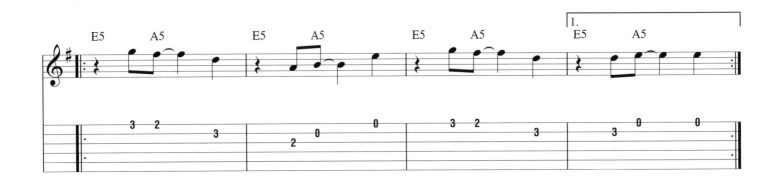

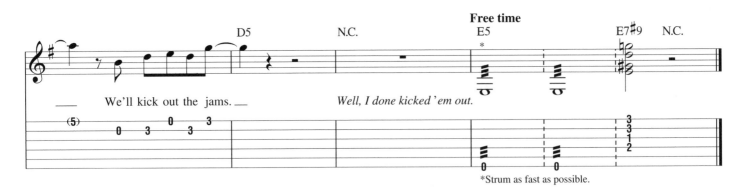

*Strum as fast as possible.

Additional Lyrics

2. Well, I'm startin' to sweat,
   Oh yeah, my shirt's all wet. What a feelin' now, baby.
   The sound that abounds and resounds
   And rebounds straight off of the ceiling.
   You gotta have it, baby, you can't do without.
   Get that feelin', gotta kick 'em out.
   Put that mic in my hand,
   Well, let me kick out the jams.

3. So you got to give it up.
   You know you can't get enough, Miss MacKenzie.
   'Cause it gets in your brain
   And it drives you insane with the frenzy.
   The wigglin' guitars, girl, the crash of the drums
   Make me want to keep a rockin' till morning comes.
   Let me be who I am
   And let me kick out the jams.

Lit Up

Words and Music by Joshua Todd Gruber, Keith Edward Nelson, Jonathan Brightman and Devon Glenn

Strum Pattern: 2
Pick Pattern: 4

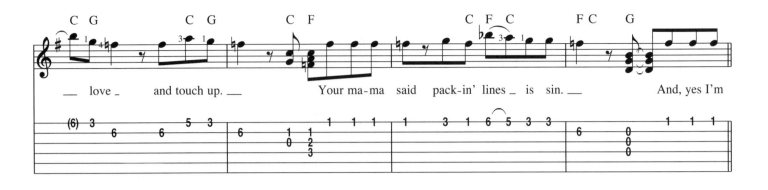

love and touch up. Your ma-ma said pack-in' lines is sin. And, yes I'm

𝄋 Chorus

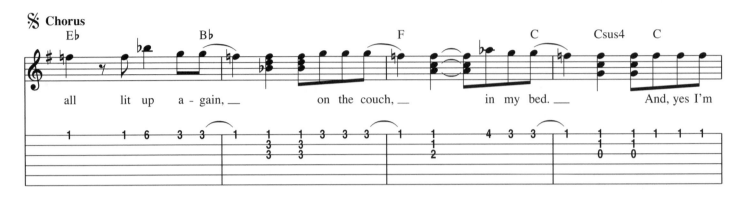

all lit up a-gain, on the couch, in my bed. And, yes I'm

all lit up a-gain, fly-in' I love the co-caine, I love the co-caine. Ma-

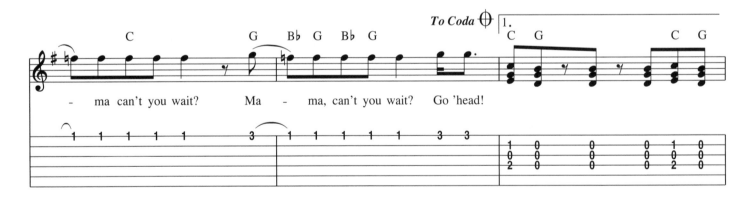

To Coda ⊕ | 1.

- ma can't you wait? Ma - ma, can't you wait? Go 'head!

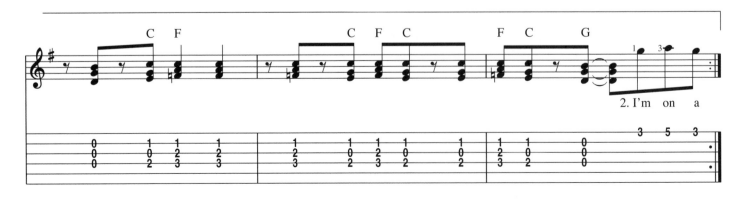

2. I'm on a

212

Bridge

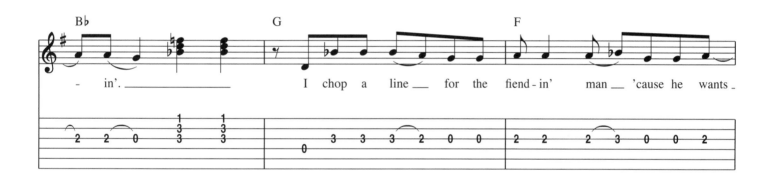

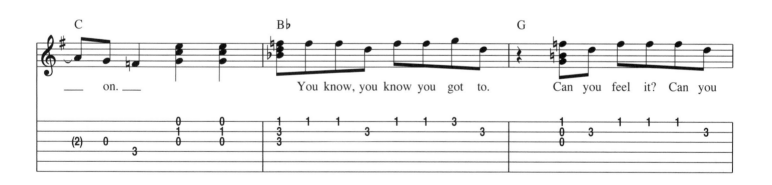

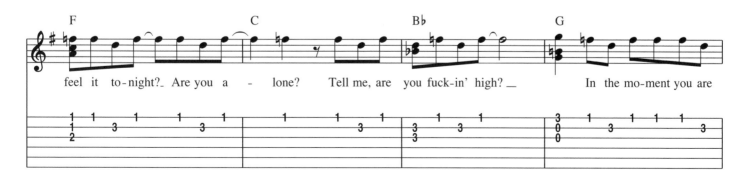

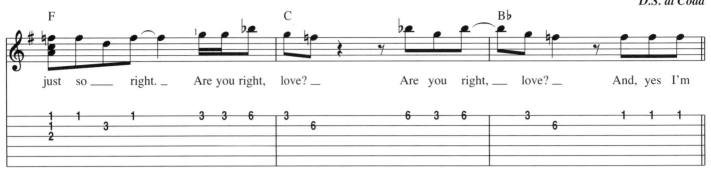

just so ___ right. ___ Are you right, love? ___ Are you right, ___ love? ___ And, yes I'm

⊕ Coda

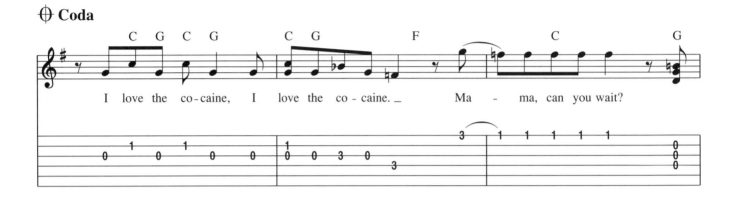

I love the co-caine, I love the co-caine. ___ Ma - ma, can you wait?

Outro

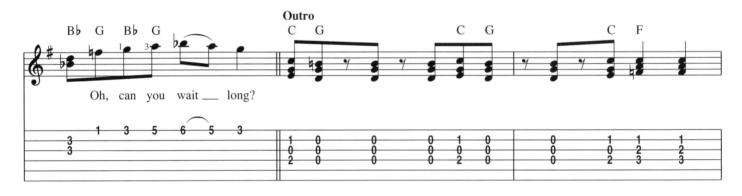

Oh, can you wait ___ long?

Oh, ___ yeah! ___

Don't wan - na fight you. ___

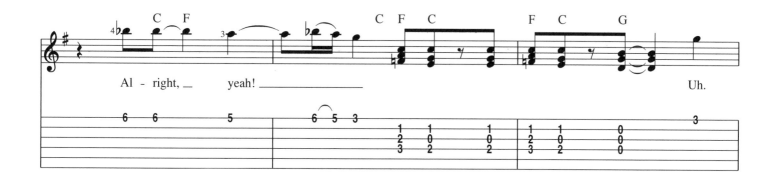

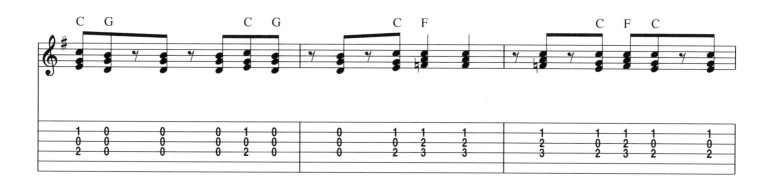

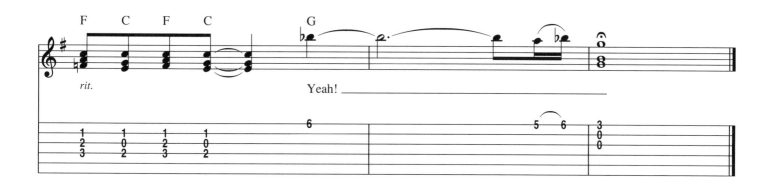

Additional Lyrics

2. I'm on a train and right on,
   You know the train is stayin' off the track.
   I'm in touch from this crutch.
   You're at ten but money I'm on eleven.

Kiss Me Deadly

Words and Music by Mick Smiley

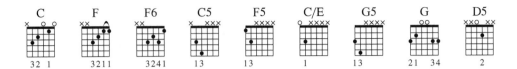

Strum Pattern: 3, 6
Pick Pattern: 1, 3

%Verse

Moderately fast Rock

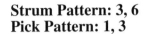

1. I went to a par - ty last Sat - ur - day night.___ I did - n't get laid. I
2. Late for my job___ and the traf - fic was bad.___ Had to bor - row ten bucks from
4. *See additional lyrics*

*Sung one octave higher throughout.

**3rd time, substitute chords in parentheses, next 8 meas.

got in a fight,_ uh - huh.___ }
my ol'___ man,_ uh - huh.___ }
It ain't no big___ thing.

3. I

Verse

went to a par - ty last Sat - ur - day night. ___ I told you that sto - ry, I'd be all right, _ uh - huh. ___
5. *See additional lyrics*

___ It ain't no big___ thing. But I know what I like. _

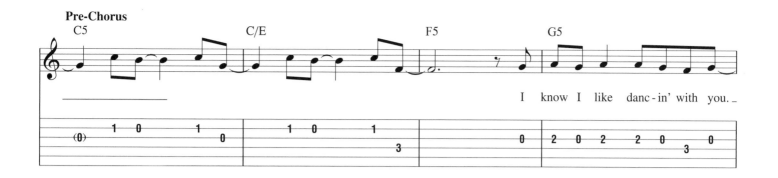

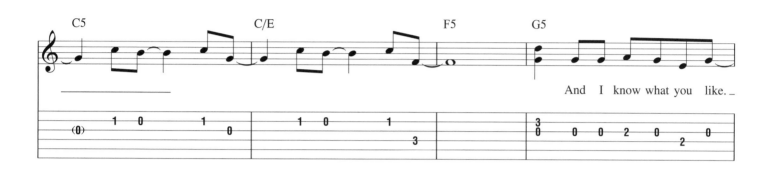

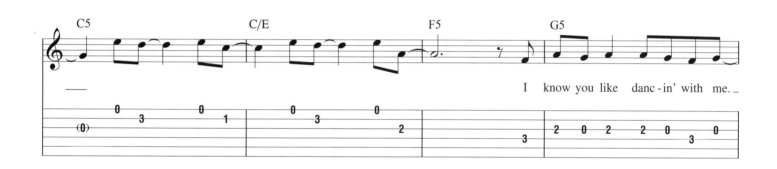

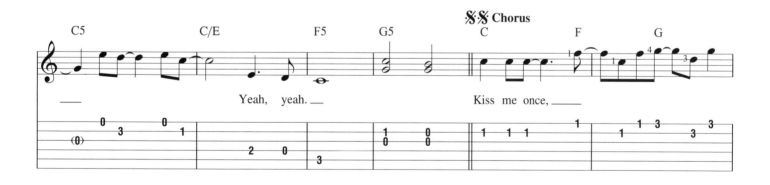

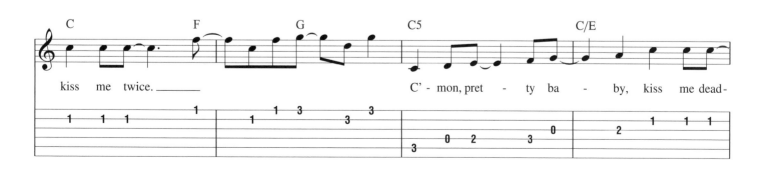

Additional Lyrics

4. Had a few beers, gettin' high.
   Sittin', watchin' the time go by, uh-huh.
   It ain't no big thing.

5. Nothin' to eat and no TV.
   Lookin' in the mirror don't get it for me, uh-huh.
   It ain't no big thing.

Love Removal Machine

Words and Music by Ian Astbury and William Duffy

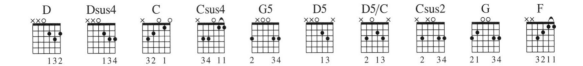

Strum Pattern: 2, 4
Pick Pattern: 3, 4

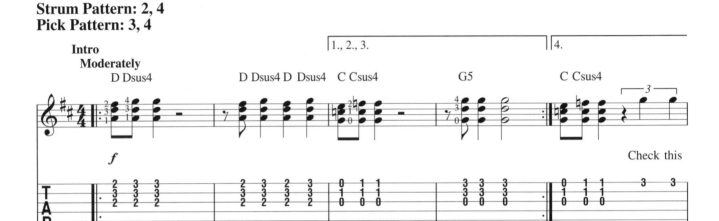

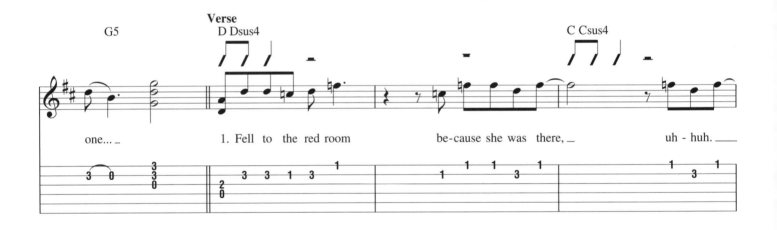

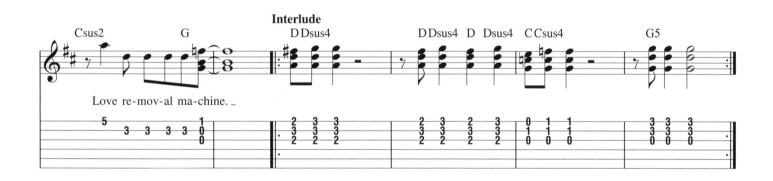

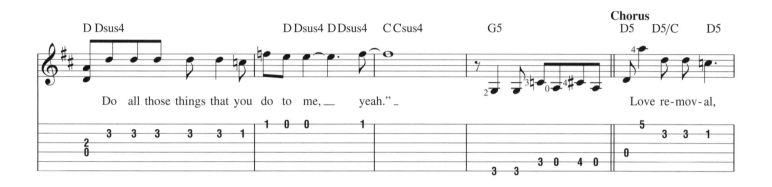

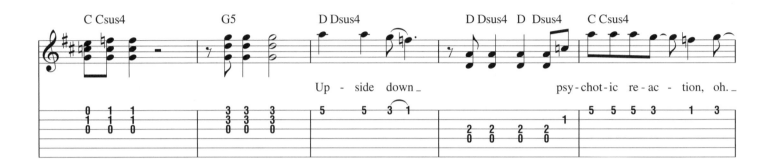

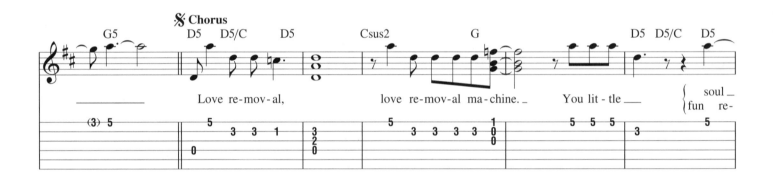

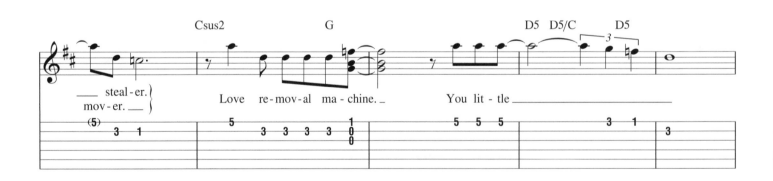

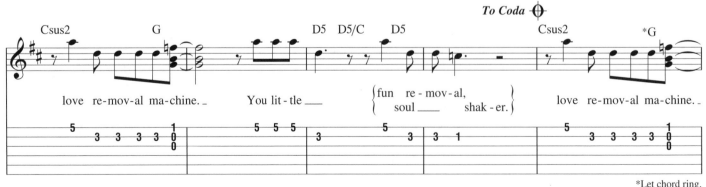

*Let chord ring.

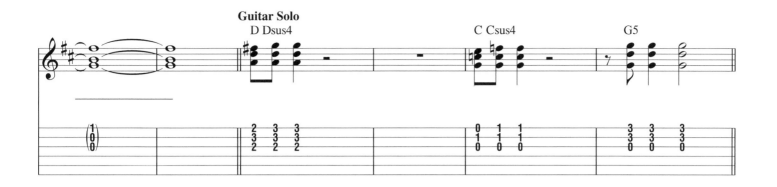

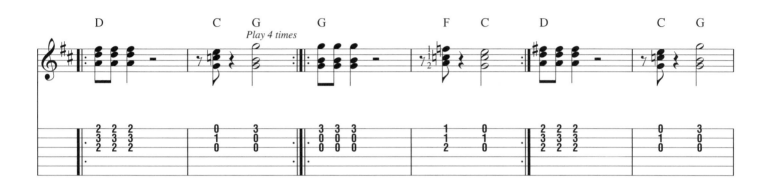

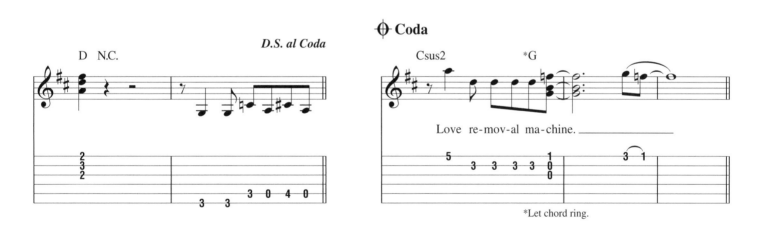

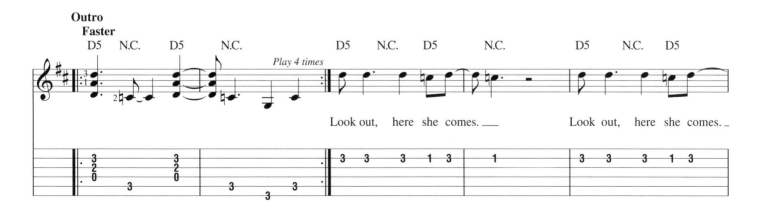

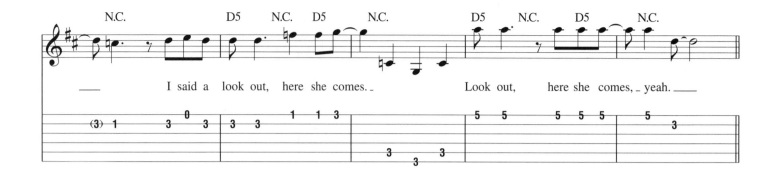

I said a look out, here she comes. Look out, here she comes, _ yeah. ___

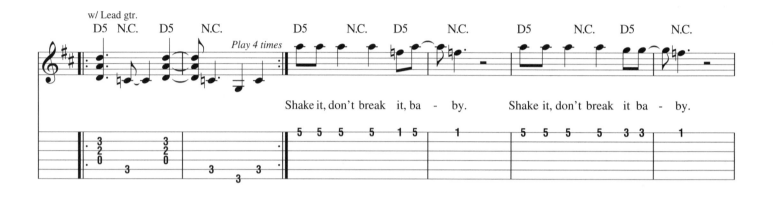

w/ Lead gtr.

Play 4 times

Shake it, don't break it, ba - by. Shake it, don't break it ba - by.

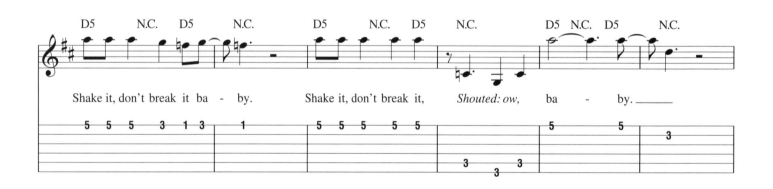

Shake it, don't break it ba - by. Shake it, don't break it, *Shouted: ow,* ba - by. _____

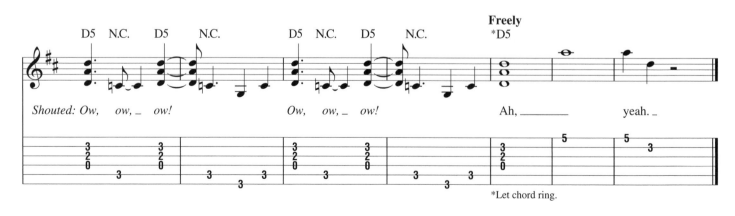

Freely

Shouted: Ow, ow, _ ow! *Ow, ow, _ ow!* Ah, _____ yeah. _

*Let chord ring.

Madhouse

Words and Music by Joseph Bellardini, Frank Bello, Charlie Benante, Scott Rosenfeld and Daniel Spitz

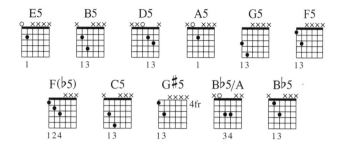

Strum Pattern: 1, 6

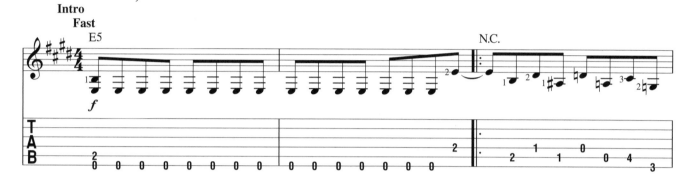

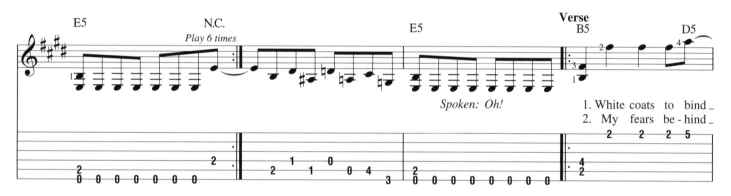

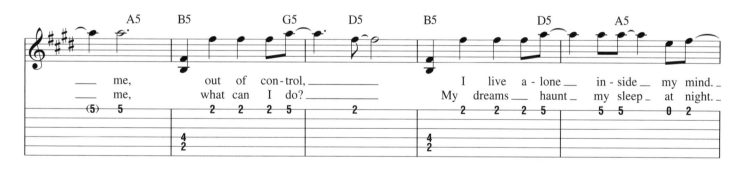

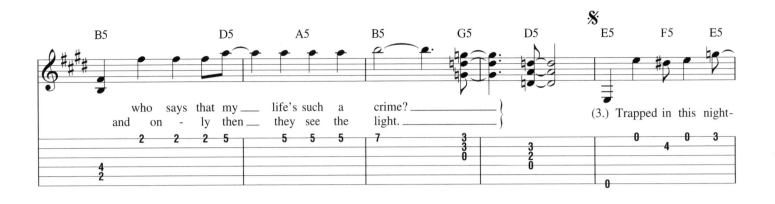

who says that my ___ life's such a crime? _____
and on - ly then ___ they see the light. _____

(3.) Trapped in this night-

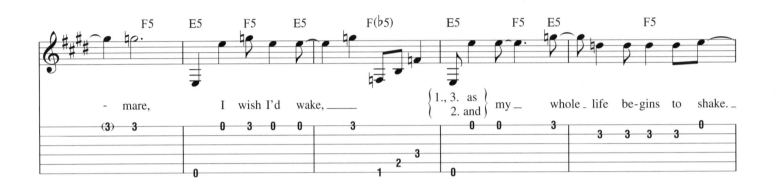

- mare, I wish I'd wake, _____ { 1., 3. as / 2. and } my ___ whole ___ life be - gins to shake. ___

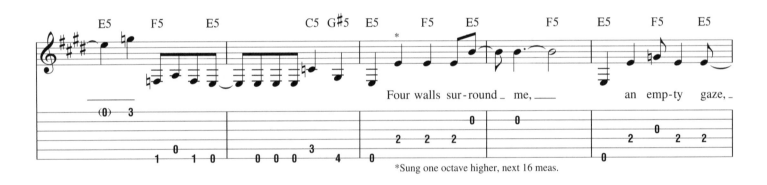

Four walls sur - round ___ me, ___ an emp - ty gaze, ___

*Sung one octave higher, next 16 meas.

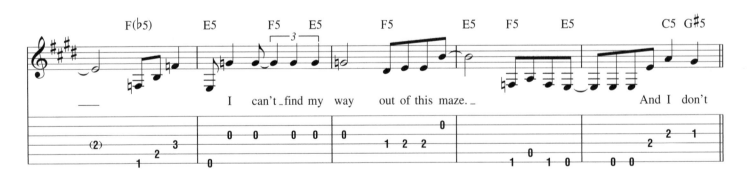

I can't ___ find my way out of this maze. ___ And I don't

Pre-Chorus

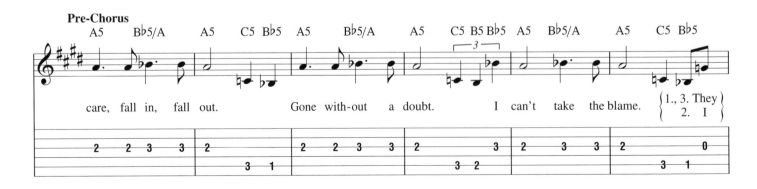

care, fall in, fall out. Gone with - out a doubt. I can't take the blame. { 1., 3. They / 2. I }

More Human Than Human

Words and Music by Rob Zombie, Sean Reynolds and Jay Noel Yuenger

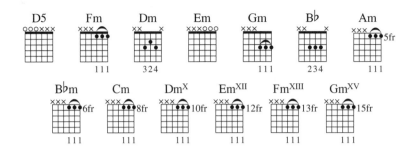

*Drop D tuning, down 1/2 step:
(low to high) Db-A b-Db-G b-Bb-E b

Strum Pattern: 1

Intro
Moderate Rock

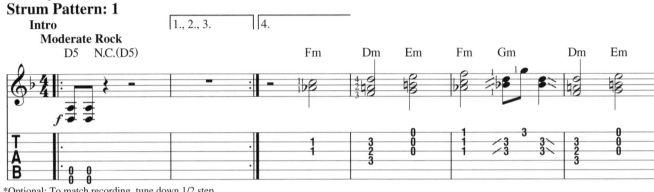

*Optional: To match recording, tune down 1/2 step.

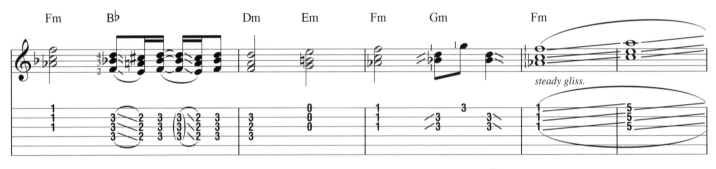

1. Yeah._____ I am the As - tro Creep, a
_ I am the jig - saw man; I

dem - o - li - tion-style hell, A - mer - i - can freak,_ yeah. I am the crawl - ing dead. A
turn the world a - round with a skel - e - ton hand._ Say, I am E - lec - tric Head, a

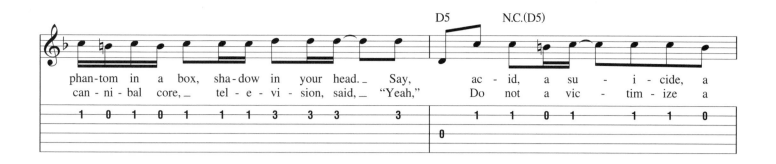

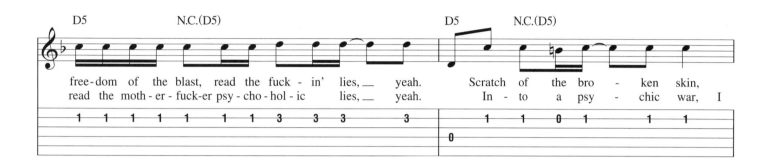

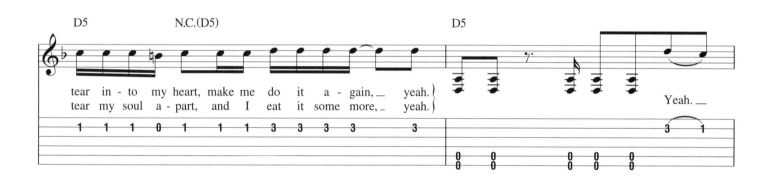

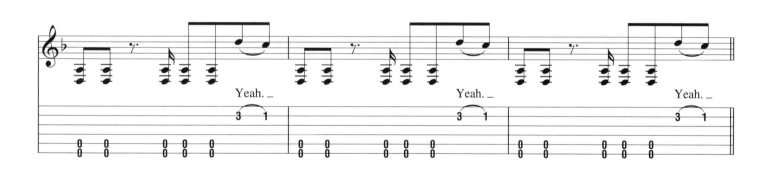

More Than a Feeling

Words and Music by Tom Scholz

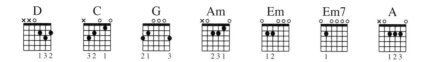

Strum Pattern: 3, 4
Pick Pattern: 2, 4

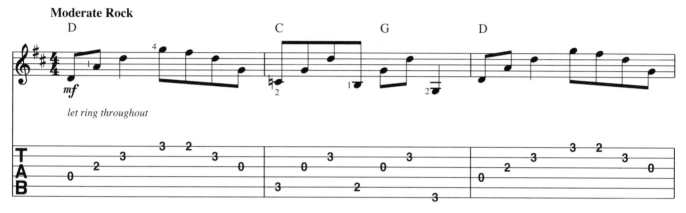

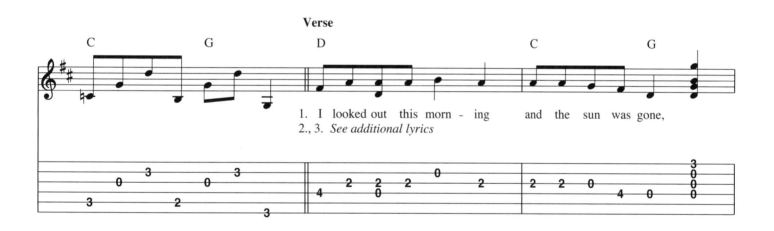

1. I looked out this morn - ing and the sun was gone,
2., 3. *See additional lyrics*

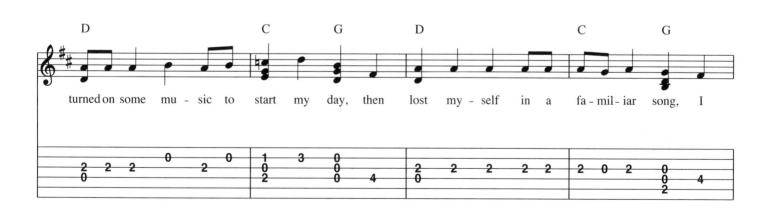

turned on some mu - sic to start my day, then lost my - self in a fa - mil - iar song, I

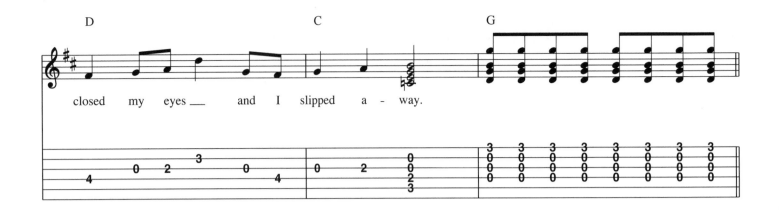

closed my eyes __ and I slipped a - way.

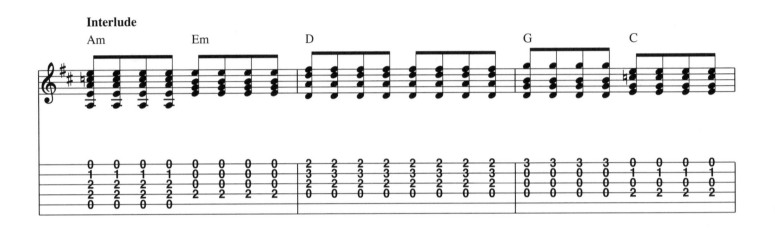

Interlude

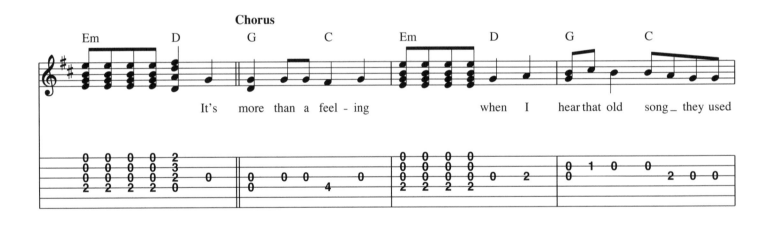

Chorus

It's more than a feel - ing when I hear that old song _ they used

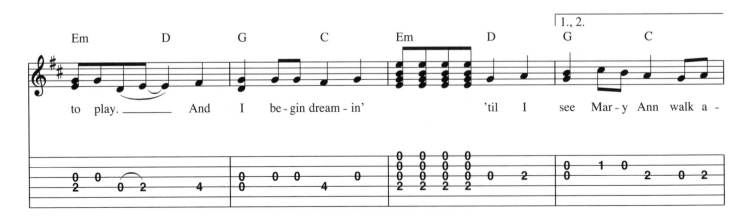

to play. ____ And I be - gin dream - in' 'til I see Mar - y Ann walk a -

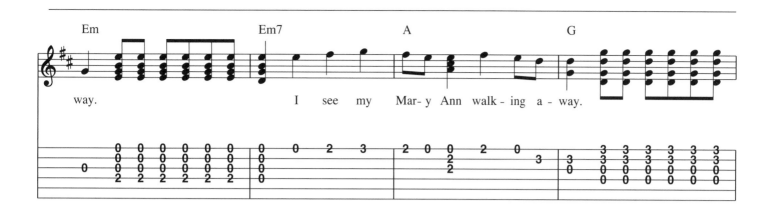

way.   I   see   my   Mar- y Ann walk - ing a - way.

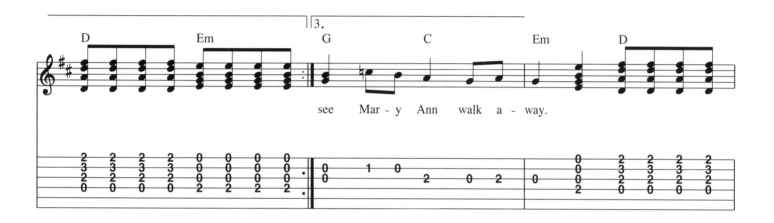

see Mar - y Ann walk a - way.

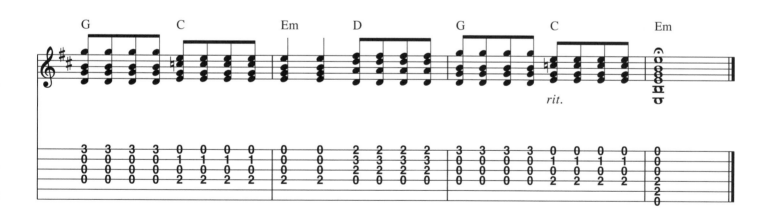

rit.

Additional Lyrics

2. So many people have come and gone,
   Their faces fade as years go by.
   Yet I still recall as I wonder on,
   As clear as the sun in the sky.

3. When I'm tired and thinkin' cold,
   I hide in my music, forget the day.
   And dream of a girl I used to know,
   I close my eyes and she slipped away.

Mountain Song

Words and Music by Jane's Addiction

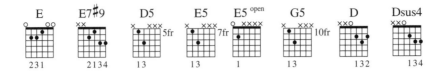

Strum Pattern: 4

Intro

Moderately slow, in 2

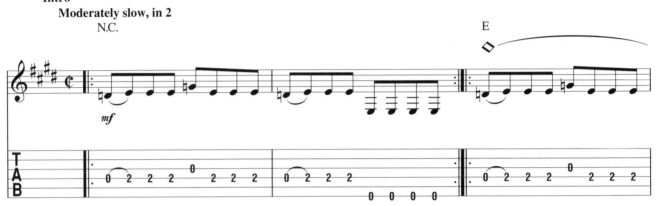

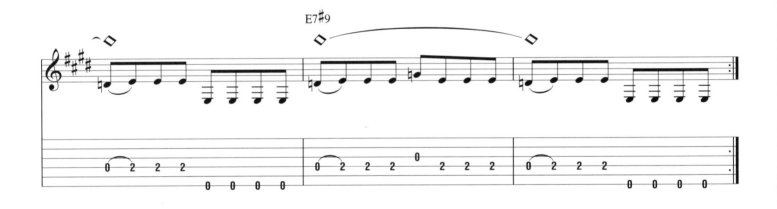

Verse

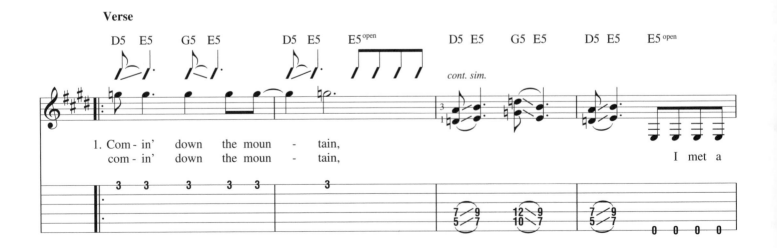

1. Com-in' down the moun - tain,
   com-in' down the moun - tain,
   I met a

one of man-y chil - dren. _____
child, man, she had dark ___ eyes. _____
We

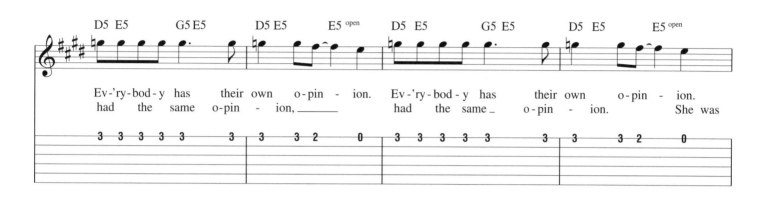

Ev-'ry-bod-y has their own o-pin - ion. Ev-'ry-bod-y has their own o-pin - ion.
had the same o-pin - ion, _____ had the same _ o-pin - ion.
She was

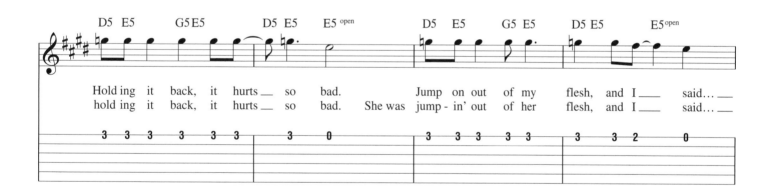

Hold ing it back, it hurts ___ so bad. Jump on out of my flesh, and I ___ said... ___
hold ing it back, it hurts ___ so bad. She was jump-in' out of her flesh, and I ___ said... ___

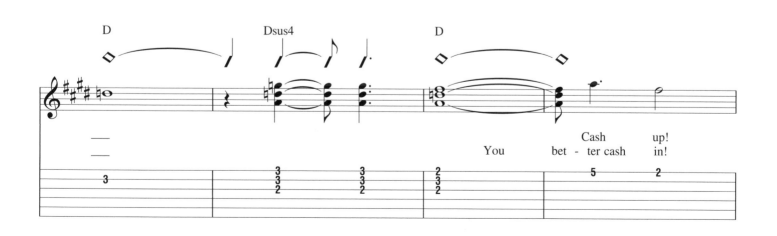

___ Cash up!
___ You bet - ter cash in!

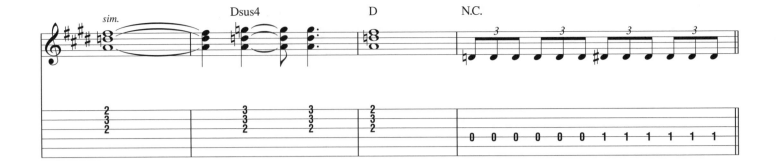

Chorus
w/ Verse rhythm

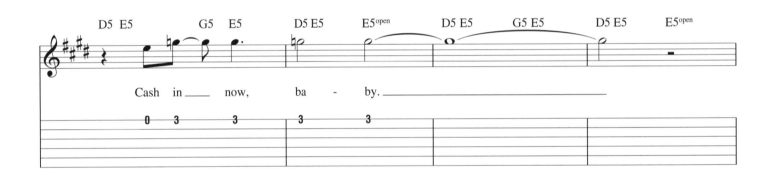

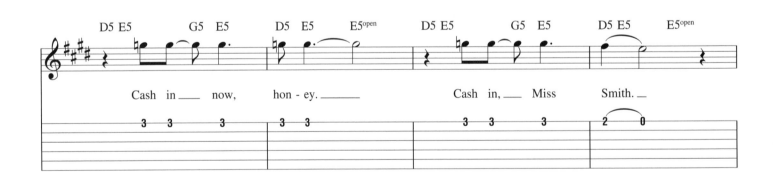

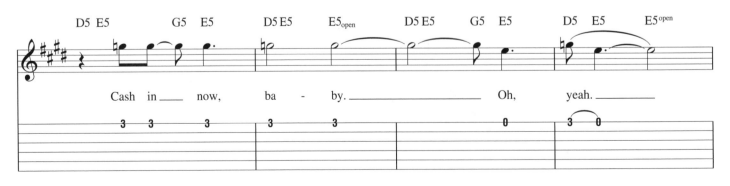

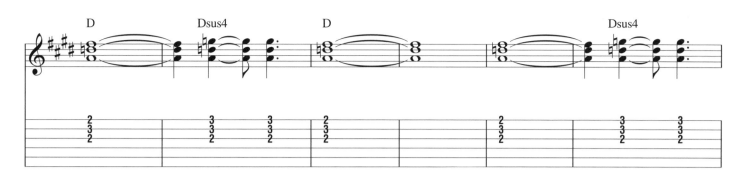

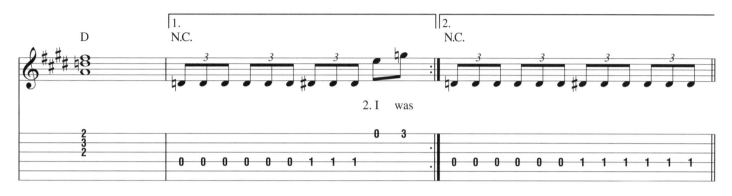

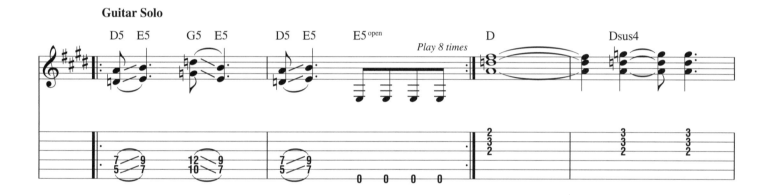

Guitar Solo

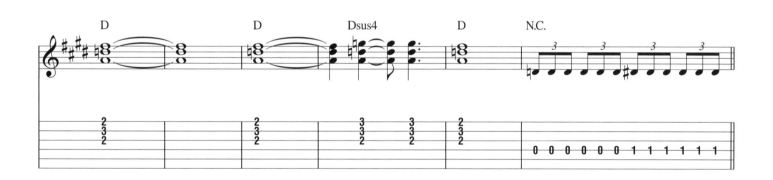

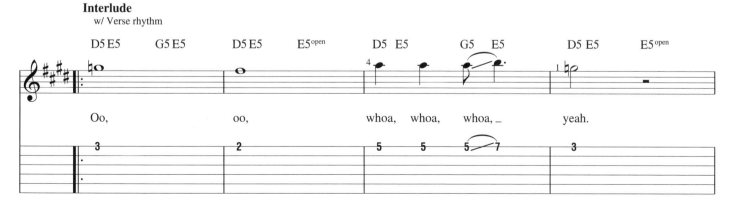

Interlude
w/ Verse rhythm

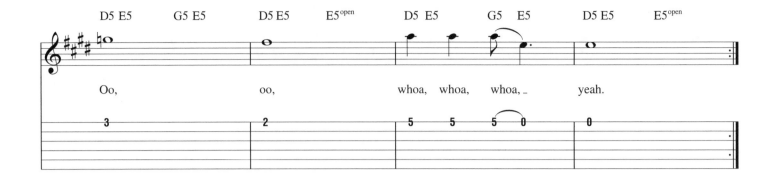

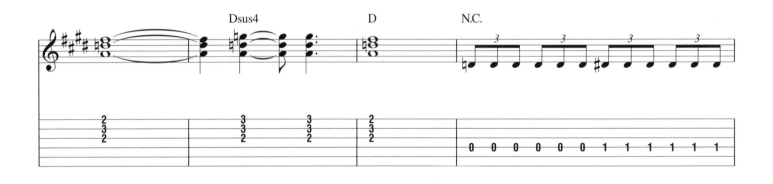

Outro

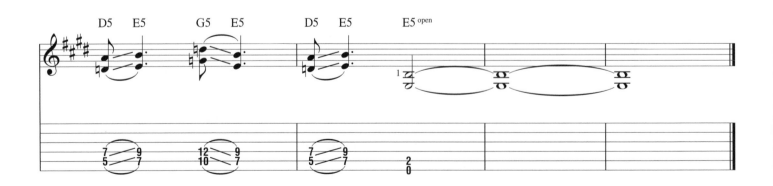

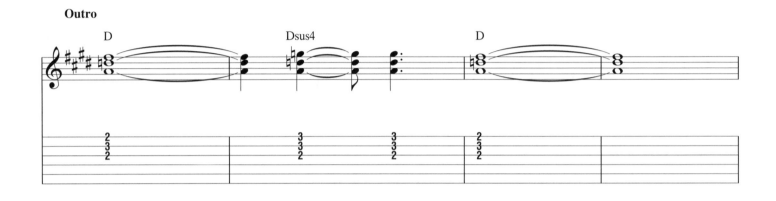

Paranoid

Words and Music by Anthony Iommi, John Osbourne, William Ward and Terence Butler

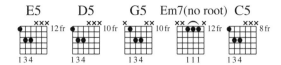

Strum Pattern: 1

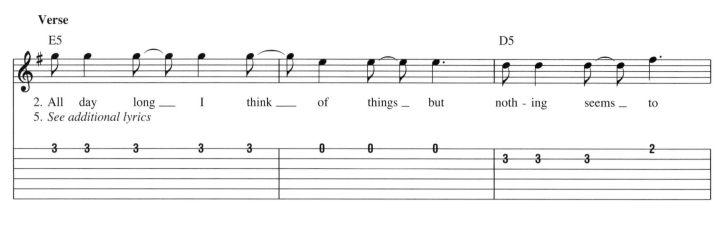

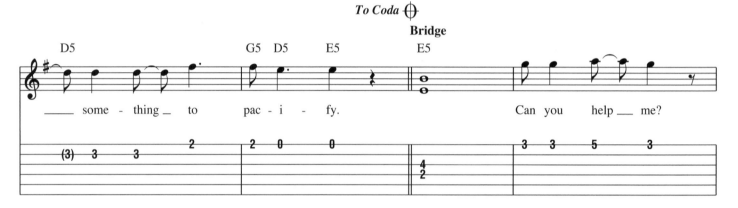

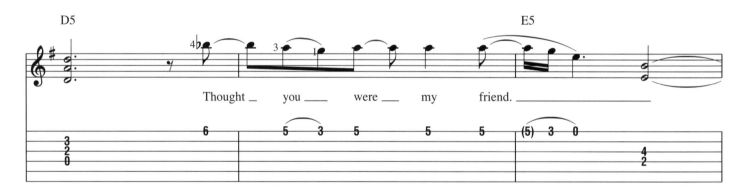

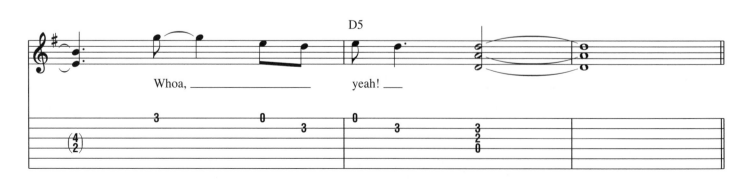

Interlude

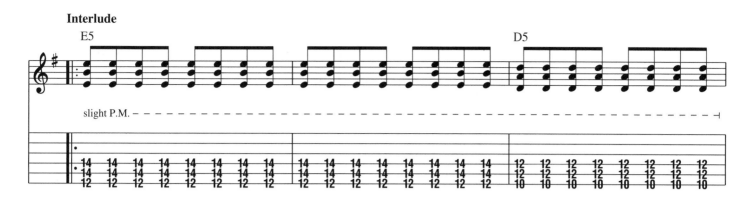

Verse

3. I need some - one to _____ show me _____ the things _____

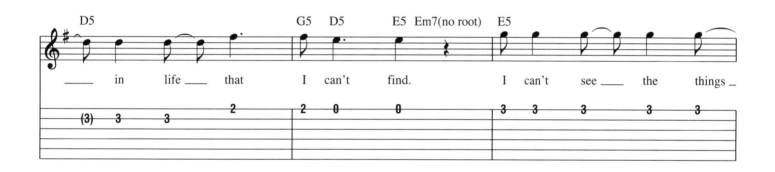

_____ in life _____ that I can't find. I can't see _____ the things _____

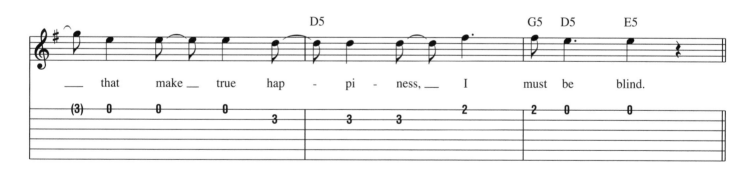

_____ that make _____ true hap - pi - ness, _____ I must be blind.

Guitar Solo

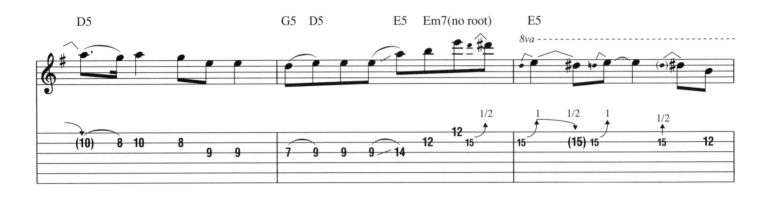

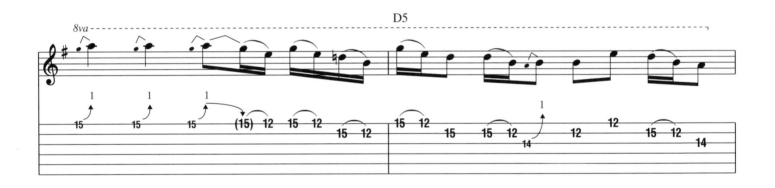

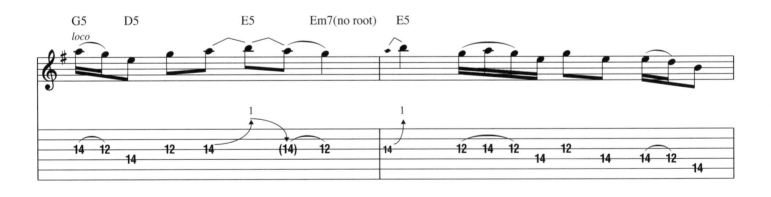

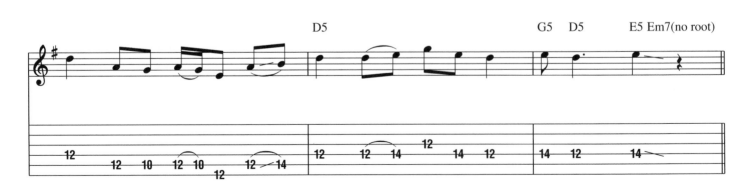

Interlude

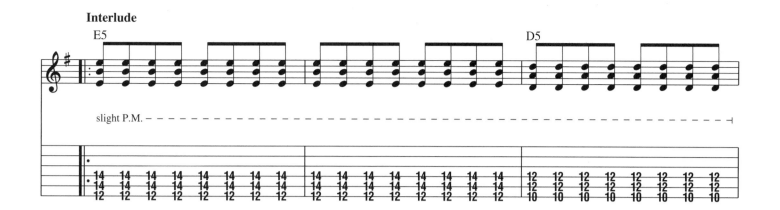

⊕ Coda

2nd time, D.S. al Coda

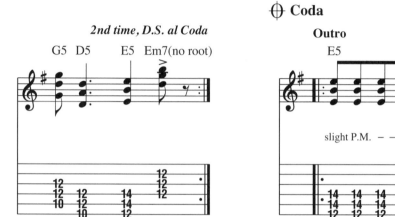

Outro

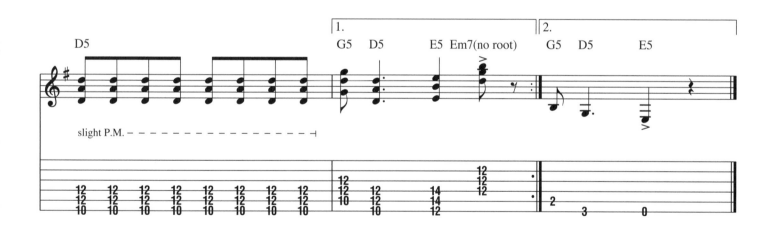

Additional Lyrics

4. Make a joke and I will sigh
   And you will laugh and I will cry.
   Happiness I cannot feel
   And love to me is so unreal.

5. And so as you hear these words
   Telling you now of my state.
   I tell you to enjoy life,
   I wish I could but it's too late.

My Generation

Words and Music by Peter Townshend

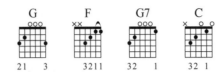

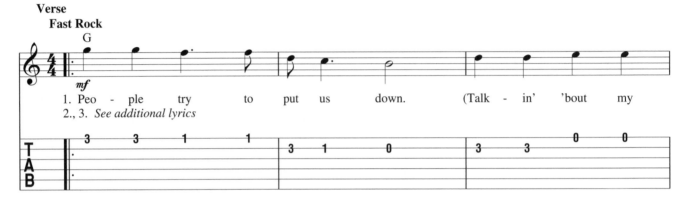

Strum Pattern: 4
Pick Pattern: 5

Verse
Fast Rock

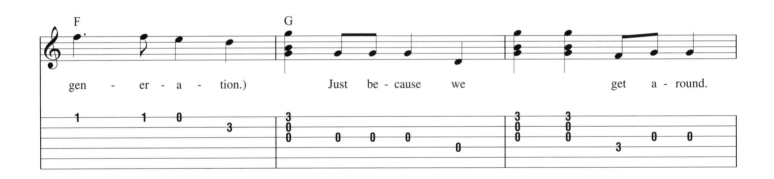

1. Peo - ple try to put us down. (Talk - in' 'bout my

2., 3. *See additional lyrics*

gen - er - a - tion.) Just be - cause we get a - round.

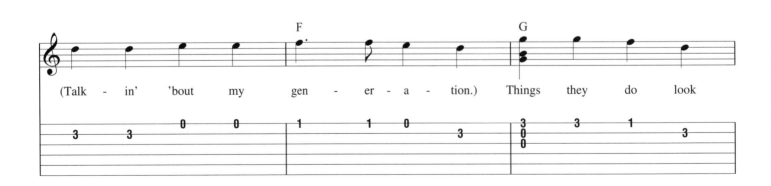

(Talk - in' 'bout my gen - er - a - tion.) Things they do look

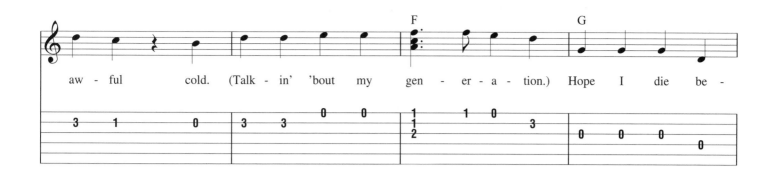

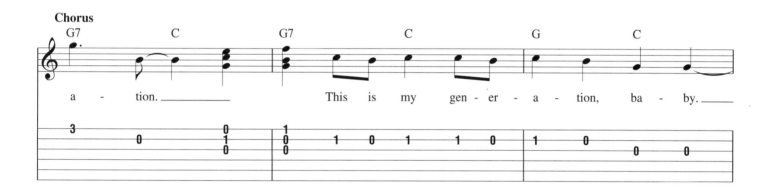

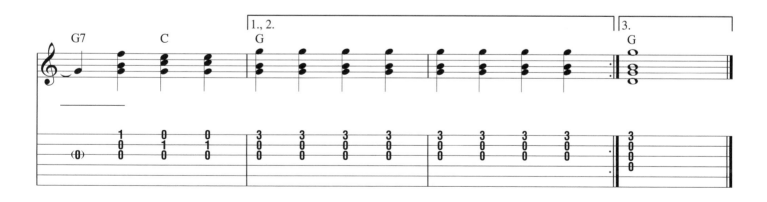

Additional Lyrics

2., 3. Why don't you all fade away? (Talkin' 'bout my generation.)
Don't try to dig what we all say. (Talkin' 'bout my generation.)
I'm not tryin' to cause a big sensation. (Talkin' 'bout my generation.)
I'm just talkin' 'bout my generation. (Talkin' 'bout my generation.)

Party Hard

Words and Music by Andrew Wilkes-Krier

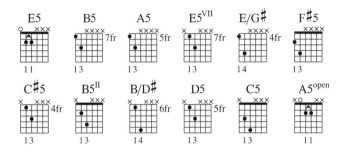

Strum Pattern: 1, 2

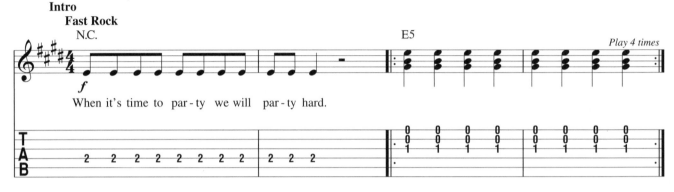

Intro
Fast Rock

When it's time to par-ty we will par-ty hard.

Play 4 times

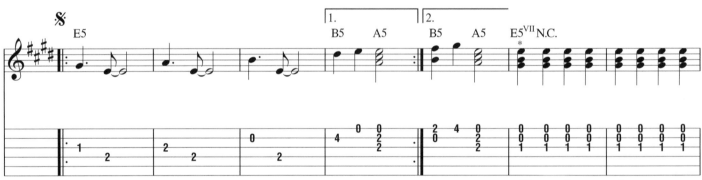

Piano arr. for gtr., next 2 meas.

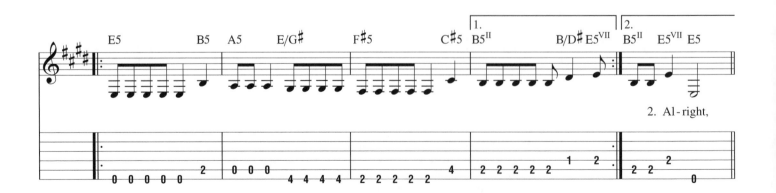

2. Al-right,

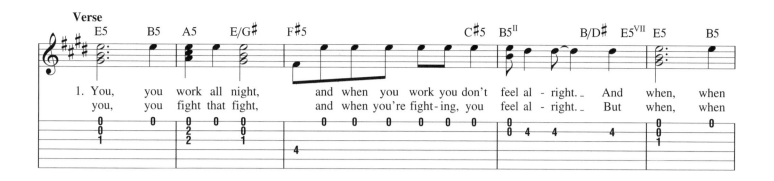

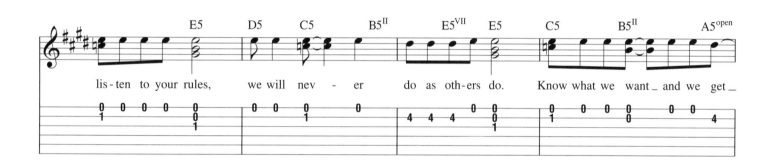

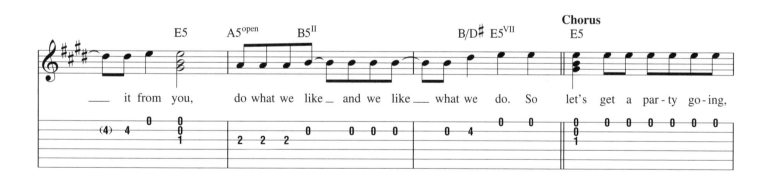

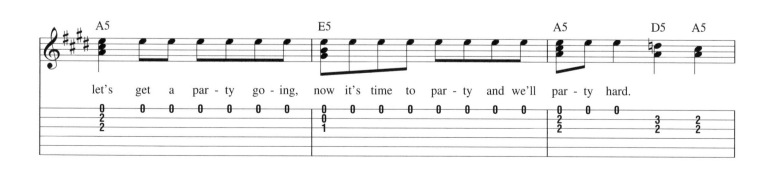

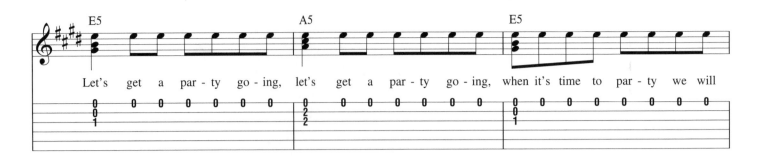

Let's get a par-ty go-ing, let's get a par-ty go-ing, when it's time to par-ty we will

To Coda ⊕

Interlude

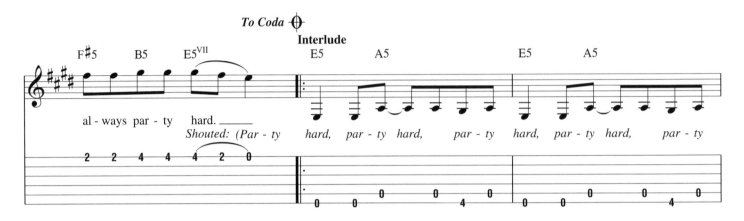

al-ways par-ty hard. _____
Shouted: (Par - ty hard, par - ty hard, par - ty hard, par - ty hard, par - ty

1.   2.   ***D.S. al Coda***
                                                                                     (take repeats)

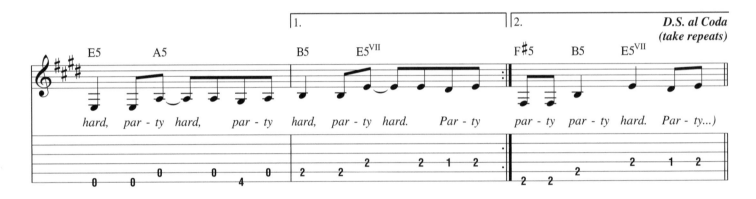

hard, par - ty hard, par - ty hard, par - ty hard. Par - ty par - ty par - ty hard. Par - ty...)

⊕ **Coda**

Outro

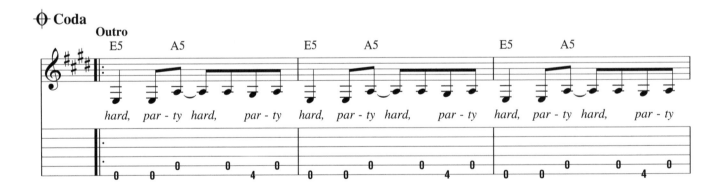

hard, par - ty hard, par - ty hard, par - ty hard, par - ty hard, par - ty hard, par - ty

1., 2., 3.   4.

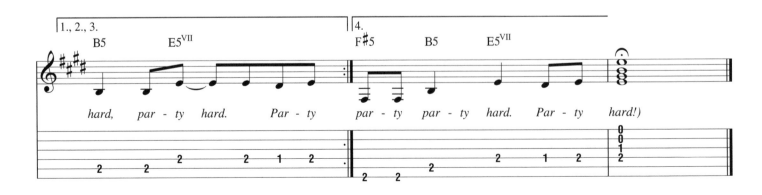

hard, par - ty hard. Par - ty par - ty par - ty hard. Par - ty hard!)

Peace Sells

Words and Music by Dave Mustaine

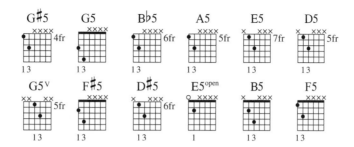

Pick Pattern: 1

*Bass arr. for gtr.

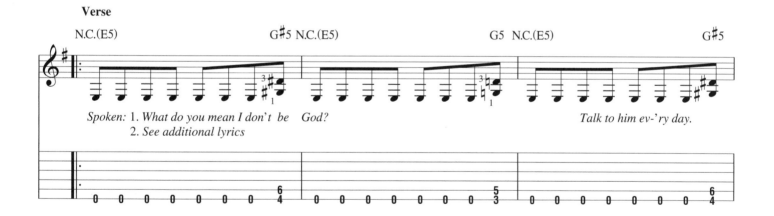

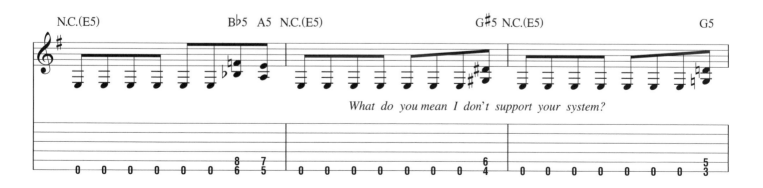

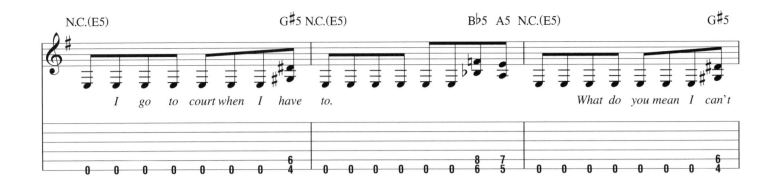

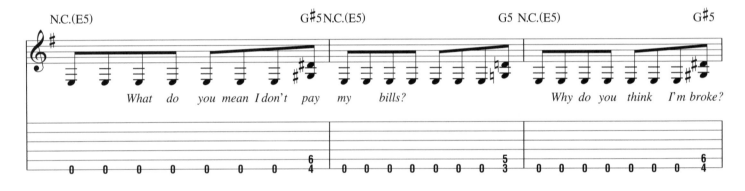

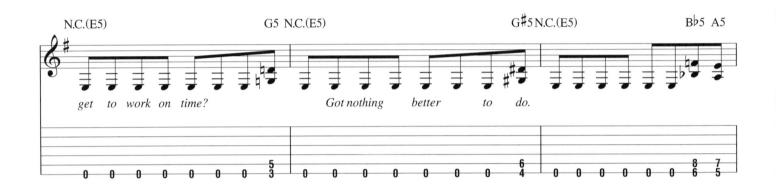

Chorus

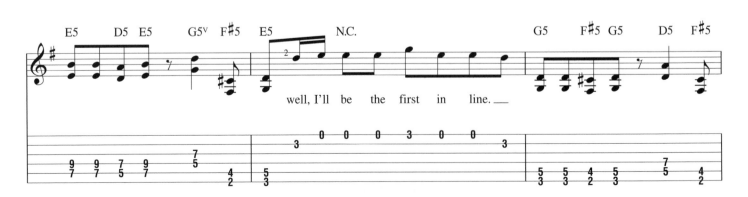

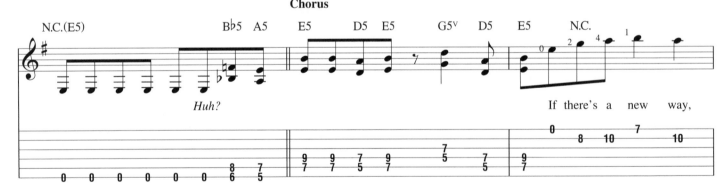

Additional Lyrics

2. *Spoken: What do you mean I hurt your feelings?*
   I didn't know you had any feelings.
   What do you mean I ain't kind?
   Just not your kind.
   What do you mean I couldn't be the President
   Of the United States of America?
   Tell me something, it's still,
   "We, the people," right?

Photograph

Words and Music by Joe Elliott, Steve Clark, Peter Willis, Richard Savage, Richard Allen and R.J. Lange

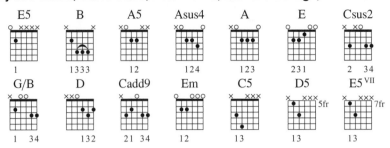

Strum Pattern: 1, 2
Pick Pattern: 2, 4

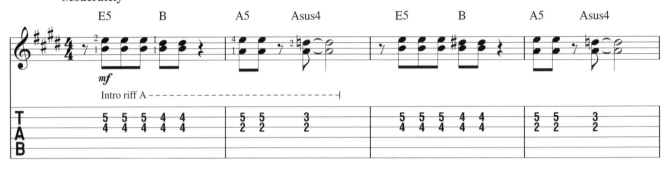

*Sung one octave higher throughout.

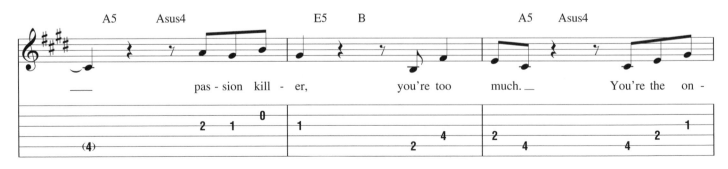

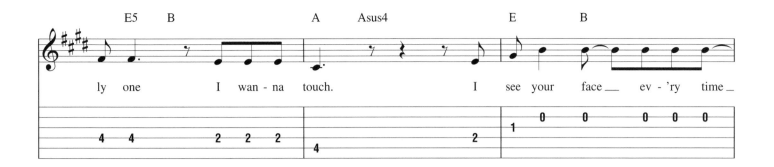

ly one   I   wan - na   touch.   I   see   your   face __   ev - 'ry   time __

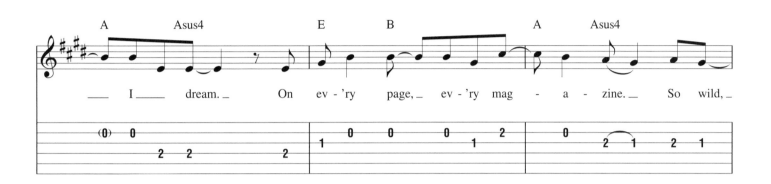

__   I __   dream. __   On   ev - 'ry   page, __   ev - 'ry   mag - a - zine. __   So   wild,

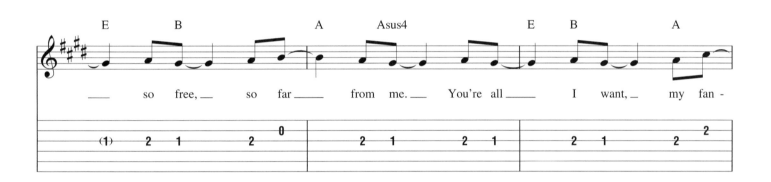

__   so   free, __   so   far ___   from   me. __   You're   all ___   I   want, __   my   fan -

𝄋 Pre-Chorus

- ta - sy.   Oh,   look   what   you've

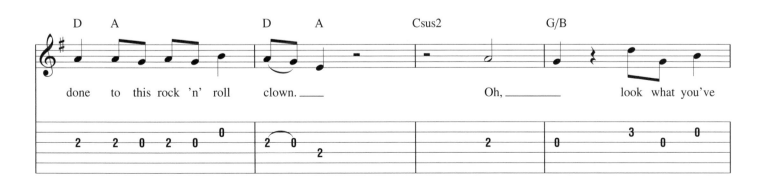

done   to   this   rock   'n'   roll   clown. __   Oh, _____   look   what   you've

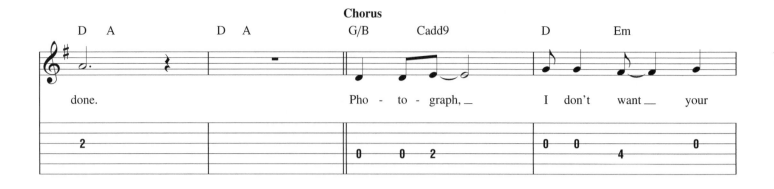

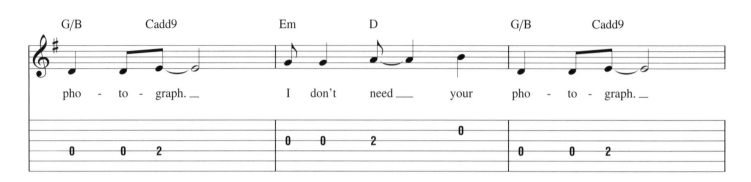

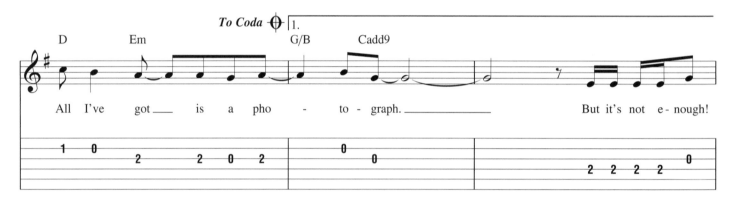

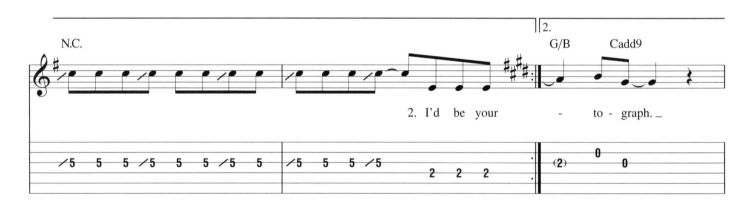

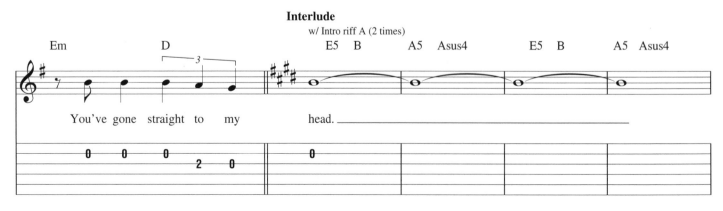

Coda

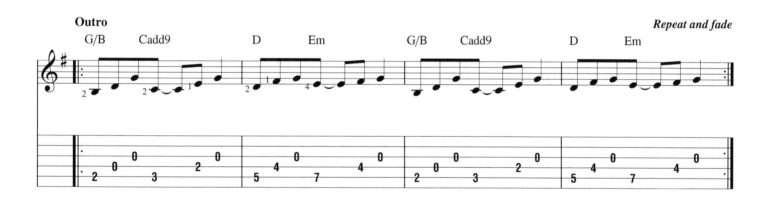

Outro

Repeat and fade

Additional Lyrics

2. I'd be your lover, if you were there.
   Put your hurt on me, if you dare.
   Such a woman, you got style.
   You make ev'ry man feel like a child.
   You got some kind a hold on me.
   You're all wrapped up in mystery.
   So wild, so free, so far from me.
   You're all I want, my fantasy.

Rebel Yell

Words and Music by Billy Idol and Steve Stevens

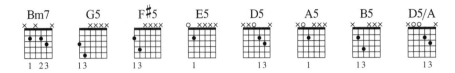

Strum Pattern: 1, 6

Intro

Moderately fast

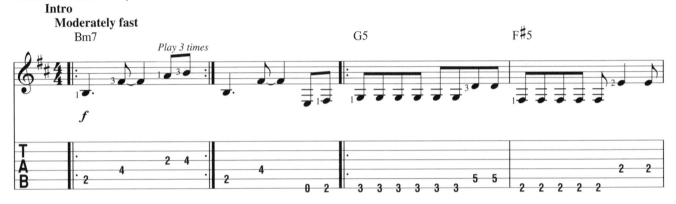

*Let chord ring.

Verse

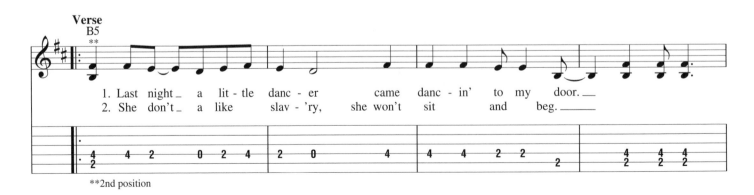

1. Last night _ a lit - tle danc - er came danc - in' to my door. _
2. She don't _ a like slav - 'ry, she won't sit and beg. _____

**2nd position

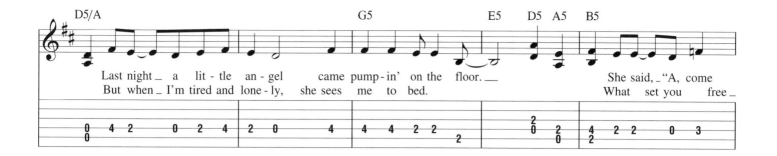

*1st position

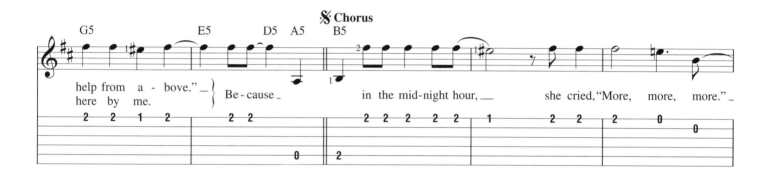

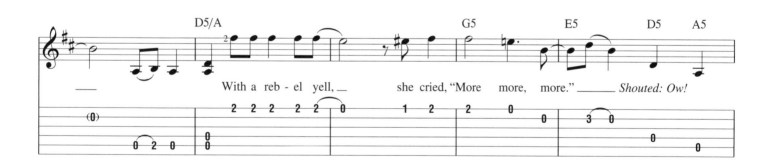

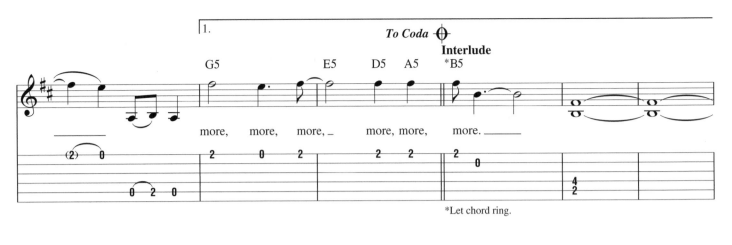

*Let chord ring.

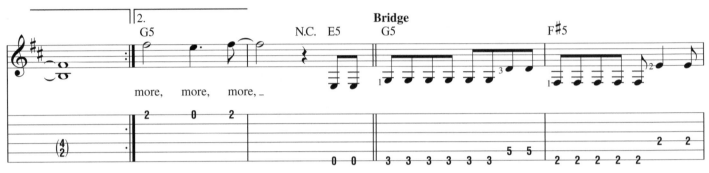

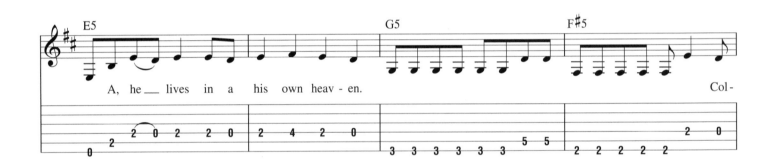

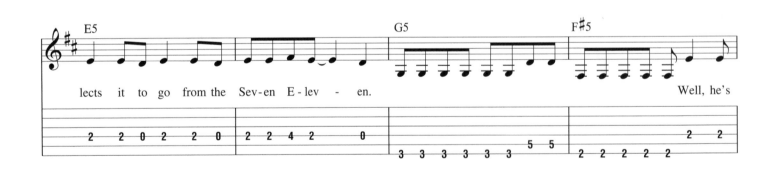

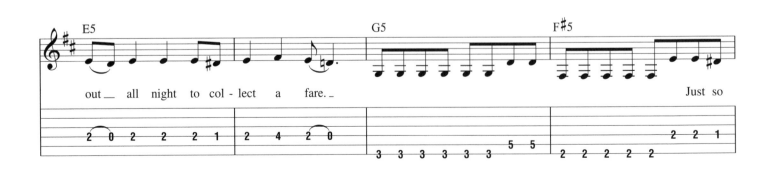

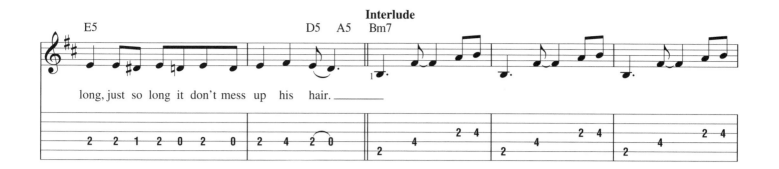

long, just so long it don't mess up his hair. _____

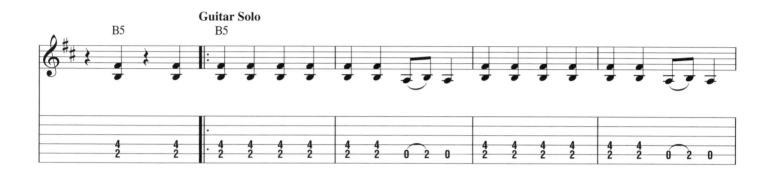

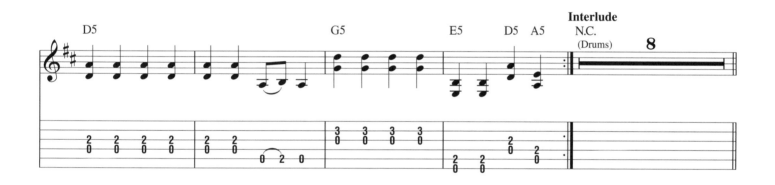

3. I ___ walked the walk ___ for you, ___ babe.   A thou - sand miles ___ for you. ___
4. I'd ___ sell my ___ soul for you, ___ babe, ___   for mon - ey to burn _____ for you. ___

*Let chord ring throughout Verse.

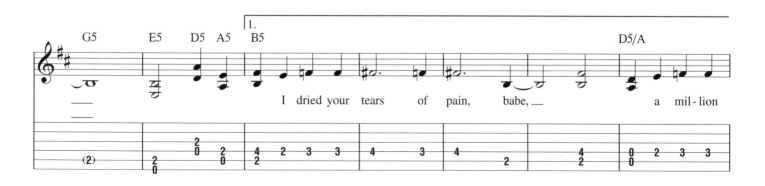

I dried your tears of pain, babe, ___ a mil - lion

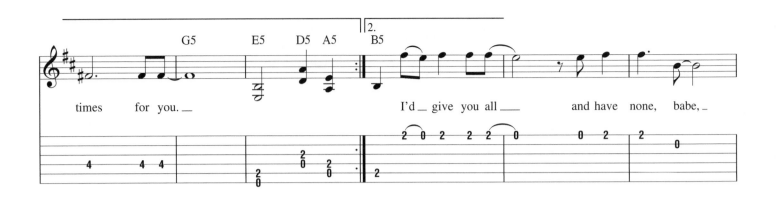

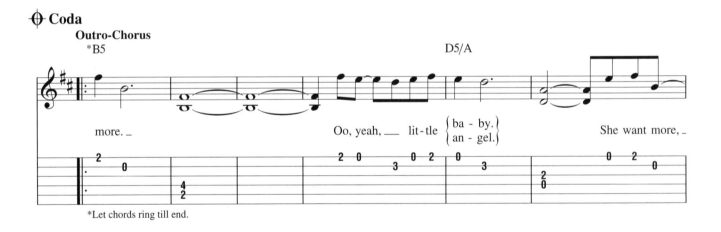

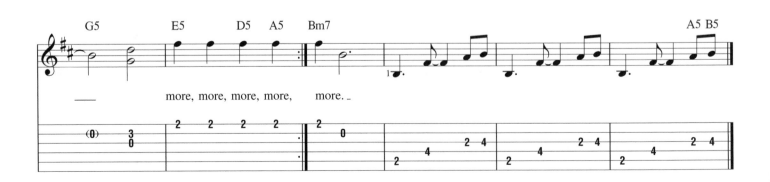

Rock and Roll All Nite

Words and Music by Paul Stanley and Gene Simmons

Strum Pattern: 2
Pick Pattern: 4

1. You show us ev - 'ry -
2. You keep on say - in' you'll

thing you've got.
be mine for a - while.

You keep on danc - in' and the room gets hot.
You're look - in' fan - cy and I like your style.

You drive us wild; we'll drive you cra - zy.
And you drive us wild; we'll drive you cra - zy.

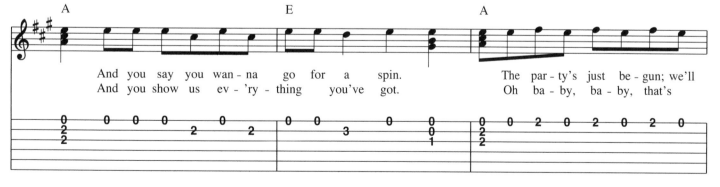

And you say you wan - na go for a spin.
And you show us ev - 'ry - thing you've got.

The par - ty's just be - gun; we'll
Oh ba - by, ba - by, that's

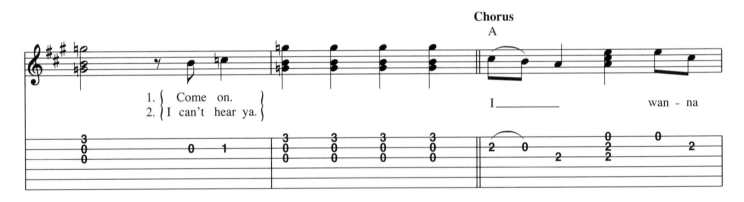

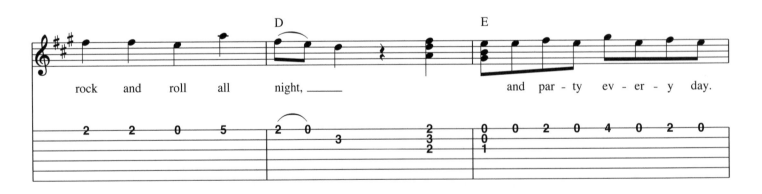

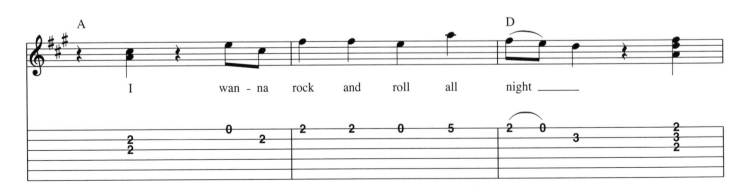

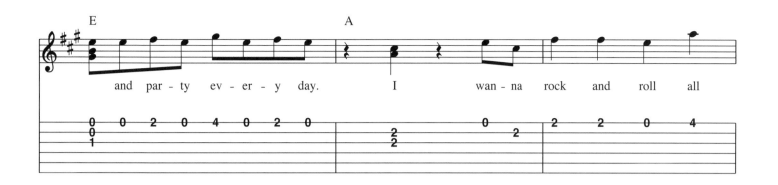

and par - ty ev - er - y day.　　　　I　wan - na rock and roll all

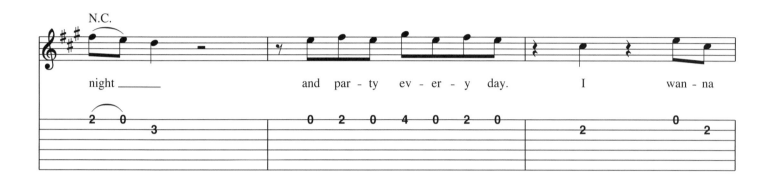

night _____ 　　　and par - ty ev - er - y day.　　　I　wan - na

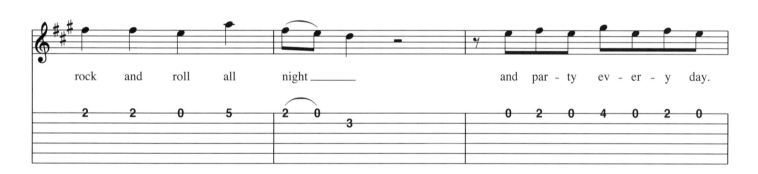

rock and roll all night _____ 　　　and par - ty ev - er - y day.

Outro

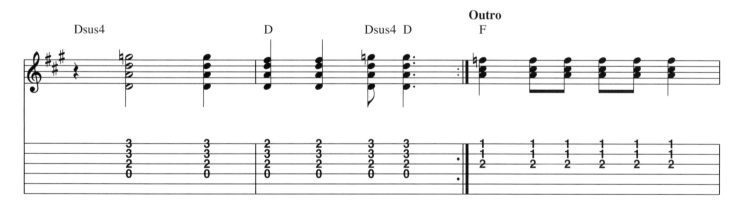

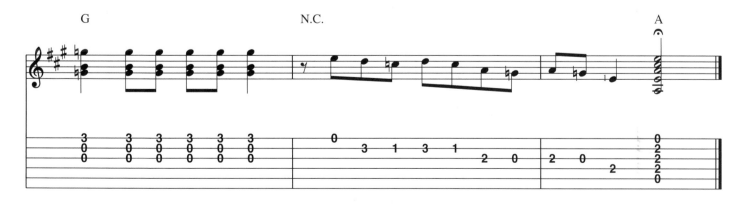

Rock You Like a Hurricane

Words and Music by Rudolf Schenker, Klaus Meine and Herman Rarebell

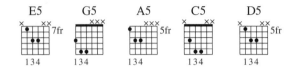

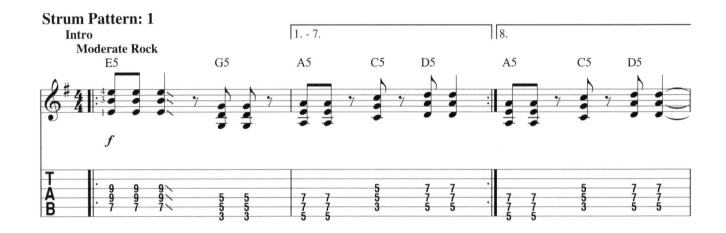

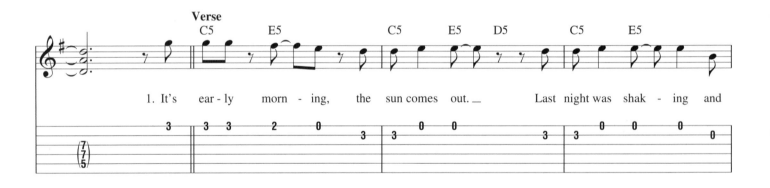

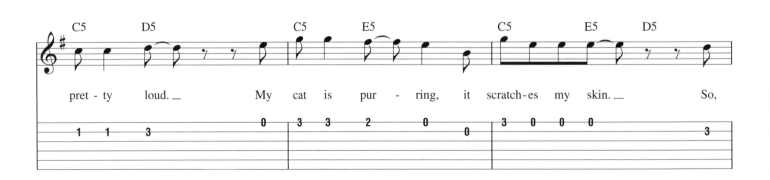

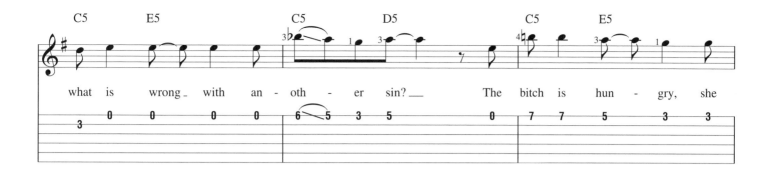

what is wrong _ with an - oth - er sin? _ The bitch is hun - gry, she

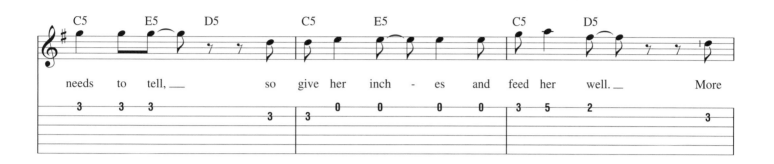

needs to tell, __ so give her inch - es and feed her well. _ More

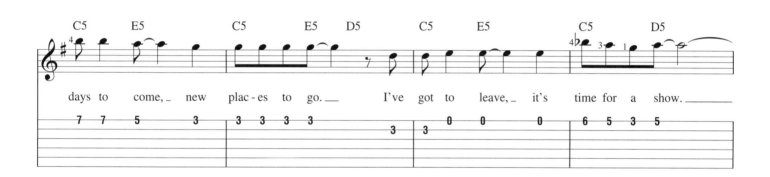

days to come, _ new plac - es to go. _ I've got to leave, _ it's time for a show. _____

Chorus
w/ Intro pattern

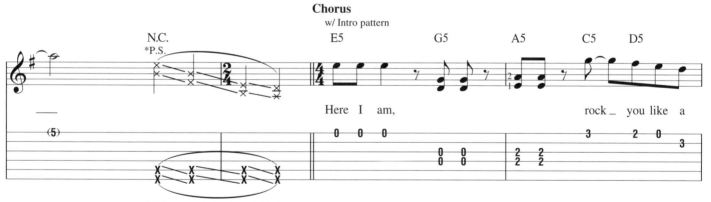

__ Here I am, rock _ you like a

*Pick scrape: Rub edge of pick down the
strings, producing a scratchy sound.

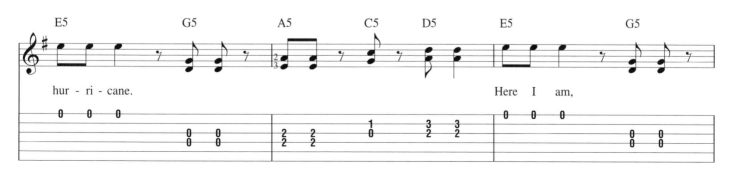

hur - ri - cane. Here I am,

rock _ you like a hur - ri - cane. _____   2. My

%. Verse

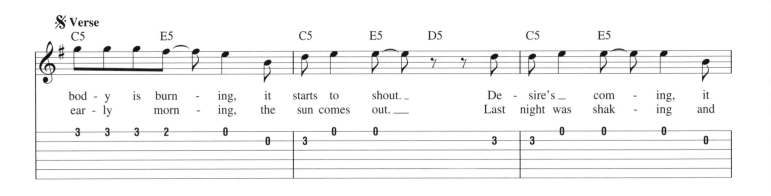

bod - y   is   burn - ing,   it   starts   to   shout. _   De - sire's _   com - ing,   it
ear - ly   morn - ing,   the   sun comes   out. _   Last   night was   shak - ing   and

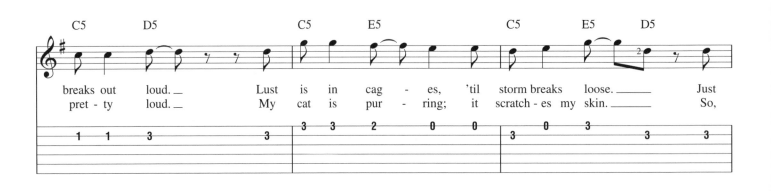

breaks out   loud. _   Lust   is   in   cag - es,   'til   storm breaks   loose. _____   Just
pret - ty   loud. _   My   cat   is   pur - ring;   it   scratch - es my   skin. _____   So,

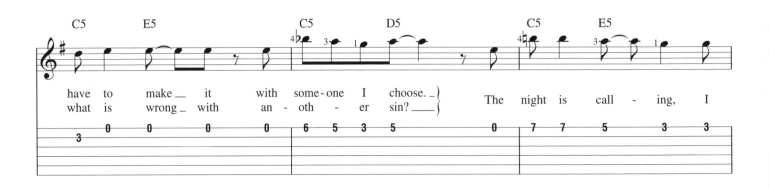

have   to   make _ it   with   some - one   I   choose. _   The   night   is   call - ing,   I
what   is   wrong _ with   an - oth - er   sin? _____

268

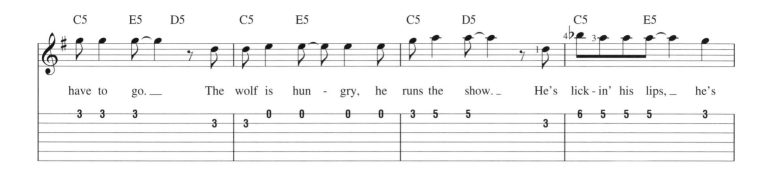
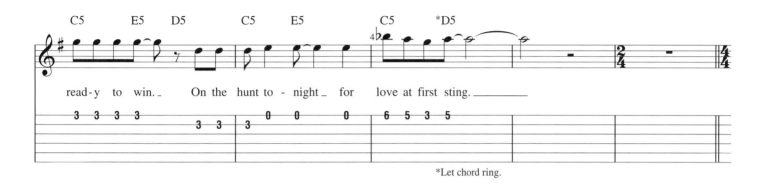
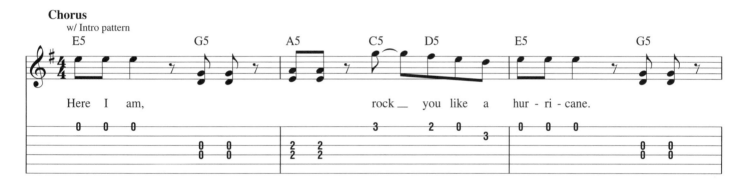
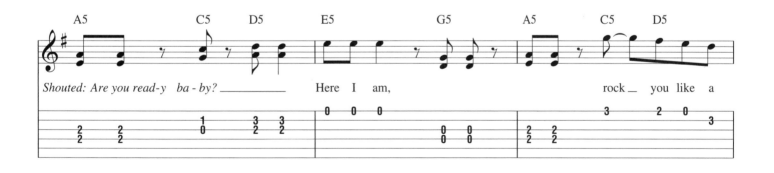
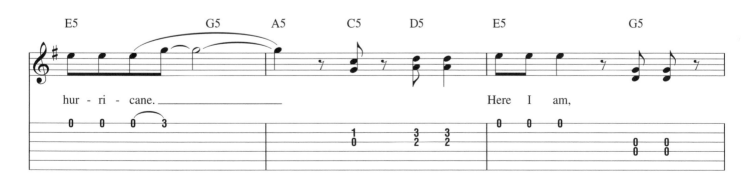

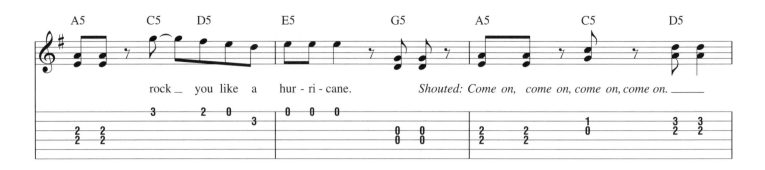

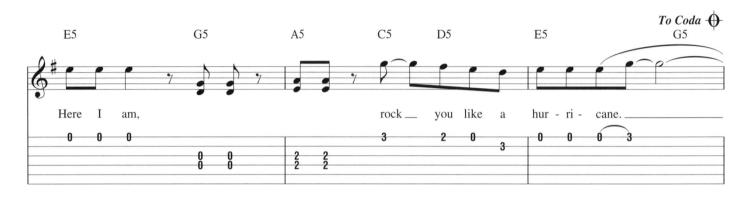

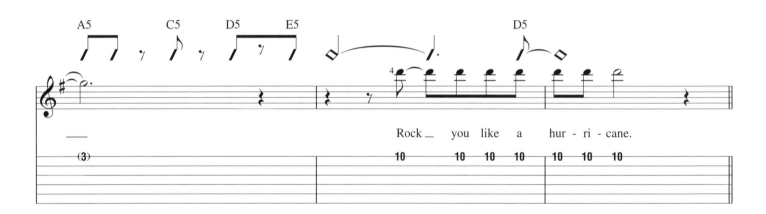

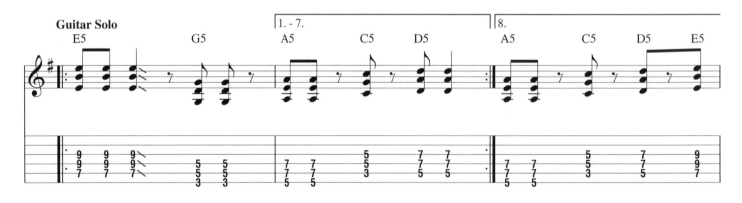

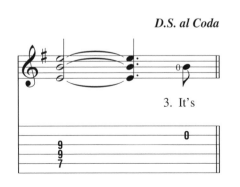

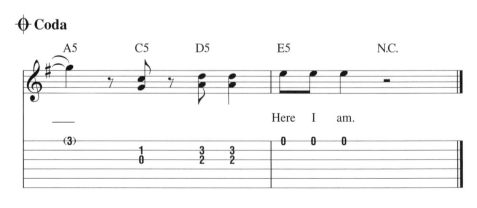

Round and Round

Words and Music by Robbin Lantz Crosby, Warren DeMartini and Stephen E. Pearcy

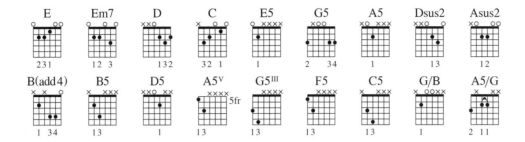

*Tune down 1/2 step:
(low to high) Eb-Ab-Db-Gb-Bb-Eb

Strum Pattern: 1
Pick Pattern: 5

Intro
Moderate Rock

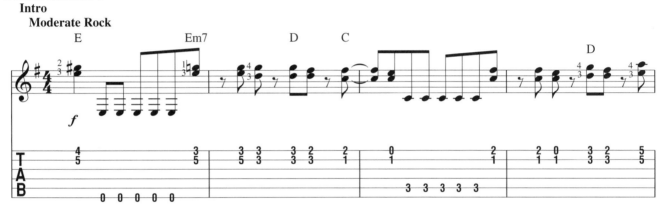

*Optional: To match recording, tune down 1/2 step.

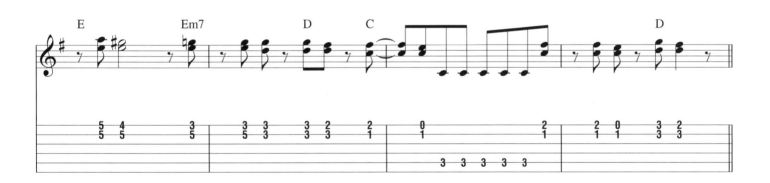

§ Verse

1., 3. Out on the streets,   that's where we meet. __   You make the night,   I al-ways cross a   line. __
    2. *See additional lyrics*

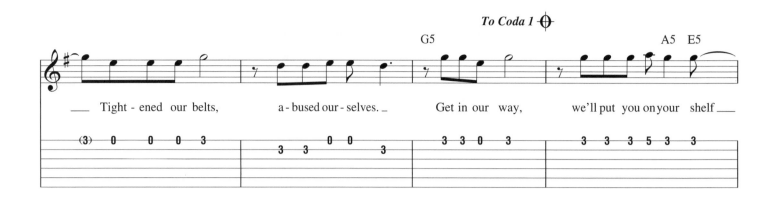

Pre-Chorus

273

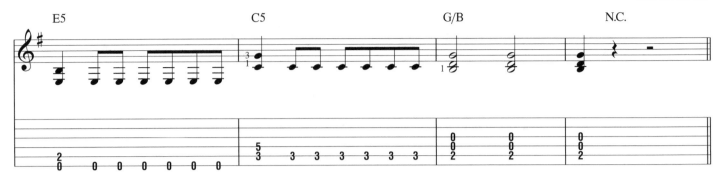

Coda 1

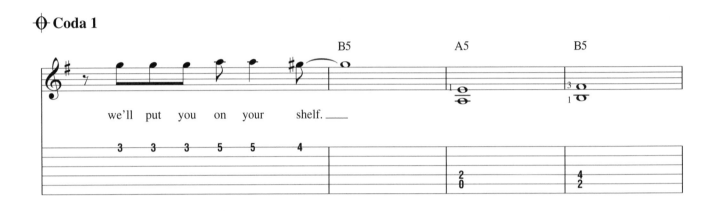

we'll put you on your shelf. ____

D.S.S. al Coda 2   **Coda 2**   **Outro**

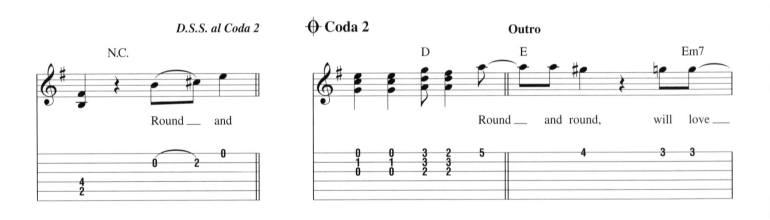

Round ____ and   Round ____ and round, will love ____

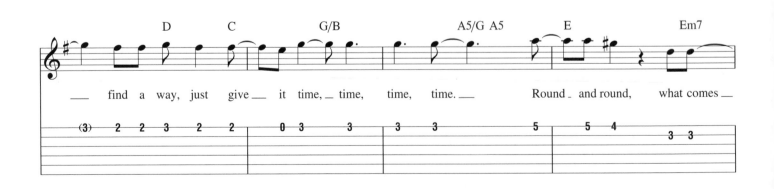

____ find a way, just give ____ it time, ____ time, time, time. ____   Round ____ and round, what comes ____

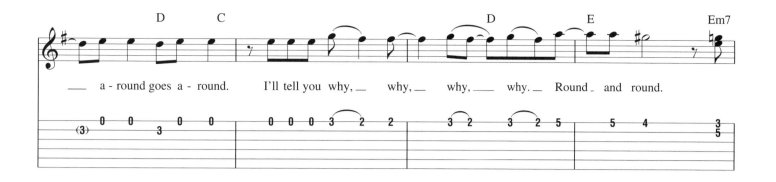

___ a - round goes a - round.   I'll tell you why, ___ why, ___ why, ___ why. ___ Round ___ and round.

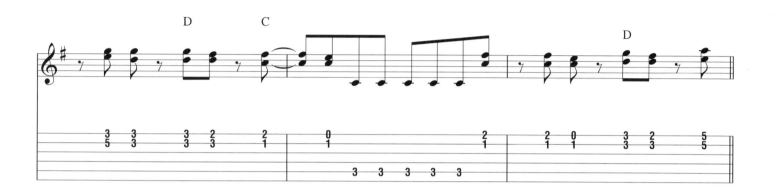

Repeat and fade

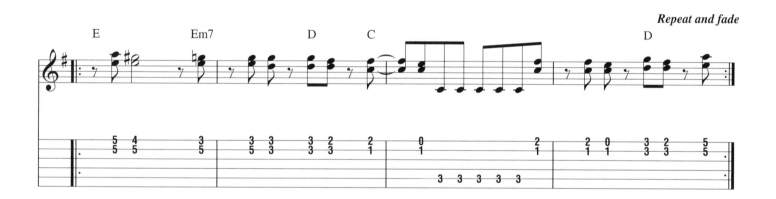

Additional Lyrics

2. Lookin' at you, lookin' at me.
The way you move, you know it's easy to see
The neon lights on me tonight.
I've got a way, we're gonna prove it tonight.
Like Romeo to Juliet,
Time and time I'm gonna make you mine.
I've had enough, we've had enough.
"It's all the same," she said.

Run to the Hills

Words and Music by Steven Harris

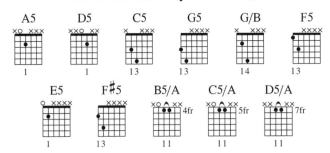

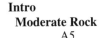

Strum Pattern: 3
Pick Pattern: 3

Intro
Moderate Rock

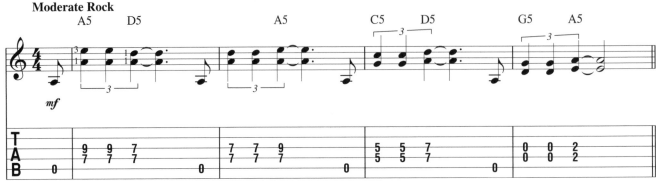

Verse

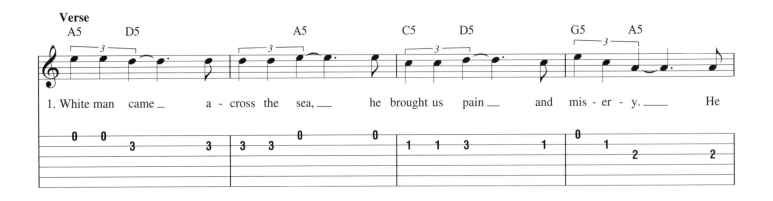

1. White man came __ a - cross the sea, __ he brought us pain __ and mis-er-y. __ He

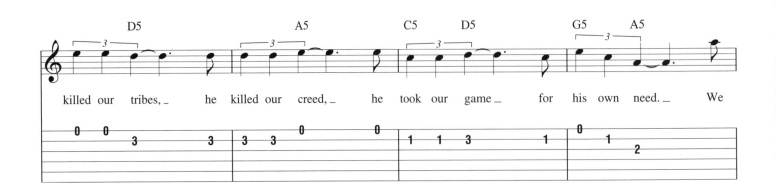

killed our tribes, __ he killed our creed, __ he took our game __ for his own need. __ We

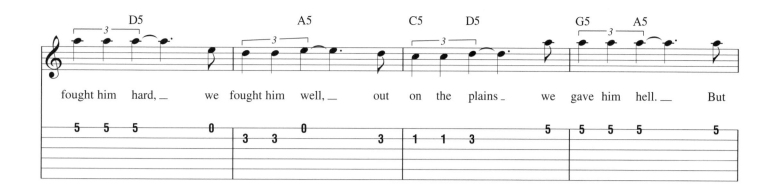

fought him hard, __ we fought him well, __ out on the plains __ we gave him hell. __ But

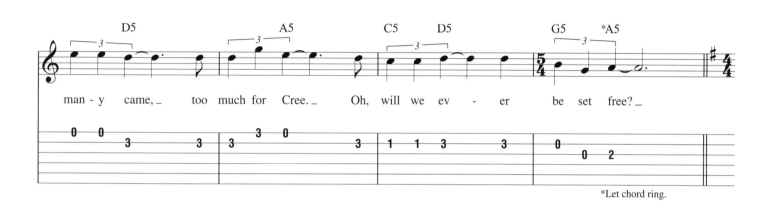

man - y came, __ too much for Cree. __ Oh, will we ev - er be set free? __

*Let chord ring.

Interlude
Faster

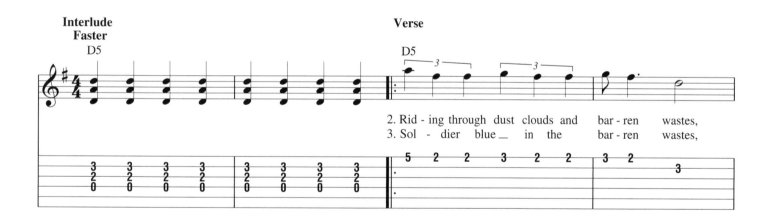

Verse

2. Rid - ing through dust clouds and bar - ren wastes,
3. Sol - dier blue __ in the bar - ren wastes,

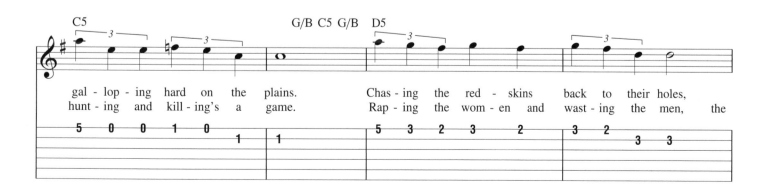

gal - lop - ing hard on the plains. Chas - ing the red - skins back to their holes,
hunt - ing and kill - ing's a game. Rap - ing the wom - en and wast - ing the men, the

fight - ing them at their own game. Mur - der for free - dom, a stab in the back,
on - ly good in - juns are tame. Sell - ing them whis - key and tak - ing their gold, en -

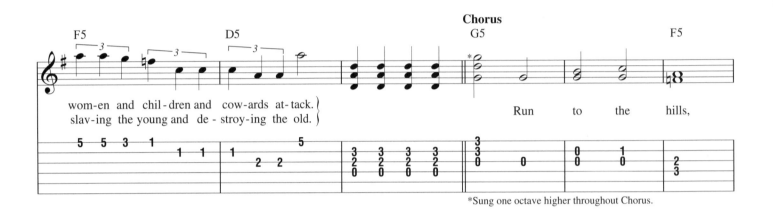

wom-en and chil - dren and cow-ards at- tack. }
slav-ing the young and de - stroy-ing the old. }

Run to the hills,

*Sung one octave higher throughout Chorus.

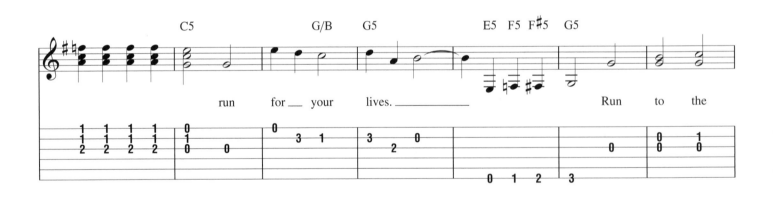

run for __ your lives. _____ Run to the

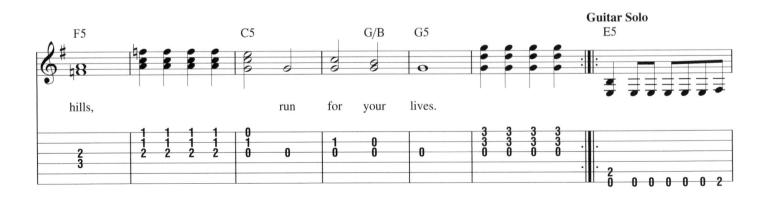

hills, run for your lives.

278

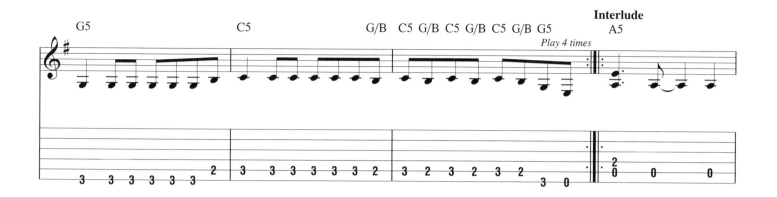

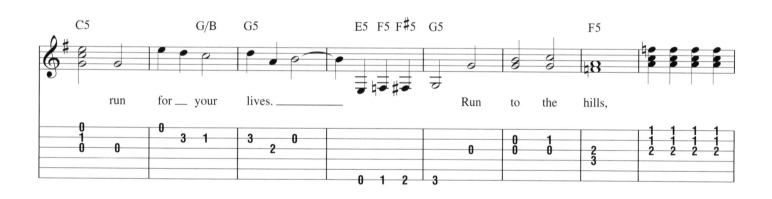

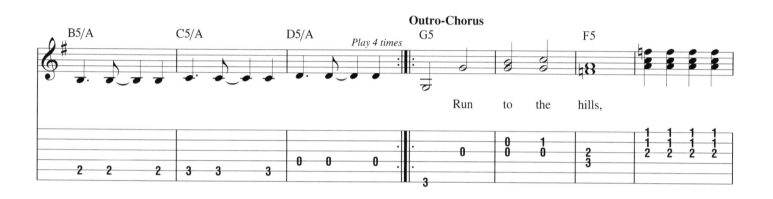

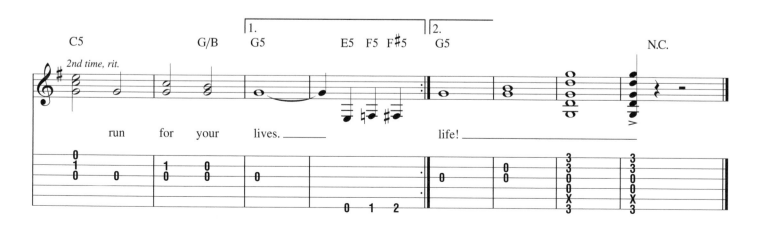

Runnin' with the Devil

Words and Music by David Lee Roth, Edward Van Halen, Alex Van Halen and Michael Anthony

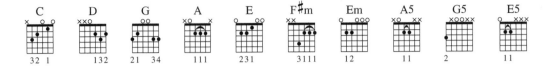

*Tune down 1/2 step:
(low to high) Eb-Ab-Db-Gb-Bb-Eb

Strum Pattern: 5, 6
Pick Pattern: 2, 5

Intro
Moderately

*Optional: To match recording, tune down 1/2 step.

**Bass arr. for guitar.

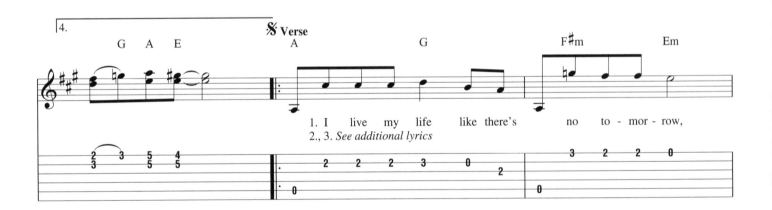

1. I live my life like there's no to-mor-row,
2., 3. *See additional lyrics*

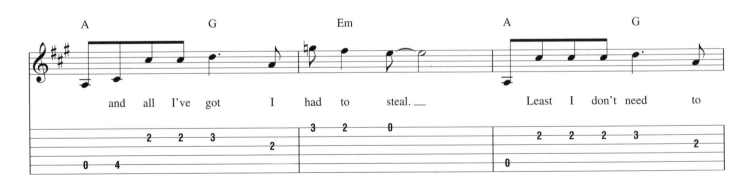

and all I've got I had to steal. Least I don't need to

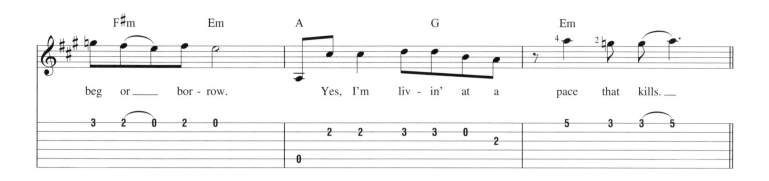

beg or ___ bor - row.   Yes, I'm liv - in' at a   pace that kills. ___

Chorus
w/ Voc. ad lib

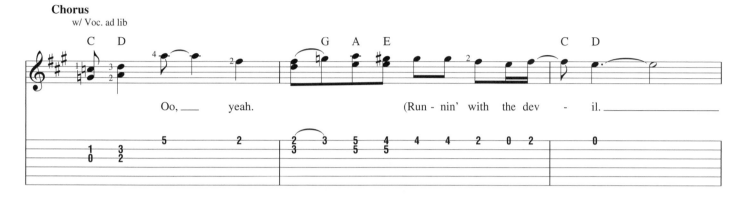

Oo, ___ yeah.   (Run - nin' with the dev   -   il. ___

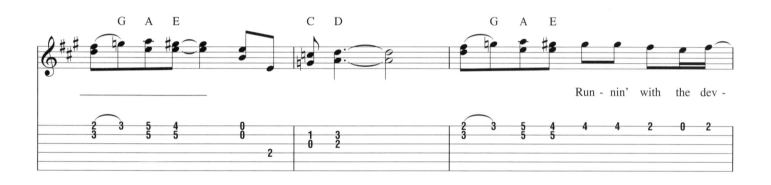

___   Run - nin' with the dev -

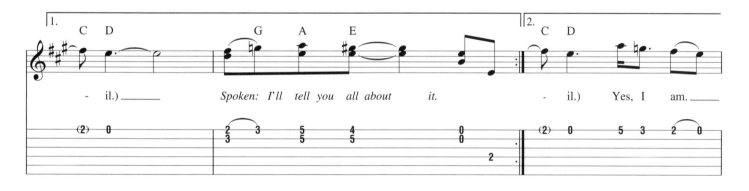

- il.) ___   *Spoken: I'll tell you all about   it.*   - il.)   Yes, I   am. ___

Guitar Solo   *To Coda* ⊕

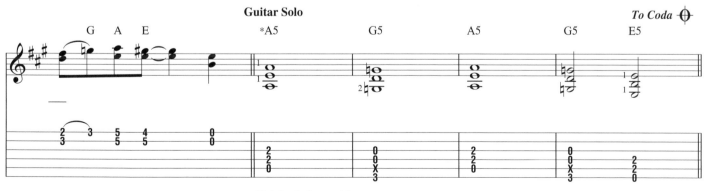

*Let chords ring, next 4 meas.

Interlude

D.S. al Coda
(take 2nd ending)

Spoken: 3. You know, uh.

Coda
Outro-Chorus
w/ Voc. ad lib. till end

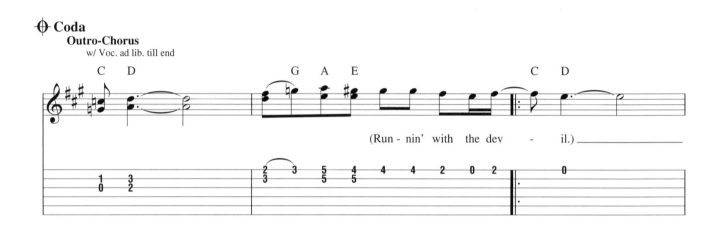

(Run - nin' with the dev - il.) _____

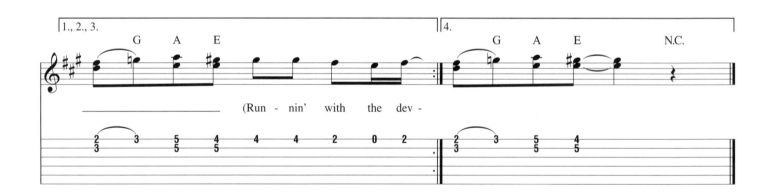

_____ (Run - nin' with the dev -

Additional Lyrics

2. I found the simple life ain't so simple,
   When I jumped out on that road.
   I got no love, no love you'd call real.
   Ain't got nobody waitin' at home.

3. I found the simple life weren't so simple,
   No, when I jumped out on that road.
   Got no love, no love you'd call real.
   Got nobody waitin' at home.

Search and Destroy

Written by Iggy Pop and James Williamson

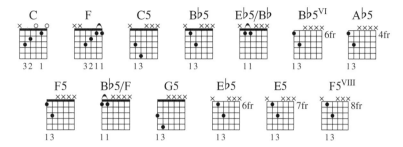

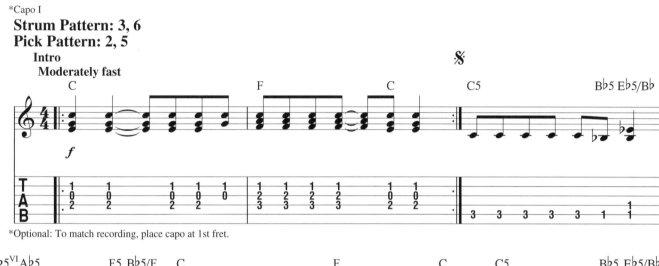

*Capo I

Strum Pattern: 3, 6
Pick Pattern: 2, 5

Intro
Moderately fast

*Optional: To match recording, place capo at 1st fret.

street-walk-in' chee - tah with a heart full of na - palm.
2., 3. Look out, hon - ey, 'cause I'm us - in' tech-nol - o - gy.

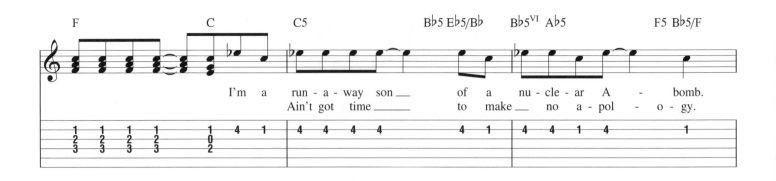

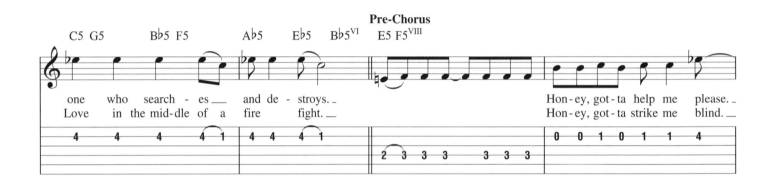

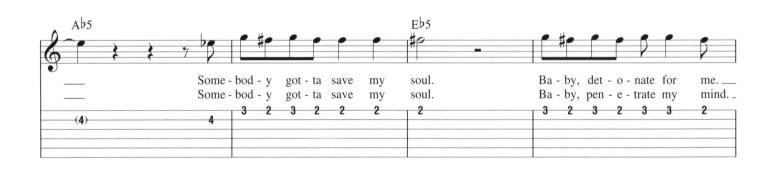

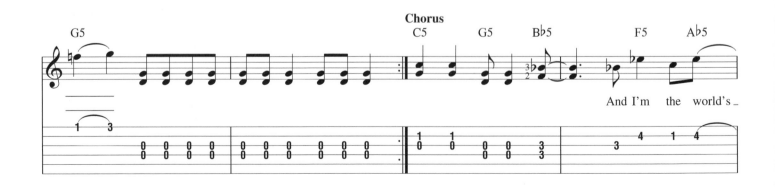

School's Out

Words and Music by Alice Cooper and Michael Bruce

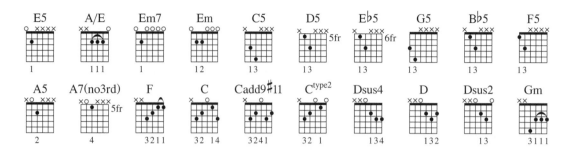

Strum Pattern: 3
Pick Pattern: 1

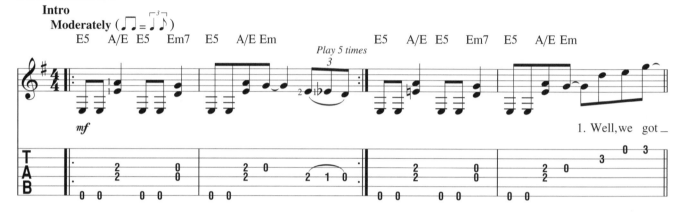

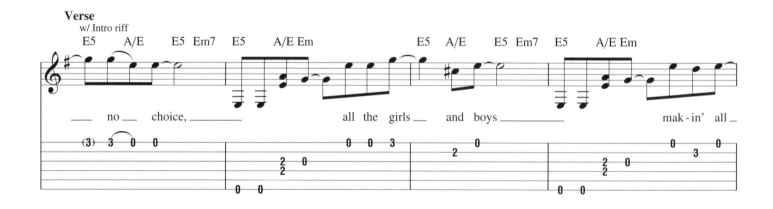

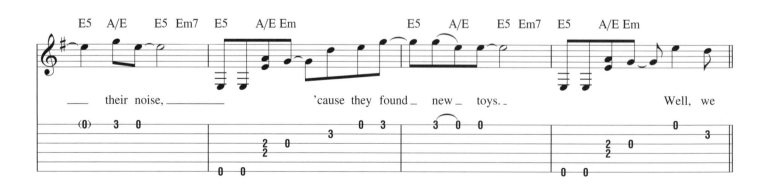

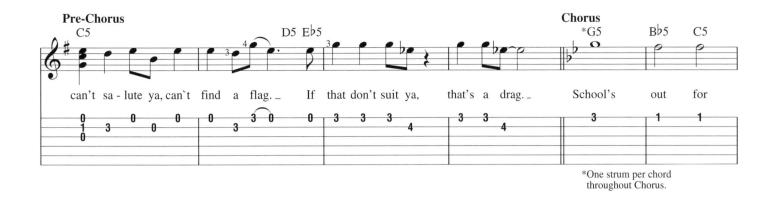

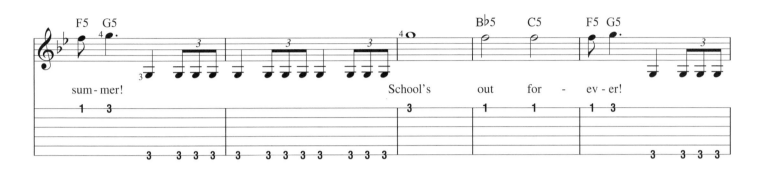

*One strum per chord throughout Chorus.

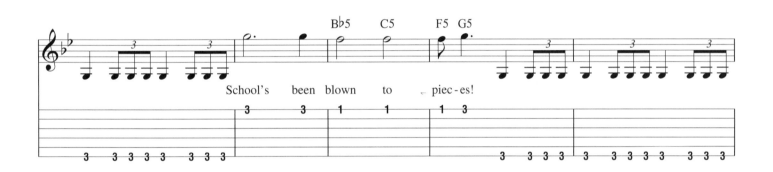

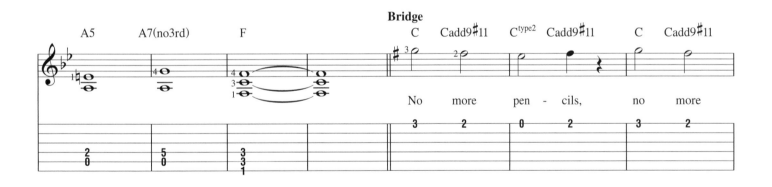

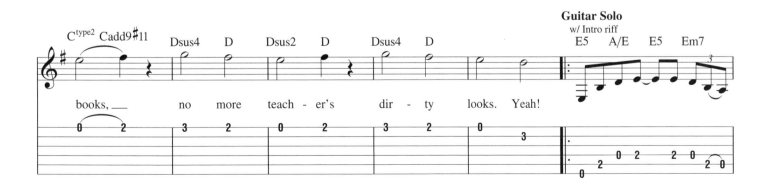

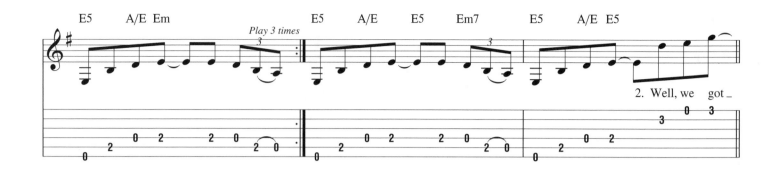

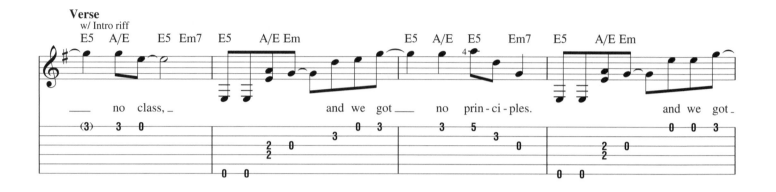

Verse

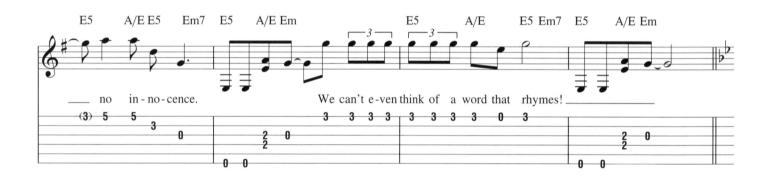

Chorus

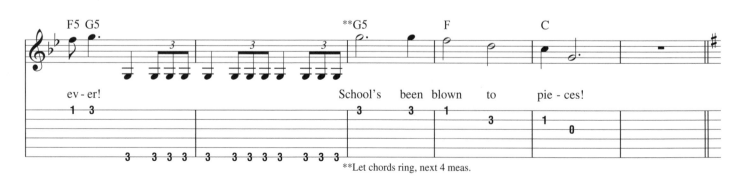

*One strum per chord, next 8 meas.

**Let chords ring, next 4 meas.

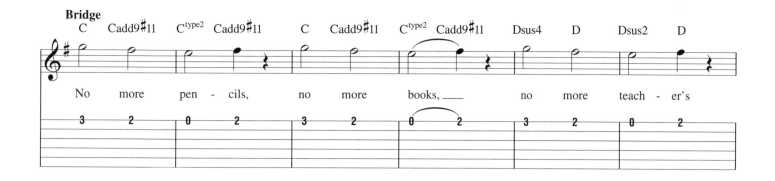

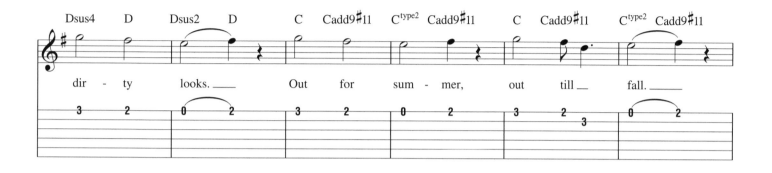

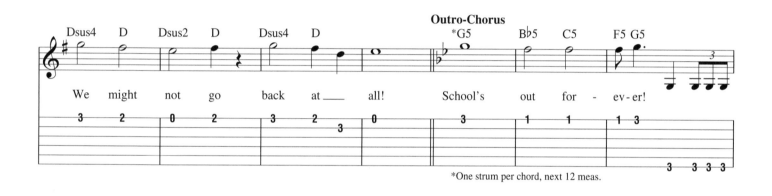

*One strum per chord, next 12 meas.

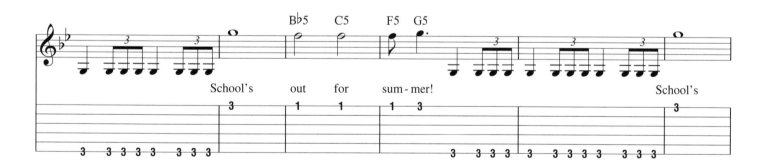

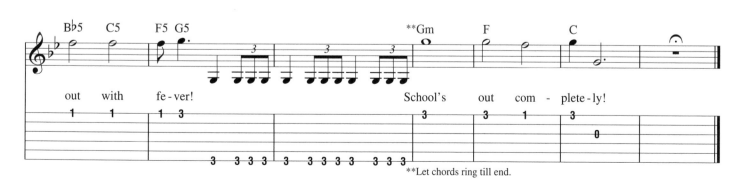

**Let chords ring till end.

Seven Nation Army

Words and Music by Jack White

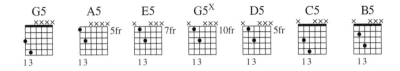

Strum Pattern: 2, 3

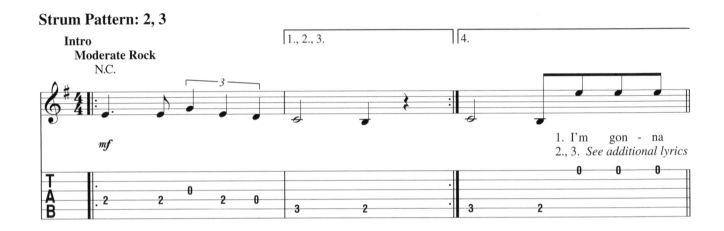

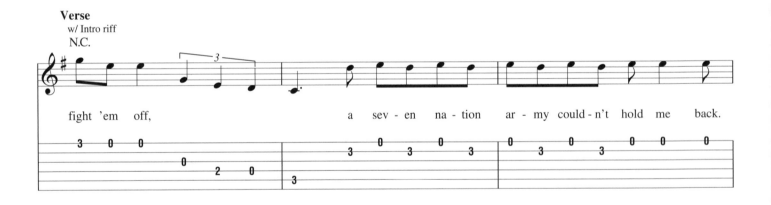

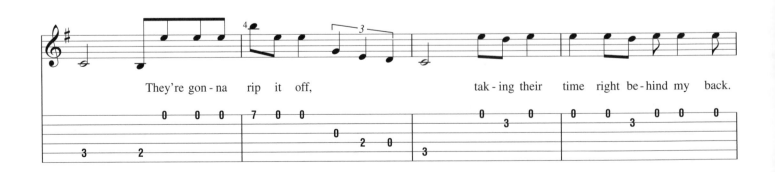

And I'm talk - ing to my - self at night ___ be - cause I can't for - get.

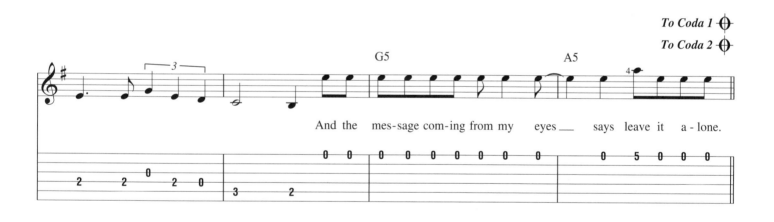

Back and forth through my mind ___ be - hind a cig - a - rette.

To Coda 1 ⊕
To Coda 2 ⊕

And the mes - sage com - ing from my eyes ___ says leave it a - lone.

Interlude

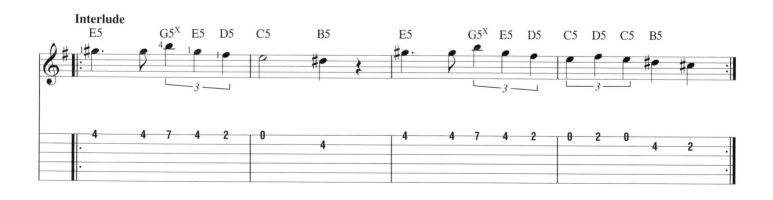

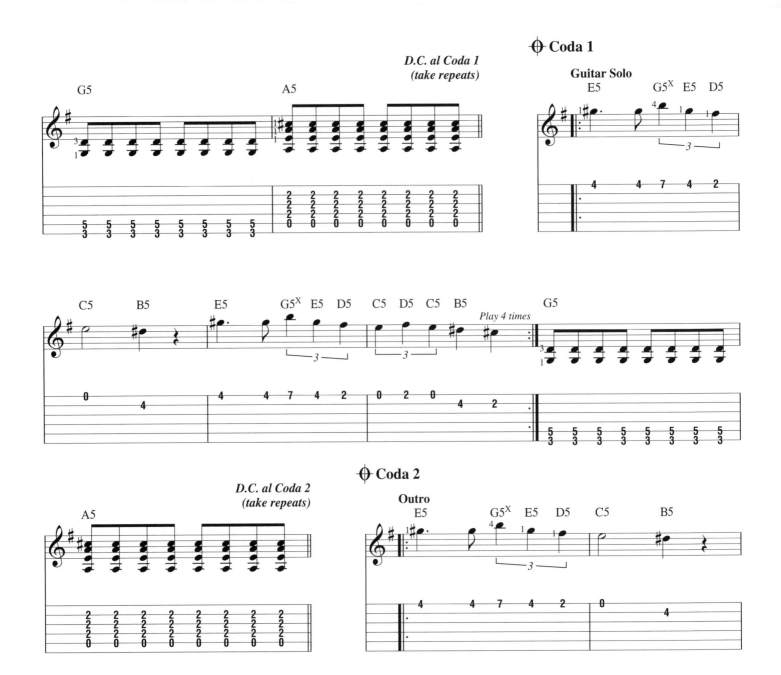

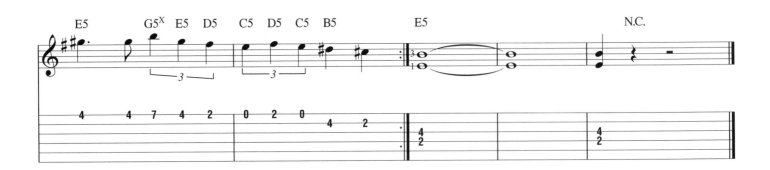

Additional Lyrics

2. Don't wanna hear about it,
   Ev'ry single one's got a story to tell.
   Ev'ry one knows about it
   From the Queen of England to the hounds of hell.
   And if I catch it coming back my way
   I'm gonna serve it to you.
   And that ain't what you want to hear,
   But that's what I'll do.
   And the feeling coming from my bones says find a home.

3. I'm going to Wichita,
   Far from this opera forevermore.
   I'm gonna work the straw,
   Make the sweat drip out of ev'ry pore.
   And I'm bleeding, and I'm bleeding, and I'm
   Bleeding right before the Lord.
   All the words are gonna bleed from me
   And I will think no more.
   And the stains coming from my blood tell me go back home.

Seventeen

Words and Music by Kip Winger, Reb Beach and Beau Hill

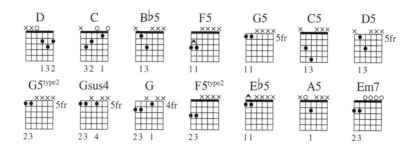

*Drop D tuning, capo I:
(low to high) D-A-D-G-B-E

Strum Pattern: 3
Pick Pattern: 4

Intro
Moderate Rock

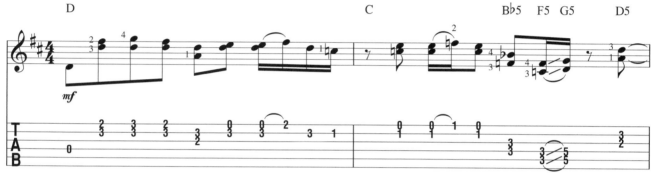

*Optional: To match recording, place capo at 1st fret.

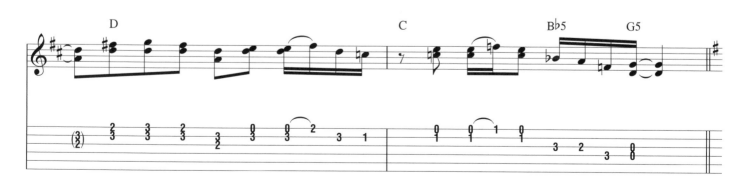

§ Verse

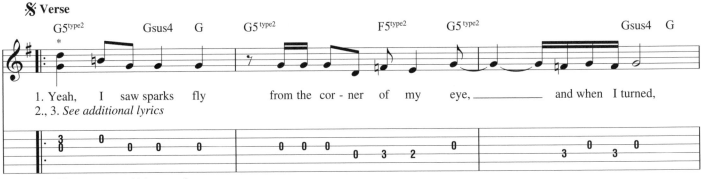

1. Yeah, I saw sparks fly from the cor-ner of my eye,_____ and when I turned,
2., 3. *See additional lyrics*

Sung one octave higher, next 8 meas.

ooh, it was love at first sight. I said, "Please ex-cuse me, I did-n't catch your name. _ Whoa, _

To Coda ⊕   **Pre-Chorus**

_____ it'd be a shame not to see you a-gain." _____ And just when I thought she was

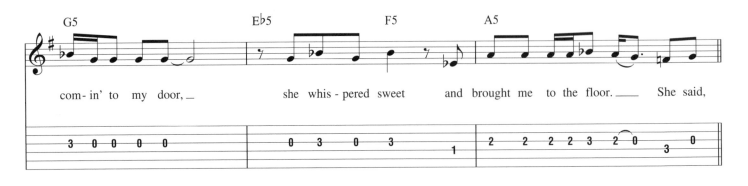

com-in' to my door, _ she whis-pered sweet and brought me to the floor. ____ She said,

Chorus

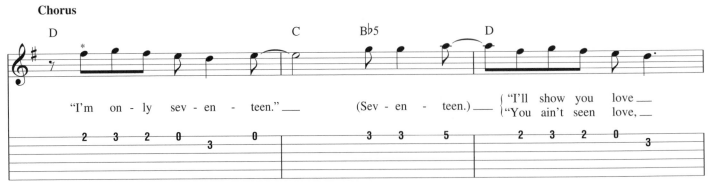

"I'm on-ly sev-en-teen." _ (Sev-en-teen.) _ {"I'll show you love _
{"You ain't seen love, _

Sung as written throughout Chorus.

294

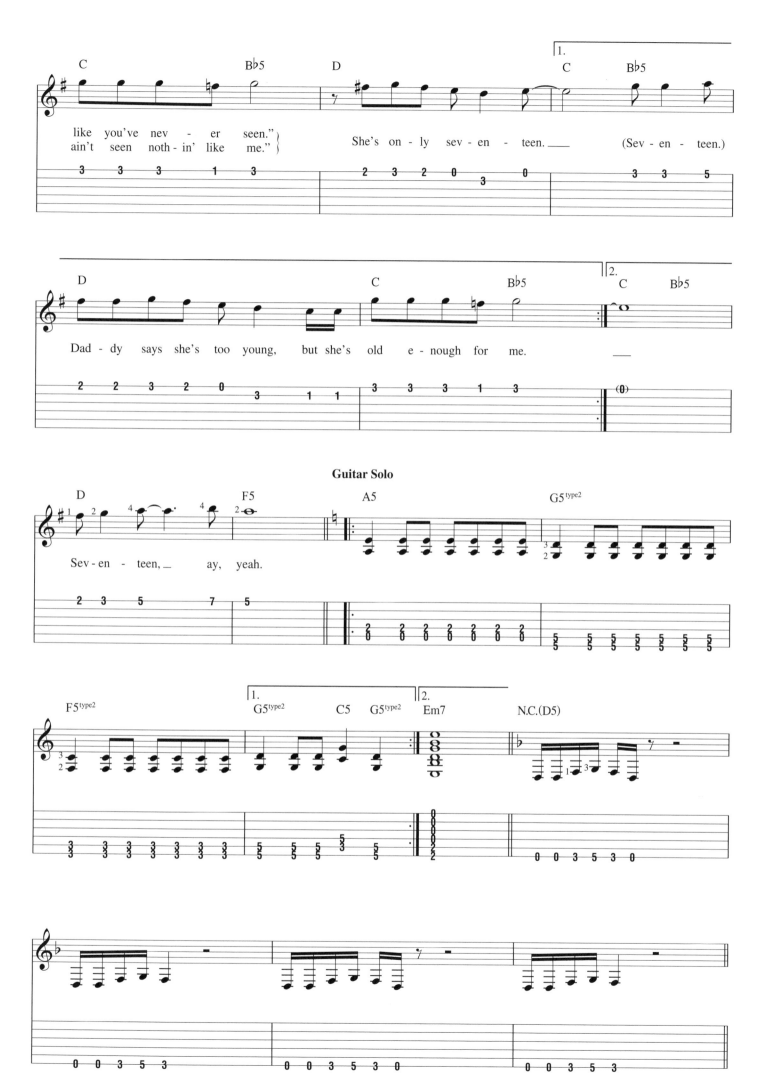

Interlude

N.C.(D5)

D.S. al Coda

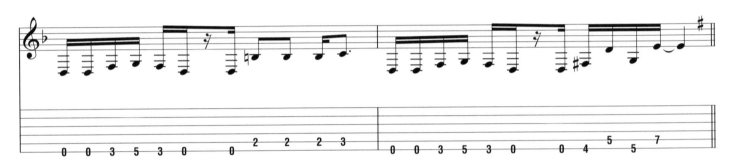

⊕ **Coda**   **Outro-Chorus**

G5 type2   C5   D

It must be love. _____   me. _____ She's on - ly sev - en - teen. __
                                                                              Yeah,   yeah. __

*Sung as written till fade.

C   Bb5   D   C   Bb5

___   (Sev - en - teen.) ___   That girl, she gives me love   like I've nev - er seen."
___   Yeah, yeah.   *2nd time, Instrumental till fade*

296

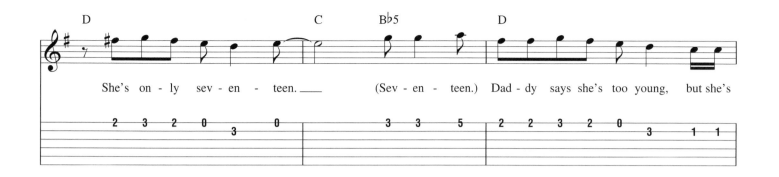

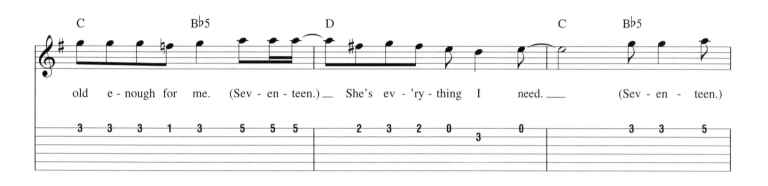

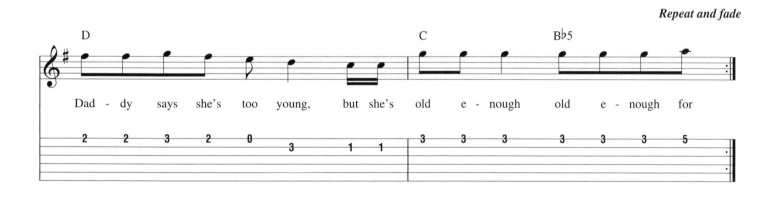

Additional Lyrics

2. Mm, come to my place; we can talk it over,
Oh, ev'rything going down in your head.
She says, "Take it easy, I need some time.
Time to work it out, to make you mine."

3. Yeah, such a bad girl, loves to work me overtime.
Feels good, hah, dancing close to the borderline.
She's a magic mountain, she's a leather glove.
Oh, she's my soul. It must be love.

Should I Stay or Should I Go

Words and Music by Mick Jones and Joe Strummer

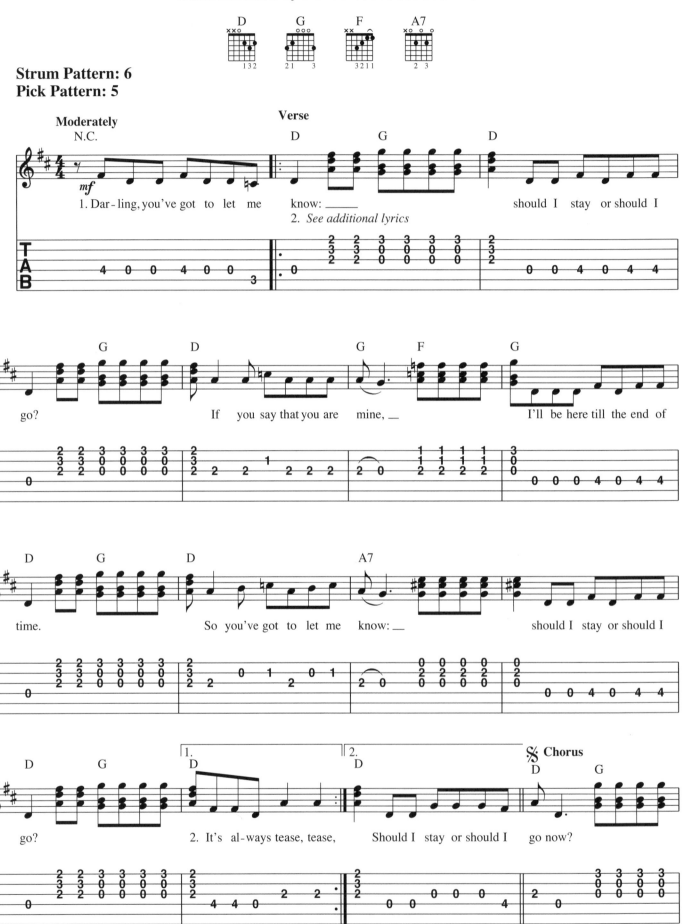

Strum Pattern: 6
Pick Pattern: 5

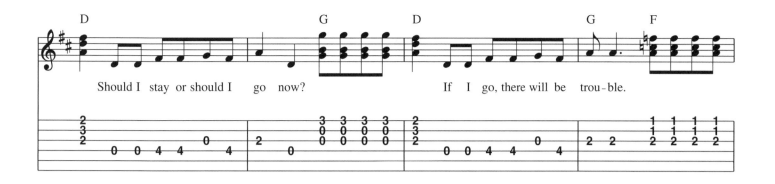

Should I stay or should I go now? If I go, there will be trou-ble.

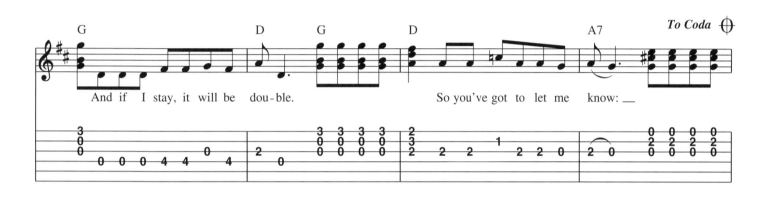

And if I stay, it will be dou-ble. So you've got to let me know: ___

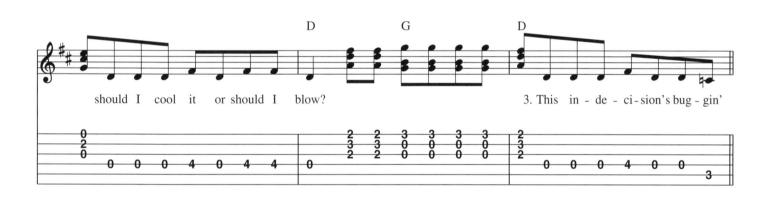
should I cool it or should I blow? 3. This in-de-ci-sion's bug-gin'

Verse

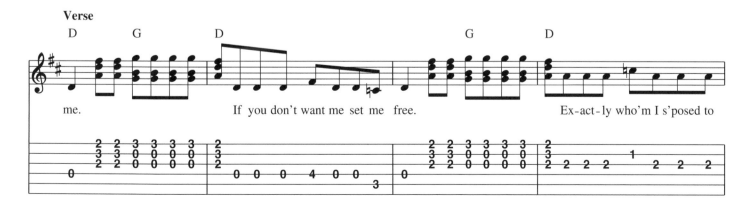

me. If you don't want me set me free. Ex-act-ly who'm I s'posed to

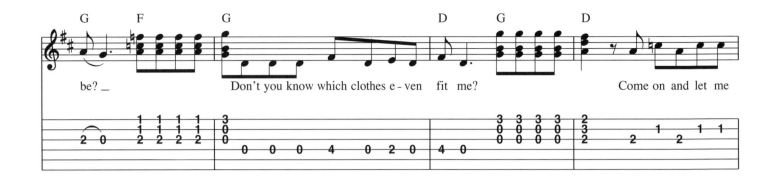

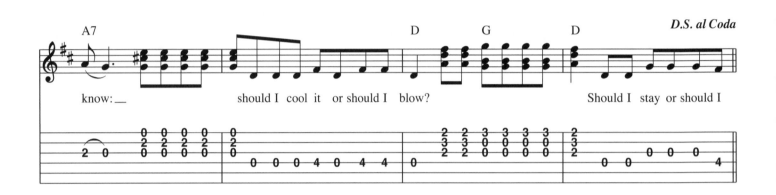

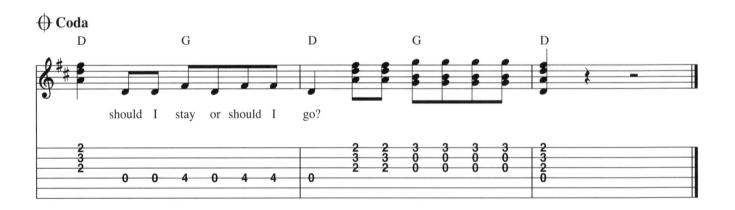

Additional Lyrics

2. It's always tease, tease, tease.
   You're happy when I'm on my knees.
   One day is fine and next is black.
   So if you want me off your back,
   Well, come on and let me know:
   Should I stay or should I go?

Slow Ride

Words and Music by Lonesome Dave Peverett

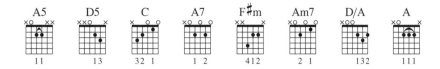

Strum Pattern: 2, 3
Pick Pattern: 3, 4

Intro
Moderately

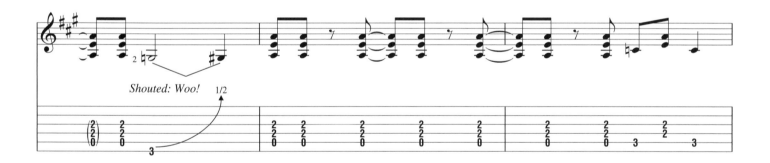

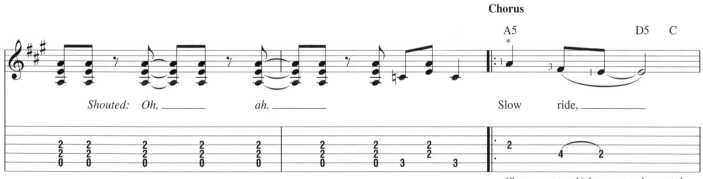

*Sung one octave higher, except where noted.

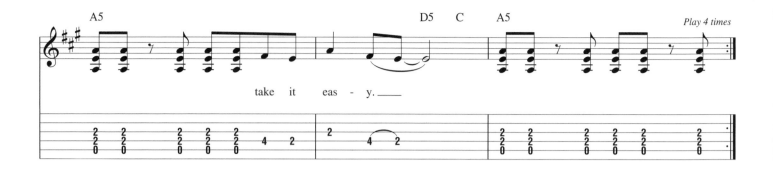

Verse

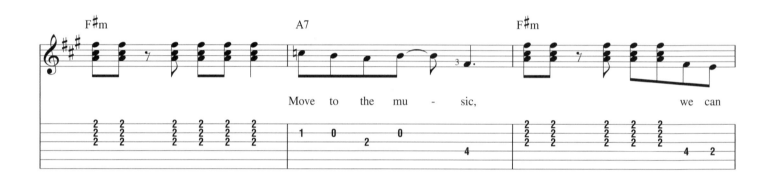

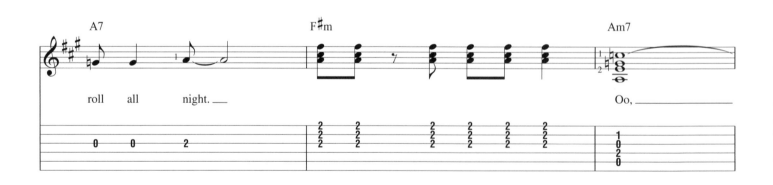

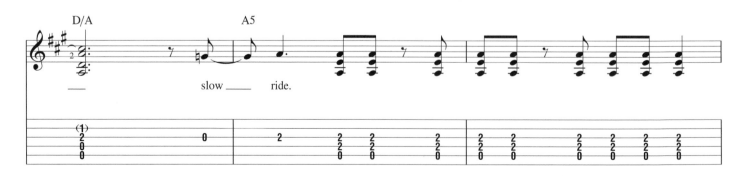

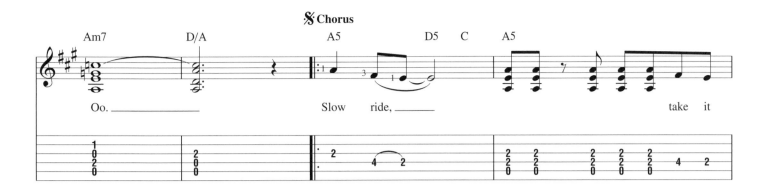

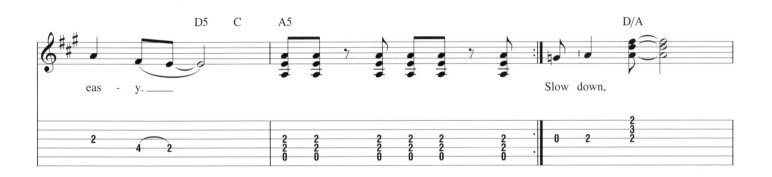

*Sung as written, next 2 meas.

*Sung as written, next 2 meas.

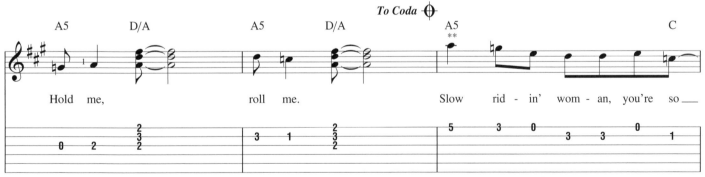

**Sung as written, next 2 meas.

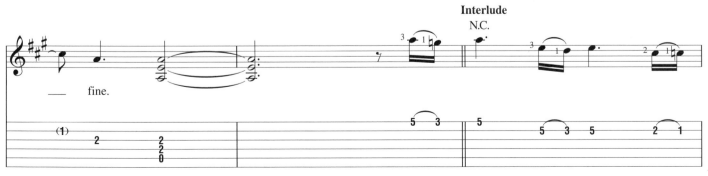

Spoken: Woo!

Verse

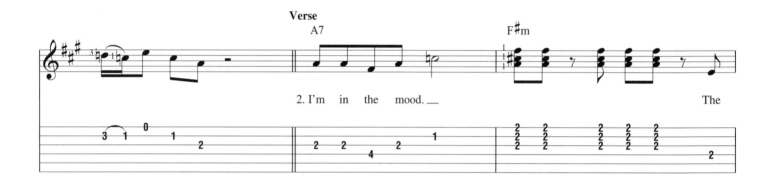

2. I'm in the mood. __   The

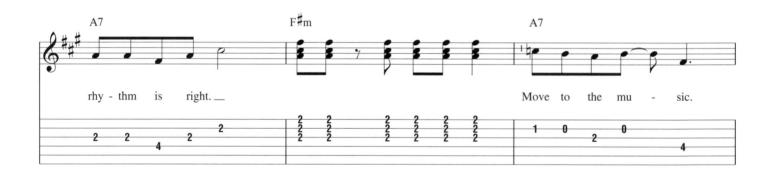

rhy - thm is right. __   Move to the mu - sic.

Yeah, __   we can roll all night, __   yeah. _____

*Sung as written, next 2.5 meas.

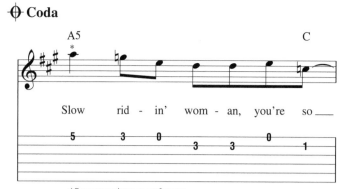

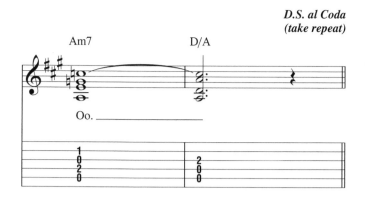

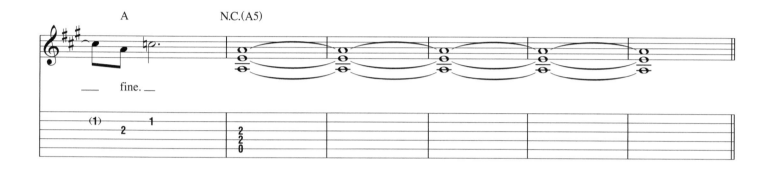

*Sung as written, next 2 meas.

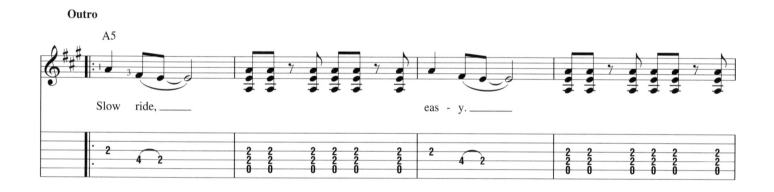

Outro

Repeat and fade

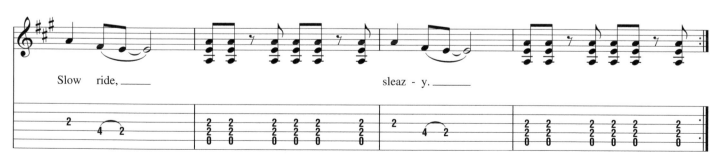

Since You've Been Gone

Words and Music by Russell Ballard

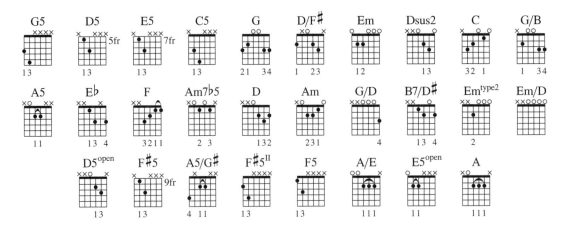

Strum Pattern: 1, 6
Pick Pattern: 2

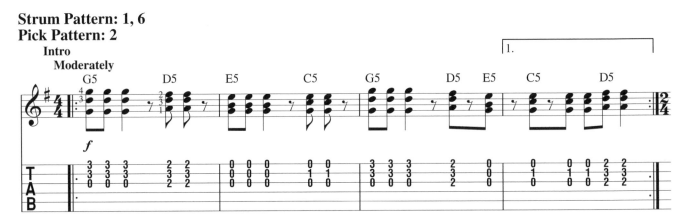

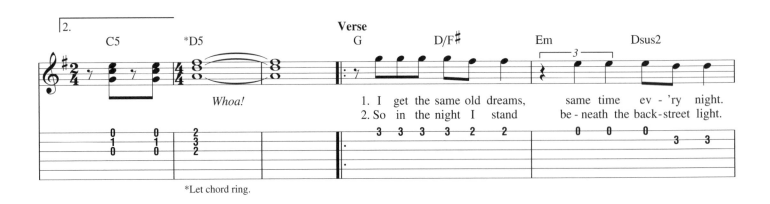

Whoa!

*Let chord ring.

1. I get the same old dreams, same time ev-'ry night.
2. So in the night I stand be-neath the back-street light.

Fall to the ground and I wake up. So I get out-ta bed, put
I read the words that you sent to me. I can take the af-ter-noon, the

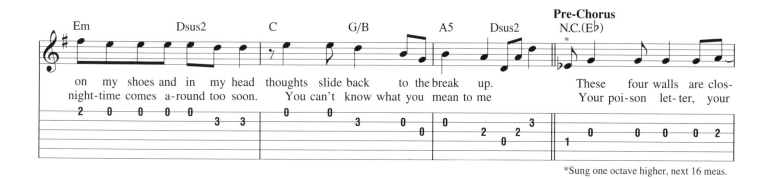

on my shoes and in my head thoughts slide back to the break up.
night-time comes a-round too soon. You can't know what you mean to me

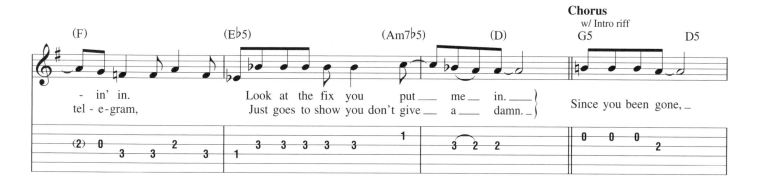

*Sung one octave higher, next 16 meas.

- in' in.
tel - e - gram,
Look at the fix you put __ me __ in. __
Just goes to show you don't give __ a __ damn. __
Since you been gone, __

since you been gone, __ I'm out-ta my head, __ can't take ___ it.

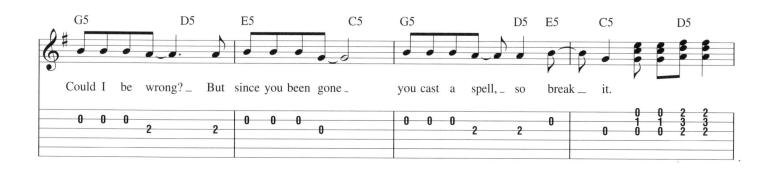

Could I be wrong? __ But since you been gone __ you cast a spell, __ so break __ it.

Oh. _____ Whoa. _____ Whoa. _____ Since you been gone.

307

Bridge
Half-time feel

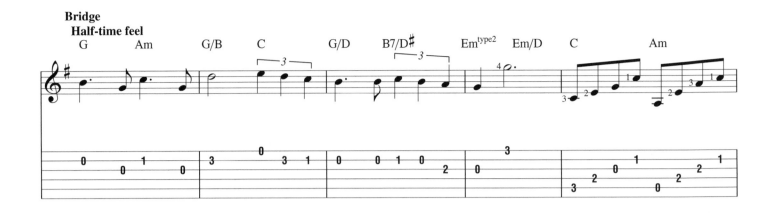

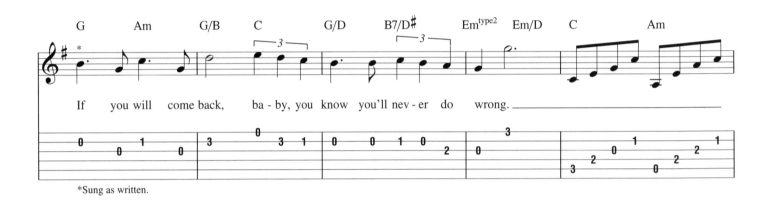

If you will come back, ba - by, you know you'll nev - er do wrong._____

*Sung as written.

Chorus
End half-time feel

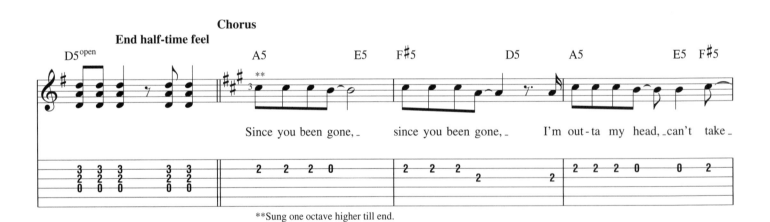

Since you been gone,_ since you been gone,_ I'm out - ta my head, can't take_

**Sung one octave higher till end.

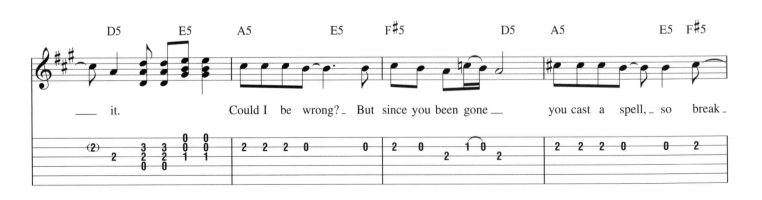

___ it.   Could I be wrong?_ But since you been gone ___ you cast a spell,_ so break_

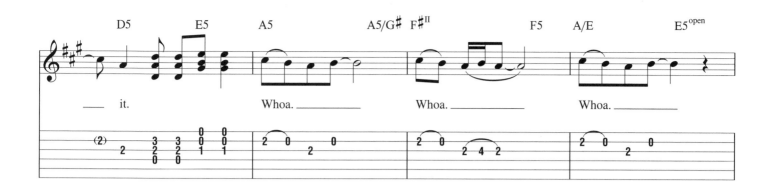

it. Whoa. Whoa. Whoa.

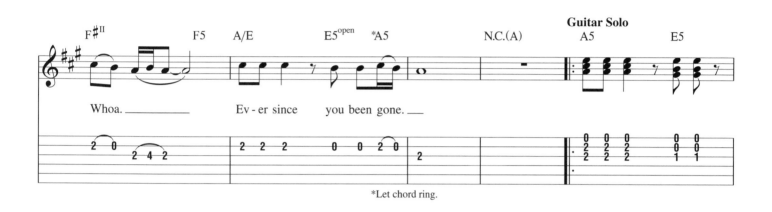

Whoa. Ev-er since you been gone.

*Let chord ring.

Guitar Solo

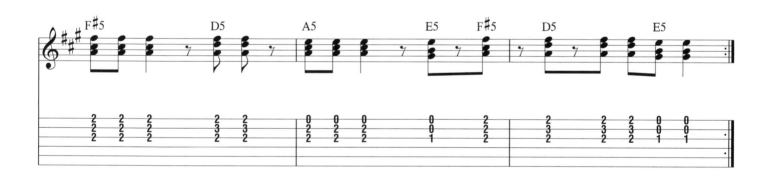

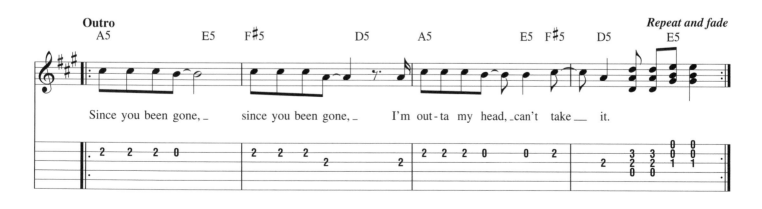

Outro

Repeat and fade

Since you been gone, _ since you been gone, _ I'm out-ta my head, _ can't take _ it.

Slither

Words and Music by Scott Weiland, Slash, Duff McKagan, Matt Sorum and Dave Kushner

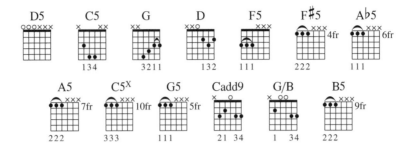

Drop D tuning:
(low to high) D-A-D-G-B-E

Strum Pattern: 1, 2

Intro
Moderately
Half-time feel

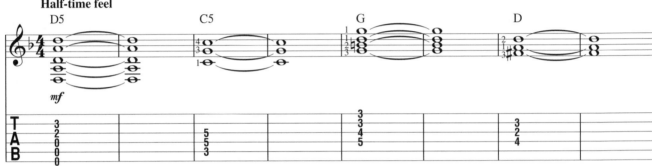

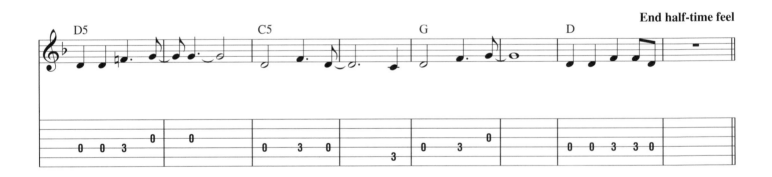

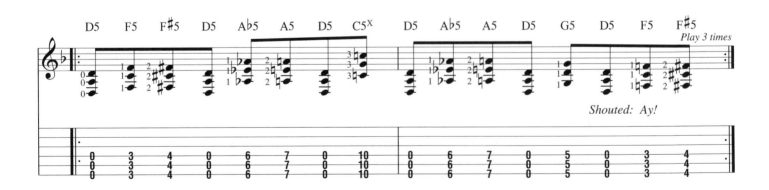

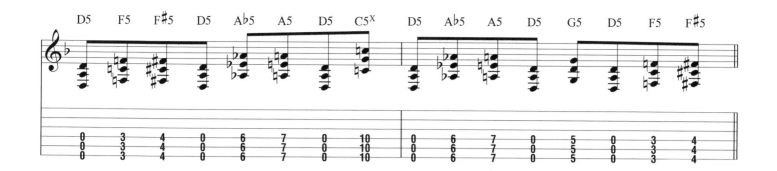

Verse

*w/ Intro pattern

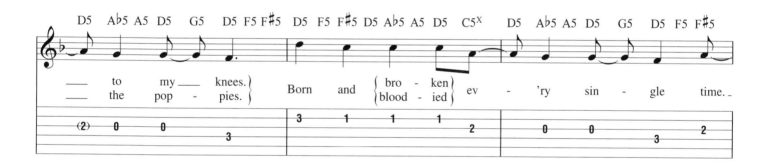

1. When you look, you see _____ right through _ me. Cut the rope, I fell _
2. When you seek me, you'll _ de - stroy _ me, rape my mind and smell _

*Play on 6th str. only, next 6 meas.

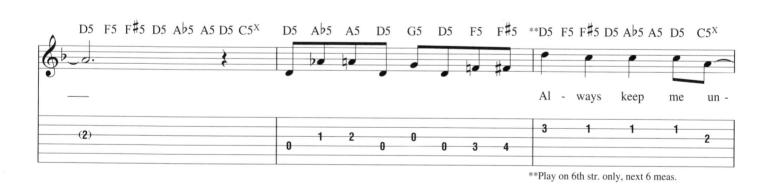

_ to my _ knees.⎬ Born and ⎰ bro - ken⎱ ev - 'ry sin - gle time. _
_ the pop - pies.⎬ ⎱blood - ied⎰

Al - ways keep me un -

**Play on 6th str. only, next 6 meas.

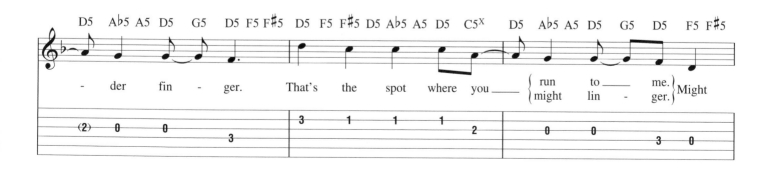

- der fin - ger. That's the spot where you _____ ⎰run to _____ me.⎱ Might
⎱might lin - ger.⎰

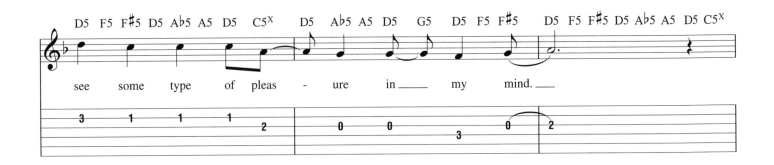

see some type of pleas - ure in my mind.

𝄋 Chorus
Half-time feel

Yeah, here comes the wa - ter.

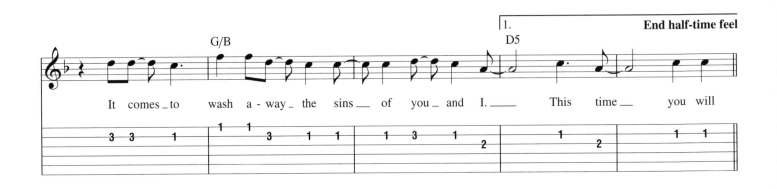

It comes to wash a - way the sins of you and I. This time you will

Interlude

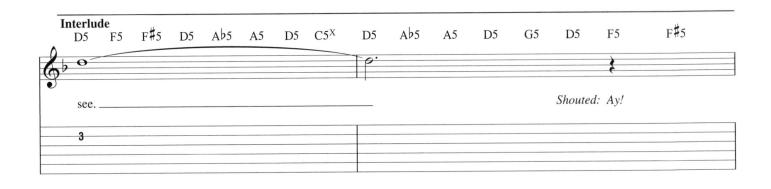

see. *Shouted: Ay!*

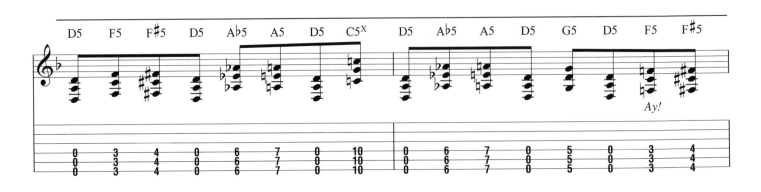

Ay!

312

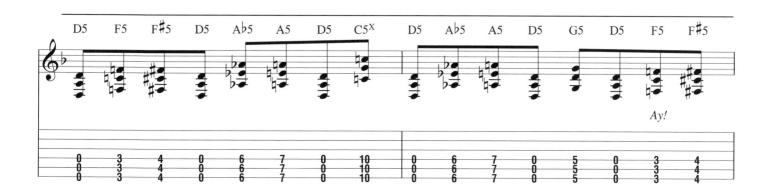

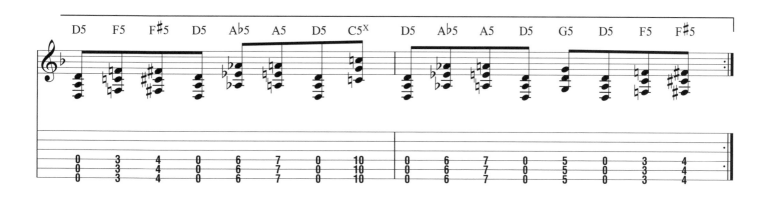

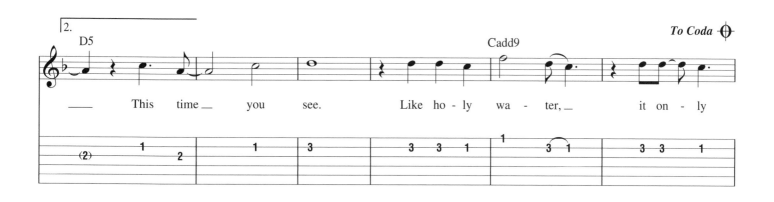

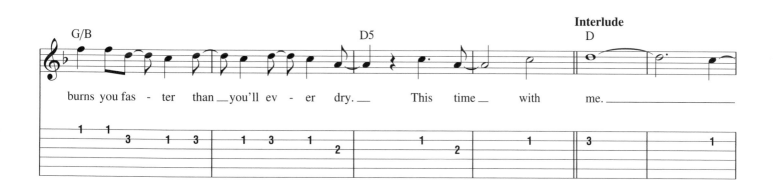

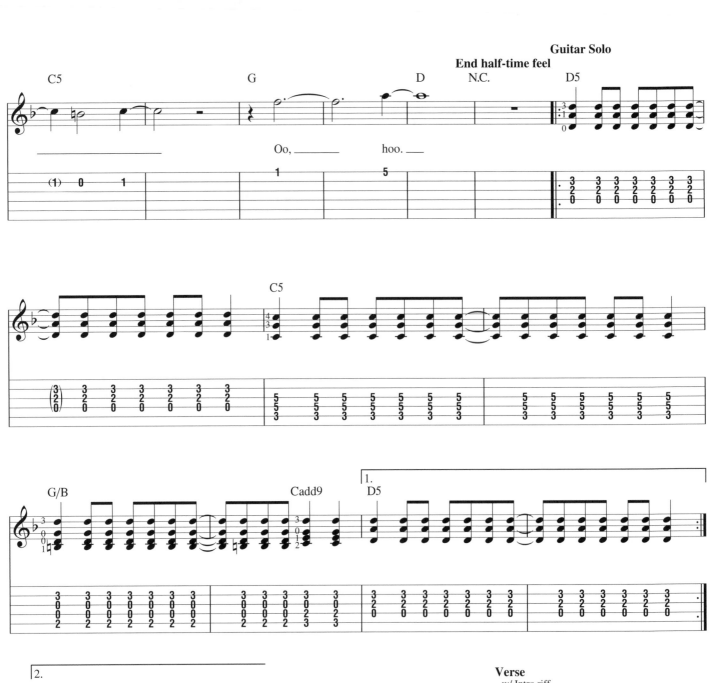

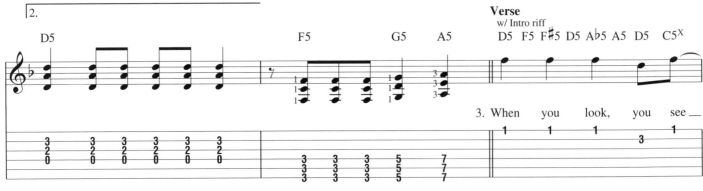

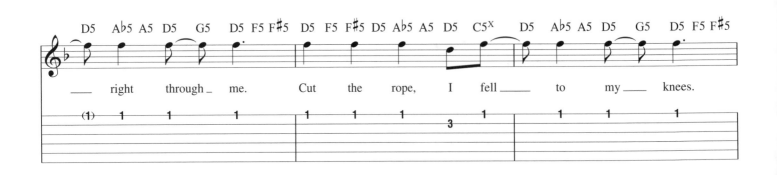

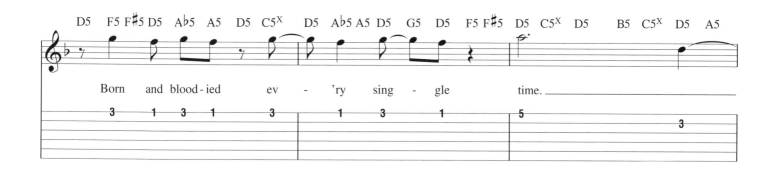

Born and blood-ied ev - 'ry sing - gle time.

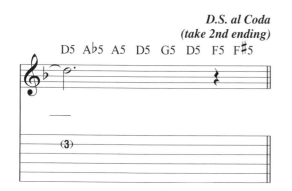

D.S. al Coda
(take 2nd ending)

⊕ Coda

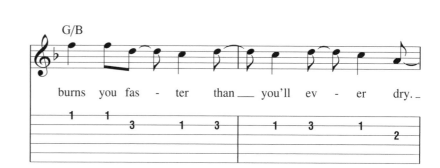

burns you fas - ter than you'll ev - er dry.

Outro
w/ Intro pattern

End half-time feel

This time with me.

Shouted: Ay!

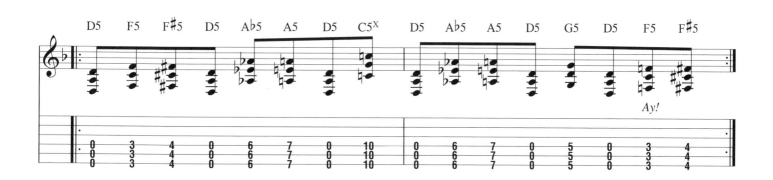

Ay!

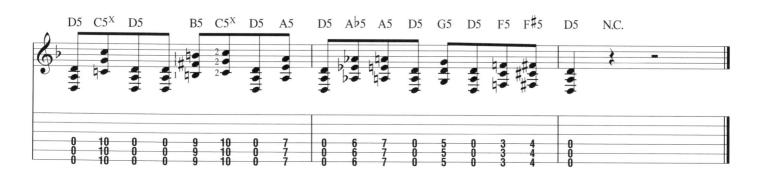

315

Smells Like Teen Spirit

Words and Music by Kurt Cobain, Krist Novoselic and Dave Grohl

Strum Pattern: 1, 3
Pick Pattern: 2, 4

Additional Lyrics

2. I'm worse at what I do best,
   And for this gift I feel blessed.
   Our little group has always been
   And always will until the end.

3. And I forget just why I taste.
   Oh yeah, I guess it makes me smile.
   I found it hard, it was hard to find.
   Oh, well, whatever, nevermind.

The Stroke

Words and Music by Billy Squier

Strum Pattern: 3, 4

Verse
Slow Rock, in 2

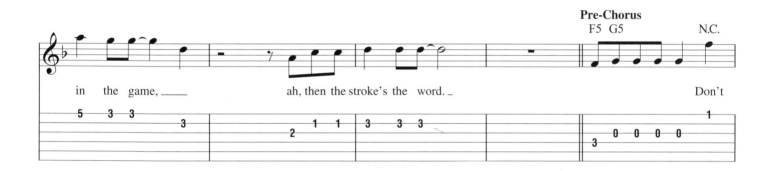

1. Now, ev - 'ry-bod - y, ah, have you heard? _____ If you're

in the game, _____ ah, then the stroke's the word. _ Don't

take no rhyth-m, don't take no style. _ Got a

Interlude

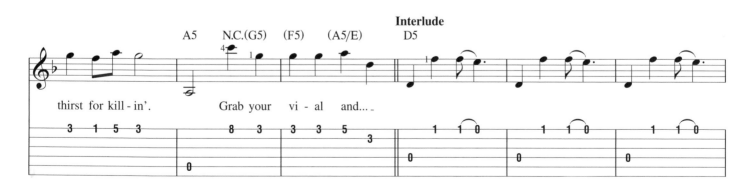

thirst for kill - in'. Grab your vi - al and.... _

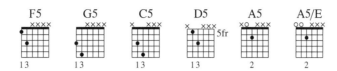

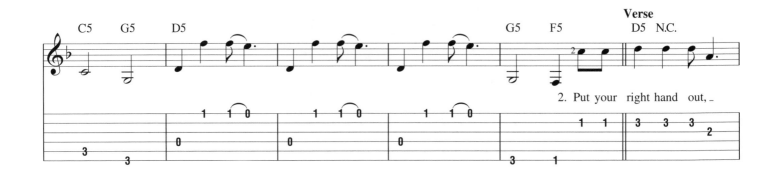

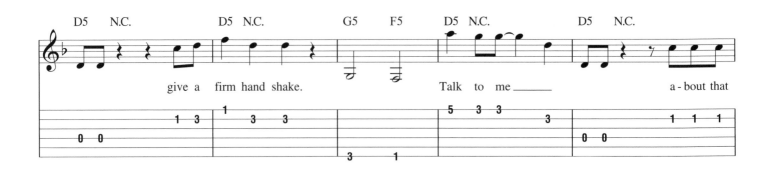

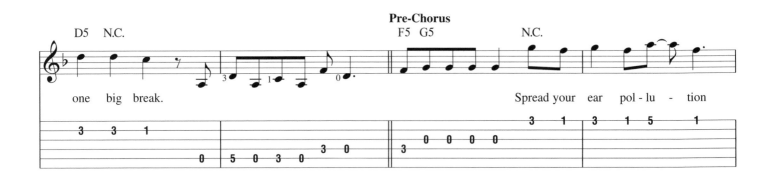

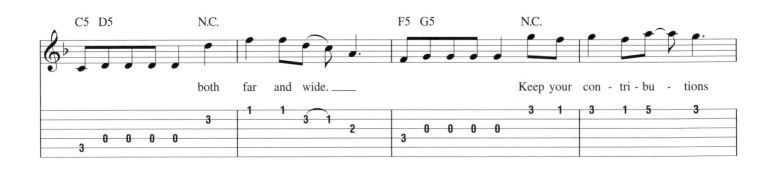

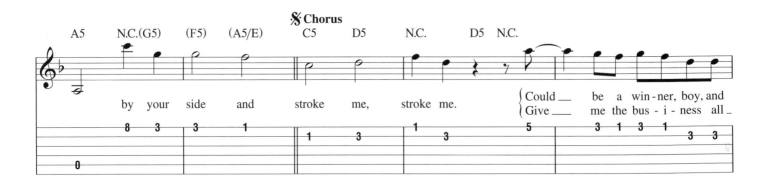

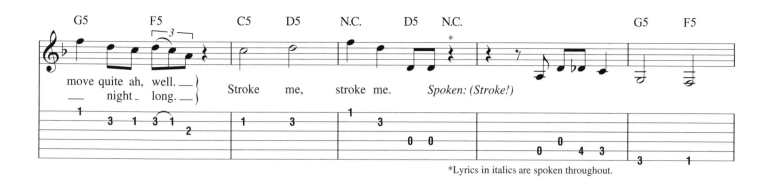

*Lyrics in italics are spoken throughout.

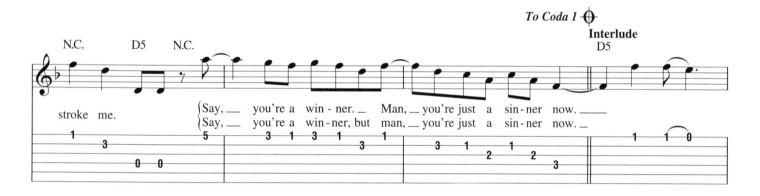

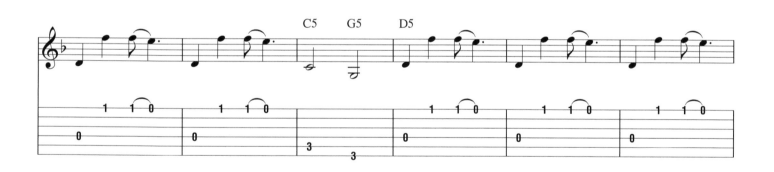

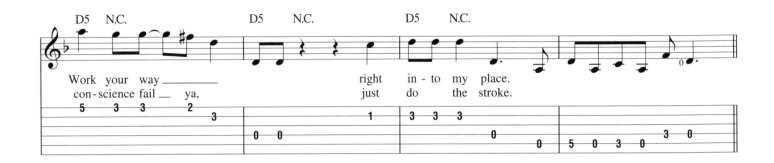

Work your way _____ right in-to my place.
con-science fail __ ya, just do the stroke.

Pre-Chorus

First you try to bet __ me, you make my back-bone slide.
Don't you take no chanc - es, keep your eye on top.

D.S. al Coda 1
To Coda 2 ⊕

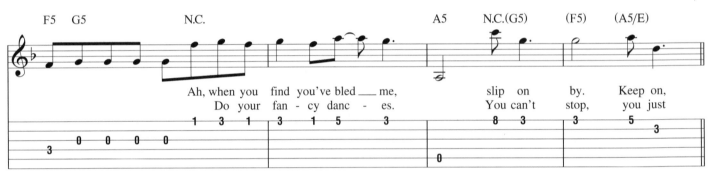

Ah, when you find you've bled __ me, slip on by. Keep on,
Do your fan - cy danc - es. You can't stop, you just

⊕ **Coda 1**

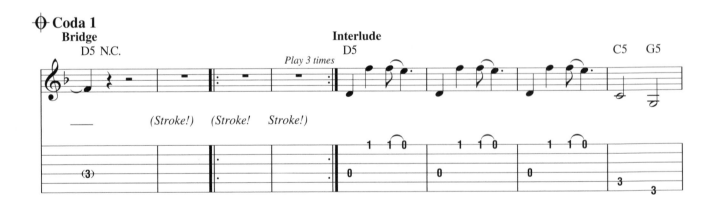

Bridge

___ (Stroke!) (Stroke! Stroke!)

Interlude

Play 3 times

⊕ **Coda 2**

D.S.S. al Coda 2

4. Bet-ter

Outro-Chorus

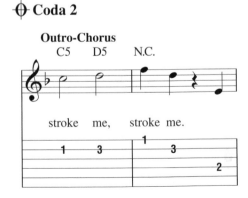

stroke me, stroke me.

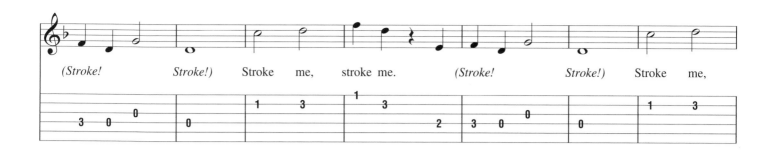

(Stroke!) Stroke!) Stroke me, stroke me. (Stroke!) Stroke!) Stroke me,

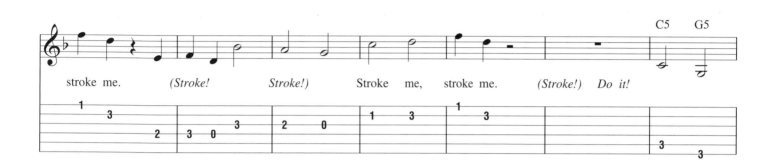

stroke me. (Stroke!) Stroke!) Stroke me, stroke me. (Stroke!) Do it!

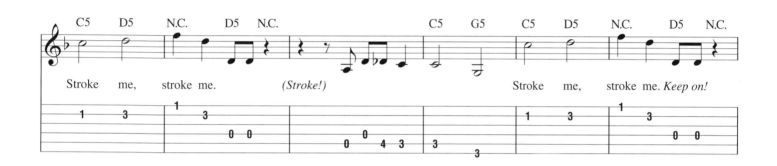

Stroke me, stroke me. (Stroke!) Stroke me, stroke me. Keep on!

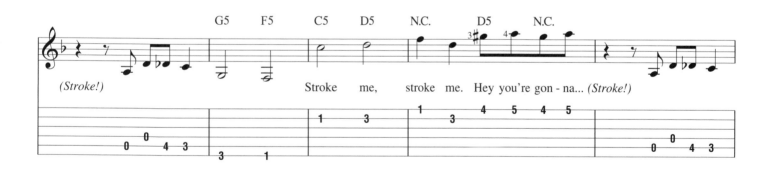

(Stroke!) Stroke me, stroke me. Hey you're gon - na... (Stroke!)

Stroke me, stroke me. Say __ you're a win - ner. __ Man, __ you're just a sin - ner now.

Smoke on the Water

Words and Music by Ritchie Blackmore, Ian Gillan, Roger Glover, Jon Lord and Ian Paice

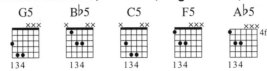

Strum Pattern: 1, 3
Pick Pattern: 3, 4

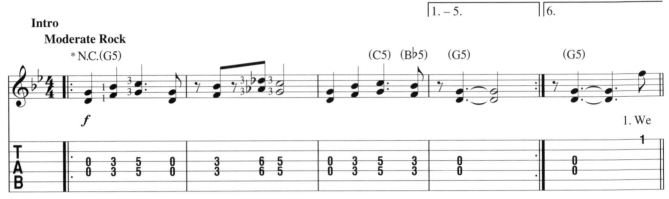

*Chords implied by bass, 3rd time.

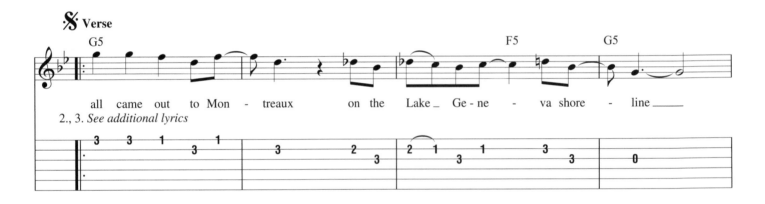

2., 3. *See additional lyrics*

all came out to Mon - treaux on the Lake _ Ge - ne - va shore - line _____

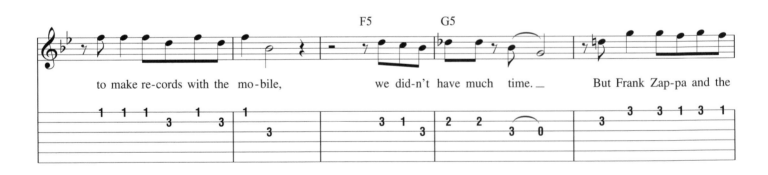

to make re-cords with the mo-bile, we did-n't have much time. _ But Frank Zap-pa and the

Moth-ers were at the best place a - round. _ But some stu-pid with a flare gun

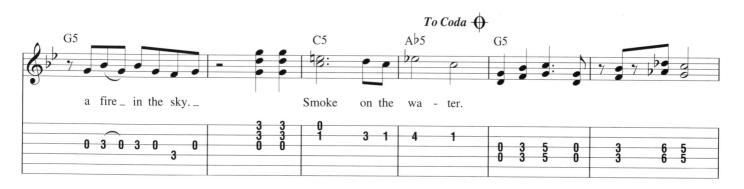

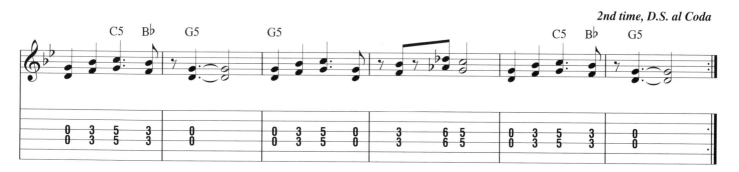

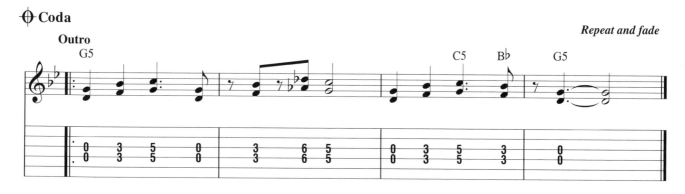

Additional Lyrics

2. They burned down the gambling house,
   It died with an awful sound.
   A Funky Claude was running in and out,
   Pulling kids out the ground.
   When it all was over,
   We had to find another place.
   But Swiss time was running out;
   It seemed that we would lose the race.

3. We ended up at the Grand Hotel,
   It was empty, cold and bare.
   But with the Rolling truck Stones thing just outside,
   Making our music there.
   With a few red lights, a few old beds
   We made a place to sweat.
   No matter what we get out of this,
   I know, I know we'll never forget.

Stone Cold Crazy

**Words and Music by Freddie Mercury,
Brian May, Roger Taylor and John Deacon**

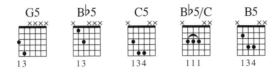

Strum Pattern: 1

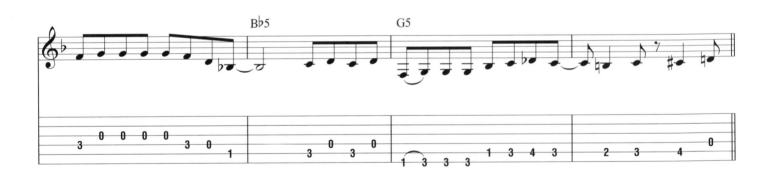

1. Sleep-in' ver-y sound-ly on a Sat-ur-day morn - ing, I was dream-ing I was Al Ca - pone.
3. *See additional lyrics*

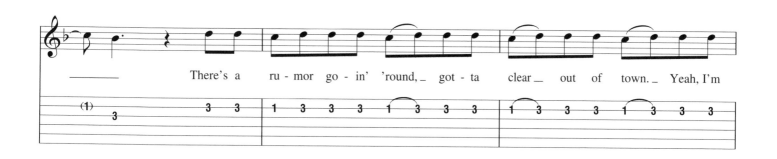

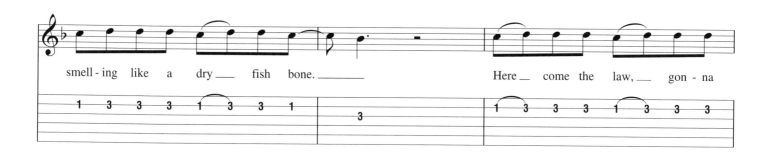

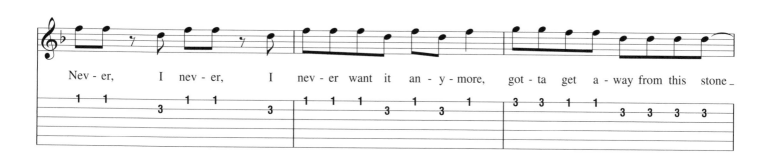

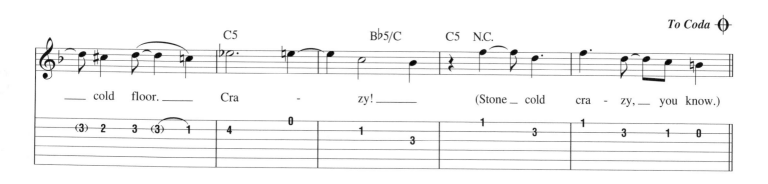

Bridge

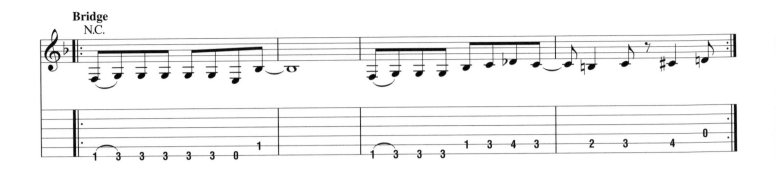

Guitar Solo

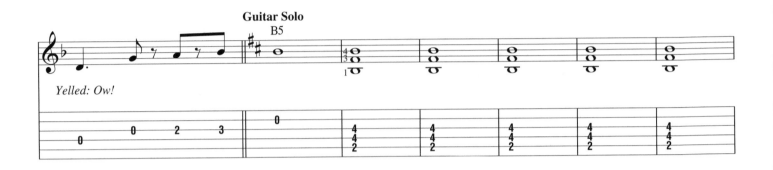

Yelled: Ow!

Bridge

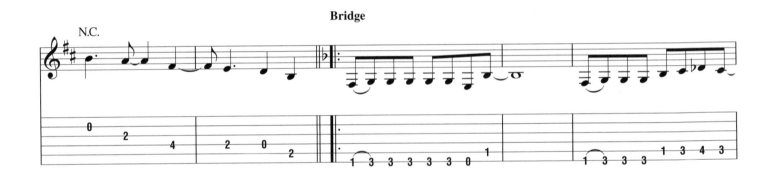

Verse

2. Rain - y af - ter - noon I got - ta blow a ty - phoon, an' I'm

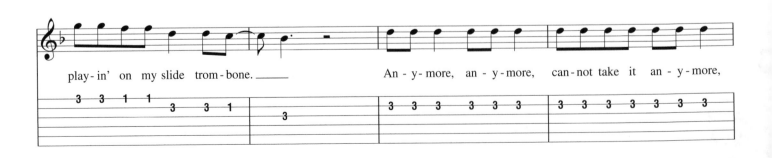

play - in' on my slide trom - bone. _____ An - y-more, an - y-more, can - not take it an - y-more,

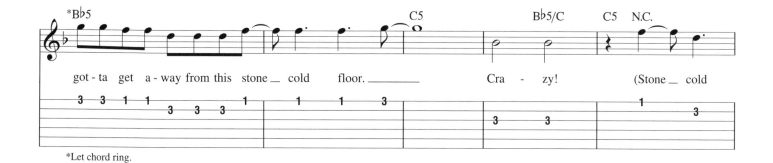

got-ta get a-way from this stone __ cold floor. _____ Cra - zy! (Stone __ cold

*Let chord ring.

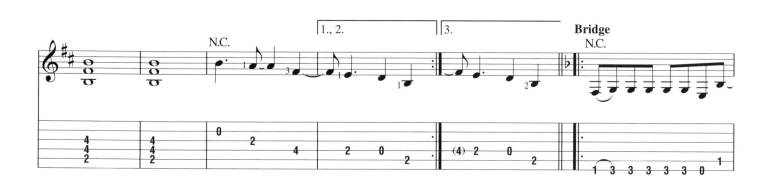

Guitar Solo

cra - zy, __ you know.)

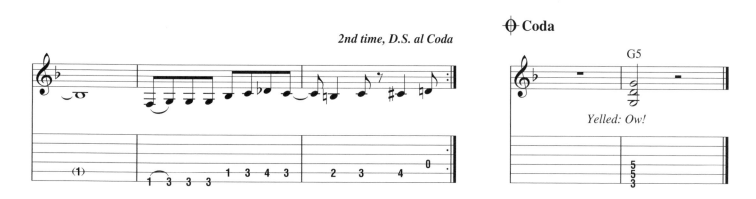

Bridge

2nd time, D.S. al Coda

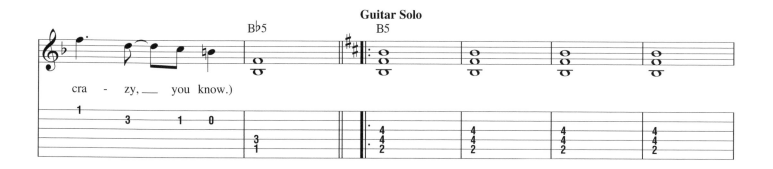

⊕ **Coda**

Yelled: Ow!

Additional Lyrics

3. Walkin' down the street,
   Shootin' people that I meet,
   With my rubber Tommy water gun.
   Here come the deputy,
   He's gonna come an' get me,
   I gotta get me, get up an' run.
   They got the sirens loose,
   I ran right out of juice.
   They're gonna put me in a cell.
   If I can't go to heaven,
   Will they let me go to hell?
   Crazy! (Stone cold crazy, you know.)

Sunshine of Your Love

Words and Music by Jack Bruce, Pete Brown and Eric Clapton

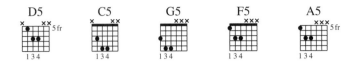

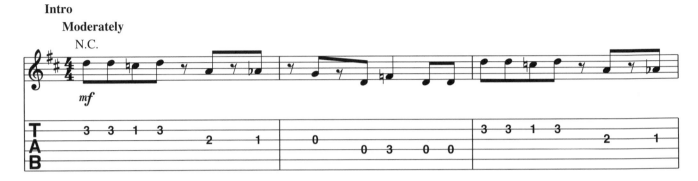

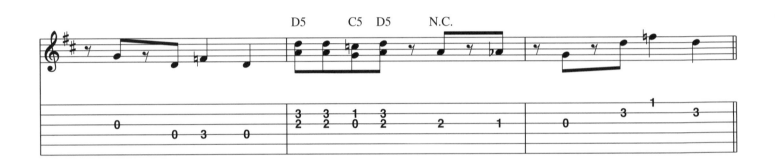

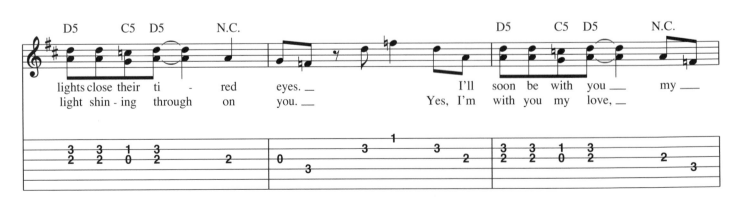

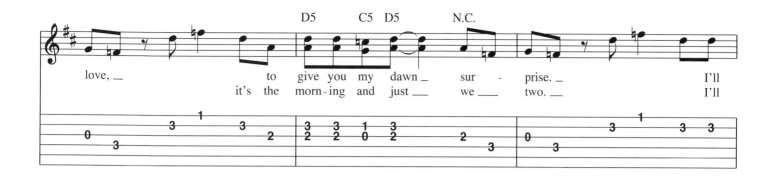

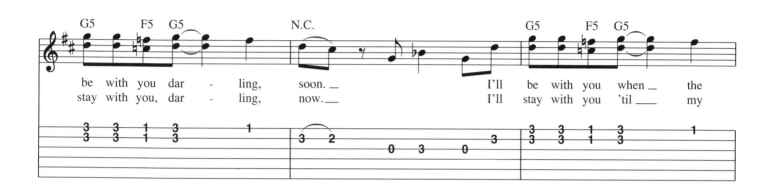

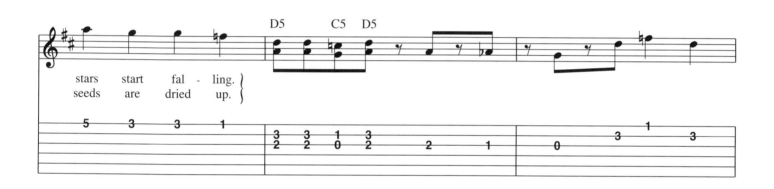

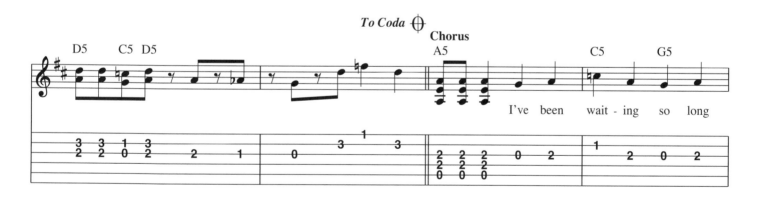

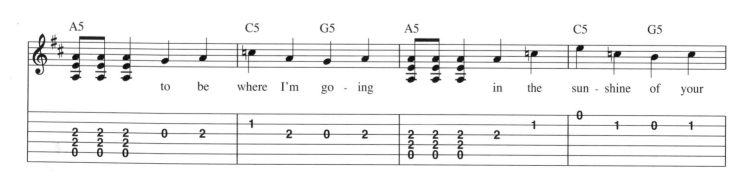

331

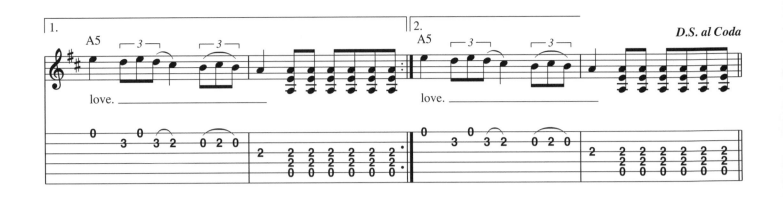

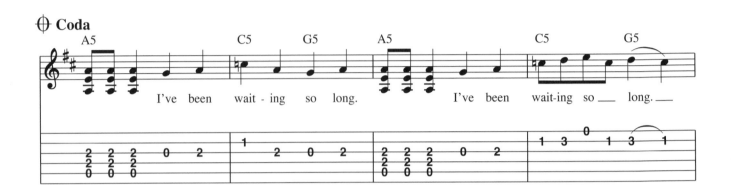

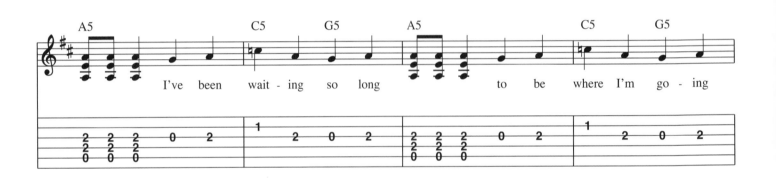

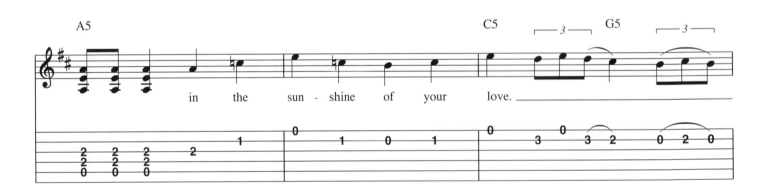

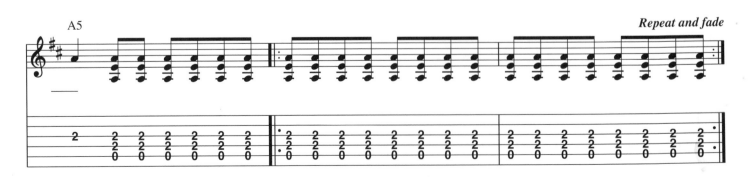

Talk Dirty to Me

Words and Music by Bobby Dall, C.C. Deville, Bret Michaels and Rikki Rockett

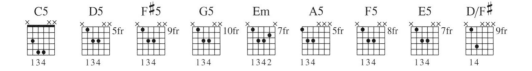

*Tune down 1/2 step:
(low to high) E♭-A♭-D♭-G♭-B♭-E♭

Strum Pattern: 1, 2
Pick Pattern: 4

Intro
Moderate Rock

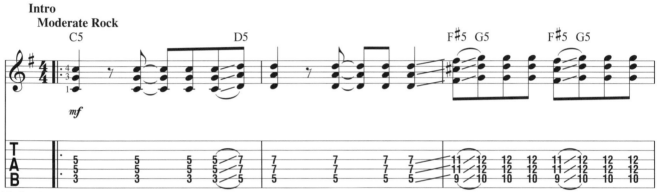

*Optional: To match recording, tune down 1/2 step.

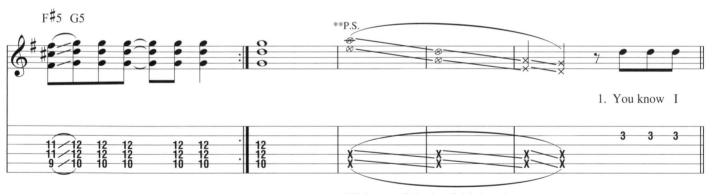

**Pick scrape: Rub edge of pick down the strings, producing a scratchy sound.

1. You know I

Verse

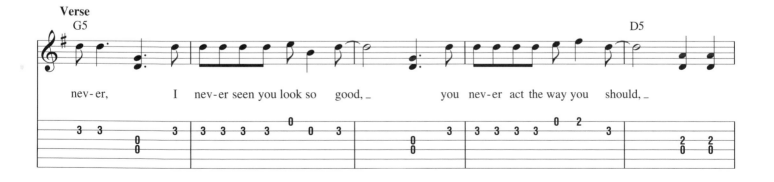

nev-er,   I nev-er seen you look so   good, _   you nev-er act the way you   should, _

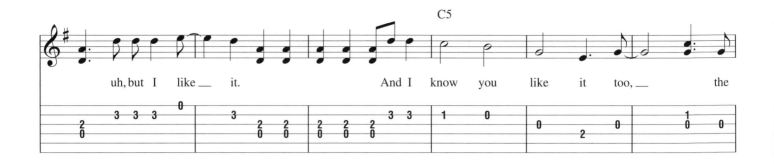

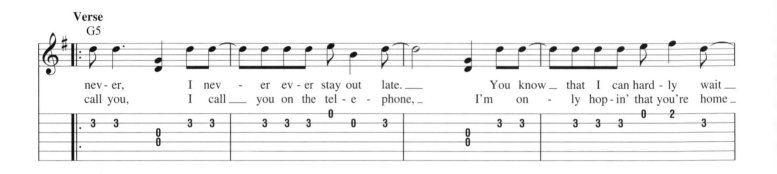

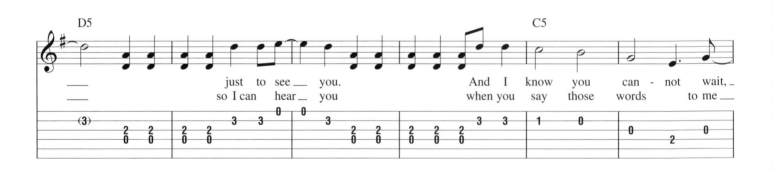

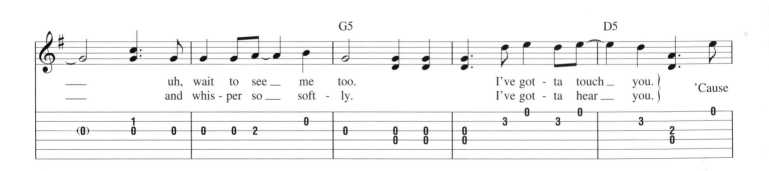

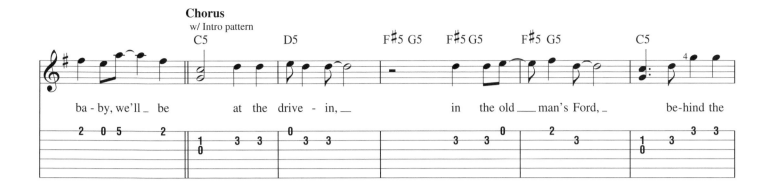

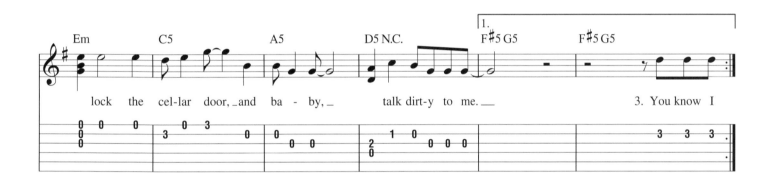

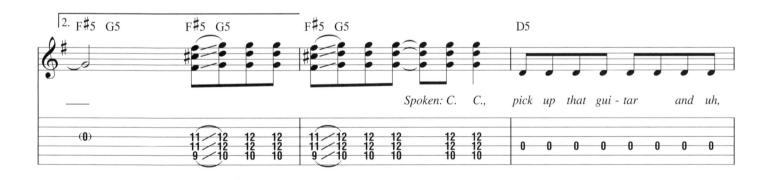

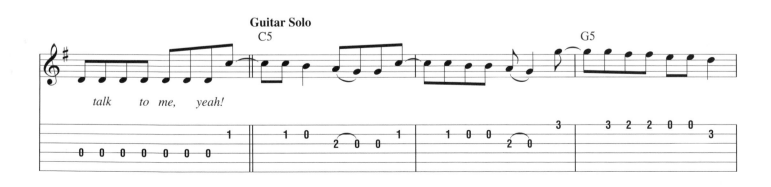

335

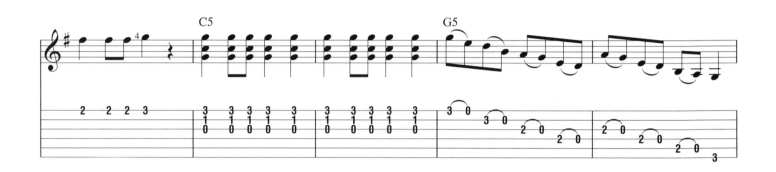

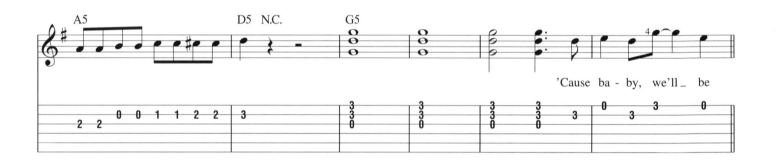

Chorus

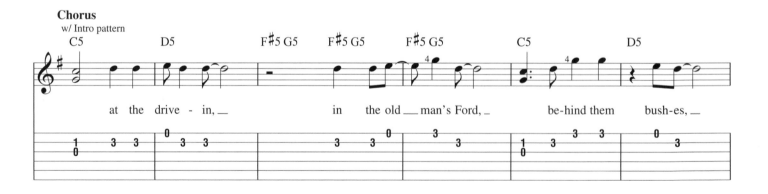

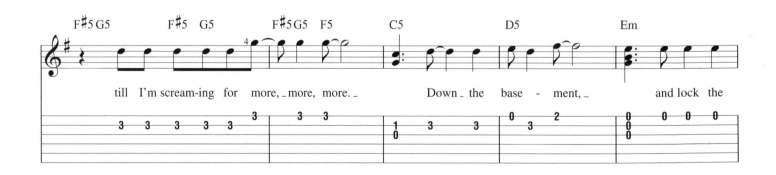

cel-lar door, _ and ba - by, _ talk dirt-y to me, _____ yeah. _ And ba - by, _

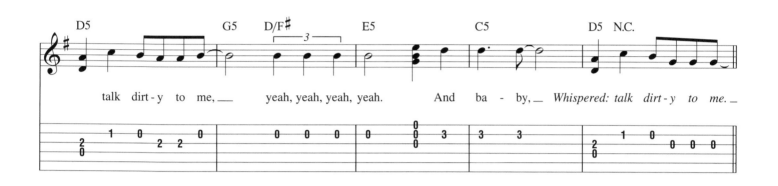

talk dirt-y to me, ___ yeah, yeah, yeah, yeah. And ba - by, _ *Whispered: talk dirt-y to me.* _

Outro

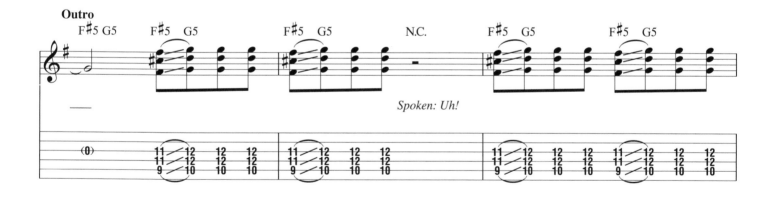

Spoken: Uh!

Whoo! ___ *Whispered: That's the way I like it, baby!* Ooh, yeah!

Tom Sawyer

Words by Neil Peart and Pye Dubois
Music by Geddy Lee and Alex Lifeson

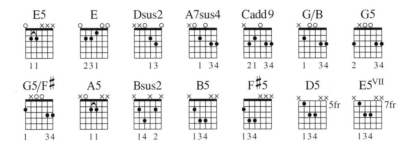

*Strum Pattern: 3, 4
*Pick Pattern: 1, 3

Intro
Moderately, in 2

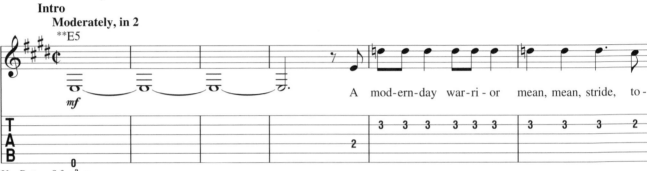

*Use Pattern 8 for ⅜ meas.
**Let chord ring for 8 meas.

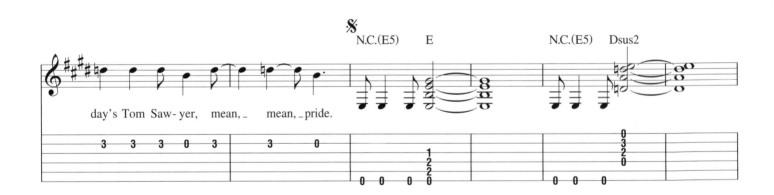

day's Tom Saw-yer, mean,_ mean,_ pride.

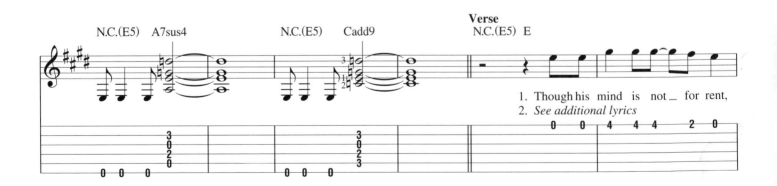

1. Though his mind is not _ for rent,
2. *See additional lyrics*

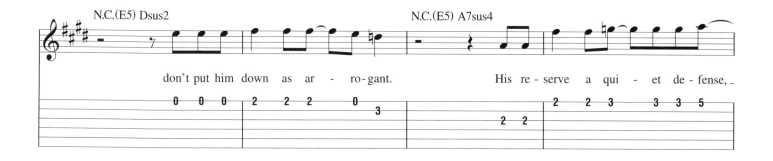

don't put him down as ar - ro-gant.   His re - serve a qui - et de - fense, _

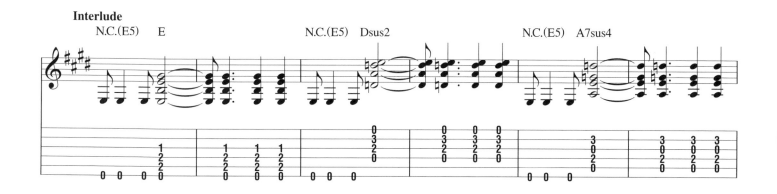

— rid - ing out the day's _ e - vents.   The riv - er.

Interlude

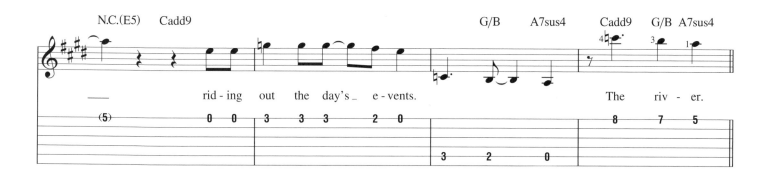

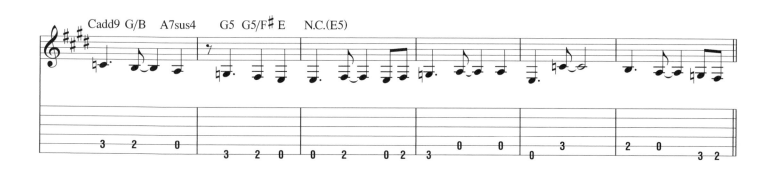

Pre-Chorus

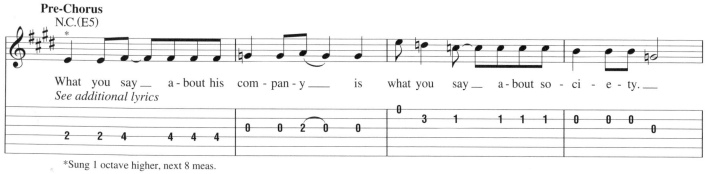

What you say _ a - bout his com - pan - y _____ is what you say _ a - bout so - ci - e - ty. ___
See additional lyrics

*Sung 1 octave higher, next 8 meas.

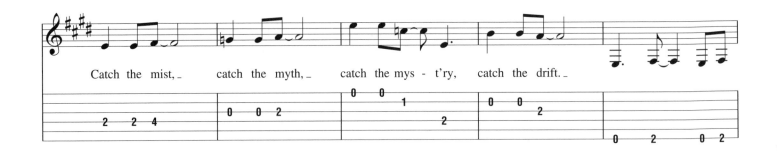

Catch the mist, _ catch the myth, _ catch the mys - t'ry, catch the drift. _

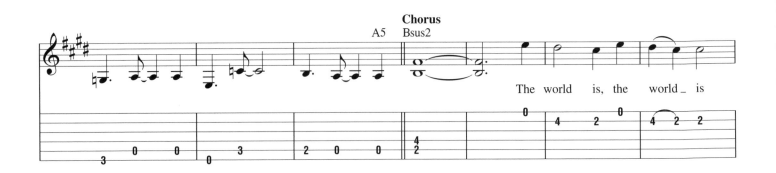

Chorus

A5   Bsus2

The world is, the world _ is

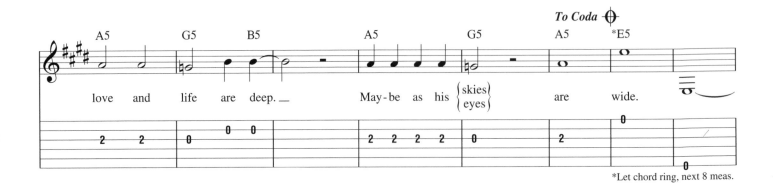

To Coda ⊕

A5   G5   B5   A5   G5   A5   *E5

love and life are deep. _ May-be as his {skies}/{eyes} are wide.

*Let chord ring, next 8 meas.

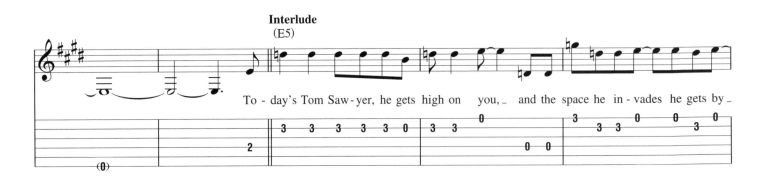

Interlude

(E5)

To - day's Tom Saw - yer, he gets high on you, _ and the space he in - vades he gets by _

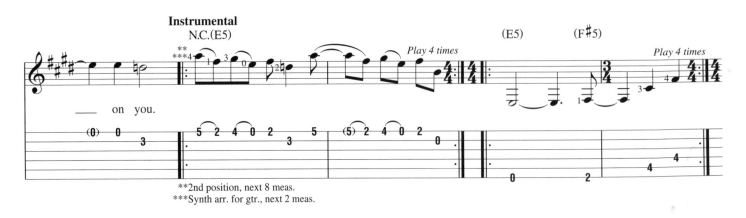

Instrumental

N.C.(E5)   (E5)   (F#5)

Play 4 times   *Play 4 times*

_ on you.

**2nd position, next 8 meas.
***Synth arr. for gtr., next 2 meas.

(E5)

Guitar Solo
*N.C.(E5)

*Bass arr. for gtr., next 20 meas.

A5   B5   D5

N.C.(E5)

(A5)

341

Coda

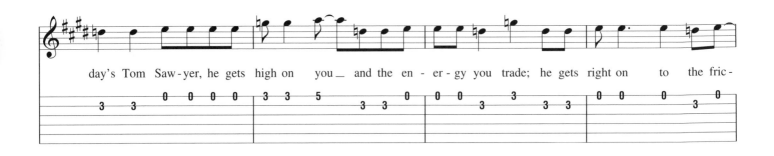

Let chord ring, next 10 meas.

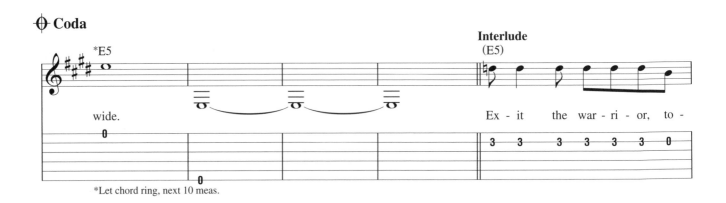

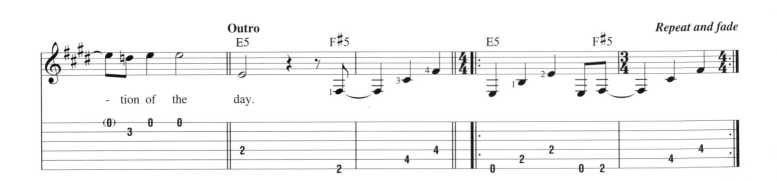

Additional Lyrics

2. No, his mind is not for rent
   To any god or government.
   Always hopeful, yet discontent.
   He knows changes aren't permanent,
   But change is.

Pre-Chorus And what you say about his company
   Is what you say about society.
   Catch the witness, catch the wit,
   Catch the spirit, catch the spit.

We're an American Band

Words and Music by Donald Brewer

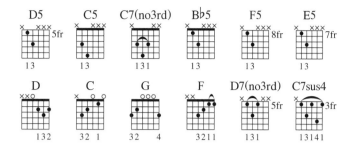

Strum Pattern: 3, 5
Pick Pattern: 1, 3

Intro
Moderate Rock

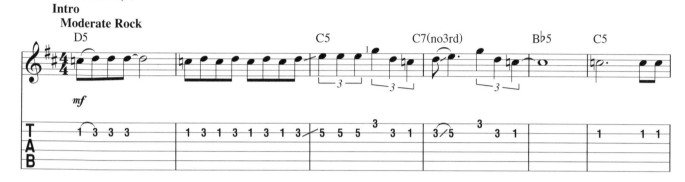

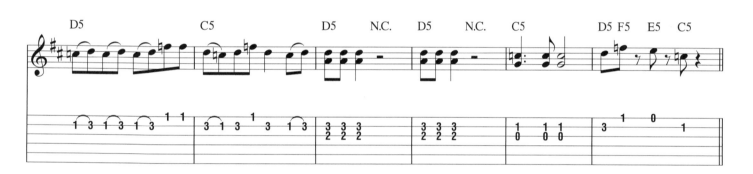

Verse

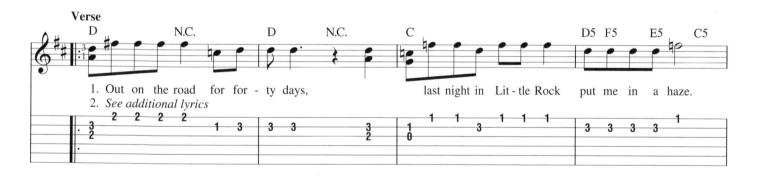

1. Out on the road for for-ty days,   last night in Lit-tle Rock   put me in a haze.
2. *See additional lyrics*

Sweet, sweet Con-nie   a   do-in' her act,   she   had the whole show, and that's a   nat-'ral fact.

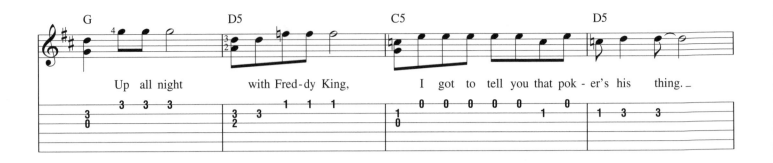

𝄋 Chorus

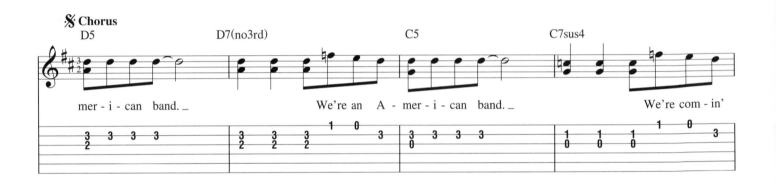

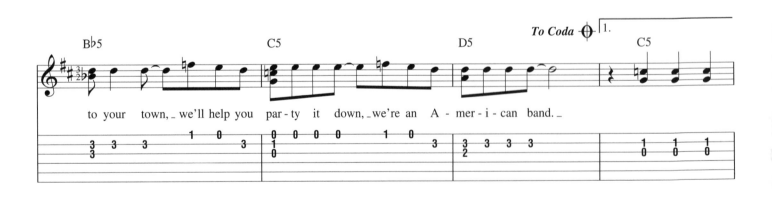

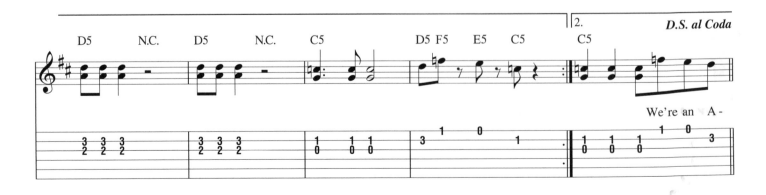

Additional Lyrics

2. Four young chiquitas in Omaha
   Waitin' for the band to return from the show.
   Feelin' good, feelin' right, it's Saturday night,
   The hotel detective, he was out of sight.
   Now, these fine ladies, they had a plan,
   They was out to meet the boys in the band.
   They said, "Come on, dudes, let's get it on,"
   And we proceeded to tear that hotel down.

Turn Up the Radio

Words and Music by Steve Isham, Steve Lynch, Steven Plunkett, Randy Rand and Keni Richards

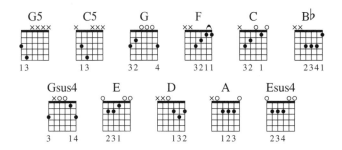

*Tune down 1/2 step:
(low to high) E♭-A♭-D♭-G♭-B♭-E♭

Strum Pattern: 1, 2
Pick Pattern: 2, 3

Intro
Moderately

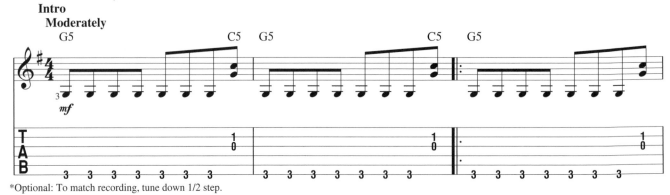

*Optional: To match recording, tune down 1/2 step.

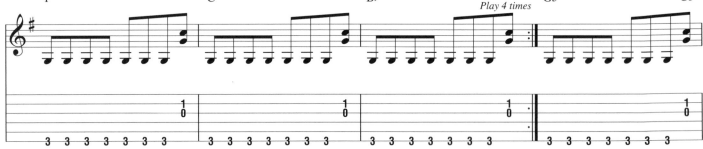

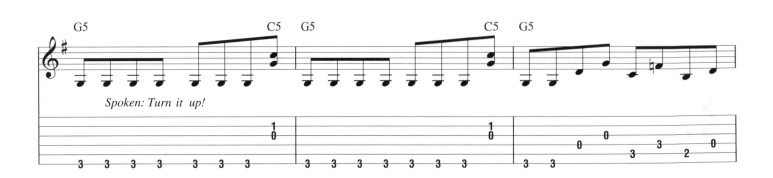

Spoken: Turn it up!

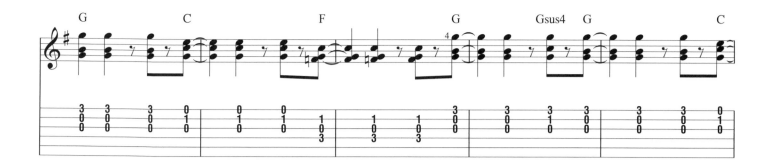

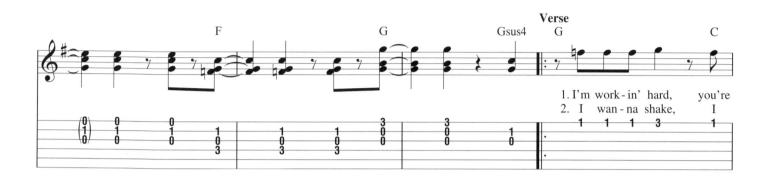

1. I'm work-in' hard,   you're
2. I wan-na shake,   I

work-in' too,   we do it ev - 'ry day. ___
wan - na dance,   so count it off, a one, two   three... ___

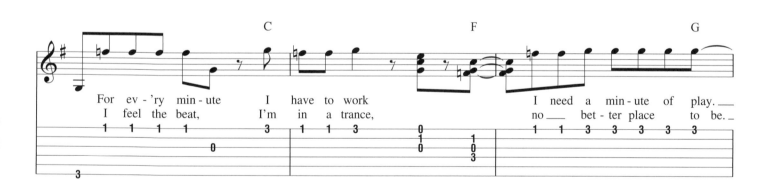

For ev - 'ry min - ute   I have to work   I need a min - ute of play. ___
I feel the beat,   I'm in a trance,   no ___ bet - ter place   to be. _

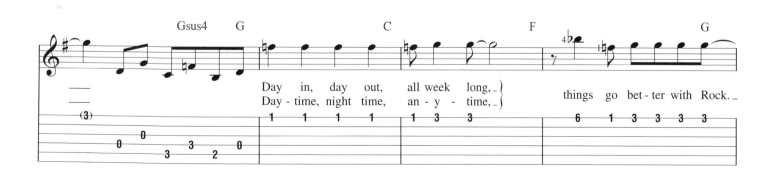

___   Day in, day out,   all week long, _
___   Day - time, night time, an - y - time, _   things go bet - ter with Rock. _

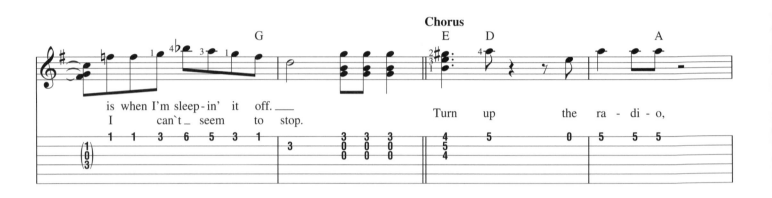

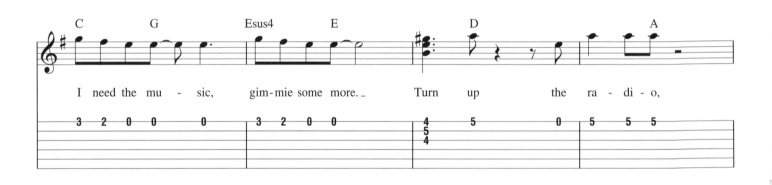

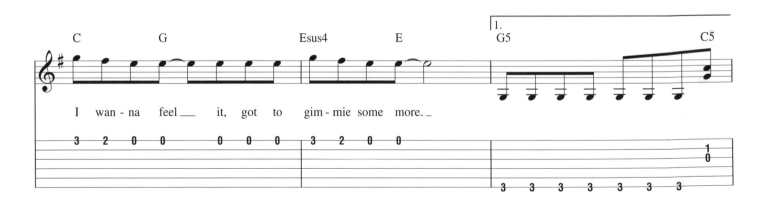

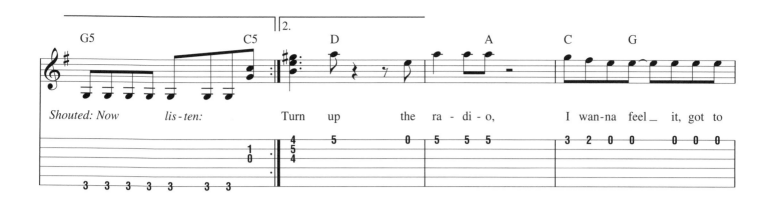

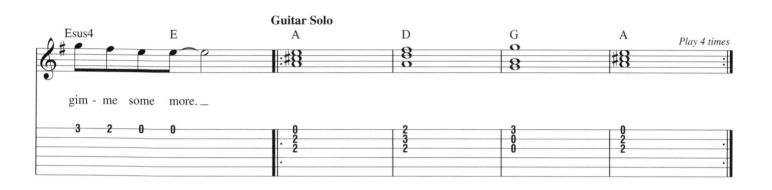

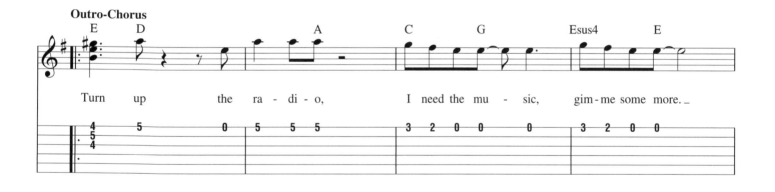

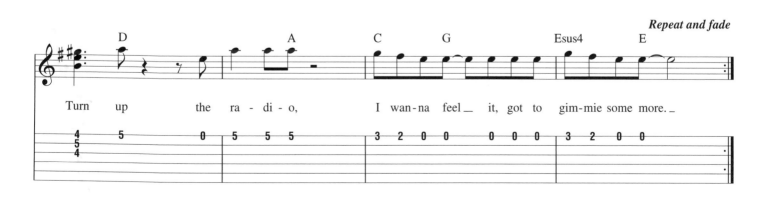

Tush

Words and Music by Billy F Gibbons, Dusty Hill and Frank Lee Beard

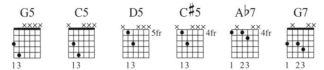

Strum Pattern: 1

Intro

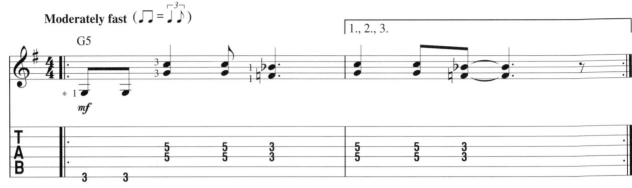

*Optional; Thumb on 6th string

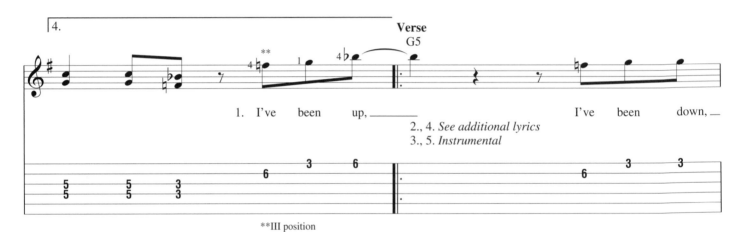

1. I've been up, _____ I've been down, _____

2., 4. *See additional lyrics*
3., 5. *Instrumental*

**III position

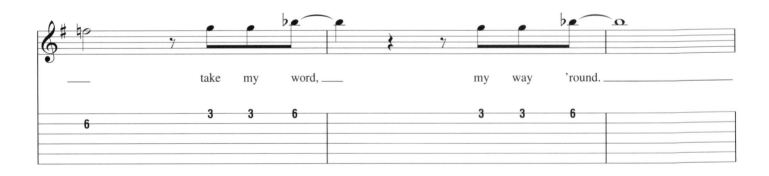

_____ take my word, _____ my way 'round. _____

_____ I ain't ask - ing for much. _____

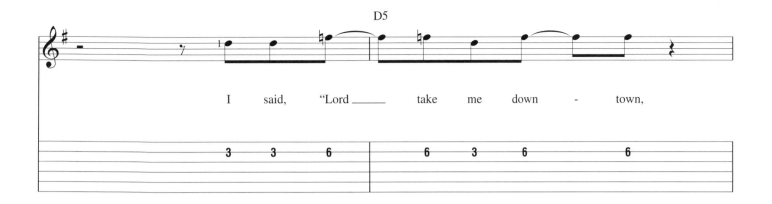

I said, "Lord _____ take me down - town,

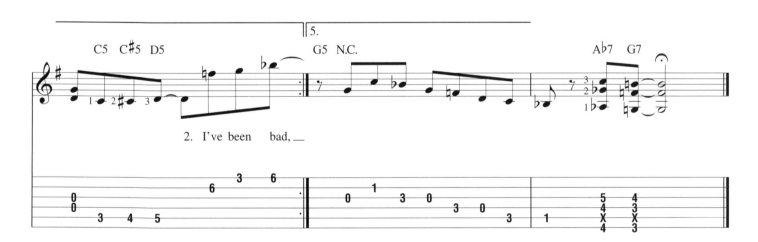

I'm just look - ing for some tush." ___

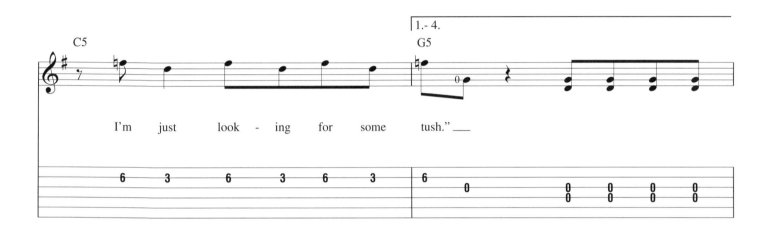

2. I've been bad, __

Additional Lyrics

2. I've been bad,
   I've been good,
   Dallas, Texas, Hollywood.
   I ain't asking for much.
   I said, "Lord take me downtown,
   I'm just looking for some tush."

4. Take me back,
   Way back home,
   Not by myself, not alone.
   I ain't asking for much.
   I said, "Lord take me downtown,
   I'm just looking for some tush."

Walk This Way

Words and Music by Steven Tyler and Joe Perry

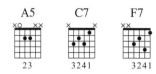

Strum Pattern: 2
Pick Pattern: 3

Intro
Moderate Rock, in 2

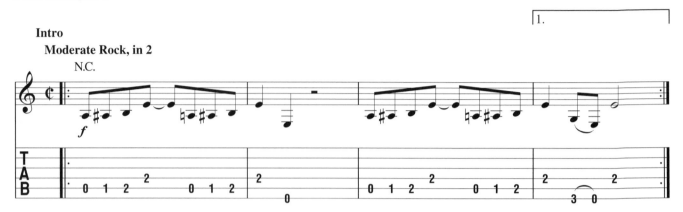

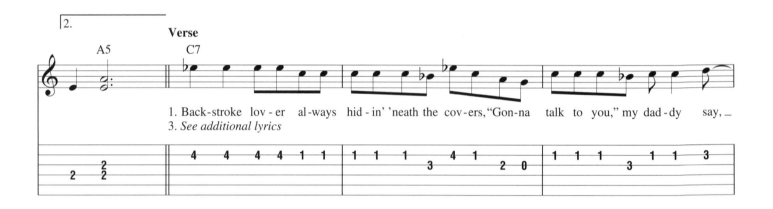

1. Back-stroke lov-er al-ways hid-in' 'neath the cov-ers, "Gon-na talk to you," my dad-dy say,—
3. *See additional lyrics*

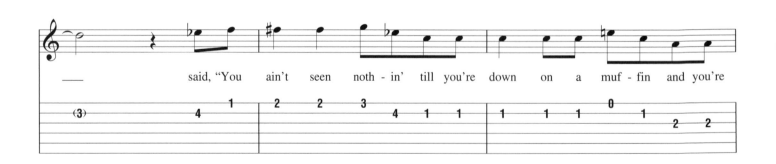

— said, "You ain't seen noth-in' till you're down on a muf-fin and you're

sure to be a-chang-in' your ways." ____ I met a cheer-lead-er, was a

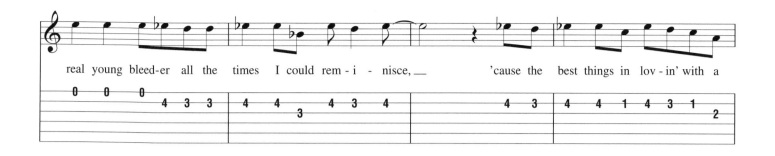

real young bleed-er all the times I could rem - i - nisce, ___ 'cause the best things in lov - in' with a

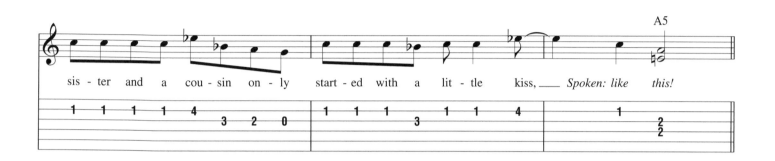

A5

sis - ter and a cou - sin on - ly start - ed with a lit - tle kiss, ___ *Spoken: like this!*

Interlude

N.C.

1.

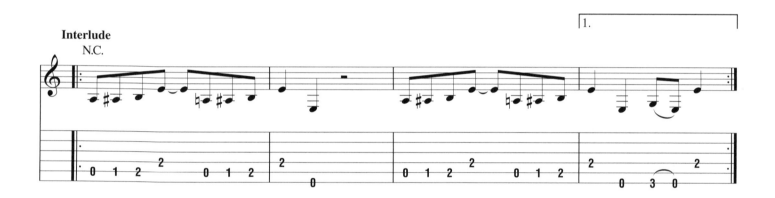

2.

A5   **Verse**

C7

2., 4. See - saw swing - in' with the boys in the school and your

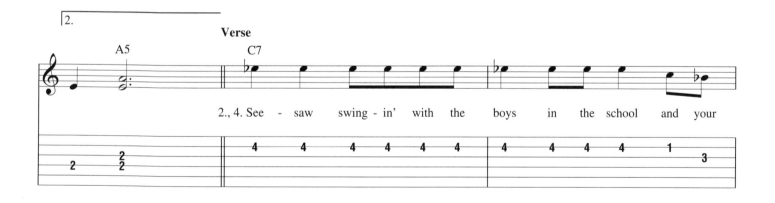

feet fly - in' up in the air, ___ I sing, "Hey did - dle did - dle" with your

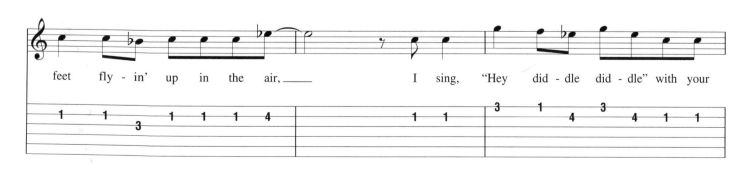

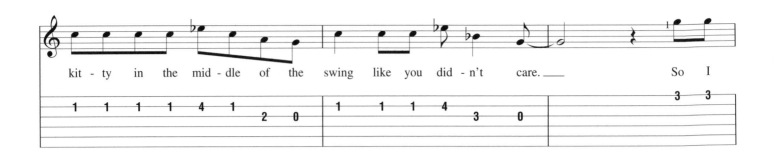

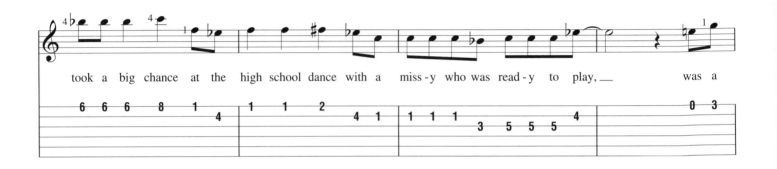

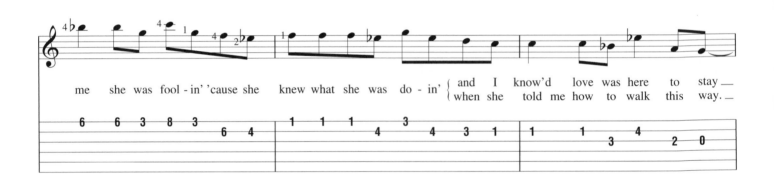

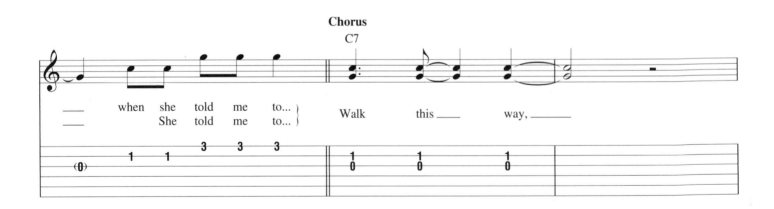

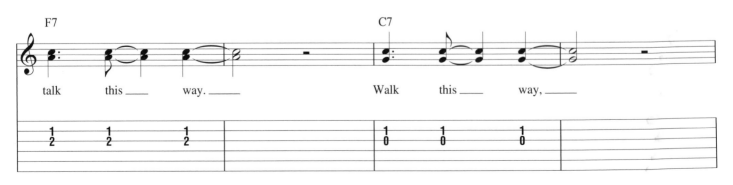

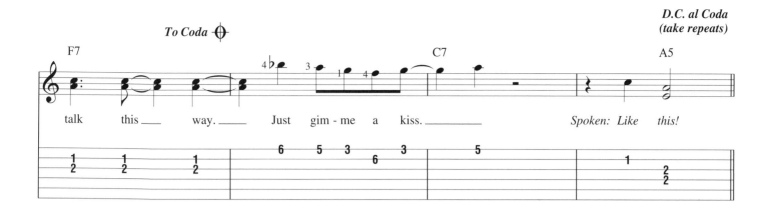

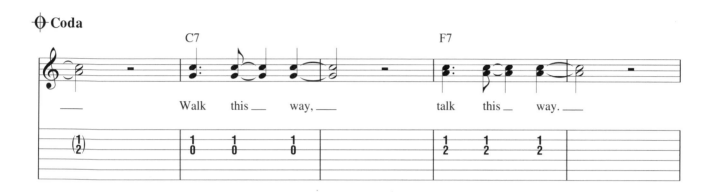

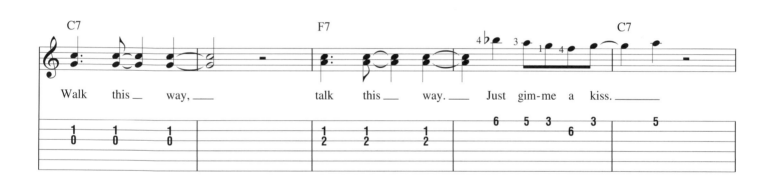

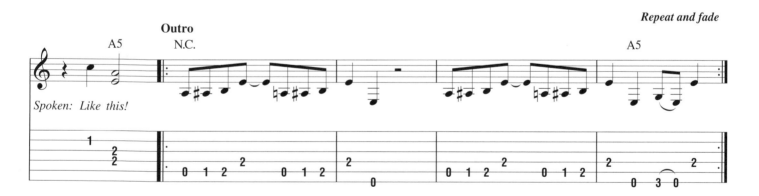

Additional Lyrics

3. School girl skinny with a classy kinda sassy
   Little skirt's climbin' way up her knee,
   There was three young ladies in the school gym locker
   When I noticed they was lookin' at me.
   I was a high school loser, never made it with a lady
   'Til the boys told me somethin' I missed,
   Then my next door neighbor with a daughter had a favor
   So I gave her just a little kiss, like this!

Welcome to the Jungle

Words and Music by W. Axl Rose, Slash, Izzy Stradlin', Duff McKagan and Steven Adler

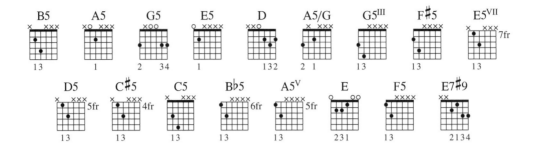

*Tune down 1/2 step:
(low to high) E♭-A♭-D♭-G♭-B♭-E♭

Strum Pattern: 1, 2

Pick Pattern: 2, 4

Intro
Moderate Rock, in 2

*Optional: To match recording, tune down 1/2 step.

**Let chords ring, next 16 meas.

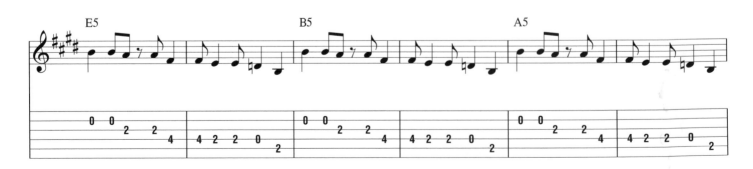

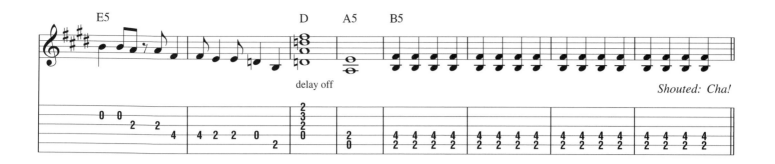

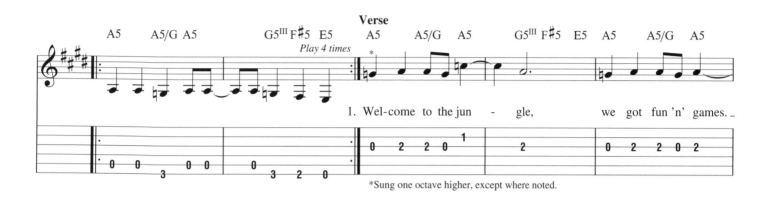

*Sung one octave higher, except where noted.

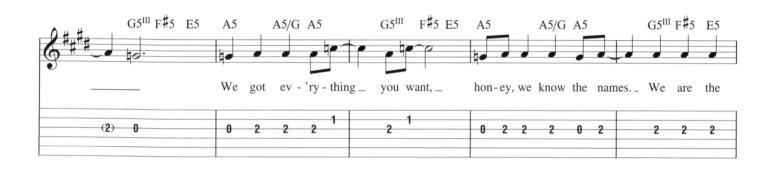

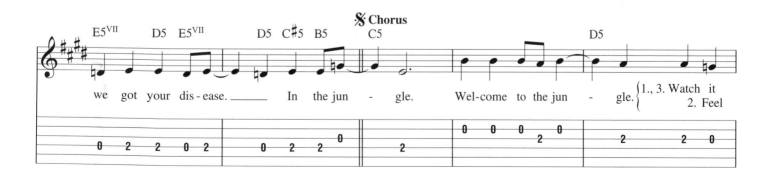

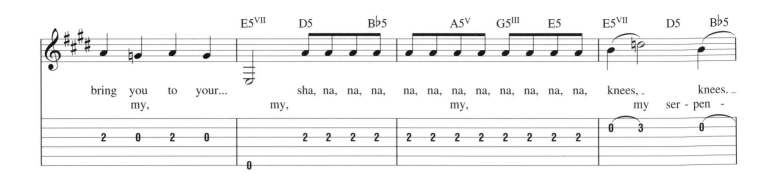

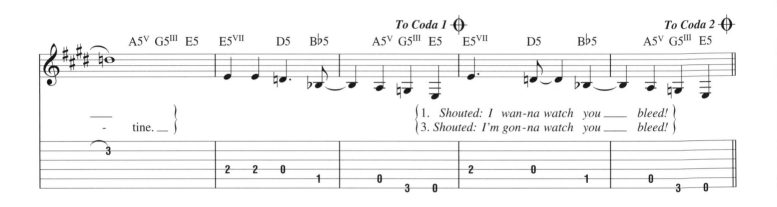

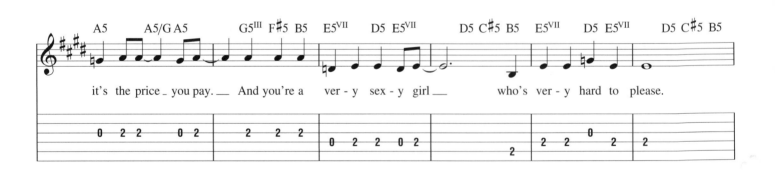

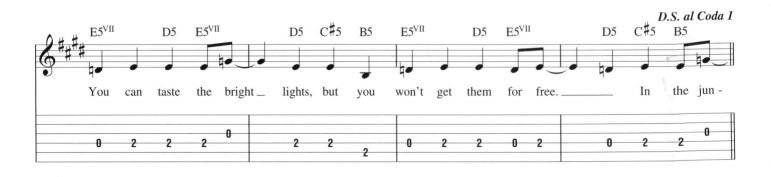

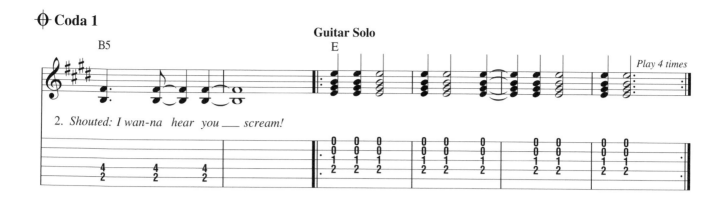

Coda 1

Guitar Solo

2. *Shouted: I wan-na hear you ___ scream!*

Verse

3. Wel-come to the jun - gle, it gets worse here ev-'ry day. ___ You learn to live_ like an

an - i - mal,_ in the jun - gle where we play. ___ If you got a hun-ger for what you see, ___ you'll

take it e - ven - tu'l-ly. ___ You can have an-y-thing you want,_ but you bet-ter not take it from me. ___

Coda 2

D.S. al Coda 2

Bridge

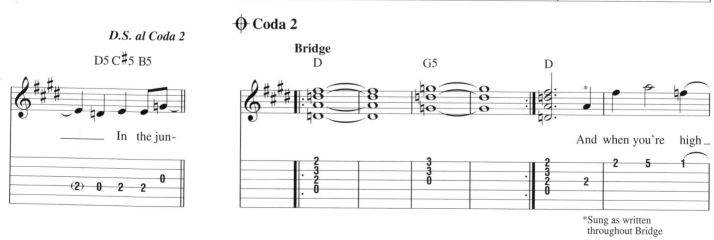

___ In the jun-

And when you're high_

*Sung as written throughout Bridge

you nev - er   ev - er want to come down, _____   so down, _

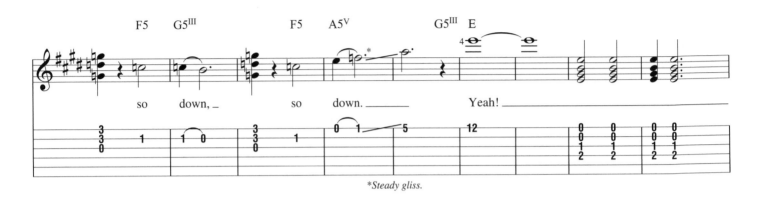

so down, _   so down. _____   Yeah! _____

Steady gliss.

Guitar Solo

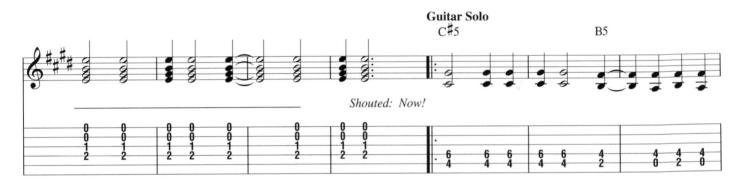

Shouted: Now!

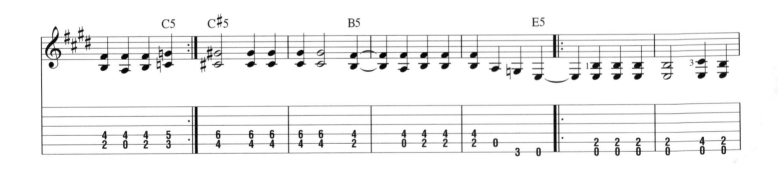

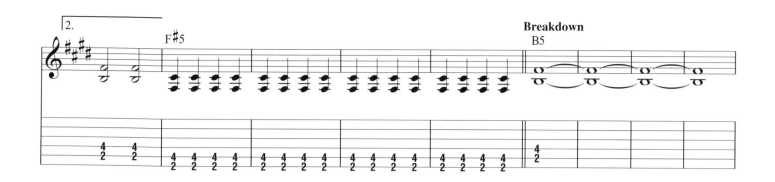

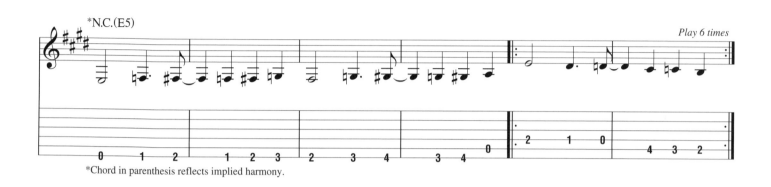

*Chord in parenthesis reflects implied harmony.

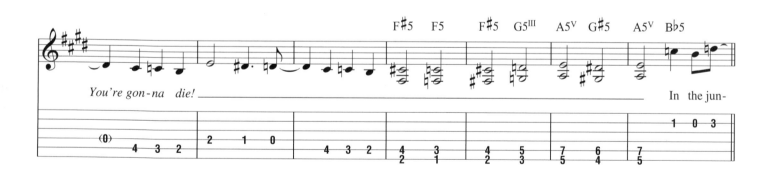

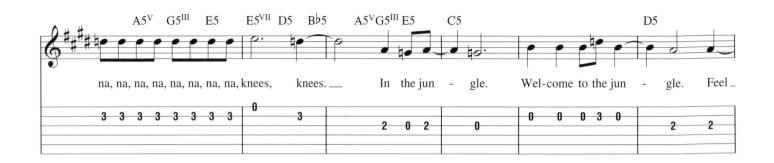

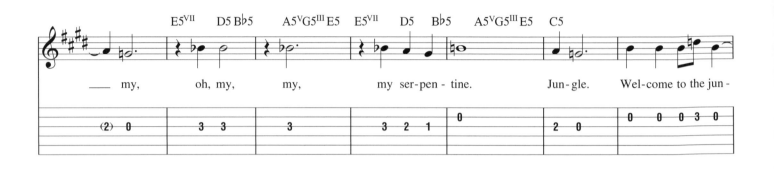

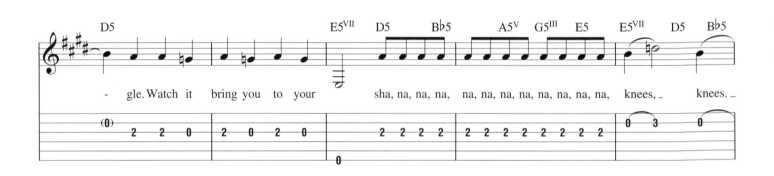

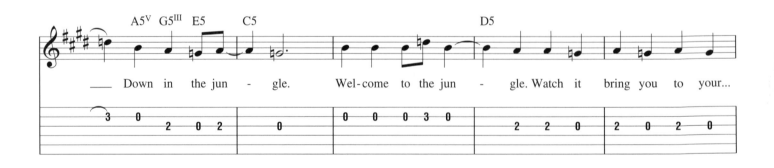

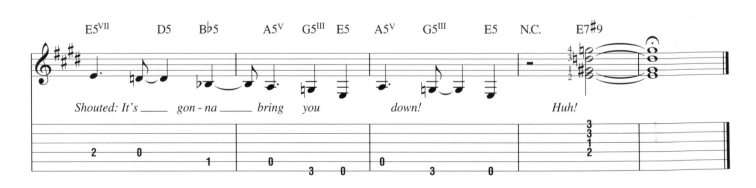

You Give Love a Bad Name

Words and Music by Jon Bon Jovi, Desmond Child and Richie Sambora

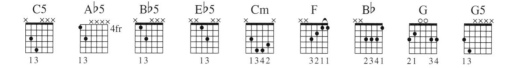

Strum Pattern: 5, 6

Intro
Moderately

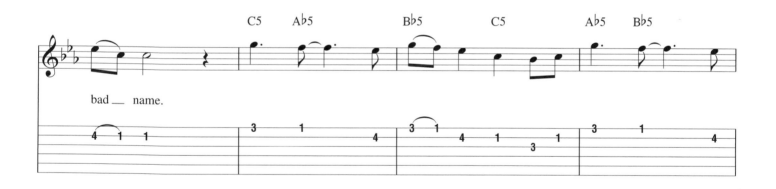

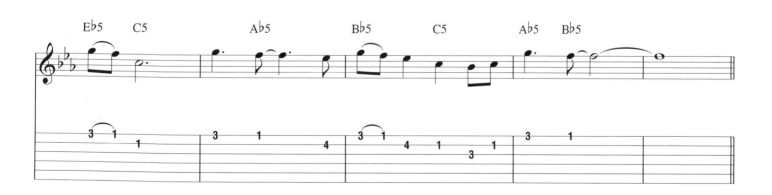

Verse

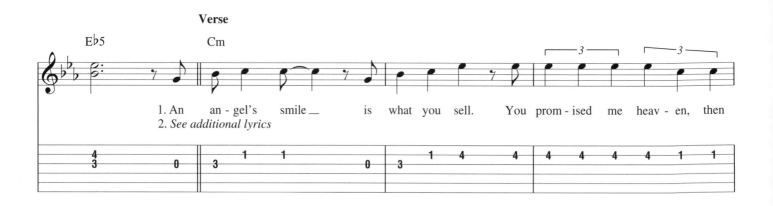

1. An an - gel's smile ___ is what you sell. You prom - ised me heav - en, then
2. *See additional lyrics*

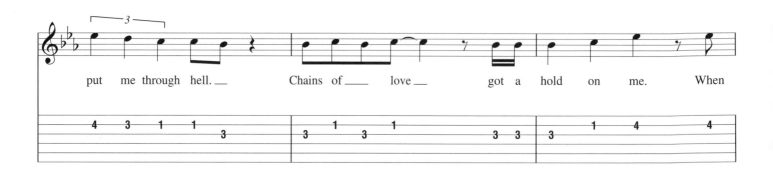

put me through hell. ___ Chains of ___ love ___ got a hold on me. When

Pre-Chorus

pas - sion's a pris - on you can't break ___ free. Whoa, ___ you're a load - ed gun. ___

Whoa, _____ there's no - where to run.

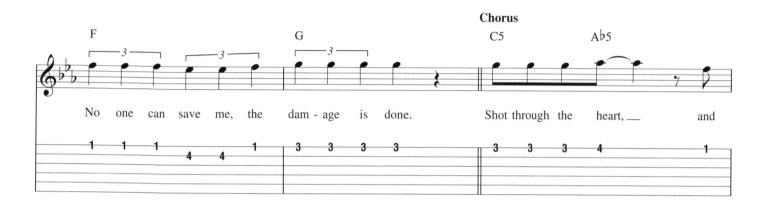

Chorus

No one can save me, the dam - age is done. Shot through the heart, _____ and

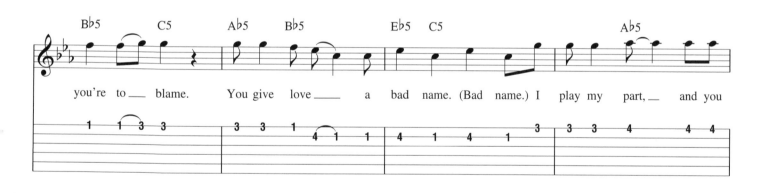

you're to _____ blame. You give love _____ a bad name. (Bad name.) I play my part, _____ and you

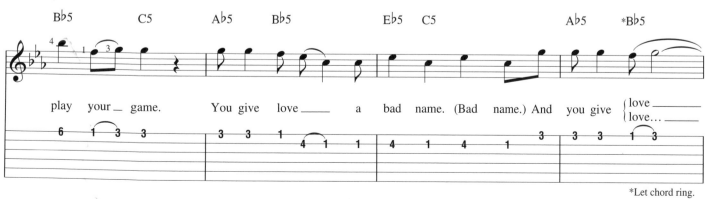

play your _____ game. You give love _____ a bad name. (Bad name.) And you give {love _____ {love...

*Let chord ring.

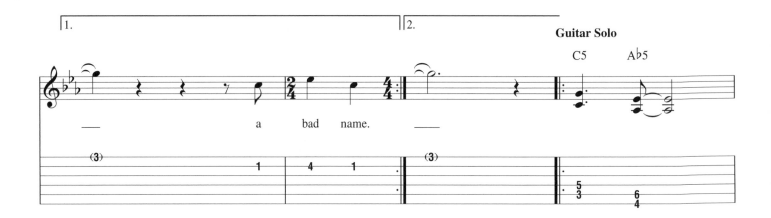

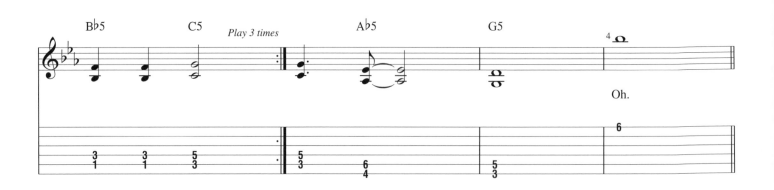

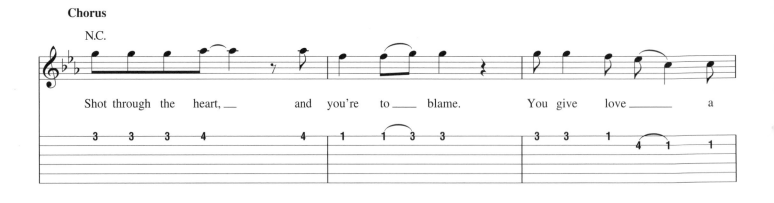

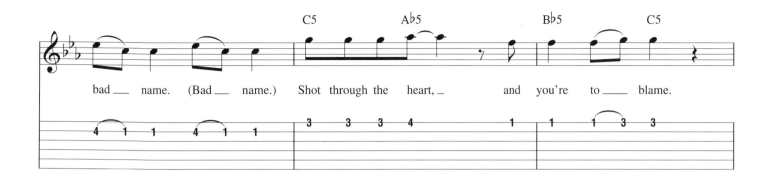

bad __ name. (Bad __ name.) Shot through the heart, __ and you're to __ blame.

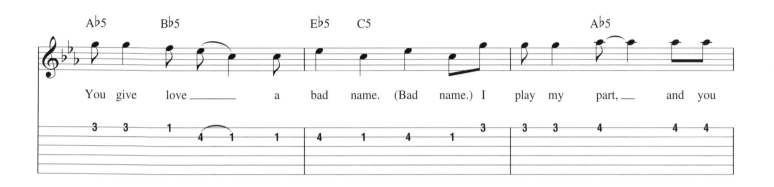

You give love _____ a bad name. (Bad __ name.) I play my part, __ and you

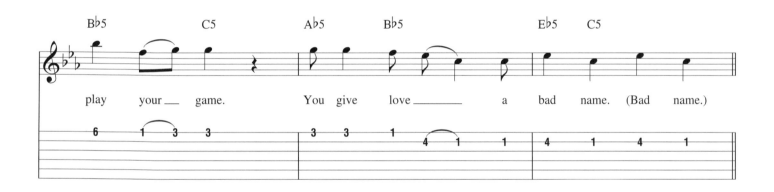

play your _ game. You give love _____ a bad name. (Bad __ name.)

Outro

Repeat and fade

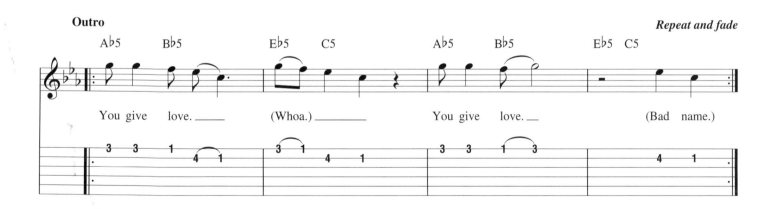

You give love. ____ (Whoa.) _____ You give love. __ (Bad name.)

Additional Lyrics

2. You paint your smile on your lips,
Blood-red nails on your fingertips.
A school boy's dream, you act so shy.
Your very first kiss was your first kiss goodbye.

Won't Get Fooled Again

Words and Music by Peter Townshend

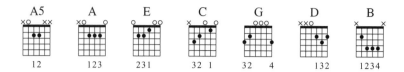

Strum Pattern: 5
Pick Pattern: 1

Intro
Moderately fast

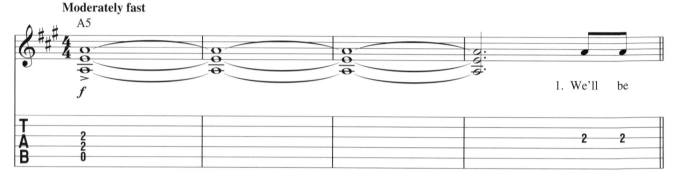

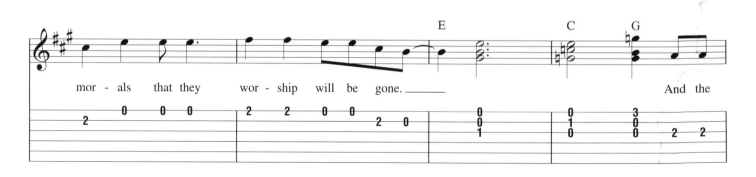

men who spurred us on _____ sit in judge-ment of all wrong, they de-

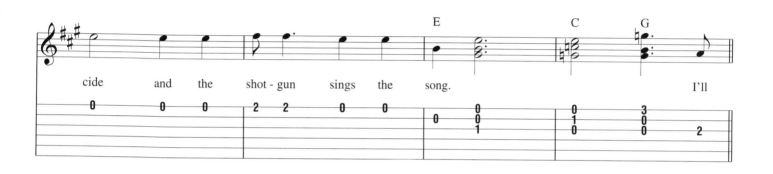

cide and the shot-gun sings the song. I'll

Chorus

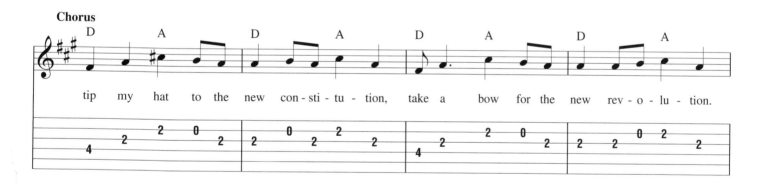

tip my hat to the new con-sti-tu-tion, take a bow for the new rev-o-lu-tion.

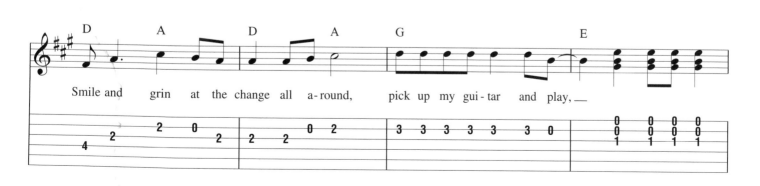

Smile and grin at the change all a-round, pick up my gui-tar and play, ___

just like yes - ter - day, ___ then I'll get on my knees and pray

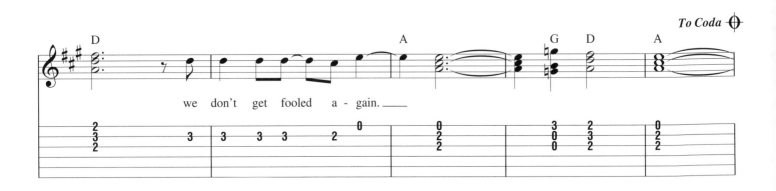

To Coda

we don't get fooled a - gain. ___

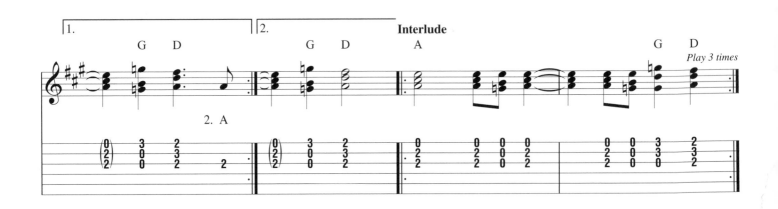

Interlude

Play 3 times

Bridge

I'll move my - self and my fam-'ly a - side, ___

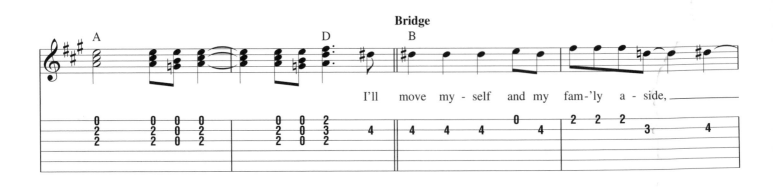

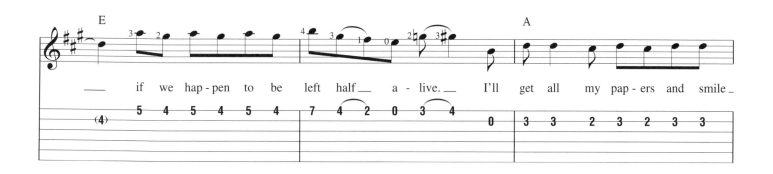

if we hap-pen to be left half __ a - live. __ I'll get all my pap-ers and smile __

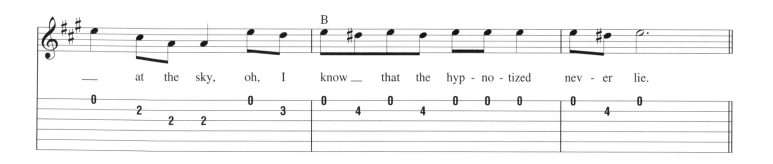

__ at the sky, oh, I know __ that the hyp-no-tized nev-er lie.

Interlude

D.S. al Coda

Play 4 times

Play 3 times

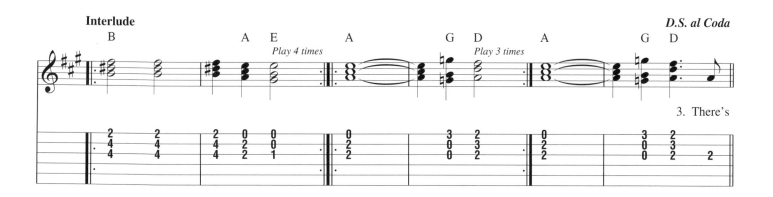

3. There's

$\oplus$ **Coda**

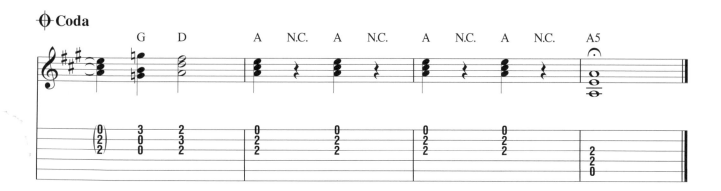

Additional Lyrics

2. A change, it had to come.
   We knew it all along.
   We were liberated from the fold, that's all.
   And the world looks just the same,
   And history ain't changed,
   'Cause the banners, they are flown in the last war.

3. There's nothing in the street
   Looks any different to me,
   And the slogans are replaced by the by.
   And the parting on the left
   Is now parting on the right,
   And the beards have all grown longer overnight.

Would?

Written by Jerry Cantrell

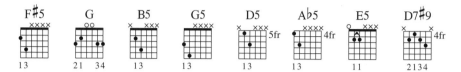

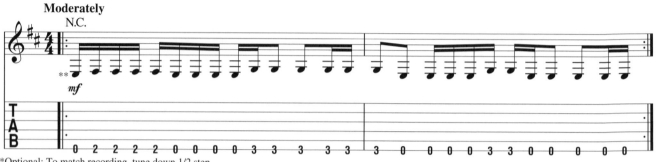

*Tune down 1/2 step:
(low to high) E♭-A♭-D♭-G♭-B♭-E♭

Strum Pattern: 2, 6
Pick Pattern: 1, 6

Intro
Moderately
N.C.

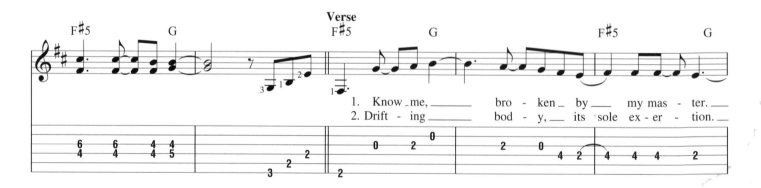

*Optional: To match recording, tune down 1/2 step.
**Bass arr. for gtr., next 2 meas.

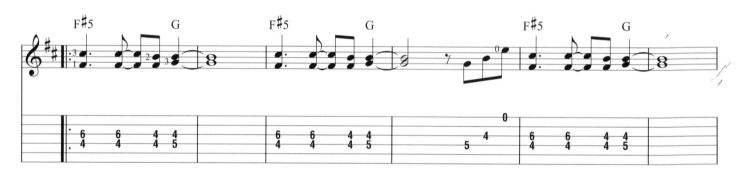

Verse

1. Know me, broken by my mas-ter.
2. Drift-ing bod-y, its sole ex-er-tion.

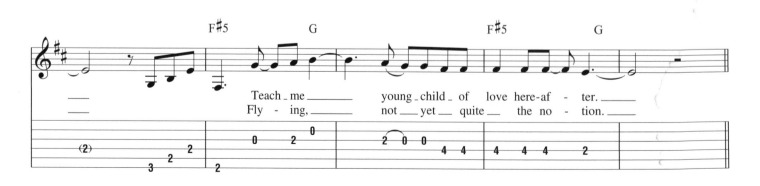

Teach me young child of love here-af-ter.
Fly-ing, not yet quite the no-tion.

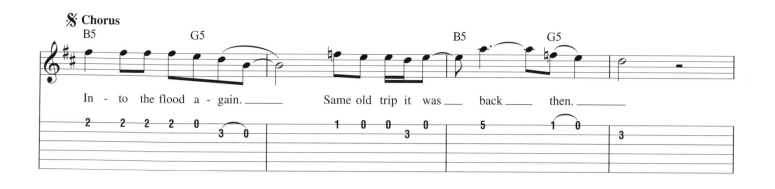

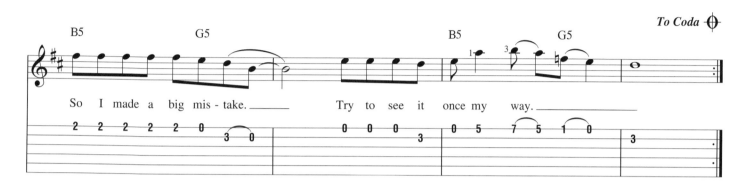

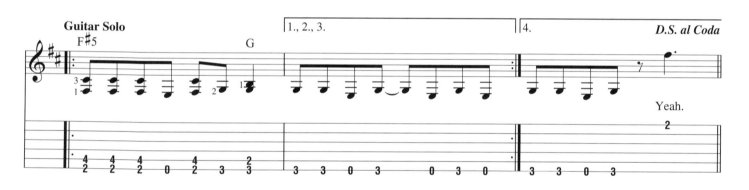

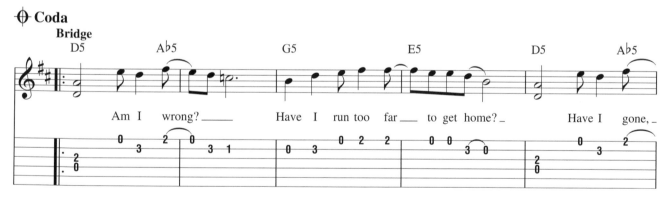

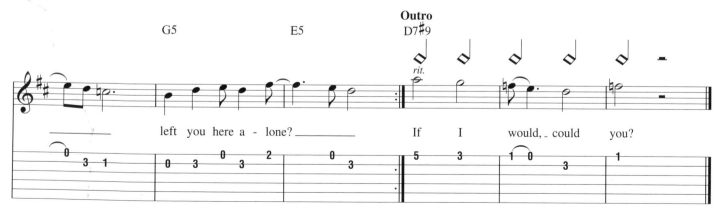

You Really Got Me

Words and Music by Ray Davies

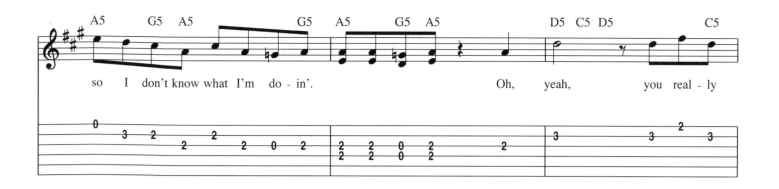

so I don't know what I'm do - in'. Oh, yeah, you real - ly

got me now. You got me so I can't sleep at night. You real - ly got me. You

real - ly got me. You real - ly got me.

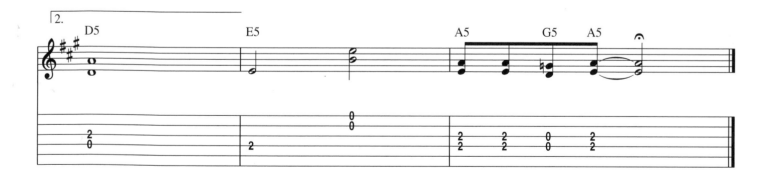

Additional Lyrics

2. See, don't ever set me free.
I always want to be by your side.
Yeah, you really got me now.
You got me so I can't sleep at night.

EASY GUITAR
WITH NOTES & TAB

This series features simplified arrangements with notes, tab, chord charts, and strum and pick patterns.

MIXED FOLIOS

00702002	Acoustic Rock Hits for Easy Guitar	$12.95
00702166	All-Time Best Guitar Collection	$19.99
00699665	Beatles Best	$12.95
00702232	Best Acoustic Songs for Easy Guitar	$12.99
00702233	Best Hard Rock Songs	$14.99
00698978	Big Christmas Collection	$16.95
00702115	Blues Classics	$10.95
00385020	Broadway Songs for Kids	$9.95
00702237	Christian Acoustic Favorites	$12.95
00702149	Children's Christian Songbook	$7.95
00702028	Christmas Classics	$7.95
00702185	Christmas Hits	$9.95
00702016	Classic Blues for Easy Guitar	$12.95
00702141	Classic Rock	$8.95
00702203	CMT's 100 Greatest Country Songs	$27.95
00702170	Contemporary Christian Christmas	$9.95
00702006	Contemporary Christian Favorites	$9.95
00702065	Contemporary Women of Country	$9.95
00702121	Country from the Heart	$9.95
00702240	Country Hits of 2007-2008	$12.95
00702225	Country Hits of '06-'07	$12.95
00702085	Disney Movie Hits	$12.95
00702257	Easy Acoustic Guitar Songs	$14.99
00702212	Essential Christmas	$9.95
00702041	Favorite Hymns for Easy Guitar	$9.95
00702174	God Bless America® & Other Songs for a Better Nation	$8.95
00699374	Gospel Favorites	$14.95
00702160	The Great American Country Songbook	$14.95
00702050	Great Classical Themes for Easy Guitar	$6.95
00702131	Great Country Hits of the '90s	$8.95
00702116	Greatest Hymns for Guitar	$8.95
00702130	The Groovy Years	$9.95
00702184	Guitar Instrumentals	$9.95
00702231	High School Musical for Easy Guitar	$12.95
00702241	High School Musical 2	$12.95
00702249	High School Musical 3	$12.99
00702037	Hits of the '50s for Easy Guitar	$10.95
00702046	Hits of the '70s for Easy Guitar	$8.95
00702032	International Songs for Easy Guitar	$12.95
00702051	Jock Rock for Easy Guitar	$9.95
00702162	Jumbo Easy Guitar Songbook	$19.95
00702112	Latin Favorites	$9.95
00702258	Legends of Rock	$14.99
00702138	Mellow Rock Hits	$10.95
00702147	Motown's Greatest Hits	$9.95
00702039	Movie Themes	$10.95
00702210	Best of MTV Unplugged	$12.95
00702189	MTV's 100 Greatest Pop Songs	$24.95
00702272	1950s Rock	$14.99
00702271	1960s Rock	$14.99
00702270	1970s Rock	$14.99
00702269	1980s Rock	$14.99
00702268	1990s Rock	$14.99
00702187	Selections from O Brother Where Art Thou?	$12.95
00702178	100 Songs for Kids	$12.95
00702158	Songs from Passion	$9.95
00702125	Praise and Worship for Guitar	$9.95
00702155	Rock Hits for Guitar	$9.95
00702242	Rock Band	$19.95
00702256	Rock Band 2	$19.99
00702128	Rockin' Down the Highway	$9.95
00702207	Smash Hits for Guitar	$9.95
00702110	The Sound of Music	$9.99
00702124	Today's Christian Rock – 2nd Edition	$9.95
00702220	Today's Country Hits	$9.95
00702198	Today's Hits for Guitar	$9.95
00702217	Top Christian Hits	$12.95
00702235	Top Christian Hits of '07-'08	$14.95
00702246	Top Hits of 2008	$12.95
00702206	Very Best of Rock	$9.95
00702175	VH1's 100 Greatest Songs of Rock and Roll	$24.95
00702253	Wicked	$12.99
00702192	Worship Favorites	$9.95

ARTIST COLLECTIONS

00702267	AC/DC for Easy Guitar	$14.99
00702001	Best of Aerosmith	$16.95
00702040	Best of the Allman Brothers	$12.95
00702169	Best of The Beach Boys	$10.95
00702201	The Essential Black Sabbath	$12.95
00702140	Best of Brooks & Dunn	$10.95
00702095	Best of Mariah Carey	$12.95
00702043	Best of Johnny Cash	$12.95
00702033	Best of Steven Curtis Chapman	$14.95
00702263	Best of Casting Crowns	$12.99
00702090	Eric Clapton's Best	$10.95
00702086	Eric Clapton – from the Album Unplugged	$10.95
00702202	The Essential Eric Clapton	$12.95
00702250	blink-182 – Greatest Hits	$12.99
00702053	Best of Patsy Cline	$10.95
00702229	The Very Best of Creedence Clearwater Revival	$12.95
00702145	Best of Jim Croce	$10.95
00702219	David Crowder*Band Collection	$12.95
00702122	The Doors for Easy Guitar	$12.99
00702099	Best of Amy Grant	$9.95
00702190	Best of Pat Green	$19.95
00702136	Best of Merle Haggard	$10.95
00702243	Hannah Montana	$14.95
00702244	Hannah Montana 2/Meet Miley Cyrus	$16.95
00702227	Jimi Hendrix – Smash Hits	$14.99
00702236	Best of Antonio Carlos Jobim	$12.95
00702087	Best of Billy Joel	$10.95
00702245	Elton John – Greatest Hits 1970-2002	$14.99
00702204	Robert Johnson	$9.95
00702199	Norah Jones – Come Away with Me	$10.95
00702234	Selections from Toby Keith – 35 Biggest Hits	$12.95
00702003	Kiss	$9.95
00702193	Best of Jennifer Knapp	$12.95
00702097	John Lennon – Imagine	$9.95
00702216	Lynyrd Skynyrd	$14.95
00702182	The Essential Bob Marley	$12.95
00702248	Paul McCartney – All the Best	$14.99
00702129	Songs of Sarah McLachlan	$12.95
02501316	Metallica – Death Magnetic	$15.95
00702209	Steve Miller Band – Young Hearts (Greatest Hits)	$12.95
00702096	Best of Nirvana	$14.95
00702211	The Offspring – Greatest Hits	$12.95
00702030	Best of Roy Orbison	$12.95
00702144	Best of Ozzy Osbourne	$12.95
00702139	Elvis Country Favorites	$9.95
00699415	Best of Queen for Guitar	$14.99
00702208	Red Hot Chili Peppers – Greatest Hits	$12.95
00702093	Rolling Stones Collection	$17.95
00702092	Best of the Rolling Stones	$14.99
00702196	Best of Bob Seger	$12.95
00702252	Frank Sinatra – Nothing But the Best	$12.99
00702010	Best of Rod Stewart	$14.95
00702150	Best of Sting	$12.95
00702049	Best of George Strait	$12.95
00702259	Taylor Swift for Easy Guitar	$12.99
00702223	Chris Tomlin – Arriving	$12.95
00702262	Chris Tomlin Collection	$14.99
00702226	Chris Tomlin – See the Morning	$12.95
00702132	Shania Twain – Greatest Hits	$10.95
00702108	Best of Stevie Ray Vaughan	$10.95
00702123	Best of Hank Williams	$9.95
00702111	Stevie Wonder – Guitar Collection	$9.95
00702228	Neil Young – Greatest Hits	$12.99
00702188	Essential ZZ Top	$10.95

Prices, contents and availability subject to change without notice.

FOR MORE INFORMATION, SEE YOUR LOCAL MUSIC DEALER, OR WRITE TO:

HAL•LEONARD® CORPORATION

7777 W. BLUEMOUND RD. P.O. BOX 13819 MILWAUKEE, WI 53213

Visit Hal Leonard online at **www.halleonard.com**

0610